MIDWESTERN
PROGRESSIVE
POLITICS

MIDWESTERN
PROGRESSIVE
POLITICS

A Historical Study of Its
Origins and Development
1870—1958

By Russel B. Nye

MICHIGAN STATE UNIVERSITY
PRESS

Acknowledgment

Acknowledgment of indebtedness in the preparation of this book must first of all be made to the Trustees of the Newberry Library of Chicago and to the Board of Michigan State University, without whose assistance in the form of a grant-in-aid for Midwestern Studies and a sabbatical leave it could not have been written. In addition, I extend thanks for co-operative assistance to the librarians and staffs of the Michigan State Library, the Michigan State University Library, the University of Michigan Library, the Detroit Public Library, the Wisconsin State Historical Library, the John Crerar Library, and the Newberry Library. Thanks are also due to those correspondents who willingly gave me the benefit of personal opinion and experience—McAlister Coleman, Bruce Nelson, Morris Rubin, S. A. Olsness, Oswald Garrison Villard, Paul Douglas, Jacob S. Coxey, and others.

Russel B. Nye

East Lansing, Michigan

Contents

MIDWESTERN
PROGRESSIVE
POLITICS

The Midwestern Problem

I

The West is the most American part of America; that is to say, the part where those features which distinguish America from Europe come out in strongest relief. What Europe is to Asia, what England is to the rest of Europe, what America is to England, that the Western States and Territories are to the Atlantic States, the heat and pressures and hurry to life always growing as we follow the path of the sun.

LORD BRYCE, *The American Commonwealth*, 1888

"THE VOICE OF THE WEST," said Woodrow Wilson in 1911, "is a voice of protest." As historian, political scientist, and campaigning candidate, Wilson knew what he was talking about, but like others who heard it, he found that voice easier to identify than to explain. Students of American history and politics have long puzzled over exactly what "the West" is, and why it protests.

What Wilson meant by the West, of course, was that vast and vaguely defined region which, after the settlement of the Pacific Coast and desert-mountain areas, became known as the

Middle West. What he referred to was the political conten-
tiousness that seemed to affect the settlers as soon as they
crossed the outermost fringe of settlement. Theirs was a
tradition of independence that stretched unbroken from the
farmers of Shays' Rebellion to Sockless Jerry Simpson, Ignatius
Donnelly, William Jennings Bryan, and Old Bob La Follette,
the spirit that raised more hell than corn in Kansas in the
eighties and dumped milk in Iowa in the 1930's. Theirs was
not the spirit of the roaring camps of the gold trail, nor the
Billy-the-Kid lawlessness of the cattle states, nor the rebellious-
ness of the city workers of the East, the coal miners of Pennsylvania and West Virginia, or the textile workers of the South-
east. It was not a class protest, nor a struggle of labor against
capital in the Marxian sense. The Midwest's spirit of protest
is simply its own, compounded out of its geography, its culture, its economic and social history. There is nothing else
quite like it in the world.

The exact boundaries of what Wilson meant by the "West"
are hard to set. Lord Bryce could only say that the West was
that which was not East, and most foreigners like most Easterners considered all that lay beyond the Allegheny Mountains
to be Western. One cannot blame Bryce or Boston, for Midwesterners themselves cannot wholly agree upon their own
geographical limits. They agree that there is a Midwest, but
the region is too fluid, too subdivided and disunified, to be
defined as more than a state of mind, a regional self-conscious-
ness that knows no clear demarcation lines.

Certain facts about the region are clear. The Midwest is a
large and imperial land, larger than the heartland of central
Europe. It is new: its first state to enter the Union—Ohio—
was admitted in 1803, and the last states—North and South
Dakota—in 1889. Its culture is diverse, both Protestant and
Catholic; France, Britain, and Spain have claimed or occupied
it, and the migrations that poured into it have made it one
of the most polyglot areas in the world. It is rich in mines,
lakes, and forests. It is pioneer in spirit, though its frontier

phase has passed; it is individualistic, materialistic, self-reliant, politically independent, often suspicious of the East and the Old World.

Geographically the name Midwest may be said to include the old Northwest Territory states of Ohio, Indiana, Illinois, Michigan, and Wisconsin, plus the newer Northwest states of Minnesota, Iowa, North Dakota, South Dakota, Nebraska, and Kansas. The apparent unity of the group, partially imposed by the pattern of its history and settlement, is an illusion, for the area is obviously divided and redivided into smaller units. Ohio, Indiana, Illinois, and Michigan, for economic and social reasons, retain closer connections to the East, yet are not really of it. Wisconsin, which historically belongs with the old Northwest group, clings more to the north central states of Minnesota, Iowa, and the Dakotas. Nebraska and Kansas, border states, have much in common with the states to the north of them, but at the same time are drawn toward Missouri, Oklahoma, and the Southwest. Midwest, then, is simply a generic term that can be applied with only relative accuracy to portions of the Ohio-Mississippi-Missouri basin, an area that shades off imperceptibly into East, Southwest, and West. Akron feels closer to Pittsburgh than it does to Chicago, and Madison closer to Minneapolis than Bismarck does to St. Louis.

Part of the Midwest's regional diversity is a reflection of its economic and social history. Originally agricultural and self-sufficient, the area in the later nineteenth century gradually developed economically specialized subdivisions. Corn became a market and feed crop in the rich lands of Ohio, Indiana, Illinois, Iowa, and parts of Nebraska and Kansas. The plains states of Minnesota, Kansas, and the Dakotas and parts of Nebraska raised wheat. Wisconsin, Michigan, and parts of Iowa turned to dairying, hay, corn, livestock, tobacco, and beans. The early settler of Wisconsin might have begun raising wheat, switched to corn, and ended up as dairyman and truck farmer.

The thrust of nineteenth-century industrialism into what

had been an agricultural area produced a double-barreled economy that helped separate one portion of the Midwest from another. The opening of the great iron and copper ranges, the development of cheap lake transportation, and the expanding network of rail lines after 1860 made the region a semi-agricultural, semi-industrial area like no other part of the nation, one in which steel worker and dairy farmer worked within sight of each other, and cities were ringed by farms. The impact of industrialism was strongest in the older states, where cities like Detroit, Chicago, Gary, Toledo, Akron, and Cleveland came to have much in common with New York, Pittsburgh, Baltimore, and Boston.

The transition from forest clearing to industrial center in these states was exceedingly swift. Ohio, Michigan, Illinois, and to a lesser extent Indiana became offensive outposts for an expanding Eastern industrialism and defensive forts of a shrinking Western agrarianism. In other states to the west and north, the shift was neither so rapid nor so complete. Wisconsin's lake edge became fringed with industry, but the broad expanses of its land remained primarily agricultural. Duluth-Superior and Minneapolis-St. Paul grew into urban islands in a sea of wheat, and the rolling cornfields of Iowa and Nebraska and the wheatfields of Kansas engulfed the industrial towns that dotted them. The Midwest is still the farmer's stronghold.

The Midwest, of course, was settled from the East. Yet it inevitably changed men, institutions, and ideas into something different, new, and native. The settler in Ohio and Michigan and Illinois established a New England town with its square or common, put up a church modeled after the Congregational church back home, and brought his law from the seaboard courts. Outwardly the East was there, but the new land changed things. The commons disappeared into Main Street. The preacher's rock-ribbed Congregationalism gave way to frontier revivalism. The precedents of Blackstone and Coke yielded to the cracker-barrel practice of a local justice of the peace. The

6

shipbuilder built a different vessel for the Great Lakes and for the wide, treacherous rivers. The farmer found different soil and different crops, and evolved new agricultural methods. The merchant found different markets at new distances. Still, the influence of the East remained strong on the settler in the Midwest. His fashions in dress, architecture, and ideas came from there; so did his money and much of his government. He subscribed to newspapers from New York, Philadelphia, and Boston, read Eastern books, listened to Eastern speakers at the lyceum. If he could afford it, he sent his children East to school; if he could not, he sent them to one of the numerous "Yales" or "Harvards of the West" that dotted the Midwest, or to a state university staffed from the East. The Midwest was of the East, and yet not of it, different from and yet part of the culture which had settled it.

Throughout the nineteenth century and well into the twentieth, the Midwest suffered from a colonial complex—the result of its newness and of its dependence on the East for population, ideas, credit, and culture. Not until the late nineteenth century did the Midwest begin to feel itself a regional entity, and then it occasionally squirmed uneasily under the attacks of literary New Yorkers and Bostonians and Midwestern expatriates such as Ed Howe, Sinclair Lewis, and Glenway Westcott who looked at their homeland as a sort of spiritual and cultural desert. Thus, Richard Harding Davis, in typical Eastern fashion, pitied "those men who would excel in a great metropolis, . . . wasting their energies in a desert of wooden houses in the midst of an ocean of prairie."

Another Eastern concept, current at the turn of the century and unfortunately long after, was that the Midwest, especially in its trans-Mississippi reaches, was politically "wild and woolly," a happy alliteration based on the appearance in politics of such men as William Peffer, Sockless Jerry Simpson, and William Jennings Bryan. The staid *Congregationalist Record* of Boston spoke in 1900 of the "dangerous characters of the inflammable and covetous West," while Lyman Abbott complained later of the Western "medicine man" who set up his campaign tent to hawk "one medicine which will cure all the ills to which humanity is subject." "The East," remarked a Western editor in 1886, "thinks the West is barbarous, and that its ignorance should forbid its being listened to in matters of legislation."

The Midwesterner, of course, was neither ignorant nor isolated. Books, newspapers, periodicals, and farm journals reached the farmer quickly; the lyceum and later the Chautauqua circuit put him in touch with practically every intellectual current of his time. Nor was the West "wild and woolly," a term no more accurate than its alliterative and inevitable counterpart, the "effete East." Political intransigence has never been confined to any section of the United States, though in the West and South it may have seemed more persistent and pyrotechnical. Yet the fable persisted, and perhaps still persists. After careful study of the question, C. S. Gleed, assistant general solicitor of the Santa Fe railroad and a well-educated and well-traveled observer, concluded in 1893 that "the East has treated the West . . . [with] an amused tolerance of its foibles and a rather smug sense of its inferiority."

So there remained in the region, until recent times, an apologetic air of colonialism. While Professor Blatchford of Chicago Seminary in 1885 might call the Midwest "the center of the nation's commonwealth towards which are gravitating forces material, spiritual, intellectual, with the certainty of destiny," the provincial feeling remained, constantly coloring Midwestern thinking. Part of the feeling came, no doubt, from the settler's nostalgia for the civilization he left behind him. The Harvard or Bowdoin graduate, lost in the vast prairie with a one-room school, a farmer's journal, and an itinerant lecturer for intellectual stimulation, might fondly remember the gentler and far more civilized culture he had known. Some of the feeling came too from the people who poured in from Scandinavia and Germany, outlanders with foreign ways whose

contrast with the older native "Yankees" gave them a feeling
of foreignness which is still noticeable, though unadmitted, in
the heavily Norwegian, Swedish, Finnish, Polish, and German
settlements of the Midwest. Though these immigrants were
quickly absorbed, they were always subject to the natural self-
consciousness of late and foreign arrivals.

This diversity of population, true of no other section of the
nation in the nineteenth century, gave Midwestern culture a
distinctive flavor. New York Staters rubbed elbows with
Virginians, Maine down-Easters with Pennsylvania Dutchmen,
later with Germans, Norse, Irish, Scotch, and Holland Dutch,
and still later with Poles and Italians, Finns, Czechs, and
Hungarians. The end product was the Midwesterner, who
owed something to Williamsburg and Boston, to William Byrd
and Cotton Mather, William Penn and John Winthrop, to
Count Zinzendorf and Martin Luther and Jonathan Edwards
and Peter Cartwright, to Canterbury and Rome, and to a
thousand other places and people and traditions.

The postwar revolution in agriculture brought a set of completely new economic problems to the Midwest. The Homestead Act of 1862 opened the fertile plains to hordes of settlers
who streamed west to take up 160-acre units of tough prairie
sod. Vast new areas of land went into production. Two million
farms in the nation in 1860 raised 200,000,000 bushels of
wheat; six million farms in 1900 raised 665,000,000 bushels, a
rate of increase duplicated in the production of corn, cattle,
hogs, dairy goods, and other agricultural products. The improved plows of Deere and Oliver broke the sod; new seeders
and cultivators raised the crops; new threshers, mowers, reapers,
and binders harvested them. Better strains of seed were
developed, and better methods of controlling plant and animal
diseases and pests increased production still further. By 1900
the Midwest farmer not only grew enough to feed the nation
but had millions of tons left over for export.

The new agriculture was clearly capitalistic—not the simple,
self-sufficing system of frontier days. The Midwest farmer raised

a money crop to sell so that he could purchase staples and luxuries from the industrial East. He was a businessman, selling at home and abroad in a free market in competition with the farmers of Europe and South America, buying from a protected Eastern market the clothes, shoes, machinery, and transportation that he needed. And as a capitalistic businessman, he faced peculiar hazards. His crops were too often at the mercy of the violent and unpredictable moods of Midwestern nature. Drought, disease, pests, hail, wind, and unreasonable changes of climate could and did play havoc with him. Kansas and Nebraska once went nearly a year and a half without measurable rain; the great grasshopper invasion of 1874 denuded whole counties, and corn borers and chinch bugs took heavy toll in other years. Every crop he raised was a speculative venture, and the farmer of the Midwest, once a self-sufficient individualist, became an agricultural capitalist with a heavy investment in land, crops, and machinery, at the mercy of a strange and terrifying set of natural phenomena and economic laws.

His most serious problems were transportation, money, credit, and tariffs. To get his crop to market he depended chiefly upon the railroad. The Midwest had neither the population nor the industrial facilities to absorb the products it raised; neither did it have any other means besides the railroad of obtaining the necessities it needed—coal, oil, cloth, and so on. Unlike his position in the earlier days of water transportation, the farmer now depended for his communication with markets on a means which was under not public but private control. Freight rates were extremely important to him, for the difference of a few cents in his shipping costs meant money in or out of his pocket. The railroads, before 1900, had consolidated into a few great lines—the Burlington, the North Western, the Illinois Central, the Northern Pacific, the Santa Fe, the Union Pacific—under the control of the Goulds, Harrimans, Hills, Morgans, and others. The Midwest farmer's economic lifeline lay under the private control of Eastern capitalists, and only a few of them at that.

He was no better off when it came to money and credit. In Iowa or Nebraska he sold his staple crops for cash to pay old debts, finance new crops, and buy necessities. Fluctuation in money values affected him swiftly and seriously, but he was not in control of currency policy, which was often shaped by Eastern financial interests which, he suspected, were inimical to his own. After the Civil War the trend toward consolidated banking affected both the farmer's money and his credit. Local banks grew fewer and fewer, less and less autonomous, their reserves deposited in larger banks, which in turn were tied to still larger banks in the financial centers of the East, where fiscal policy was made. Since the farmer usually began with little capital besides land, he needed to borrow heavily on a long-term basis to buy machinery, improvements, even seed. His homestead was a relatively large speculation which had to pay off, but he was forced to use a credit system better adapted to manufacturing than to agriculture. He needed insurance, too, to protect his investment in buildings, crops, stock, and machinery, but insurance companies were mostly Eastern and, like the railroads and the banks, under private control. So too were the flour mills, elevators, and packing houses to which he sold his products.

The tariff was the Midwest farmer's third major problem. The protectionist policy of the enactments of 1862 and 1864 continued long after the Civil War, and an even more rigorous protective schedule replaced it in the nineties. The issue was simple, though its ramifications were wide. The farmer sold in an unprotected market and bought in one protected by a tariff whose schedules were set in favor of Eastern industrial and financial interests. Therefore he wanted more protection for the markets to which he sold and less for those from which he bought.

The extent and nature of a farmer's difficulties naturally depended on the type of farming he did and the area in which he did it. The corn and livestock producers of Illinois, Iowa, Nebraska, Kansas, and Minnesota found transportation charges their most pressing problem. The dairy farmers of Wisconsin,

Minnesota, and Iowa, who sold some of their output in a home market, had smaller shipping expenses and were less subject to monopolistic control. The wheat farmer of the Dakotas, Minnesota, and Kansas faced the worst situation. Soil and climate restricted him to one crop and left him at nature's mercy. The riskiness of wheat made credit harder to obtain, and he needed a great deal of both land and machinery to raise it. The nature of the market left him open to abuse by elevators, millers, and railroads, for he was forced to depend upon someone else to buy, ship, and process his product for a distant market in open world competition. It was no accident that the greatest agrarian unrest after the Civil War centered in the wheat belt.

In general, the triple alliance of railroads, banks, and tariff-protected industry dominated Midwestern economy after the Civil War. All the problems connected with them seemed to emanate from the East. Thus "Wall Street" became very real to the Midwest as a general term including the entire body of Eastern influence—the moneylender, the high-tariff manufacturer, the market speculator, the railroad king, the trust holder, the mortgage owner. It might mean Minneapolis, Chicago, Kansas City, St. Louis, or Boston as well as New York, but "Wall Street" was a living entity, a major influence in Midwestern thinking after 1865. "I cannot recall," said one farm journal editor, "another conspiracy in the history of mankind quite equal in colossal and criminal splendor to the profound and universal plot of Wall Street," a plot "to reduce the Midwest to vassalage." The Midwestern idea of a meeting of the directors of a corporation in the eighties and nineties, as sketched by a Granger writer, ran something like this—*Order of Business:* bankrupt farmers, form new monopoly, rig market, fix prices; *Resolutions Passed:* raise interest rates, lower farm prices, instruct business through interlocking directorates to raise prices on all goods sold to farmers, order newspapers to support regular party candidates, allot money to "educate" legislatures, declare dividend, adjourn.

No wonder the Midwest was, as Wilson and others observed, an area of revolt. It was, so to speak, a "culture area" of political discontent. Spreading outward after 1870, diminishing in force as it encountered increased resistance from adjacent and politically different areas, the so-called Midwestern spirit of "progressivism" (or "insurgency" or "radicalism") became a real force in American political life. The Grangers, the Populists, the "progressives," the "insurgents," the Non-Partisan Leaguers, even the Socialists, represented phases of this movement.

Certain traits of this Midwestern spirit may be isolated and identified. In the first place, its reforms were moderate rather than revolutionary, aimed at planned experimentation rather than disintegration and upheaval. The Midwest radical was traditionally a rather conservative radical, attacking one at a time certain specific problems within the existing governmental system, requesting specific and practical solutions. His demands for changes in the established system stemmed from attempts to eradicate special grievances: commission government, direct primaries, state regulation, corrupt-practices acts, tax revisions, conservation of resources, control or ownership of utilities. Then too he asked for reforms within the current framework of politics, to be realized through traditional, legitimate political means: the ballot, the third party, fusion, and so on. Neither socialism in the nineteenth century nor communism in the twentieth ever received much support in the Midwest.

It was always difficult for demagogues to gain a Midwestern following of any significance, and hard for those who skirted the fringe of demagoguery to avoid committing themselves to any but specific and pertinent reforms. Neither Bryan nor La Follette could justifiably be classed as "radical," and even those who came closest to it—Donnelly, Simpson, possibly Weaver, and others—proposed concrete ways of dealing with immediate problems of railroads, currency, and credit, rather than demanding sweeping political revolutions. In the same way, it was virtually impossible for a single man or a small group of men to create a Midwestern movement. Traditionally, Midwestern protest came from the people first and a leader followed, or if no leader appeared, the movement proceeded without one, as did the Grange and the Farmers' Alliance. Midwest movements seemingly could not be organized from the top downward, as abolitionism had been in the East.

Midwest politics was consistently socialized politics, that is, politics which attempted to give the state some positive and systematic control over the economic and social life of the people. Its political thinking always showed a desire for positive governmental action which charted a course of economic and social reform for the common benefit. From parties like the Anti-Monopoly, Reform, Populist, and Progressive came such proposals as workmen's compensation, child and female labor laws, conservation programs, unemployment insurance, public service commissions, agricultural development programs, state planning commissions, school laws, old-age and mothers' pensions, and the like. Midwest reform politics attempted from the beginning to adjust government to the needs of the people.

Perhaps the most characteristic trait of the Midwesterner in politics was his clear and direct desire to protect his own interests. If railroads overcharged, the voters passed a law and fixed the rates. If grain elevators monopolized the field, the farmers tried to establish a state elevator. If farm machinery cost too much, they formed a co-operative and bought or made it. If the dollar deflated, they asked for currency laws to reinflate it. Call these things socialism or anarchism—the Midwest never minded. Most of its radicalism was nothing but a series of perfectly logical attempts to find some sensible method of removing certain threats to Midwestern interests. It was an essentially common-sense, agrarian, frontier radicalism, a thoroughly indigenous compound of various elements in Midwestern history.

Finally, the Midwest was in the process of swift change during the nineteenth century. Many of its settlers came West to escape political, social, or economic discrimination; movement rather than adaptation was the traditional Midwestern means of solving problems. With the gradual disappearance of free land, the Midwest found itself forced to face new conditions, willy-nilly: there was no place left to move to. The accelerated rate of change made adaptation more difficult than in the older regions, where the problems of wealth, monopoly, railroads, urbanism, and population had evolved slowly and gradually. Trends of national development were speeded up in the Midwest. The East, for example, had half a century to work out the conflict between public and private interests in the use of natural resources; many Western states had only a decade or so. Political compromises between antagonistic interests take time, and the Midwest had little of it.

The primary problem of America after 1865 was to resolve the clash between the old ideals of agrarian democracy with the new industrialism, to reconcile political liberty with economic expansion. The postwar period was the age of business, of the captain of industry, of the empire builder. To him the country offered more raw materials than any country except Russia. The whole West, with its forest, mines, lakes, and fields, waited for the entrepreneur. Inventions, already developed or about to be, were too many to list—the cotton gin, the reaper, the improved plow, the railroad, the steamboat, and the stone breaker (which made track and railroad ballast available, and later concrete). The huge iron deposits and timberlands of the West, and the oil pools and coal fields of the West and South, were ready at hand. The opportunities for the young man of 1870 dwarfed those of the young man of 1860. A whole nation, its vast resources and markets virtually untouched, lay before him, and the devil take the hindmost.

Now that the Civil War had settled the question of political unity, there was much to be done—the West to populate, illimitable natural resources to tap, millions of machines to be made, and nothing in the way. Andrew Carnegie expressed the mood perfectly in 1886, saying, "The old nations of the earth creep at a snail's pace; the Republic thunders past with the rush of the express. The United States, in the growth of a single century, has already reached the foremost place among nations, and is soon to outdistance all the others in the race." America had the best political system, the most money, and the most intelligent leaders and farseeing businessmen of any in the world. The job ahead simply lay in making the land more prosperous. True, injustice, graft, and corruption might creep in, but when the task was done America might then pause to brush some of the sand out of the gears of the social and economic machinery.

The laissez faire, or "let alone," theory of economy was ingrained in the American tradition, deriving not only from eighteenth-century economics but from pioneer experience, when a man's success depended on his own energy and skill in outwitting and subduing the wilderness. The economic thinkers of the pre-Civil War period erected the principle into a shrine. Postwar industrialism fitted perfectly into the pattern, for laissez faire was ideally adapted to the business of exploiting a continent. Emerson's self-reliance was perhaps never meant to produce a Jay Gould or a J. P. Morgan, but in the new industrial age it seemed to justify him. Though American business, it is true, never actually adopted laissez faire wholeheartedly, it used the theory as a convenient weapon to silence opposition. The real attitude of late nineteenth-century business was Hamiltonian: it assumed that the function of government was to protect and encourage business development, guaranteeing an industrial prosperity which percolated down to the people.

Nevertheless, with huge resources to draw upon, large and available markets, free trade between states, government subsidies both direct and indirect, tariff protection from foreign competition, and popular confidence, business began to find hard going almost at once. The competition was terrifically intense. In the struggle for economic survival a manufacturer or businessman in the seventies and eighties was much more likely to go to the wall than to succeed. Bitter rate and price wars wiped out firms overnight; witnesses appearing before the Industrial Commission in the nineties agreed that competition in some business areas was so vigorous that "nearly all competing establishments were destroyed." The laissez-faire theories of Adam Smith and the economists were well enough in the books, but the slogan of "free enterprise and individualism" that had grown naturally out of the eighteenth century no longer really fitted the new nineteenth-century industrial economy.

It became perfectly clear to many a businessman, no matter how much he respected the system of laissez-faire competition, that there were certain advantages to be gained from avoiding or suppressing it. It was only logical for rival firms, instead of ruining each other in wasteful price wars, to split up the market, leaving each a tidy profit and, even more important, allowing each to survive. Economist Franklin Giddings pointed out that "the competition that wastes resources and ruins competitors is an abnormal process." "Fortunately," remarked another, "men have learned a better regulator [than competition]—combination. Joining hands is the industrial order of the day." In the 1850's and 60's, for example, there had been two hundred different firms manufacturing farm machinery, four hundred and fifty different companies mining coal, several thousand oil producers, thirty horsecar companies competing in New York alone, and seventeen different railroad lines between New York and Chicago. From the standpoint of efficiency, such multiplication was foolish; from the standpoint of profits, it was suicidal. Consolidation was an advantage to all concerned.

Thus was a loophole found in the popularly accepted Darwinian idea of the elimination of the unfit. It was simply the common-sense principle of "If you can't lick 'em, jine 'em."

By combining instead of competing, businesses could cut costs in production and marketing, control prices, fix profits, and suppress rivalry. To say that competition was the life of trade, commented one businessman in 1888, was simply to repeat "a moldy old proverb." Combination was more efficient than unbridled competition; it was a logical means, as Giddings said, of "restraining conduct that is mutually injurious."

It was not a new thing in business, for combinations had been known in colonial days, but the period after the Civil War, marked by the most savage competition in economic history, brought its greatest expansion. The businessman of Lincoln's youth knew what monopoly was—he knew the Astor Fur Company and Western Union—but he would have been amazed by the industrial juggernauts of Cleveland's time. The first step in controlling competition was the development of the corporation, that legal but fictitious creation which H. C. Adams remarked reduced the moral element to its minimum while retaining the rights of a person. The pool, (a "gentlemen's agreement" among corporations to control profits and prices) was popular in the seventies because it seemed specially adapted to the needs of the railroads. When it was finally forbidden by the Interstate Commerce Act of 1887, the pool was already being replaced by the more efficient trust, in which the stockholders of competing firms or related firms agreed to deposit controlling portions of their stocks with a board of trustees in return for trust certificates. These, said *Bradstreet's*, with magnificent understatement, "promise to furnish some highly interesting problems for solution by the statesmen and economists of the near future." The trust worked very well indeed, and as a form of control it dominated business into the twentieth century.

The evolution of the great trust is perhaps best represented by the development of the Standard Oil Company. In Cleveland, shortly after the Civil War, a quiet young man named John D. Rockefeller began refining oil when the average profit was approximately 30 per cent. By good management he was able to do much better than that, and in 1870 his was the largest business in the Midwest. Persuading twelve other refiners to join him, he formed the South Improvement Company, forced railroads to grant it rebates, enlarged his own capital, and bought out his rivals. Next he formed a pool with other refiners, controlling roughly four fifths of the national oil output. For nine years he carefully bought or forced out rivals, and in 1882, with the assistance of an astute corporation lawyer, Samuel C. T. Dodd (who is generally credited with developing the trust), he united them all in one huge trust. Broken by the Ohio courts in 1892, Standard Oil reorganized in New Jersey under more lenient law and proceeded on its way.

Though Standard Oil was one of the earliest big trusts, its basic pattern was repeated in almost every important industrial field. The railroads, beginning with Vanderbilt and continuing through Gould, Harriman, Hill, Morgan, and Belmont, followed it fairly closely. Andrew Carnegie, a shrewd little Scotsman, built up an organization that culminated in 1901 with the United States Steel Company, whose capitalization under Morgan was larger than the entire national wealth in Washington's day. Rockefeller and Morgan organized banking chains or "trusts" which interlocked with railroads, insurance companies, and manufacturing concerns until by 1912 the combined Morgan and Rockefeller interests held directorships in 341 firms with a total capitalization of $22,000,000,000 and more. The McCormick farm machinery trust, the Swift and Armour packing combines, the Guggenheim copper trust, and the Duke tobacco trust followed the pattern, and so did trusts in cottonseed and linseed oil, sugar, whisky, rubber, matches, lead, leather, silver, nickel, salt, carbon, gas, electricity, and so on. Roughly two hundred firms in 1900 did half the nation's business, and a government committee in that year found 185 combinations pursuing business with capitalizations of more than $3,000,000,000. Four years later John Moody reported 319 firms capitalized at $7,000,000,000 or more, of which 234 had been organized since 1898.

All this, said Andrew Carnegie, was "triumphant democracy,"

concrete proof of the tremendous energy of laissez-faire capitalism. The leaders of finance and industry were "builders," men who built railroads, opened banks, dug up and cut down or converted huge national resources, and made the nation rich. It was a wonderful structure they reared, but it was not "triumphant democracy," as the pre-Civil War United States understood it. The public began to think of the corporation as a giant octopus with tentacles stretched into every man's life, controlling his destiny from cradle to grave; even then, as Ignatius Donnelly remarked, he might be buried in a coffin made by a coffin trust. The real extent of control over widespread economic areas exerted by a single individual or firm is difficult to establish, and was perhaps never so great as the general public imagined or feared. Morgan the younger testified in 1913 that "it is preposterous to suppose that every interlocking director has full control in every organization," and Louis Brandeis claimed that past a certain point in bigness the individual businessman simply lost track of affairs and control over them. Nevertheless, a large segment of the American public refused to believe other than that the trusts were in complete control of the economic life of the nation, and from what it could observe it had no reason to change its mind.

The new trend toward "big business" demanded a new type of businessman, quite different from the conservative European who was satisfied with 10 per cent profit and safety. The American businessman, operating in a fluid and unstable economy, either won or lost heavily; as an English visitor wrote wonderingly, "Most of the fortunes at New York have been made and remade over again. Millions rise and fall by turns, like the waves of a troubled sea." Conservatism and timidity did not pay off in a world of fierce economic competition: they were more likely to invite disaster. Like the frontier trader, the late nineteenth-century businessman had to be aggressive and daring to survive.

But if the risks of business were great, so were the rewards. The nation's population was increasing swiftly, the American public was a fairly homogeneous group of calculable demand, and good service at a cheap price was always well rewarded. If a businessman could gain some advantage over his competitor, or avoid competition by monopolizing the field, he could be richer than any of his predecessors in history. A Minnesotan showed by an analysis of the mining-railroad interests how great a margin of profit could really be secured through monopoly and agreement. Iron ore in 1896 sold in Cleveland at $2.65 a ton. Of this, $1.60 represented the cost of production and transportation; roughly 50 cents went to Rockefeller (who leased the land), 25 cents to the owner of the land, 35 cents to the mining company, and 1 cent to the state as tax. Since the Mesabi range in Minnesota produced about four million tons of ore a year, the accrued profit to all concerned was obviously considerable.

To reap the rewards of business under such conditions demanded a man's entire time, brains, and energy. So the "captain of industry" emerged, a peculiarly American type, ruthless, almost savage in his business dealings, a man of boundless imagination and daring. The earliest of the breed was the individualist, the gambler who staked everything on a single throw, the real primordial laissez-faire survivor of the struggle of the fittest in business. "Crazy" Harper conceived the staggering idea of cornering all the wheat in the West, missed for the lack of a mere million dollars, and went quietly to prison. "Old Hutch" Hutchinson did corner it in 1888. Joe Leiter once actually entered into negotiations for the purchase of the Great Wall of China, while "Bet-You-A-Million" Gates introduced $150,000 antes in poker circles.

These were the pioneers. Their successors, who took over in the eighties and nineties, were cold, shrewd men of business: Vanderbilt the second (who added ninety million to his father's fortune in six years), Harriman, Carnegie, Rockefeller himself, and the king of them all, J. P. Morgan, Sr. They changed business from a rough-and-tumble individualism to corporate co-operation; they absorbed rather than competed, slicing up the national economy like a melon. Morgan shut the door on the old era in 1889 when, after bitter rate wars in the West, he called together eighteen railroad presidents and told them to stop fighting. "This is not elsewhere customary in civilized communities, and no good reason exists why such a practice should continue among railroads." After that it was not like the old days, when the robber baron fled with the bonds a step ahead of the posse. Now the individual was lost in a maze of faceless corporations—the "interests." The men who ran them avoided the headlines, contributed to churches and charities, and lived solidly respectable lives in comparative obscurity. None of them would have bet, as Gates is supposed to have done, on the course of a raindrop down a windowpane; the high living of "Diamond Jim" Brady inspired nothing but righteous horror in the breasts of churchgoing Christians like Rockefeller, Carnegie, or Morgan. They were precise, austere, calculating, and mercilessly thorough. The difference between them and their predecessors was quite evident to a Minnesota farmer who once remarked that if the railroads were going to clean him out he'd prefer to have the old buccaneers back, in place of Morgan or Harriman, for the old ones "left a little for seed."

The wealth amassed by these men was enormous, and so was the power that followed it. Abram S. Hewitt, the wealthy New York ironmonger, thought no man was rich unless he had twenty million or more, while the *New York World* remarked in 1888 that "millionaires are as thick as hops." Carnegie's annual income approached twelve and a half million; his total fortune totaled a billion dollars, of which he gave away three hundred and fifty million. Rockefeller amassed one and a half billion, and E. S. Harkness, his partner, three quarters of a billion. The Guggenheim interests took two billion from the copper ranges of Montana, and John Gates a hundred and ninety million from a barbed-wire combine. Morgan's fortune equaled Carnegie's and Ford's, and those of Commodore Vanderbilt, Gould, Harriman, Stanford, Huntington, and

Cooke (railroads), Stewart (real estate and stores), Swift and Armour (packing), and Duke (tobacco) were not far behind. The economist Charles Spahr calculated in 1890 that 125,000 men controlled at least half the national wealth. Business was life to these men. They measured existence in terms of economics, and thought of the state as an antagonist or an ally, depending upon its attitude toward them.

Nor was there, in the light of contemporary ethics, any reason why these fortunes should not rest in their hands. The function of government, it was assumed, was to see that all men had a chance to obtain wealth. As one spokesman put it, "All that government ought to do is to give every man, woman, and child an equal opportunity to get wealth by industry, economy, and intelligent management and temperance." Though possibly skeptical, and certainly envious, a good many people probably agreed with Senator Ingalls of Kansas that "Great private fortunes are inseparable from high civilizations. . . . All the great enterprises that exalt and embellish existence and ameliorate the conditions of human life—come from the conception of money in the hands of the few."

But as industrialism widened its sphere of influence, some Americans began to note a growing discrepancy between the nation's traditions and beliefs and its social and economic (especially the latter) development. People listened to press and pulpit and business proclaiming the United States "the richest nation in history," with "the highest standard of living in the world," and asked quite naturally, "Where is all this wealth, and who profits by it?" Some people continued to believe in and to insist upon practicing the principles of freedom, equality, and opportunity, but in actuality some wondered if they really possessed any of these things. Obviously the wage earner was not his own master, nor was the farmer. The traditionally independent American yeoman was now in debt to a bank, his selling prices controlled by buyers and his buying power controlled by sellers. He was apparently not the economic equal of the industrialist, the railroad magnate, the grain speculator, the miller, or the company executive whose decisions influenced his life. Rapid concentration of capital was creating class divisions nearly as clear as those of Europe. The American believed in opportunity, in the right of the individual to improve himself by his own courage and initiative; if he failed he had only himself to blame. But only a smaller and still smaller minority found the doors of opportunity open; courage and initiative alone seemed not enough. People felt that in attempting to establish democracy they were attempting something impossible, and began to question whether or not they really had a fair chance to establish it.

After 1870 industrialism was in the saddle, booted and spurred. It was hard, in the midst of tremendous material progress surrounding them, for the farmer and the worker to understand their failure to share equitably in it—the paradox of poverty amidst progress was puzzling. Carping critics could not find an answer. Supporters of the status quo pointed to the quadrupling of the national wealth since 1865, to new inventions, great factories, thousands of miles of railroads, and asked how anyone could be discontented. There might be evil, inequality, and injustice in the system, but one need not burn down the barn to get rid of rats. There were, it was true, poor and rich, a fact that squared with nature and Biblical prediction. Equality was an admirable philosophical abstraction, but a poor principle in economic and social practice. It was some little time before the malcontents found the answer: that all this industrial "progress" served private rather than public ends, that government was perverted and corrupted so that it might continue to do so. The answer came slowly and dimly, but it came.

As the fierceness of competition forced the American businessman to become a single-minded specialist in money-making, so did it change his attitude toward politics. The pre-Civil War businessman had time to pursue some cultural activities, dabble in politics, and in general develop a well-rounded set of interests over and beyond business matters—

witness the Adamses, Lawrences, and Lowells of an earlier day. But as his affairs increased in size and scope, the postwar businessman found little time to vary his routine. Survival outweighed all other considerations, and while a tycoon was serving in Congress, reading the classics, or playing diplomat in Europe, he might very well find his industrial empire cut out from under him by some shrewd rival who tended to his knitting. Yet, at the same time, the businessman realized that politics concerned him directly, for his affairs conflicted at many points with both law and public interest. He could gain an advantage over a competitor by the passage of one kind of law or lose it by the passage of another. He needed an ally, one who could be trusted to handle affairs on the political front so that he might give his undivided attention to economic warfare. The political "boss" was the man.

The political boss was not new to American politics. He appeared before the rise of huge corporations and will probably outlast them, but in the later nineteenth century and the earlier twentieth he found in business the perfect alliance. The boss was, more than anything else, the product of the extraordinarily complex American political system, which, like the increasingly complex economic system, demanded the services of specialists. Established at a time when the populace feared centralized power, most of the states (especially in the West) evolved intricate governmental patterns. The separation of executive, judicial, and legislative branches, the short terms granted governors and judges, the special rules, long constitutions, frequent elections, and other devices characteristic of state governments were intended to make them acutely sensitive to the people's demands. But faced by such puzzling machinery, the voter was often willing to turn its operation over to a class of specialists, or bosses, who made politics their business.

The machines of Jefferson, Jackson, and the pre-Civil War Whigs were insignificant compared to those of the later nineteenth century. The growth of cities produced localized and cohesive voting groups; the flood of immigration to the cities shaped single blocs of votes, easily handled and unified in interest; the development of industry encouraged the growth of classes and class interests. The boss, carefully weighing the demands of one group against those of another, had to be able to satisfy everybody's interests without alienating any or endangering his own. His job required alertness, intelligence, skill, and consummate shrewdness; Lincoln Steffens found the political bosses as a rule to be extremely capable men, often more so than the reformers who opposed them.

Their alliance with corporations was a natural one. The industrial king needed a political watchdog to guard his holdings from interference. The boss needed funds and patronage for his army of retainers. By an exchange of services both profited. Both were logical results of an increasing need for expert leadership in the two great national vocations, business and politics. The real danger to democracy lay, of course, in the fact that both were working for particular persons or groups rather than for the public interest. Charles Francis Adams in 1870 expressed the fears of many observers when he wrote, "Our political system cannot much longer sustain the conflict with corporations. Modern civilization has created a class of powers which are too strong for the control of our governments. How long can they develop together?" And Henry L. Stoddard, who knew politics intimately from Grant to Coolidge, concluded that the influence of business in politics was "a gun held at the head of every President."

The alliance of business and politics, despite obvious advantages to both, was yet not an unmixed blessing to either. Businessmen found politics a double-edged weapon and complained of what amounted to blackmail. Powerful politicians, in return for "protecting business interests," set and collected fees, threatening embarrassing legislation if the price went unpaid. "Influencing" politicians with cash could and did turn out to be extremely expensive. *Gunton's Magazine,* the unofficial organ of business in the nineties, complained in 1901 that businessmen were heartily sick of contributing to machine politics and would welcome a thorough purging of the whole machinery of government. The La Crosse and Milwaukee Railroad in Wisconsin, for example, admitted that during one year in the seventies it spent $872,000 for "influence," including $50,000 for a governor, $10,000 for a state comptroller, $125,000 for thirteen legislators, $10,000 for a first secretary, and so on. Lincoln Steffens, pursuing his muckraking at the turn of the century, found that while businessmen were perfectly aware of the immorality of political bribery, they were often unable to protect themselves from the machines in any other way. Bosses, on the other hand, complained that businessmen often did not understand the ethics of politics, that they were likely to join reform movements that looked impressive and prone to switch allegiances, without proper notice. Nonetheless, business and politics, caught in a trap of their own devising, made the alliance work.

At any rate, the "Great Barbecue" (as Parrington has neatly phrased it) was on. Every man had his price, and scandal reached from the small-town council up to the cabinet. Lord Bryce, surveying American politics, found it shot through and through with graft. "No feature in American life," observed W. E. H. Lecky in 1896, "strikes a stranger so powerfully as the extraordinary indifference, partly cynicism and partly good-nature, with which notorious frauds and notorious corruption are viewed by American public opinion. There is nothing, I think, like this to be found in any other great country."

There were good reasons for this popular cynicism and indifference, implicit in the moral shock of war itself and in the whole ideological pattern of the age. Much of it can be laid at the door of science, for Darwin's *Origin of the Species,* thrown like a pebble into the pond of ideas in 1859, sent out concentric circles that seriously disturbed the waters of later nineteenth-century thought. Choosing Darwin's two chief principles, the theory of the variability of species and the theory of the survival of the fittest, popular and scientific thinkers read into them implications that would have amazed and worried Darwin. To the average mind, Darwinism meant change rather than stability—life was a flux, a kaleidoscopic pattern with nothing permanent or fixed. Truth, said some philosophers, was simply a word of shifting meaning, a changing product of changing conditions; it could be established only on the pragmatic basis of experience. The sociologist Lewis Morgan worked out the laws of social evolution, while William Graham Sumner at Yale showed "right" and "morality" to be merely relative terms, not at all the products of a divinely implanted conscience. Law was man's fiat, not God's—the result of human adaptation to social and ethical evolution, to be viewed with some sophistication and urbanity. Darwinism tore up the old fixed beliefs in performance, in solid stability, and left in their place nothing constant but inconstancy.

The survival-of-the-fittest theory, adapted by Darwin from Malthus, found immediate popular acceptance. Herbert Spencer and his followers, applying Darwinism to contemporary social and economic institutions, found that it fitted them admirably. Darwin placed man definitely with the animals rather than with the angels; if man was a part of nature, what could be more logical for him than to live by nature's law of survival? Worked out by the Organicists, who drew a clear analogy between social and biological evolution, the "dog-eat-dog" principle became the prevailing theory of human existence. Good, said Spencer, meant simply adaptation that insured survival; evil was nonadaptation. Thus the fittest were "good" and those who lost in the struggle were "evil." Both deserved what they got. Evolution meant progress, and if survival of the fittest was a factor in evolution, it was obviously a factor in progress as well. "Evolution," remarked a writer in *Popular Science Monthly,* "shows the automatic and irresistible nature of the process by which society evolves the structure and functions needful for its betterment. Evolution teaches us to expect further changes to be *additions* to the present state rather than anything like subversions."

Darwin and Spencer gave the answers that politicians and businessmen needed. Fairly certain that what they were doing was right, yet gnawed by the feeling that the traditional code of Christian ethics did not fit it, they eagerly accepted most of the social implications of Darwinism. "Government is force," said Senator Ingalls of Kansas. "Politics is a battle for supremacy. Parties are the armies. The Decalogue and the Golden Rule have no place in a political campaign. The object is success. . . ." In the same vein an economist remarked, "Competitive commercial life is not a flowery bed of ease, but a battlefield where the 'struggle for existence' is defining the industrially 'fittest to survive.' " If the advancement of society rested upon the disposal of the unfit, that was exactly what the businessmen and politicians were doing. Jim Hill thought the function of a railroad trust to be the elimination of weaker units by absorption into the stronger. Rockefeller saw the growth of a corporation as "merely the survival of the fittest . . . the working out of a law of Nature and of God." Carnegie read Spencer and "Light came as in a flood and all was clear." While the struggle for survival might seem cruel and unjust to the individual who lost, he wrote, the loser should comfort himself with the thought that this failure was in the best interests of society at large. Sumner labeled the millionaire as "the finest flower of a competitive society." There was no such thing as a "natural" right in the sense of the Declaration of Independence: life was a struggle, and the only "natural" right was the right to compete in that struggle. American business had already accepted laissez faire, and Darwinism inserted the missing pieces in the pattern. The political boss and the captain of industry were merely adapting and surviving, following natural law; the function of the state was to preserve conditions under which this battle for survival could continue. Thus businessmen and politicians, remarked Edgar Lee Masters in 1904, "have canonized Darwin, and driven self-conscious intelligence in the control of human destiny from the economic field."

The Darwinian point of view seeped into the thinking of people who had never actually read Darwin or Spencer, but who found in the popular concept of their ideas a satisfactory explanation of the current contrast between spiritual ideals and social practices. The whole body of social and economic Darwinism was seemingly scientific in tone, laboratory tested, and therefore, to the popular mind, trustworthy. The survival-of-the-fittest principle was easily grasped and broad enough to cover most areas of human endeavor. Best of all, it seemed to explained concretely what men were doing and wanted to do. What more could a system of thought do to provide a *raison d'être* for an age?

Yet some observers sensed that something was wrong. Henry George in 1879 pointed out the peculiar paradox of a nation that became richer and richer while more and more of its people became poorer and poorer. Despite all the twistings and turnings of John Fiske and other popular explicators, Darwinism seemed to some a denial of the basic tenets of Christianity; furthermore, those who "lost" in the so-called struggle for survival were not at all sure that they had lost by fair means, nor were they ready to be "eliminated" without a protest. The shameless buying and selling of democracy in the market place impressed others, as it did young Henry Adams, as a betrayal of all that America stood for. There was a mood on the people, a suspicious and restless mood, no matter what Darwin and Spencer said or Adam Smith implied. The Philadelphia *North American* in 1900 polled prominent citizens for opinions on what the twentieth century had in store. The outlook, all agreed, was gloomy; some predicted socialism, others revolution and bloodshed, and the paper remarked on the shock of finding "such a tremendous undercurrent of dissatisfaction."

In the period after 1870 there was a growing conviction that old-style democracy was gone, or was going fast. "The only question which occupies the ruling class," Brooks Adams concluded, "is whether it is cheaper to coerce or to bribe." E. L. Godkin, in his detached, coldly intellectual comments on *The Unforeseen Dangers to Democracy,* thought the rise of the city and the corrupting influence of money doomed traditional democracy. For that matter, Godkin agreed with President

Eliot of Harvard that its disappearance might not be wholly undesirable, since popular government was "absolutely incapable of dealing with great subjects." Harry Thurston Peck called for recognition of a "leader class," an aristocracy of wealth, taste, and worth. J. Sterling Morton, a stern Nebraska conservative, thought that in any proper government "the rights of the unintelligent should be defined and defended by the intelligent." A writer in *Gunton's Magazine* tied up Darwin, Spencer, and democracy in one neat package by saying, "Liberty never did and never will imply equality . . .; the strong will emerge, the weak founder." In the same vein President George Harris of Amherst told his students in 1899, "We have outgrown the crude notion that democracy is equality and that it has no use for an aristocracy. . . . Its problem is to place its best men in its highest places, to put power in the hands of the wisest and most capable, to recognize superiority. . . ."

American democracy, for these reasons, had reached a turning point by 1870. The nation still paid its respects to the traditional concepts of liberty and equality expressed so brilliantly by the eighteenth century, but at the same time developments in economics and politics, especially, pointed directly away from them. The amassing of huge fortunes, the stifling of individual opportunity by monopoly, the corruption that inevitably followed politics-in-business and business-in-politics, the stratification of society that economic consolidation seemed to bring about—all these made it extremely hard to adjust old democratic ideas to contemporary practice. Yet the "struggle between democracy and plutocracy," as William Graham Sumner called it, had to be resolved. The task of reconciliation fell chiefly on the Midwest.

Perhaps no other portion of the nation at the time was better adapted to the task. The conflict between pioneer ideals and the new industrialism was peculiarly a Midwestern problem. The Midwestern states, only recently settled as frontier communities and now rapidly becoming semi-industrial areas, were a focal point for the collision of old and new ideologies. They had cities and farms, factories and mines, laborers and farmers, forests and railroads, an economy that was and still is both agrarian and industrial in fairly even balance. They had passed abruptly from log hut to big city, from simple frontier settlement to complex industrial society, compressing into a few decades the experiences of two centuries on the Atlantic Coast. They had a characteristic revolutionary heritage, a hell-for-leather frontier radicalism that had little use for precedent and stability. The Midwest held both the elements of frontier democracy and nineteenth-century industrialism—the Cleveland tycoon stood on its Eastern boundaries and the Kansas farmer on its Western, with varying shades of opinion lying between.

The problem, as the Midwest conceived it, was to reaffirm eighteenth-century democratic faith and to preserve it against the rising tide of skepticism, cynicism, and, as they called it, "plutocracy." But how could an agrarian democracy exist in an industrialized America? How could the political philosophy of Jefferson and Jackson be grafted onto the system of Spencer, Darwin, and Rockefeller? In the process of solving the problem it appeared that the Jeffersonian system of limited government might have to be exchanged for the Hamiltonian system of powerful government, that Jeffersonian ends might be accomplished by Hamiltonian means. The continuous conflict between individualism and collectivism, reform and reaction, agrarianism and industrialism turned the Middle West into a battleground.

This was the background of Middle Western progressivism—diversity, change, conflict, traditionalism, individualism, co-operation—a mélange of old and new tendencies. The whole tangled skein of American democratic thought was thrown into its lap for unraveling. The result was a regional movement—chiefly political, but with religious, economic, and social overtones—that was new, indigenous, and characteristically American.

Thunder in the West,
1870–1892

II

He came West, perhaps, to take up a section of free land, under the Homestead Act or to buy his acres from a development company. Others from his home country—York State, New England, Pennsylvania, perhaps Norway, Sweden, or Germany—arrived before him and sent back glowing reports of the fertility of the soil, the purity of the water, the salubrity of the climate. "—You must come, Joel, you can have your choice of buying on the river or farther back on timbered land or prairie. The land is dry and the water good, and few who are here now have ever been sick. I hope you will not fail to come to see." In Nebraska it was claimed that "a poor man may live richer, and a rich man easier" than in any other part of the world, and Kansas exclaimed that it was "a life of ease, perpetual June weather. . ., milk and honey." So he came, borrowed from the bank, put in his seed, raised a crop, and shipped it to market.

THE FIRST MUTTERINGS of protest came from the farm areas, where economic problems were most intense. The American farmer was never given to reticence when his interests were threatened, and the Midwestern farmer believed he had legitimate cause for complaint. It did little good to point out to him as the *Nation* did in 1873, that he was much better off than his grandfather had been, or that his troubles were primarily his own fault. With typical directness, he tried to do something about it, and before he finished he had brought into question the whole concept of American democracy.

The Midwestern farmer's situation in the 1870's and 1880's was the result of a decade and more of confused economics. The panic of 1873 called attention to the possibilities of Western lands; the nation needed a new source of wealth; the West needed settlers; the settlers needed railroads and credit; speculative capital needed settlers and railroads. Therefore banks, railroads, and states themselves campaigned to lure farmers to the West. Railroads advertised, state and county immigration boards and commissions sent out literature, and rumors of the great opportunities to be found in the Mississippi-Missouri Valley sped through the East and Europe. Land was cheap or free, credit easy, climate and soil good, chances for wealth excellent (one man cleared $10,000 in seven years on his crops). In the early seventies settlers began to pour in, and after the panic of 1873 they were much easier to lure. The million and a half men discharged from the Union armies and two million unemployed provided plenty of recruits, while immigration, at first checked by the war, brought more.

Eastern capital followed the settlers, for the new settlements needed improvements and the railroads needed money. Loans to the West from New Hampshire alone totaled twenty-five million in one year (1899), and the railroads in Nebraska sold $50,000 worth of stock for every mile of track laid in the state. Real estate boomed, land values doubled, trebled, quadrupled and then soared out of sight. "Double Your Money in Thirty Days!" cried a Kansas newspaper, "Do not be afraid of going into debt. Spend money for your city's betterment as free as water. . . ."

New land, new farmers, easy credit, and technological improvements all combined to release a flood of agricultural products, with a corresponding decrease in prices. Pressure of competition from the new states farther west, and from the farmers of Russia, Argentina, Canada, and Mexico, drove the value of crops down still more. The production of corn from 1866 to 1880 increased 98 per cent, but the price dropped 15 per cent; the production of wheat rose 221 per cent while the price dropped 27 per cent. Since these were the staple crops of the great Midwest area, the results were disheartening. Overproduction could be explained to the farmer, perhaps, but at the same time he knew that people in the United States and Europe were starving and freezing while he burned his corn for fuel, since it was not worth shipping.

Burdened with debts and plagued by pests, drought, and disease, the Midwest farmer was angry. Looking about, he could find plenty of people to blame—the railroad owner, the manufacturer, the banker, the middleman, the mortgage holder, the tariff protectionist—most of them in the East. "The East," said one editor, "has placed its hands on the throat of the West and refused to afford us that measure of justice which we, as citizens of a common country, are entitled to receive." If he was ever to receive justice, the farmer concluded, he would have to wrest control of transportation, credit, markets, currency, and land from the hands of those whose interests were inimical to his own.

The most concrete personification of all that was anathema to the farmer was the railroad. It was his lifeline, his single means of getting a crop to market and receiving goods in return, almost as important to him as his capacity to raise a crop. When reminded that if there had been no railroad, there would have been no farmer and no West, he retorted that if the railroads persisted in oppressing him, there was likely to be neither farmer nor West. Neither the farmer nor the railroad was wholly at fault for contemporary prices, and certainly part of the responsibility lay in historical and economic conditions which neither had caused.

The tremendous need for transportation in the newly opened West after the war caused a frenzy of railroad building. Without transportation the West was useless, so after 1870 the upper Mississippi Valley and the plains began to be covered by a lacework of trackage. The Union Pacific was chartered in 1862, the Northern Pacific in 1864, the Atlantic and Pacific (later the Santa Fe) in 1866, the Texas Pacific in 1871, and after them the Burlington, the Southern Pacific, the Rock Island, the North Western, the Milwaukee, and others that reached into every producing area. All this construction required huge amounts of capital, far more than private sources could provide; the nation, the states, and the local governments pitched in to help. The federal government held title to western lands which it granted either directly to the railroads or to the states, which in turn passed them on to the railroads. Towns, counties, and states gave loans or donations or floated bonds, and the companies themselves issued stock for sale to speculators and settlers. Much of the railroads' capital, however, came from land—between 150,000,000 and 190,000,000 acres in all. In Iowa, they received an acreage larger than the area of Connecticut and Rhode Island combined, and in Minnesota, it was double the size of Massachusetts. Railroad grants in the Dakotas and Kansas were as large as New Jersey, and in Nebraska larger than New Hampshire.

The temptations involved in the handling of almost illimitable amounts of other people's land and money proved very great. Instead of selling land to settlers, some railroad companies withheld it for speculation or sold it to land companies. Some found it convenient to issue stock and water it, or to disregard wasteful methods of construction, or to accept grants and then fail to build. Jay Cooke, once sold $37,000,000 in bonds and incurred $3,000,000 in indebtedness on six hundred miles of second-rate railroad. Where the real cost of building in the flat West ran from $8,000 to $12,000 a mile, companies sometimes spent as much as $66,000 a mile, much of it construction-ring graft. The complex convolutions of stock issues, receivership, and reorganization left the investor confused, usually with a handful of worthless stock. Some railroads organized, received charters and grants, sold stock and made loans, went into receivership, reorganized, and issued stock again without laying a mile of track. Since the railroads had been subsidized for the good of the public, especially in the West, the farmer's bitter antagonism toward them is understandable.

Once construction was finished, and the railroads actually began to serve the Midwest, another set of conflicts appeared. From the farmer's point of view, the railroad had been built to haul goods. From the point of view of the railroad, it was a capitalistic venture intended to make a profit for the investors while rendering reasonable service. The point of conflict between the two concerned chiefly rates and services, the farmer demanding those which gave him the greatest profit on his crop shipments, the railroad those which allowed it the greatest margin of operating profit. Before 1870 the farmer generally assumed that competition between lines would keep rates down, but it soon became clear that, as Charles Francis Adams pointed out, the very nature of the railroad business precluded competition. It was economically wasteful to have two or more rail lines serving every point, and even if it were possible, the stronger and more efficient company would soon drive out or absorb the weaker.

The farmer complained too that the railroads' habit of undervaluing themselves for tax appraisals and overvaluing themselves for rate-making or stock-issuing purposes was nothing but simple theft. In Illinois the railroads were capitalized at $42,450 a mile but assessed for taxes at $7,800 a mile; in Iowa they were capitalized at $35,000 a mile and taxed at $5,000, while in Nebraska and Kansas they were capitalized at

$40,000 and $52,500 a mile, respectively, and taxed at $5,800 and $6,500. Already paying heavy taxes to discharge local and state debts incurred by loans to railroads (Kansas alone lent $175,000,000) and perhaps the holder of a few shares of extremely watered stock himself, the farmer claimed with some justice that the whole railroad business was a monumental steal.

He had a point. A million bushels of wheat in one Wisconsin county in the sixties and seventies were worth a dollar a bushel at the railhead; shipping it to a lake port cost another dollar a bushel, and from there to New York another fifty cents a bushel; thus of the two and a half million dollars the wheat brought in market, one and a half million went to the railroads. Ignatius Donnelly in 1873 noted that it cost as much to ship wheat from Minneapolis to Milwaukee as to ship the same wheat from Milwaukee to Liverpool. Furthermore, the railroads instituted the "transit rate," a device by which the shipped paid in advance the full freight to the easternmost terminal, no matter where the shipment went; thus a shipment to Minneapolis was charged the rate to Chicago or Milwaukee. In addition, the railroads made agreements with elevator companies, commission agents, and others to control both shipping and market rates. With thousands of bushels of wheat or corn to sell, the farmer was forced to deal with the railroad, elevator, or buyer nearest him; there was no way he could force the railroad to come to him on his terms.

The arrogance of some of the railroad kings in the seventies and eighties had much to do with the farmer's hatred of the railroad. With the Dartmouth College case at their backs, the railroads flatly denied that the public possessed any right whatsoever to interfere wtih the operation of a private business. Hired publicists and sympathetic journalists insisted interminably that the railroads had done far more for the settler than he had ever done for them. Railroads had opened the West, populated it, and gave it markets. Justice Paine of the Wisconsin supreme court thought railroads had "done more to develop the wealth and resources, to stimulate the industry, reward the labor and promote the general comfort and prosperity of the country than any other and perhaps all other mere physical causes combined." Farmers knew nothing about railroad operation and had best keep their noses out. "Given a company of men pursuing a lawful and useful occupation," asked Sidney Dillon, president of the Union Pacific, "why interfere with them? Why empower a body of other men . . . to dictate to these citizens how they should manage their private affairs?" Granted that the railroads, like most institutions, could stand reformation, who was fit to reform them except railroad men?

And the railroad kings were really kings. Lord Bryce observed that they constituted the nearest thing to dynasties that America possessed, for they had wealth, fame, power, and regal influence. A. B. Stickney recalled touring the West in his private train in the eighties, with merchants and businessmen of each town waiting respectfully at the stations, hats in hand, with furs for his wife and a case of champagne for him. Railroads had special clerks who did nothing but issue free passes; they hired editors and newspapers, retained the best attorneys, controlled the least and the most influential public officials. Senators and representatives did not consider it unethical to appear on railroad payrolls as lobbyists. The Pennsylvania provided special trains for newspaper conventions and gave free trips each year to seaside resorts to members of Congress. One reporter who came to Washington, determined to expose the railroads, in a few days had collected passes to his home and return, three to New York and return, and a three-day pass to Cape May.

Every railroad of consequence maintained lobbies in the capitals of every Midwestern state and by lavish use of money and passes dominated legislation with relative ease. Richard T. Ely knew one state senator in Wisconsin who distributed two thousand free passes in a single legislative session. It did not pay to buck the system. When Edward Russell, a small-town editor in Iowa, tried it, the railroad refused to deliver his coal for his press, and he had to dig his own from a seam in his yard to keep going. A hardware dealer who supported Russell found his shipping charges suddenly doubled; the freight agent blandly told him, "We reserve these rates for those who antagonize us." Another Iowan, who fought a claim against the railroad in court and lost, rode home on the train from the county seat with the judge, several jurors, his own attorney, and the railroad's—every one of them rode free on a pass except the farmer.

Next in importance to the Midwestern farmer was the matter of credit. The settler who came west, unless he was fortunate enough to bring cash with him, was usually in debt from the moment he arrived. He borrowed to buy land, machinery, tools, and seed. His day-to-day supplies he bought on credit from a local dealer, while to buy machinery and implements he used company credit or a bank loan. A crop failure or a drop in prices brought him face to face with either foreclosure or further debt. Usually unfamiliar both with good financial practices and efficient farming methods, the farmer was not wholly blameless. Yet he was victimized by high rates of legal interest and the smooth talk of loan and mortgage companies' agents.

Most of the money the farmer borrowed came from the East. New Hampshire in 1888 held eighteen and a half million in Western mortgages, while *Rhodes' Journal of Banking* estimated that 40 per cent of the amount in the savings banks of New Hampshire and Vermont was so invested. The St. Louis *Republican,* though its figures were only approximate, claimed that interest payments from the Midwestern states to Eastern mortgage holders ran to $180,000,000 a year. The *Iowa Tribune* spoke bitterly of a "Mortgage Cow" with her forefeet in the Mississippi Valley and her hind feet on the Atlantic seaboard, pointing out that "nearly all of the farmers of the West help to feed her while all her milk and cream and butter go to a favored few in the East."

The system began with individual brokers, who accepted money from Eastern investors and lent it to Midwestern farmers, with the broker taking the difference between the interest rate the farmer could pay and the rate the investor would accept—from 6 to 8 per cent on land and from 10 to 18 per cent on chattels as a rule, though instances of 5 per cent a month were recorded. After the drought years of the eighties, rates of from 18 to 24 per cent became common, with a high of 40 per cent noted now and then. Nebraska in the late eighties, it was said, "raised three crops—corn, freight rates, and interest."

The individual broker gave way to the loan corporation whose agents traveled from farm to farm in buggies, drumming up business. "There is scarcely a town of 500 inhabitants that is not supplied with an agency for Eastern Capitalists," wrote a Kansas editor in 1888. The Eastern investor deposited his money with the corporation, which in turn lent the money to the farmer, taking a commission of from 10 to 15 per cent on a ten-year loan. This commission itself was secured by notes and a second mortgage, payable to the company in ten semi-annual installments, the default of one bringing the entire commission due. The company then made out the mortgage to itself and assigned it to the investor, with a partial or full guarantee of payment backed by bonds or other mortgages. The borrower promised to pay taxes on his property, maintain, and insure it. On default of an interest payment, or on the failure to keep any of the agreements, the whole amount fell due. If the farmer could not pay, the company either offered him a loan (at interest up to 24 per cent in some states) or bought his farm at the tax sale. In the event of foreclosure (and in some Kansas counties 90 per cent of the farms were foreclosed in one bad year) the company could either pay off the investor and keep the farm and sell it or turn it over to the mortgage holder. Since the first method allowed financing a new loan to a new buyer, the companies found it more profitable.

In the defense of the system, the loan corporations pointed

out that the risk involved in this type of investment justified high rates and rigid specifications. The investor depended upon someone else's judgment, for he rarely saw the mortgaged land and knew nothing of Western conditions. Land booms made values fluctuate crazily, and faulty titles (especially in Indian lands) occasionally caused trouble. The worst risk of all to the investor was the agent, who lived on commissions and was likely to grant loans that should never have been made. However, the amount of profit made by most loan companies indicated that it was a relatively safe and highly lucrative business. There were two hundred such firms in Kansas and Nebraska by 1890, and five of them in Kansas City reported $68,000,000 outstanding that year. Though it warned that Western land investments were far from being gilt-edged securities, the Boston *Journal* in 1889 concluded that "There is no longer any doubt, even in the minds of the most conservative and careful investors, that money can be safely invested in Western mortgages."

A great deal of what the farmer in the Midwest needed he purchased from Eastern firms—machinery, sewing machines, clothes, shoes, coal, oil, fertilizer, and so on. At the same time he sold to Eastern corporations the wheat, beef, corn, and other products that he raised. In effect, he sold to companies that could fix his selling price, and bought from those that he could fix the price for what he bought. It was actually possible, for example, to buy an American-made reaper in Europe for less than its price in Kansas. Therefore, the price-fixing monopoly (later the trust) became another target of the farmer's ire. The farmers' convention of 1873 in Springfield, Illinois, called monopolies "detrimental to the public prosperity, corrupt in their management, and dangerous to republican institutions." Governor Larrabee of Iowa repeated in 1886 that "through trusts and combinations, the prices of many of the necessities are greatly increased, to the undoubted disadvantage of the farmer," and the theme ran through Midwestern thought into the next century.

The farmer was in no position to bargain with the monopoly. A wheat farmer, for example, sold his grain to the elevator nearest him, for he could not ship it about looking for the best price. The elevator, usually owned by a syndicate or by the railroad near which it stood, bought at the price set by the syndicate. Many a farmer found his No. 1 wheat graded as No. 2, or as wet, frozen, weedy, or smutted, with a corresponding decrease in price, while those who followed the course of their grain to the miller found it mysteriously upgraded again. The state railroad commission of Minnesota once figured that farmers lost an average of at least five cents a bushel by dishonest grading practices. Similarly, when the farmer bought a plow, he found himself dealing with a syndicate once more; quite possibly he bought it through an agent who collected a commission for the sale, and more than likely he bought it on credit at a high rate of interest. Manufacturing concerns holding patents on articles used by the farmer guarded them jealously. The profits obtained by the holders of patents, such as the McCormicks, were enormous. Patent rights near expiration were often extended by various ruses, and furthermore the federal patent office occasionally gave patents on ideas long in common use, such as the Teal sliding gate, which was finally declared unpatentable after a long fight by Michigan farmers.

High on the farmer's list of grievances—next to the railroads, the loan companies, and the monopoly—were national currency and tariff policies. Post-Civil War deflation hit him hard, and the crash of 1873 aggravated the currency problem. The debts he incurred were sometimes paid in currency worth from 15 to 20 per cent more than that which he had originally borrowed. The protective tariff policy, adopted originally as a means of revenue and continued after the war for the benefit of manufacturing, added to his troubles. "Why is agriculture depressed?" asked the *Minneapolis Farm, Stock and Home*. "Because we are compelled to pay tribute to millions and billions of fictitious values, to protected classes, to capitalistic conspiracies, and to a thousand and one artificial and vicious

influences." Though it was estimated by farmers that the prevailing tariff schedules cost them $600,000,000 a year, pressure
from manufacturing interests in the East prevented not only
any revision of the tariff but also any real study of the problem. Garfield's statement, "If I had my way, if I were king of
this country, I would put a duty of $100 a ton on pig iron
and a proportionate duty on everything else," was perfectly
representative of the protectionist policy of Congress throughout the period. It bore hard on the farmer who sold his staple
crops in a free world market and bought in a protected home
market.

The whole interrelated problem of credit, monopoly, currency, and tariff fused into one major issue in the Midwest—
the impoverished farmer versus the Eastern "money king." The
railroad man, the monopolist, the speculator, the banker, the
mortgage holder, the manufacturer, all merged into a single
composite creature, the "plutocrat," whom the farmer hated
and feared. The "plutocrat" planted no corn or wheat, built
no towns, farmed no land, and battened on the labor of those
who did; he foreclosed mortgages, raised freight rates, charged
high interest, stole public lands, and bought legislatures. When
the farmer read about the "Swan" dinner at Delmonico's
(where swans swam in a thirty-foot lake in the banquet room),
or about the "gold" and "diamond" dinners at which each
guest received a ring or bracelet, or about the Astor wedding
where the presents were valued at two million, or about the
Kansas City bankers' dinner at $20,000 a plate, and then
thought of mortgages at 18 per cent on half the farms in the
West, he was not in a pleasant mood.

Traditionally any discontented group in the United States,
if its grievances are sufficiently strong and its numbers sufficiently large, turns to political action for redress. The Midwest farmer of the postwar period found himself in a peculiarly
disadvantageous position when he tried to do so. The dominant party, the Republican, was controlled by and for the

Northeastern and Middle Atlantic states. It was an efficient and thorough machine, its grip so firm in the Midwestern area that it saw no reason to listen to the cries of debt-ridden malcontents. The farmer was, for all practical purposes, unrepresented in state and national governments under the Republican regime. Of the Forty-third Congress, which met in the seventies, for example, 61 per cent were lawyers, 16 per cent businessmen, and 7 per cent farmers, though of the national population 47 per cent were engaged in agriculture. In Illinois in the same period, where more than half the population of the state was agricultural, one sixth of the senate and less than one quarter of the house were farmers. Other Midwest legislatures showed about the same percentages, a situation largely the fault of the farmer and of the conditions under which he lived. Ignorant of political methods, clannish and suspicious, confused about the issues and often uncertain of exactly what he did want, committed by blind loyalty to a party that did not represent him, the Midwest farmer was simply lost in a political wilderness.

In 1866 the Agricultural Bureau sent a clerk through the South to gather statistical material. This young man, Oliver Hudson Kelley of Itasca, Minnesota, was impressed among other things by the absence of organization and unity among farmers. An ardent Mason, Kelley conceived of a agricultural secret society to educate farmers and advance their interests. After entering the Post Office Department as a clerk a year later, he enlisted the aid of several other government workers and organized such a society in 1867. Its aim was educational and social; it admitted women equally with men and placed great stress on reading and discussion to stimulate the farmer's interest and increase his fund of knowledge, generally as well as specifically. "Our order is right," wrote Kelly. "Its foundation is laid on *solid nothing*—the rock of poverty—and there is no harder material."

The official title of the order was the Patrons of Husbandry, but it soon became known as the Grange. The pattern of the organization provided for state granges (called "divisions") and for local granges covering roughly a township, called "subordinate granges." The local groups might, if membership warranted, band together in a "district grange." The masters of state granges and their wives, in later phases of the organization, made up the National Grange—the controlling legislative body with policy-making powers.

The local grange admitted anyone over fourteen years of age whose interests were "closely connected with agriculture." The presiding elected officer was called the Master; under him were twelve other officers, the most important being the Lecturer, who arranged programs and handled the educational work. Meetings were held weekly or semiweekly, usually consisting of a business session, a recess for social gathering, and the "Lecturer's Hour," a program of readings, discussion, music, debates, essays, and so on. The ritual, intended to encourage cohesion and fraternity, consisted of signs, passwords and secrets, while the order granted seven degrees—four by the subordinate grange, one by the state grange, and two by the National Grange. Most granges built and owned their own halls, with an audience room, a smaller meeting room, and a kitchen for the preparation of "feasts."

The Grange was avowedly nonpolitical, affirming that "no Grange, if true to its obligation, can discuss political or religious questions, or call political conventions, or nominate candidates, or even discuss their merits at meetings." But on the other hand the Granger as a citizen was pledged to "take a proper interest in the politics of his country . . . , put down corruption, bribery, and trickery in his own party," and see to it that "competent, faithful, honest men, who will unflinchingly stand by our industrial interests, are nominated." This obviously equivocal stand caused some confusion. It was almost impossible to prevent farmers from talking about freight rates or high taxes after 1870, and as a result there developed political "clubs" or "associations" which had no official connection with the Grange but grew out of it.

Kelly and the others organized the first subordinate grange, Potomac No. 1, in Washington, but soon realized that someone would have to tour the farm states and organize on the spot. Kelley therefore left to work through the East, reaching Minnesota in 1868. The organizing trip did not go well; an order was established at Newton, Iowa, and another at St. Paul, the first permanent granges in the West. The latter, the famous North Star Grange, had the brilliant Colonel D. A. Robertson at its head, and with his assistance Kelley revised and sharpened his techniques. "The Grange," wrote one observer, "was advertised as if it were a patent medicine." Another year saw thirty-seven subordinate granges in Minnesota, and from there the movement fanned out into Iowa, Wisconsin, Illinois, Nebraska, Kansas, and Indiana. The high point came in 1873-74, when twenty-three thousand subordinate granges claimed 750,000 members. By 1880 the number of chapters had dropped to four thousand, and after the turn of the century it remained strong in only a few areas of the Midwest.

A good many members agreed with Ignatius Donnelly's statement that a nonpolitical farmers' organization was like a gun that wouldn't shoot. After 1876 Granger leaders decided that "agitation for desirable legislation was acceptable," and soon the Granger "special committee" appeared as a lobbying group. Candidates for office were questioned, mass petitions and letters sent to congressmen, and—not very subtly—Grange conventions were held in capital cities while legislatures were in session. Legislators found it a sobering experience to walk through a crowd of overalled Grangers on their way to vote on a bill affecting farmers.

Though the Grange itself was never actually a political party, there was nothing to prevent its members from engaging in pressure politics. The farmers wanted to clip the wings of the railroads. They wanted educational benefits, better schools and more extensive agricultural training in them, cheap textbooks, better instruction. They wanted tax-law revisions—no exemption of railroad properties, a tax on mortgages but not

on mortgaged property, a more equitable adjustment of the
tax burdens on persons and corporations. They wanted reduced rates of interest and a more liberal credit system. They
wanted less expensive and better government. "Give us cheap
coal, cheap bread, cheap transportation, cheap clothing," wrote
James McCabe, the Grangers' historian. "We want the price
of every necessary article of consumption or daily use lowered,
and whatever man or combination of men who seek to prevent
the realization of this demand is the enemy of the public." All
this boiled down to three major demands that ran consistently
through Granger political thinking—remove special interest
from government, make it more responsible to the people, and
broaden its concept to include economic and social welfare.
Grangerism was the earliest form of Midwestern progressivism.
Bryan and La Follette built on this foundation.

In the post-Civil War period it was hard to find a political
outlet for such ideas. The two major parties were controlled
either by leaders who preferred not to notice the new issues or
by practical politicians who cleverly used old issues to divide
sentiment and distract attention from the new ones. The Democrats had little influence in Midwest politics, for the old prewar coalition between Southern and Western farmer was
broken. The Democratic party had, after all, been "the party
of treason and secession"; as one Kansan said, "Hell is peopled
by two kinds of folks, those who don't read the Bible and those
who vote Democratic." As Brand Whitlock said later of his
Midwestern boyhood, any self-respecting person knew that
Republicanism was "a fundamental and self-evident thing, like
life, liberty, and the pursuit of happiness, or like the flag, or
the federal judiciary."

War and reconstruction made the Republican party a powerful, unified, energetic organization. It had the most effective
slogans ever possessed by a political party—"Vote the way you
shot," and "The party that saved the nation must rule it." It
was also corrupt, so patently so that a "Liberal" Republican

element broke off in 1872 in an unsuccessful attempt to drive out the "boodlers" and clean up national politics. But the party withstood reformers without much difficulty; theirs was the party of Lincoln, Grant, and Sherman, a party of loyalty, military allegiance, and a colorful past. How could a farmer, or a workman, or a veteran disown the party that had saved the nation? Republican politicians traded shamelessly on the unreasoning loyalty and *esprit de corps* that drew men to it. It was clear in the seventies and eighties that it would do the Midwestern Democratic party little good to change its course, and the Republican party need not. The only effective outlet for Granger activity in politics seemed to lie in a third party.

Between 1873 to 1876 the Midwest was dotted with small, abortive parties under various names, composed of Grangers, Liberal Republicans, and other reformers, parties which either eventually fused with the Democrats or retained a precarious independence. Though never really successful, they did force some concessions from the dominant Republicans simply by existing, but the great majority of these independent political groups were either absorbed into major parties or dead by 1876. Republicanism in the Midwest was simply too strong for a third-party movement; the farmers' only hope lay in capturing a major party, a virtually impossible feat at the time. The lingering distaste of many Midwesterners for the Democrats ruled out that party, and the Republicans refused to harbor malcontents. The minor third parties possessed neither real leadership, effective organization, nor a stable and trustworthy following—they had nothing with which to challenge the smooth, powerful machine the Republicans had built. Then too, the farmer did not yet have a really popular issue. True, times were bad, freight rates high, and prices low, but campaign promises and the hope of a good crop next year always encouraged defection from independent ranks.

The platforms of these parties, however, and the minor successes they did enjoy, were prophetic. Almost unanimously, they demanded state regulation of corporations, especially of railroads. The Northwest Farmers' Convention, meeting in Chicago in 1873 with delegates from seven states, drew up a typical list of those Granger issues adopted by most of the independent parties: federal regulation of transportation rates, outlawing of subsidies to corporations, government-built and owned railroads, encouragement of decentralized manufacturing, no tariff protection for industry, and revision of the credit system. Granger resolutions and conventions in other states followed this pattern fairly closely.

The Granger-independent movement of the seventies concentrated most of its political energy on that *bête-noire* of the farmer, the railroad—to keep it out of politics, reduce its rates, and subject it to popular control as a public service corporation. The railroads, with millions in cash to spend and an expensive array of lobbyists and legal talent, held the contest to at least a draw. In Illinois, where antirailroad legislation had already been introduced in the sixties, the farmers forced a clause into the new state constitution which directed the legislature to act further on the matter. In 1871 the legislature responded with a new set of rate laws for railroads and elevators and a plan for the establishment of a board of railroad and warehouse commissioners to enforce them, but the state supreme court declared them all invalid. By 1873 the farmers were stronger and passed a stiffer bill, again tossed out by the same chief justice who ruled on the 1871 laws. The matter eventually went to the federal Supreme Court which, in the famous "Granger Decisions" of the late seventies and early eighties, found for the farmers. Though provisions for their enforcement were generally inadequate, the Illinois "Granger laws" established two principles that became fundamental to the progressive movement later—the right of the state to control corporations, and the use of commissions as a device for their regulation. Despite constant agitation by the railroads, the "Granger laws" remained on the books.

The clearest manifestations of Granger power outside of Illi-

nois appeared in Minnesota, Wisconsin, and Iowa. Minnesota
in 1871 passed two laws, one fixing rates and the other appoint-
ing a railroad commissioner, but the railroads immediately
snarled them in litigation. In 1874 another set of laws, modeled
on the Illinois pattern, had sharper teeth, but the decline of
Grangerism and the growth of railroad opposition blunted
them to the point of uselessness. In Iowa, ruled by the Burlington, Grangers and the Anti-Monopolists pushed through a
passenger-rate schedule in 1873 and a fixed-rate freight act
not long after. The Burlington obtained an injunction against
the laws, tying them up until settlement came with those of
Illinois, Minnesota, and Wisconsin in the Supreme Court.
Constant attacks by the railroad interests finally forced modifications in the laws by 1878. In Wisconsin the Grange and the
Reform party belabored the Republicans into accepting an
antirailroad plank, and a Democratic-Reform coalition victory
in 1873 brought about the Potter Law, a complex piece of
legislation apparently designed to be so bad that it would have
to be repealed.

In other states the Grangers achieved little. Nebraska and
Kansas, completely under railroad domination, produced
nothing. Ohio passed a rate-fixing bill with no means of enforcing it. Indiana Grangers asked for railroad legislation and
got none, and Michigan appointed a commissioner with
nothing more than supervisory duties. By the time the Granger
cases were settled, sniping by the railroads had reduced most
of the statutes to impotence, and the solution to the railroad
problem was left to later and more powerful movements. The
railroads were victorious for the time being. "There was a
time when railroad men were badly off-color in this state,"
wrote a Milwaukee official from Wisconsin in 1878, "but by
fasting and prayer and self-sacrifice they are now able to look
an honest Granger in the left eye and charge him 4¢ a mile."

The railroads, naturally, replied to the Grangers by appealing to legal precedent, laissez faire, and individual enterprise.
In the first place, they argued, the rates the farmers complained

of were quite necessary, since the cost of building and maintaining railroads was enormous and high rates were needed to pay off debts and stock dividends. How could investors be persuaded to furnish capital for new lines, or to increase services for the old ones, if Granger laws frightened them away? The railroads also possessed the perfectly valid argument that interference with their business was illegal, for they were fully protected by the fourteenth constitutional amendment. And even if it were legal to fix rates, the complexity of railroad business was such that only an expert railroad man could do it, not some "bucolic legislator" or commissioner who was "the willing agent of demagogues." For the most effective argument of the Grangers, that the railroads had been built by funds raised from the sale of public land grants and were therefore under public control, they had an equally effective reply. If this principle held, suggested Perkins of the Burlington, why should not the federal government fix the prices of farm products raised on land given to the settler under the Homestead Act?

Most of all, the railroads claimed the whole Granger platform was un-American, an interference with private affairs that amounted, bluntly, to communism—an endlessly repeated epithet. J. Sterling Morton of Nebraska termed the Grange "a national humbug, a sort of huge bunko establishment . . . an organized, active, and influential idiocy" under "the red flag of communism." Godkin of the *Nation* thought that the Grangers were defiling the pure springs of American democracy with "the dregs of European communism." A Wisconsin judge said that the Potter Law was "the spirit of communism in disguise," a spirit "born in the seething brain of France" which had finally "traversed the ocean and established itself upon our shores." Coupled with the demands of city laborers for "ten hours pay for eight hours' work," Granger policies led straight to communism. The scarehead of radicalism and un-Americanism undoubtedly influenced large segments of public opinion, but it never bothered the Grangers.

The attack on the railroad was the most bitterly fought portion of the Granger war on monopoly, but not the only one. The farmer's anger at the manufacturer and middleman resulted in an attempt to beat them down by going into business for himself—in co-operative ventures aimed at breaking monopolistic control of the market. Some subordinate granges made deals with local merchants for discounts in return for cash trade. Others appointed or hired an agent, who took orders from Grange members and bought directly from wholesalers and jobbers, and in the early seventies thousands of rural dollars were saved in this fashion. Some firms made special bids for Granger trade, and one of them, Montgomery Ward and Company, developed a mail-order business aimed directly at the farmer. Farmers banded together to purchase implements, machinery, clothing, feed, seed, and other necessities otherwise available only through manufacturers' agents or local stores.

Iowa granges were the most successful in co-operative buying ventures, but the movement spread into every Grange state from Kansas to Ohio. It was only a step from agency buying to agency selling, which led to the co-operative store. The importation of the British Rochdale plan gave co-operatives a great boost; some of them, first established under Granger auspices, are still in business. In the same way the farmers attempted to break price-fixing monopolies in beef, pork, and grain by organizing co-operative selling groups and by buying elevators. In Iowa it was reported in 1872 that one third the grain elevators and warehouses were Granger-owned or controlled. Millions of bushels of grain and thousands of cattle and hogs were shipped directly to buyers at a savings of from 10 to 40 per cent to the farmer.

Eventually the Grange was forced into business for itself, since the majority of manufacturers disliked the agent system and refused to deal with it. Twenty-two plow manufacturers met in 1873, for example, and agreed to sell no plows to granges except at retail prices. In reply the granges started their own factories to smash the "machinery rings" and the "monopolists." Nebraska Grangers attempted to manufacture headers (a device used to gather only the heads of grain) and sold them at half the prevailing price; bad machines and worse management killed the enterprise and very nearly killed the Grange in Nebraska. The most successful venture was a factory for the manufacture of the Werner harvester, located in Iowa, which made and sold good harvesters for about half-price. Plans were projected for plants in Minnesota and Nebraska, and the Grange bought up patents for cultivators, seeders, reapers, mowers, and dozens of other implements. The whole project blew up in 1875, plagued by defective machines, patent suits, and insufficient capital, and as Grangerism died, so did co-operative manufacturing. A few Granger banks were founded in protest against the "bankers' ring," and also a number of mutual insurance ventures. The banks lasted only briefly; the fire insurance companies operated fairly well, but the life insurance companies did not. The only Granger business that survived the final wreckage was the co-operative creamery, cheese factory, mill, or packing plant, built to provide a market for local products. These still survive in many parts of the Midwest, particularly in dairy country.

The Grangers' attempt to break monopoly failed, as it was bound to, for obvious reasons. The spirit of the co-operative movement did not fit the temper of rural life in the seventies, for the farmer was traditionally a self-reliant, independent individualist, totally unaccustomed to co-operative responsibility. Some of the enterprises were not at all suited to the co-operative system, particularly those involving manufacturing processes that required considerable engineering and supervisory skill. The Grangers were not accustomed to business, unfamiliar with the dangers of granting indiscriminate credit, and lacking in working capital. They faced, in addition, the unremitting hostility of local merchants, manufacturers, buyers, and bankers. The co-operatives were not equipped to compete with better-financed private businesses, which could declare and win a price war. Wider use of the Rochdale system might have saved them, but even that is doubtful.

The Granger movement was not a failure, though it left few marks on the statute books. The first large-scale attempt to organize the farmer, it prepared the way for the Farmers' Alliance, Populism, insurgency, and progressivism. The farmer found in the Grange that joint action got results—the first modification of the old pioneer individualism. The third parties disappeared, but they gave the Midwest a taste of independent politics that it did not forget. Broken once, the bonds of party loyalty might be broken more easily again.

Most important, the Granger movement marked the beginning of the end for the unregulated development of the corporation. The railroads won, and the co-operative did not succeed in breaking monopoly, but during the Granger years the farmer in the Midwest spent a great deal of time thinking about business, hitherto untouchable by law. If the law made corporations, he reasoned, it could also unmake them. Natural law and competition were not enough to secure economic justice, it seemed, and the idea of state control and regulation, a radical departure from the old Jeffersonian concept of weak government, seeped into Midwest political thinking. Faced by an oppressive combination of shipper, manufacturer, supplier, and creditor, the farmer had but one agency left to which to appeal for help—the state. According to the rules of the laissez-faire Darwinian game, the defeated farmer should have bowed to the victor, the corporate genius of business, and accepted his leadership. The Granger broke the rules and resorted to political action (always possible under the American system), hoping to gain by politics what he could not gain by open struggle. He did not gain much in the seventies, but he caught the idea. When the Midwest developed leaders of its own, he gained more.

The vacuum left by the disappearance of the numerous Granger-independent parties was almost immediately filled by a new third party—the Greenback—the first appearance (but not the last) of the currency issue in Midwest politics. The plank upon which the Greenbackers built dated back to the early days of the Republic, to the old argument of "hard" versus "soft" money, but the immediate currency problem was chiefly a result of the Civil War. During the war, as gold gradually disappeared from circulation, Congress authorized the issuance of paper money, "greenbacks," supported by nothing but the national credit. They were strictly a war-financing measure, but the man who borrowed under this system of cheap and plentiful money found that it suited his purposes quite well. At the end of the war some $400,000,000 in greenback currency was out, as well as an unknown amount of government securities in use as currency. In the postwar years, the Treasury planned to retire the greenbacks and resume payment in specie, thus reducing the amount of currency, high prices, and inflation.

From the South and West, where borrowing had been heavy, the Treasury's policy aroused violent protest. A farmer in Iowa who had borrowed $2,000 in paper money worth seventy-five cents on the dollar would now be paying it back in gold or gold notes worth one hundred cents on the dollar. As in all currency disputes, the creditor wanted debts paid in dear money, the debtor in cheap money. "The relation of the West to the East is that of debtor to creditor," wrote one Western editor in an admirably clear-sighted summary of the argument. "It is for this reason that the Eastern influence is always exerted toward a contraction of the volume of the currency, while the tendency of the West is toward inflation. Until the West becomes rich enough to be independent of the East in financial matters, this contest will continue."

Various solutions to the greenback impasse were proposed, none satisfactory. Congress delayed action on greenbacks until the panic of 1873 brought the question up once again. Hard times, argued the greenback men, were caused by too little money; if the government would issue money equal in amount to that in circulation in 1865, when times were booming, they would boom again. The Republicans, who controlled Congress, vacillated between the demands of creditor and debtor, until finally in 1875 they decided to resume gold payments in 1879 and redeem the greenbacks. Howls of disapproval came from the debt-ridden Midwest, and Greenbackism momentarily merged with the railroads and the trusts as a political issue.

The Greenback movement in the Midwest was a continuation of the several Reform, Independent, and Anti-Monopoly parties that drew Granger support in the early seventies. Whereas in the Granger period the farmer sought a solution to his difficulties by lowering transportation costs through the control of freight rates, or by eliminating the monopolist and middleman through co-operatives, he now tried to accomplish the same result by currency inflation. Greenbackism itself came originally from the East, but after the 1873 crash it found fertile territory in the Midwest. "Our people out West," said Weaver of Iowa to Congress, "do not like the feast you set before them. . . . There is a screw loose in Federal legislation, and the people have found where it is."

Currency did not displace the railroad, monopoly, and credit as political issues, but absorbed them. The Greenbackers asked for control of corporations, honesty in government, conservation of natural resources, and for other reforms besides paper money—"a free ballot, a fair count, and equality for all classes," said General Weaver. The new party had also certain advantages over its predecessors, besides having a new and larger issue. It was better organized, had more experienced leaders, and drew support from dissatisfied debtors outside the Midwest. It organized on both national and state levels, running Peter Cooper, the millionaire Eastern reformer, in the presidential campaign of 1876 and placing tickets in most of the Western states. But it was never an important factor in national politics, and Cooper polled only 81,000 votes, mostly in Indiana, Illinois, Michigan, and Kansas. In certain of the Midwestern states, however, Greenbackism seriously threatened

Republicanism, and brought into politics men like James Baird Weaver of Iowa, "Roaring Bill" Allen of Ohio, "Blue Jeans" Williams of Indiana, Edward Allis of Wisconsin, and Ignatius Donnelly of Minnesota—real Western mavericks who prepared the soil for Bryan's harvest.

The national Greenback party in 1878 polled a million votes and put fifteen men in Congress. In 1880, with Weaver running for President, it cast 307,000 votes, and later with General Ben Butler at its head (a joint nomination with the Anti-Monopolists) only 173,000. Thus Greenbackism died a quick death. The return of prosperous times, the complexity of the currency problem, the lack of a leader, and the dominance of the Republican party killed it. The issue had to wait for Bryan.

With the collapse of the minor third parties a new farmers' movement, the real successor to the Grange, took shape in the Midwest. As early as 1874 local farm groups calling themselves "alliances" sprang up in the East, South, and West, emerging as the Southern Alliance and the Northwestern Alliance, separate organizations designed to serve regional needs. The organizing spark of the powerful Northwestern Alliance was Milton George, editor of the Chicago *Western Rural,* who founded the first local in Cook County, Illinois, in 1880. Under George's direction, the Alliance spread over the Midwest, claiming in 1882 eight state alliances, two hundred local alliances, and a total membership of a hundred thousand.

Unlike the Grange, the Alliance had no secret ritual, was loosely organized, and was admittedly political in character. Its aims, in order of their importance, were social, educational, financial, and political. Socially it encouraged meetings, picnics, and dinners; educationally it disseminated agricultural information, sponsored lectures, libraries, and newspapers, and encouraged reading on contemporary issues. Many a farmer read Bellamy's *Looking Backward,* Donnelly's *Caesar's Column,* Weaver's *Call to Action,* Powderly's *Thirty Years of Labor,* or

Henry George's *Progress and Poverty* on the recommendation of Alliance reading lists. Like the Grange, the Alliance involved itself in co-operatives—stores, elevators, grain-marketing organizations, insurance companies, and the like—whose successes varied with the skill of their managers.

Politically the Alliance rested upon much the same foundation as had the Grange—hard times—and the antimonopoly, antirailroad resolutions adopted by its state and local organizations were practically indistinguishable from those of the independent parties of the seventies. The new agriculture was in full swing in the Midwest by 1880, producing wheat, corn, hogs, and beef, dependent upon the railroad and Eastern markets—an invitation to monopoly control. The Eastern farmer, perhaps, was as much under the thumb of monopoly as the Midwestern, but he felt the pressure less. The Eastern monopoly was not engaged in direct exploitation of the farmer; the Western monopoly was. In the Midwest, the farmer met big business face to face—railroads, grain, lumber, banks—and saw it clearly. The fluctuation in the price of agricultural products, along with drought, hoppers, and debt, brought hard times, and Alliance membership grew on the issue of "ten cent corn and ten percent mortgages."

From a postwar high of $1.50 a bushel wheat fell to 67 cents in 1868, when the Grange first organized. Climbing back up to a dollar, wheat dropped to 87 cents in the years of the independent parties. Up to $1.05 by 1877 as these parties disappeared, it fell to 80 cents in the early years of the Alliance. By 1887, when the drought years began, it was down to 67 cents. Eight of the next ten years were too dry for good crops, with chinch bugs, killing frosts, and wind, and eleven thousand farms were foreclosed in a four-year span. Gloom settled over the farms of the Midwest, and Hamlin Garland, in his *Son of the Middle Border,* recalled how men in "this great new land" fell into "a slough of discouragement." Significantly, eighteen thousand prairie schooners crossed the Missouri in the year 1891, heading East.

As they had before, the farmers looked to political action for help. "The West should drop political lines and vote as a unit for the man of its choice," said the *Omaha Herald,* "and thus serve notice upon the Eastern capitalistic and monopoly element that it cannot run the country." The mood of the West showed in the 1880 elections. Garfield's victory by a plurality of slightly more than ten thousand in a major party vote of almost nine million indicated an extremely delicate state of balance in politics. Both parties, fearful of alienating even a small bloc of votes, avoided commitments on anything and left themselves practically issueless. The situation was potentially explosive.

Third parties seemed to be the only solution for the farmer's political problems. In the South, however, the Alliance felt that it must work through the dominant Democratic party, since with three parties in the field the Negro might be able to sell his vote to the highest bidder in return for social and economic privileges. The advantages of working with labor in a third party were evident, and some attempts were made at a farmer-labor coalition. In 1887 a Union Labor party, intended to draw support from Alliance, Greenback, Grange, and industrial elements, named a national ticket. State tickets appeared in Kansas, Iowa, and Wisconsin, and in Missouri, Arkansas, and Texas, but the "union" label, after the industrial troubles of 1885 and 1886, conjured up visions of strikes and violence and damaged the party's chances. Attempts were made again to consolidate the Northwestern and Southern Alliances with the Knights of Labor into a third party, but no basis of agreement could be found on questions of the Negro, hourly wages, strikes, and so on, and the proposed coalition came to naught.

In 1889 the Northwestern Alliance called a convention because, as it stated, "by reason of new systems of business and combinations against us, we are not, as an agricultural class, enjoying equal privileges with the manufacturing and commercial classes," and announced itself ready to do political business in twenty-five states. The result was a sudden resurgence of third-party activity—the People's party of Kansas and Nebraska, the Industrial party of Michigan, the Independent party of Iowa, South Dakota, Minnesota, and Indiana. Though it might not be successful, remarked the *New York Sun,* the Alliance would have the satisfaction of knowing that it had caused a near panic in both Republican and Democratic circles.

The platforms of these parties repeated the issues of the seventies. They asked for government ownership and regulation of railroads, economy and honesty in government, cheap money, tax reforms (including an income tax), tariff reductions, antimonopoly laws, control of the land policy, better credit systems—familiar themes of Midwest politics. A new "subtreasury" scheme was added, providing for federal warehouses in every farming district in which farmers might store crops and receive in return certificates worth 80 per cent of the market price. Used as currency, these certificates would really give the farmer credit, hold his crops off the market until the price rose, and inflate the currency. And also the issue of "free silver" (that the government should coin all silver offered it at a rate of sixteen grains of silver to one of gold, rather than eight to one) began to lift its head. But the farmer's old antagonists, the banks and the railroads, were still the chief targets. As William Peffer of Kansas put it, the Alliance represented a "defensive movement" against "the most powerful and active agencies in modern civilization, whose work is clearly traceable in our recent history—railroads, middlemen, and banks."

Alliance-sponsored third parties rang up some notable victories, especially in Kansas, Nebraska, South Dakota, and Minnesota, and some of lesser note in Michigan, North Dakota, and Indiana, where at least they cut sharply into Republican power. (It was an off-year election in Illinois and Iowa.) "The Republican party can hold nothing in the West without fighting for it," remarked a St. Louis paper after the 1890 elections. "The specter of the Farmers' Alliance overshadows all other political considerations here," said the *New York Herald,* while the *Philadelphia Times* lamented that "there is not a sure Republican state left in the West." "Hayseed socialism," "a monstrous system of paternalism," "fantastic, cheap-John politics," "a mad platform," said other Eastern papers. A Cleveland journal piously advised the recalcitrant farmers to abjure radical nonsense and return to the fold, for "Republicanism, strongly and faithfully supported, is the best and only agent through which reformers . . . can attain their end."

The Midwest farmer paid little attention to the warnings. A strong Alliance "wedge" went to Congress after the 1890 elections: two senators, Kyle of South Dakota and Peffer of Kansas (joined in 1892 by William Allen of Nebraska), and eight representatives—Halvorsen and Boen of Minnesota, Simpson, Clover, Baker, and Davis of Kansas, and Kem and McKeighan of Nebraska. In addition, there were some forty Democrats in Congress who owed their elections either to Alliance support or to the split it caused in the Republican vote; Hamlin Garland thought about fifty congressmen either were Alliance men or had Alliance sympathies.

Regarded more or less as curiosities (the press made great sport of Peffer's fearsomely luxuriant beard and "Sockless Jerry" Simpson's supposed aversion to socks) the third-party congressmen were able to do little of practical value for their discontented constituencies. True, they introduced a good many bills—for rural free delivery, a stronger Interstate Commerce Commission, a federal income tax, pure food and drug laws, industrial safety regulations and so on, every one of which later became law—but their bills usually died in committee. Yet their presence in Congress was a constant reminder to the old parties of the dissatisfied Midwest that had sent them there. The Interstate Commerce Act of 1887, though it chiefly affected transportation, and that only nominally, was partly the result of twenty years of farmer agitation, and the Sherman Anti-Trust Act of 1890 showed that the powerful antimonopoly protests of the Midwest were beginning to show results. The Sherman Silver Purchase Act of 1890, which doubled the amount of silver purchased annually and paid for it in currency notes redeemable in silver and gold, was at least a partial sop to Alliance and Greenback demands. The real accomplishments of the Alliance came not in Congress, however, but in the states.

Kansas, perhaps the hardest-hit financially of the Midwest states, reacted most strongly. By 1890 the farmer's situation in Kansas was extremely serious. Between 75 and 90 per cent of all Kansas farms were mortgaged at an average interest of 9 per cent. Lyon County, regarded as one of the more prosperous, had a total valuation of $6,500,000 and a mortgaged indebtedness of $5,500,000; about one third of all farm mortgages in the state were foreclosed in the decade 1880 to 1890, and in the first six months of 1890 ten thousand more were foreclosed. Farmers burned their corn and buried eggs; the drought of 1887 made the state so dry that one editor wryly claimed that "you had to prime the mourners at a funeral so they could shed tears for the departed."

In the fall elections of 1889 reform tickets under various names began to pop up here and there in Kansas. A "People's Convention" won in Cowley County, and in 1890 it joined the Alliance, single taxers, Knights of Labor, Grangers, and other groups, put up a state and congressional ticket, and began a campaign the like of which had never before been seen in the Midwest. It was a crusade, a fanatic upthrust of thousands of angry, dispossessed farmers, who met in lamp-lit one-room schoolhouses, at picnics, and in the fields to hear Jerry Simpson, Colonel Sam Wood, Annie Diggs, and dozens of others flay the Republicans. Mary Ellen Lease, "The Kansas Pythoness," gave the campaign its slogan—"Raise less corn and more hell"—and they did. Irish-born, with a powerful voice, snapping black eyes, and an unparalleled gift for invective, she left a trail of fire through the state. The incumbent Republican senator, John J. Ingalls, a cultured and dignified lawyer, she tagged as "a dishonest, soulless, shameless charlatan." Kansas, she said, "suffers from two great robbers, the Santa Fe Railroad and the loan companies. . . . The people are at bay, let the bloodhounds of money who have dogged us beware."

The Republicans simply could not stand against it. The hated Ingalls went down. William Peffer, single-taxer Jerry Simpson, and three others went to Congress from the People's party; but the new party took only the lower house of the legislature in the local elections, losing most of the state offices by narrow margins. Blocked at every turn by a Republican senate, the party could do little in the way of legislation, and watched a freight-rate bill, a passenger-fare bill, an anti-railroad-pass bill, an interest-rate bill, a corrupt practices act, and various other reform bills all go down the drain in the 1891 session.

Nebraska, dominated by Republicanism and railroads, felt the pulse of revolt too. The Democrats, under the guidance of J. Sterling Morton, pursued a middle way, joining occasionally in some elections with the discontented farmers without winning anything important. Though the Republicans had narrow squeaks in 1882, 1884, and 1886, they kept control of the state by granting token concessions to the third-party groups, but in 1890 the accumulated pressure of thirty years broke through. The Alliance called a convention for the creation of a People's Independent party, drew promises of support from the Knights of Labor and Liberal Republicans, and launched the wildest campaign in Nebraska history.

There were rallies, picnics, and barbecues—sixteen hundred wagons were counted at Hastings hitching posts for one People's party meeting. Farmers' glee clubs sang songs about Bartlett Richards (president of the Nebraska Land and Feeding Company), Tom Burton (of the Western Exchange Fire and Marine Insurance Company), and John Thurston (attorney for the Union Pacific). They were bitter songs, sung to familiar tunes, such as to "Marching Through Georgia."

No banks shall corner the exchange provided by the State,
No speculator shall get rich on wealth that we create,
No railroad e'er again shall tax three-fourths our crop for freight,
For we are marching for freedom.

Or, to the tune of "Save a Poor Sinner Like Me."

I was once a tool of oppression
As green as a sucker could be,
And monopolies banded together
To beat a poor hayseed like me.

The railroads and old party bosses
Together did sweetly agree
And they thought there would be little trouble
In working a hayseed like me.

But now I've roused up a little
And their greed and corruption I see.
And the ticket I vote next November
Will be made up of hayseeds like me.

The Republicans called Alliance farmers "shiftless, lazy, and improvident" people who "kept hogs in the parlor," but they swept the senate, shut the Republicans out of Congress, and nearly won the governorship. In the following legislative session they pushed through an Australian ballot law, a free-schoolbook law, mutual insurance company acts, and a bank-reform bill. A railroad-regulation bill passed both houses after an openly corrupt campaign against it, but Republican Governor Boyd vetoed it and an attempt to pass it over his veto failed.

Minnesota's story was much the same. By 1886 the Alliance replaced the Grange as a political force (it had 438 locals) and made overtures to the Knights of Labor. It sent some independents to the legislature that year, but the Republicans kept tight control of the state. Two years later the Alliance and the Knights established a Farmer and Labor party—one of the first real attempts in the Midwest to fuse the industrial and rural vote—based on votes for women, industrial safety laws, accident compensation, an eight hour day, and the Australian ballot. Though the Republicans won, and again in 1890, the revolt was well started in Minnesota. The Alliance hired Ignatius Donnelly as lecturer, and plans for a third party took shape, with popular election of senators, reduced interest rates, tariff revision, income taxes, and government ownership of railroads as the chief planks in its platform.

Third-party strength in Iowa was never great, but Granger pressure in the seventies made the Republican party pay attention to its demands. In the late seventies, Greenbackers sent General James Weaver and E. H. "Heifer-calf" Gillette to Congress, and again in the middle eighties resurgent farmer strength forced concessions from the Republicans. Governor Larrabee, who took office in 1886, was a Liberal Republican, an expert on railroad legislation, and sympathetic with the farmers. In his terms, 1886 to 1890, Republican legislatures enacted some concretely progressive legislation—an antitrust law aimed at coal, oil, lumber, grain, and other interests, and a bill empowering the state railroad commission to adjust rates, outlaw passes, and control stock issues. The farmers themselves broke the barbed-wire trust in Iowa and beat a patent trust in well-digging equipment after nine years of litigation.

The railroads, however, were strong in Iowa, and Judge Hubbard, the North Western's counsel, was always a powerful behind-the-scenes figure. In 1886 forty-five antirailroad bills were defeated in the House and sixteen in the Senate, while the few that did pass were all modified and weakened in later years. But in 1890 the Democrats, in one of the occasional upsets of Iowa politics, put Horace Boies in the governor's chair. At the same time the Farmers' Alliance, after a convention in Des Moines, formed a Union Labor Industrial party. Though unsuccessful at the polls, the new party split the

Republican vote sufficiently to insure Boies' re-election in 1891. Iowa, too, was on the doubtful list.

The two Dakotas, admitted as states in 1889, showed similar signs of restlessness. South Dakota, when still under territorial government, had formed a weak antimonopoly party, but after its admission to the Union an Alliance People's party quickly took fifty-seven seats in the state legislature and joined with the Democrats to send Senator Kyle to Washington. Working with the twenty-seven Democrats already in the legislature, the People's party men enacted the Australian ballot and passed a corrupt practices act and new election laws. North Dakota, like its sister, had a strong farmers' movement which swept the state elections in 1892. This legislature asked for a national income tax, the direct election of senators, government control of the telegraph, and the removal of duty on imported binder twine—an attempt to break a twine monopoly. It also appropriated $100,000 for construction of a state-owned elevator at Duluth or Superior for North Dakota wheat, an experiment wiped out by the depression of 1892 but not forgotten.

Of the eastern group of Midwest states, only Indiana reacted to Alliance politics. With the assistance of the Farmers' Mutual Benefit Association (an all-male secret order) the Alliance placed independent tickets in county elections only. However, the Alliance backed an unsuccessful People's party in 1890, and kept up efforts to perfect some sort of a state organization.

Wisconsin was Republican ridden. Lumber and railroads controlled the state, and from 1855 to 1893, except for one Granger-Democratic hiatus in the seventies, every governor was a Republican who owed his office to "Uncle Ike" Stephenson, Philetus Sawyer, or John C. Spooner, the party bosses. But in 1886 there were signs of trouble. Labor riots in Milwaukee were put down by troops sent by Governor Rusk (who supposedly said, "I seen my duty and I done it"), and a People's party formed at La Crosse, gathering together Green-

backers, Alliance farmers, and labor groups. The movement
came to nothing, but some Republicans, among them a young
country lawyer named Robert La Follette, began to ask for
reforms within the party.

In 1891 a survey of newspaper opinion concluded that
Alliance political power was "crumbling to pieces" because of
a revival of prosperity, good crops, the lack of appeal to a
single class, and other reasons. Yet there were clear signs of
dissatisfaction in all the states of the Middle Border. "The
West thinks the East is mercenary, and that its selfishness will
always forbid its giving honest counsel," concluded a Western
editor. "The West should be a political unit today on everything which pertains to the West or which affects Western
interests." In Kansas, Nebraska, Minnesota, Iowa, Wisconsin,
and the Dakotas, and less audibly in the more stable industrialized states of Michigan, Indiana, and Illinois, the farmer's
voice was raised, not always clearly, but loud enough to be
heard. The Republicans were still in power, it is true, but the
old slogans and loyalties were not quite so appealing as before. For nearly thirty years the people of the Midwest had
asked the major parties for relief, and had received none. Anyone could see the omens of revolt.

The Grangers and Greenbackers had lacked, among other
things, really competent leaders. In the Alliance movement of
the eighties they began to emerge—the first appearance of the
"hayseed radical," the "maverick," that native political type
that belonged solely to the Midwest. A few of them had already turned up: Larrabee in Iowa, who laid the foundation
for Cummins and the Iowa progressives later; Van Wyck of
Nebraska, the original insurgent Republican senator who
cheerfully voted against his party for six straight years; and
others. But the true type—the roaring third-party rebel—
appeared in greatest profusion in the eighties.

The first of these was Ignatius Donnelly of Minnesota, one
of the most colorful men in political history. A well-educated

Irish born lawyer, Donnelly came to St. Paul from Philadelphia in 1856 to found a model community at Nininger. After it was wiped out in the panic of 1857, he went into farming and Republican politics. Republican victories in 1859 and after made him lieutenant governor and sent him to the legislature for six years, but he broke with the party machine and was beaten in 1868. Convinced that the great battle of the future would be between humanity and property, between men and money, he enlisted then and there in the people's army. "The first right of man," he wrote in 1870, "is to have everything essential to his happiness. Whatever stands in the way of this is not law but fraud and robbery. . . . Wherever amid the fullness of the earth a human stomach goes empty, or a human brain remains deadened in ignorance, there is wrong and crime and fraud somewhere."

Donnelly's first campaign as an independent was for tariff revision. Unsuccessful as a candidate on this issue, he came back to the Republicans in 1872 as a Liberal supporter of Greeley. After the hard times of 1873 he became chief lecturer for the Minnesota Grange, pushing the Grange more and more into politics until he finally persuaded it to back an anti-monopoly party that, while it failed to elect him governor, did send him to the legislature. The thirteen reform bills he introduced, some of them unreasonably wild, all failed, and the slow death of Grangerism and the antimonopoly parties soon sent him back to private life. The temporary rise of the Greenbackers revived his fortunes; he dominated the state party, chaired the national convention at Indianapolis in 1876, and polled a large but losing vote in Minnesota for senator. Fusion of Greenbackers and Democrats with the Workingmen's party in 1876 almost sent him to Congress. William Washburn, the Republican, beat him, but Donnelly contested the election on grounds of fraud, for which he probably had a case. After a long series of hearings, Congress finally seated Washburn, and Donnelly, defeated and broke, went back to Nininger to edit a small paper, the *Anti-Monopolist.*

It was hard to keep a man of Donnelly's resilience from bouncing. In 1881 Harpers brought out *Atlantis, The Antediluvian World,* his popularly written attempt to prove the existence of Plato's lost continent in the Atlantic. The book caught on, and sales mounted—Gladstone commented on it from England, jokes circulated about it, and the magazines debated over it. *Ragnarok: The Age of Fire and Ice,* followed in 1883, an almost automatic success, and Donnelly took to the lecture platform. In 1884 he tried once more for the Senate, this time as a Democrat, with no better luck than before.

The Farmers' Alliance was growing in Minnesota, and by 1886 it carried considerable weight in state politics. Donnelly, seeing the bandwagon coming, wanted to ride, but an argument with Alliance leaders over whether to work with the Democrats or the Republicans set him to organizing a reform third party of his own. It elected him to the legislature, where he made a deal with the Republicans and became the most powerful farmer-labor leader in the state. The appearance of *The Great Cryptogram* in 1888, a book that stirred up the famous controversy over Bacon's supposed authorship of Shakespeare, made his name a household word. He lost his legislative seat that same year, however, by refusing to cooperate with the new Union Labor party and turned his organizing talents to the Alliance.

Pugnacious, learned, a brilliant and persuasive speaker, Ignatius Donnelly stood ready in 1890 to lead the Midwest revolt. He loved to battle for a cause, and he needed one. He had already fought slavery as a Republican, the corporations as an antimonopolist and an independent, and the "money power" as a Greenbacker. A born third-party man, he felt in his bones the new rumblings of unrest. True, he was too much of an individualist to work well with a group, and he was inclined to play the prima donna. But he had, to his credit, a deep sense of justice and an affection and respect for the people's will, besides a brain to go with them. "The only politics worth studying," he once said, "is the amelioration of the conditions of the great mass of mankind." The Midwest developed more skillful leaders than Donnelly, but none more sincere or colorful.

In Iowa, to the South, the same forces that produced Donnelly shaped James Baird Weaver. Born in Ohio, Weaver lived through a poverty-stricken farm boyhood, drove ox teams to California in the gold rush, and worked his way through law school. An early Iowa Republican and a brigadier general in the Civil War, he broke with his party to follow the Greenbackers in the late seventies, served in Congress for them, and was their presidential candidate in 1880. A long-time foe of banks and railroads, he was a candidate for some office as Greenbacker, Union Laborite, Populist, or Democrat in every election from 1874 until his death. Impeccably honest, puritanically uncompromising in his politics, Weaver lacked Donnelly's fire and Simpson's picturesqueness, but he was a shrewd parliamentarian, a laconic and devastating speaker, and a great vote getter among veterans. Erect, thin, wiry, and with a vein of energy that belied his mild appearance, Weaver was, as Herbert Quick later called him, "one of the skirmishers who drove the pickets in" in the battle of Midwestern progressivism.

Kansas contributed Jerry Simpson, born in New Brunswick of Scotch and Welsh parents, a Great Lakes sailor for twenty-three years before he arrived in Kansas in 1878. Never formally educated, Simpson was a wide reader and an intelligent man, with a background of Burns, Victor Hugo, Tom Paine, Shelley, Blackstone, Kent's *Commentaries,* and especially of Henry George. Republican politics disgusted him, so he joined successively the Liberal Republican, Greenback, and Union Labor parties, searching for an affiliation that would satisfy him. "Of course," said Simpson during one of his early unsuccessful campaigns, "I haven't a chance to win—but great God, what if I did!" The infant People's party finally drew him in, and in 1890 he was one of the five men it sent to Congress. Victor Murdock, a young newspaperman, hung the name "Sockless

Jerry" on him after Simpson jibed at a Republican opponent for wearing silk socks. Another young newspaperman, William Allen White, expanded this to "The Sockless Socrates of the Prairie" and one appellation or the other stuck to him for the rest of his life.

But Simpson was no clown. He may have played the buffoon in the House (he almost drove Dingley of Maine distracted with jokes about his silk hat), but behind the hayseed's disguise there was a sharp mind. Champ Clark thought him the best debater in Congress, and those who once tangled with him never forgot the experience; neither Hallowell nor Ingalls ever recovered from the lacing he and Mary Ellen Lease gave them in 1890. Peffer, his companion in Congress, a Union veteran and editor of the *Kansas Farmer,* was a different sort. Hebraic in his fanaticism, morbid, introspective, Peffer was stiff necked, dignified, and difficult to approach. Neither he nor Mary Ellen Lease were ever so popular in Kansas as Simpson, who drew men to him by his good will and friendliness.

These were the early leaders, for better or worse the advance guard of Midwestern insurgency—Donnelly, Weaver, Simpson, and a host of lesser lights, representing a million disgruntled farmers. Hamlin Garland, looking down into the House chambers from the galleries in 1891 on the Alliance wedge in Congress, felt a queer thrill run through him. Something was coming, he thought, something like the Civil War, except that this time it would be West against East on the battlefield of politics.

The Storm Breaks, 1892–1900

III

"It was a fanaticism like the Crusades," said one who went through it, "a season of shibboleths and fetiches and slogans. Reason slept; and the passions—jealousy, covetousness, hatred—ran amuck. . . . Far into the night their voices rose, praising the people's will as though it were God's will, and cursing wealth for its iniquity." It was a crusade, and into it went the fear and hate of thirty years— droughts and grasshoppers, grinding debts and millstone mortgages, poverty and disillusion, the shreds of the lost American dream, the whole backwash of the frontier. They gathered in the small towns of the Midwest, farmers in overalls and their wives in faded sun- bonnets and calico, people with hard, tired faces and worn hands, come by wagon team to fight the devil—plutocracy in a checkered vest, gold watchchain, and silk hat. They gathered in the town squares, on the picnic grounds, in the small white schoolhouses and on the camp-meeting sites, singing songs of defiance to the tunes of old hymns, stamping and shaking fists at their oppressors. Out of it rose the great shout that rang in Wall Street and on the ex- changes and echoed through the nation—Bryan! Bryan! Bryan!— the peerless leader, the shining knight of the West.

THE DECADE of the nineties was an angry decade. "The mutterings of discontent grow more ominous," remarked B. O. Flower in the *Arena*. "Rights denied the weak through the power of avarice have brought us face to face with a formidable crisis." Hugh Pentecost, editor of *Twentieth Century*, believed that the struggle over graft, currency, and monopoly might soon split the country wide open. E. L. Godkin, with Olympian detachment, thought a revolution was bound to come, and could suggest nothing to do about it. Henry van Dyke analyzed the situation and came to the amazing conclusion that popular discontent came from the inability of the farmer and the worker to appreciate beauty. "Nature lovers," he added, "are seldom mob leaders."

The "hayseed radicals" of the Midwest were in no such pessimistic mood. The relatively successful maneuvers of 1890 convinced many Alliance men that there was much to be accomplished through political action. If the trouble with the country was too little money, make more of it. If monopolies fleeced the people, outlaw monopoly. If utility and railroad interests cheated the public, let the public take them over. If government did not represent the people's interests, make it do so. They were, perhaps, politically naïve, but they knew what they wanted.

The formation of the Populist and other independent parties in the Midwestern states naturally led the Alliance to conjectures about a national third party. Neither major party, its members agreed, offered much hope to the Midwestern farmer or worker. "From the present attitude of the Republican and Democratic parties," remarked Senator Kyle, "there does not appear to be a ray of light." The Southerners in general opposed the idea. As the *Atlanta Constitution* said, for the Alliance in the South "to leave the Democratic party is to sacrifice the only means it has to accomplish in any degree the great work it has undertaken." As a compromise, some Southern Alliance leaders suggested that the problem of independent political action on a national scale might well be placed on the agenda of the St. Louis convention for 1892.

Since 1892 was a presidential election year, certain impatient members of the Northwestern Alliance planned a meeting for the spring of 1891. Having had a taste of third-party success in 1890, they sent out a call which brought to Cincinnati a most extraordinary hodgepodge of Alliance men, Green-backers, Union Laborites, Georgist single taxers, Bellamy socialists, prohibitionists, and plain crackpots. "There is not one element," said the *Ohio State Journal,* "whose ideas are not violently antagonized by half-a-dozen other elements and no two elements that agree exactly upon the same thing." The credentials committee simply threw the rules out the window and admitted anyone with a grievance, about fourteen hundred delegates, the majority from the Northwestern Alliance states.

The task of imposing some sort of order on this assembly of misfits fell to the eccentric Minnesotan, Ignatius Donnelly. That a third party must be formed was assumed by most of those present; the real question was how and when. General Weaver, backed by a strong Alliance contingent, thought that the actual formation of a party might well be delayed until 1892, so that the intervening time could be used to recruit and organize. Donnelly's group held out for organizing on the spot and running candidates in the off-year elections of 1891.

The deadlock was finally broken by a compromise, worked out by Donnelly, and a platform was outlined. It was the fa-miliar Alliance platform, covering free coinage of silver, aboli-tion of private banks, institution of postal savings banks, tax reforms, direct election of senators, government ownership of telegraph and railroads, and (in deference to the labor dele-gates) an eight-hour day for industry. The national committee immediately began to print and distribute leaflets and pamph-lets, sending out speakers like Jerry Simpson, Mary Ellen Lease, Annie Diggs, and others to whip up enthusiasm in the Midwest.

The St. Louis meeting of 1892, like its Cincinnati predeces-sor, attracted an assortment of delegates representing every shade of opinion, including a large group of labor men headed by Terence V. Powderly. The Southern Alliance, which had more or less boycotted the Cincinnati meeting, was out in force ("The Blue and the Grey," said Donnelly hopefully, "are to be woven into the same banner of protest"), though probably the majority of Southeners were still unsympathetic to a third-party commitment. The reason, said Tom Watson of Georgia, "could be summed up in one word, *nigger*." It took all of Donnelly's skill to weld the convention into some semblance of unity, and even then the platform of the new People's party was endorsed over the protests of some Southerners.

It was an enthusiastic convention, singing and cheering, and the platform, primarily from Donnelly's pen, was a fighting document. There was not a single railroad president at the meeting, he pointed out, no Chauncey Depews, no rich men's creatures to be "petted, wined, and dined" in the Republican manner. "We meet in the midst of a nation," he continued,

brought to the verge of moral and material ruin. Corruption dominates the ballot-box, the legislature, the Congress, and touches even the ermine of the bench. The people are demoralized . . . , our homes covered with mortgages, labor impoverished, and the land concentrating in the hands of the capitalists. . . . The fruits of the toil of millions are boldly stolen to build up colossal fortunes for a few, unprecedented in the history of mankind; and the possessors of these, in turn, despise the Republic and endanger liberty. From the same prolific womb of governmental injustice we breed the same two great classes of tramps and millionaires.

These were winged words, said the *New York Herald,* that sped through the West "like fire on a dry prairie."

The St. Louis meeting created a party, but decided that the actual business of a nominating convention might well be left until July. A committee headed by Weaver chose Omaha as the site. Only those who unequivocally accepted the St. Louis platform were deemed eligible to attend, and it was believed to be a good omen that at Omaha, on July 4, exactly 1,776 delegates would appear under the system of representation agreed upon.

The Omaha convention was even more enthusiastic and optimistic. Not all the state organizations sent representatives (the railroads refused to follow their usual custom of granting cut-rate fares to convention delegates), but roughly fourteen hundred appeared, marching, singing, and waving banners. The platform, adopted without much discussion, was substantially the same as the St. Louis document of 1891, a ringing declaration of war against the "interests" and the usual program of reforms.

The choice of a candidate for President was rather restricted. A Northern Union veteran would not please the Southern Alliance, and a Confederate nominee would certainly alienate Northern votes. Donnelly, though obviously the most powerful figure at the convention, simply would not do. The Populists shuddered at the prospects of Republican and Democratic sport with "Ignatius Donnelly Bacon" or "Atlantis Ignatius."

The most eligible candidate was General James Baird Weaver of Iowa, an experienced campaigner, a Union veteran, an old foe of railroads, and a tireless third-party nominee. Weaver rode in without serious opposition, and to placate the South an ex-Confederate general, courtly and able James Field of Virginia, was chosen for Vice-President. So the Populist party was launched and the battle joined, to use Jerry Simpson's words, "for the final struggle between the robbers and the robbed."

The party that emerged at Omaha was the legitimate descendant of the long-dead Grange, the independent parties of the seventies and eighties, and the new Farmers' Alliance. Nearly all of its demands were old and familiar issues in the Midwest. It was an economic movement, representing the farmers' entrance into politics to fight for their causes, as the laborers were to do later. But it was also a regional movement —its platform simply stated what the Midwest wanted. The Populist party was the farmer with both feet in politics.

For relief from his problems the Midwesterner looked to the government, as he had before—another manifestation, as Frederick Jackson Turner pointed out, "of the pioneer ideals of the native American, with the added element of increasing readiness to utilize the national government." The Midwesterner had been given his land by the government, the United States Army had protected him while he settled it, his railroads had been subsidized by the government, and Washington had governed him until his state entered the Union. He therefore turned naturally, when he required help, to the agency that had always given him a hand. At the same time, however, some of the planks in the Populist platform were not peculiarly Midwestern solutions to Midwestern problems. Urban and Eastern reform ideas had filtered into Middle Western agrarian thinking and settled there. The equal rights, antimonopoly, loose currency, antibank, and anti-"money power" principles of the Locofocos of the Jackson era went west with the settlers, long before the Omaha convention, to mingle with Midwestern ideas. Antimonopolism came from many sources; the use of the state as a policeman to eliminate special privilege in government was an old Locofoco tradition; government ownership had already been expounded by Bellamy and the urban socialists, and in a different manner by Henry George. But in Populism all these took on frontier, Midwestern coloring. The ideas of Populism may have been of mixed ancestry, certainly, but nevertheless they were undeniably fitted to and possessed by the Midwest. Postwar "radicalism" depended on the block of states in the Mississippi and Missouri and Ohio valleys for its strength, the block that had produced the Grangers, the independents, and finally the Populists themselves.

The Omaha platform put into words a feeling that was growing stronger by 1892, that all was far from right with the world and democracy. The Eastern press, of course, railed at the Omaha meeting. It was a farrago of nonsense," said the *Baltimore American,* "a confession of moral and political depravity," said the New York *Commercial Advertiser,* "a new symptom of the old trouble, the discontent of the unthrifty," pronounced *Harper's Weekly.* But nevertheless the storm clouds from the West set both Republicans and Democrats to thinking of shelter. It was noticeable that both major party platforms for 1892 advocated antimonopoly legislation and suggested some compromises on the currency issue, though both hedged their planks with enough restrictions to reduce them to mere vaguenesses.

Weaver was a good campaigner, with a trick of phrasing things clearly and concisely. "The new movement," he said, "can be summed up in one sentence, 'Equal rights for all and special privileges for none.' It is simply a battle for liberty." His book, *A Call to Action,* carried the campaign to thousands of readers. The Populists, he said, intended to rescue land from the land monopolists, transportation from the railroad kings, money from bankers, and government from the "pluto-crats." Donnelly, Mary Lease, Annie Diggs, Simpson, and others repeated the theme over and over again through the farm states, and the people listened. "My gentle sirs," said Simpson, "put on your goggles and watch the buccaneers of Wall Street, the brigands of the tariff, and the whole shootin' match of grain gamblers, land grabbers, and government sneak thieves, before they steal you blind."

The Populist campaign, good as it was, had little effect on the main contest between Grover Cleveland and Benjamin Harrison. The South, where third-party sentiment was weak, did not take kindly to Weaver (he was egged there so much, said Mary Lease, that he looked like an omelet) and even Tom Watson, the most powerful Southern Populist, lost his congressional seat. Altogether, Weaver polled roughly a million votes and carried twenty-two electoral votes, concentrated in seven trans-Mississippi and five Southern states. Cleveland's majority was a safe one, but though the results were disappointing, the Populists were encouraged to note that Weaver's total was the highest any third-party candidate had polled in twenty-five years. The fact that a million people had voted for "this lunatic," as the journalist Murat Halstead called him, was in itself a warning of things to come. Weaver's sound thumping did not spell death to Populism by any means. The forces behind him in 1892 were not yet fully organized, nor the issues clear cut, but the contest was shaping up for the future. Or so the Populists thought.

In the state elections, Populist showing was inconsistent. The party's chief problem was whether to join hands with the Democrats, whom many Populists did not trust. Actually, although the two parties co-operated in various sections of the Midwest, a workable fusion was arranged only in Kansas and in North Dakota. In Kansas the Populist candidate won the governorship and the party took most of the state's congressional seats and gained a majority in the state senate, while in the lower house of the legislature it barely held even. In North Dakota a fusion of Farmers' Alliance, Democratic, and Populist elements made a clean sweep of the state. Iowa re-elected Democratic Governor Boies, but Nebraska's contest was hot and close. The question of fusion split both Democratic and Populist ranks, giving the governorship and most of the state offices into Republican hands, but the Populists helped send Silver Democrat William Jennings Bryan to Congress, and the Democrats helped send Populist Kem to accompany him. Later, after much maneuvering, Democrats and Populists in the legislature combined to elect William Allen, a Populist, to the Senate. Party strength in the legislature was fairly evenly distributed, and the sole significant Populist measure passed during the session was a bill fixing railroad rates.

South Dakota's Populists had no show in a three-cornered contest. In Minnesota the tempestuous Donnelly split the party. Anti-Donnellyites in the Alliance (and there were a good many) did not relish the idea of turning the organization over to him, and when a pro-Donnelly farmer group nominated him for governor, his Alliance opponents countered with an opposition candidate. Even had the Populists been unified behind Donnelly, it is doubtful that he could have won. The Republicans put up Knute Nelson, a free-wheeling Republican who was both a farmer and a Scandinavian, a practically unbeatable combination in Minnesota. Nevertheless, the Populists still elected a lone congressman and took twenty-four seats in the legislature, one of them Donnelly's, who prudently ran for the legislature too.

President Grover Cleveland came into office at an unlucky time. A cycle of prosperity was just ending, and almost as soon as he was inaugurated the depression struck. In 1893 seventy-four railroads went into bankruptcy (ninety-five more by late 1894) and soon the banks began to go, mostly in the West and South—national, state, private, savings banks and trust companies—nearly six hundred of them in all before the panic ran its course. Fifteen thousand businesses failed in one year; wheat dropped to forty-nine cents (the lowest price recorded since the Civil War), and corn dropped almost out of sight. Little by little the national economy slowed down, factories closed, machines stood idle, unemployed flocked the streets. "Never within my memory," said the Reverend T. Dewitt Talmadge of New York, summing up the situation, "have so many people literally starved to death as in the past few months," and a Kansas farmer spoke for the prairies, "We have reached the bottom; we cannot further reduce our rations and live."

Cleveland, serving his second term, was hardly the man best equipped to handle the crisis. Though thoroughly honest ("A public office is a public trust"), he was also monumentally stubborn. He was elected on a conservative Democratic platform which he considered he must follow to the letter, and though banks closed, businesses crashed, and strikers marched in the streets, he plowed doggedly ahead, doing the best he could. "No harm shall come to any business interest as a result of administrative policy so long as I am President," he said upon taking office, which made it clear to the Populist Midwest that the difference between the major parties was precisely that between Tweedledum and Tweedledee.

What Cleveland did for the panic of 1893 may or may not have been right, but it was certainly not good politics. For one thing, he was firmly convinced that the best cure for depression was simply to let it wear itself out. Eventually it did, but the policy failed to satisfy those who meanwhile suffered under it. For another, he was a confirmed gold man, and the repeal of the Sherman Silver Act alienated the silver wing of his own party as well as the great mass of Silver Populists in the West. Then, when the Pullman strike of 1894 seemed to be reaching a critical stage, he sent federal troops into Illinois to break it over the protests of Democratic Governor Altgeld (who had strong Populist backing), thereby losing the confidence of both labor and Western Democrats. At the same time his Attorney General, Richard Olney, another corporation lawyer, made open sport of the Populist-revered Interstate Commerce Act of 1887.

So the Sherman Act rusted while trusts ran riot, and Olney, with almost cynical amusement, used it as authority to send troops to the Pullman strike. Cleveland himself quarreled with the leaders of his party, told Henry Watterson to go to hell, and notified others of his independence in more temperate but equally definite terms. A more liberal or even a more tactful politician might have tempered the winds of 1894, but Cleveland could not or would not. When he left office, to the relief of even his own party, he had held back the tide of Populist revolt, but he had also given Populism some excellent issues. His administration, wrote one Midwestern commentator, proved vividly that relief to the farmer would come only from the West by its own efforts, that the major parties and the East offered absolutely no hope. The farmer alone "would determine the destiny of his and the nation's future."

"If anything is to become of a third party," remarked Willis Abbott of Chicago, "it must be through a union of farmer and laborer." The Northwest, where rural Populism and urban industrialism existed side by side, seemed to be the logical place to begin. As numerous Populists pointed out, laborer and farmer were really working for the same thing—a more equitable distribution of wealth—and if they joined forces they stood a much better chance of obtaining it. A strong minority of AFL men favored joining the Populist party outright, but traditional Federation resistance to party politics led instead to a more temperate resolution only "to cooperate, that the best interests of all might be served."

The difficulty was, of course, that Populist strength came from those farming areas where one set of economic conditions prevailed, and labor strength from the cities under another set. Logically, neither Populist nor labor unionist could come to anything more than a surface agreement on major issues. Railroad rates interested the city worker less than the preservation of his right to strike for higher wages. Breaking the grain, currency, and tariff "rings" were more important to the farmer, in the last analysis, than eight-hour days or industrial safety laws. The single issue on which the two might join was monopoly. Industrial combination and concentration deeply affected both farmer and worker, as Altgeld told the Grange and the Railway Trainmen conventions, but nevertheless, they affected each in different ways—the farmer as producer, the laborer as employee.

There were other reasons why Populist farmer and city laborer could not agree on a common political course. Labor itself was not convinced of the efficacy of direct political action, nor were its own ranks by any means solid. Half a dozen reform groups were represented in organized unionism—old Knights of Labor, Bellamyite socialists, Christian Socialists, single taxers, anarchists, conservatives, and the Socialist Labor party —each with a different platform and all suspicious of the others. Neither the People's party nor the labor unions possessed a real leader who was capable of uniting farm and city. Nor was the farmer, sympathetic though he might be to labor's needs, reconciled to the use of the strike, which smacked to him of violence and un-Americanism. Donnelly himself reminded laborers that rather than strike they should resort to "that peaceful and effective remedy for wrongs which in this country the ballot gives to free men."

The elections of 1894 were not marked by any great Populist successes in those states where they had joined forces with labor, nor in those where they fused with the Democrats, nor in those where they followed an independent course. In Illinois, where the alliance with labor was supposedly strongest, the results were disappointing. In Kansas, the cradle of Populism, the party disagreed over fusing with the Democrats and ran two tickets, one an independent and another a Democratic-Populist, thus practically guaranteeing an overwhelming Republican victory. In North and South Dakota the Populists were routed completely, and in Iowa even Weaver lost. In Minnesota Knute Nelson's popularity proved too great for the Populist candidate, Sidney Owen, though Owen polled twice as many votes as Donnelly had in 1892. The single bright spot was Nebraska. Here William Jennings Bryan, the Democratic candidate for senator, split the Democrats on the silver question and supported Silas Holcombe, the Populist candidate for governor. Both won.

By the close of 1894 Populism was in the peculiar position of having polled more votes than it had in 1892 and yet of having elected fewer candidates. The depression of 1893 undoubtedly helped the party, for the widespread wave of bank failures, interpreted as a result of the scarcity of gold, lent some credence to the Populist claim that free silver would cure depressions. Furthermore, Cleveland's leadership was hardly calculated to inspire Midwestern confidence in the Democrats, and more than a few edged into the Populist voting column. The total Populist vote in 1894 did exceed that of 1892, but the Populists' actual control of state governments slipped badly. Much of their loss was a result of the disagreement in both Democratic and Populist parties over the question of fusion. Since the gold Democrats were the dominant party under Cleveland, some silver men felt that there was little hope in working within that party for free silver. Some Democrats, tired of following the Populist lead, could see no point in currying Populist favor if they could win elections without it. There were two possibilities open for the Populists: they might remain a third party, independent of Democratic support; or they might join the Democratic party in the hope of capturing it from within, with the danger that they might be swallowed by the Democrats and never regain independence.

The Farmers' Alliance, as the question of fusion gained importance, rapidly lost political influence. Those who did not like the Populists left the Alliance in protest, feeling that it was now simply a political party. Those who favored third-party action could see no reason for supporting two organizations if the Populists could do the job alone. A bid by the far left wing of Populism to revamp the Alliance by reintroducing some of the ritualistic aspects of Grangerism could not revive it. The Industrial Legion (also called the National Legion), modeled on GAR lines and intended to propagate Populism as a secret order, attracted little attention and soon died.

It was also clear by 1894 that Populism had really accomplished exceptionally little in those states where it had won in 1892. Populist bills did not stand up in court tests; Populist legislation was often hasty, ill prepared, and its administration not always wise. Populists in state legislatures had been unable to work out compromises with other parties, with the result that Populist bills were often blocked. The Populists in Congress had made perhaps a better showing than those in the states; they had been especially active in promoting investigations of railroads, banks, strikes, "grain rings," and so on. In 1894 they agitated successfully for the passage of a federal income tax law, and though it was thrown out by the courts as an encroachment on state powers, the seed of the act of 1913 was planted by Populists in that session. But the fact was that Populist victories, both in Congress and in the states, had been few and minor.

The failure of the Populist party to make a real showing between 1892 and 1894 did not mean that its principles were losing ground. John Peter Altgeld, Democratic governor of Illinois, and General Jacob S. Coxey of Ohio won concrete victories for Populist principles, if not for the party. Neither had an agrarian background, and neither fitted into the Kansas-Nebraska-Minnesota mold of Midwestern protest, yet both contributed as much as the Donnelly-Weaver-Simpson group to the Midwestern tradition. Neither was a Populist by name, but both were certainly Populist in theory.

Altgeld began his political life in 1874, when the Grangers elected him state's attorney of Andrews County, Missouri. Not long afterward he moved to Chicago, where the Labor party supported him in a successful campaign for a judgeship. Meanwhile, the rapid growth of Populism convinced the politicians of both major parties in Illinois that neither could win without Populist support. The Republicans, generally regarded by farmer-labor elements as creatures of the corporations, found it hard to pump up much enthusiasm in either group, but the Democrats saw an excellent chance to capitalize on Populist strength by choosing candidates likely to attract the farmer-labor vote. So they picked Altgeld for governor, a position that he privately thought might be highly useful as a vantage point from which to launch certain political and social reforms he had in mind. In order that he might go into office owing nothing to anyone, he paid his own campaign expenses—nearly $100,000—and won in 1894 with a substantial majority.

Illinois since the Civil War had been dominated by one of the most corrupt Republican machines in the nation. Altgeld's election seemed at first to be one of those meaningless "reform" victories that collapse when the professional politicians get to work, but Altgeld was something different in the way of reformers. Unlike most Populist leaders, he was of foreign birth, born in Germany, with a background of Ohio farm life, Civil War service, factory work, and law school. His shrewdness at law and real estate made him a rich man, nearly a millionaire, but despite his wealth he had strong support from socialists, Populists, and Democrats. A homely, hare-lipped, pasty-faced man ("Hell," he said, "if I had to depend on my looks I'd have been hung long ago"), he had an overwhelming sympathy for the underdog, a strong sense of social responsibility, and great honesty and courage. Nelly Bly, the New York *World's* famous newspaperwoman, came to interview this "Midwestern anarchist" soon after his election and left with a wholesome respect for him. He seemed to be the sort, she wrote, "who would do as he thinks right every time, if the world stands still."

Altgeld's program for Illinois blended Populism and socialism in about equal proportions, though Medill's *Chicago Tribune,* which hated him bitterly, called him "a follower of Jefferson and Marx." Altgeld wanted rural and urban reform —child-labor laws, corporation laws, a better means of industry-labor arbitration, new laws for city government, collective bargaining, civil service, new tax laws, educational and penal reforms—and for these he had the support of labor, farmer, and urban leaders like Jane Addams and Henry Lloyd. His pardoning of the Haymarket rioters, his stand in the Pullman strike of 1894, and his foreign origin all conspired against him ("He apparently has not a drop of true American blood," said the *Tribune*). Nevertheless he enacted more Populism into law than any other state executive in the Midwest before 1900.

Altgeld's great battle was against the corporations. His reasoning on the matter was direct and simple, his conclusions much the same as those of the old Granger-Greenback-Anti-Monopoly leaders. The corporation, he believed, threatened the existence of democratic government because it used that government for private interests. Yet it was obvious that the giant corporation was a natural result of economic evolution, not something simply to be wiped out overnight. The answer was, therefore, to unify those forces adversely affected by monopoly and fight against it. "If we cannot prevent combination and monopoly," he wrote, "then it is idle to rant about it, and it becomes our duty to meet it as an existing fact and restrain its power for evil."

The corporations were strongly entrenched in Illinois in 1892. The railroads and stockyards, the Pullman corporation, the coal operators, the Chicago gas trust, the traction trust under the direction of Charles T. Yerkes, and others ran the state almost as they pleased. Altgeld's attack on them was double pronged. Like the Grangers, he tried to limit their powers by taxing them and also by exposing them to public view through both investigation and publicity. George Schilling, Altgeld's secretary of labor statistics, probed into corporation tax assessments and found them shamefully rigged. Revenues from dog licenses in Illinois, for example, were actually greater than the entire taxes paid by Yerkes' system of street railways. At first the legislature refused to do anything about the inequities turned up by Schilling and others, but later an inheritance-tax law was passed, and in 1895 corporation taxes were revised on a sliding scale.

In the spring of 1893 Altgeld started an investigation of a state-wide whisky trust. The result was a series of laws outlawing price fixing and railroad rebates, designed to restore competition in the trade. He began other investigations too, but his hardest fight against monopoly came in 1895. The Chicago gas and traction monopoly, tired of dealing with a blackmailing city council, decided to by-pass it and extend its control of city utilities by obtaining franchises directly from the state legislature. So Yerkes and his allies approached Springfield with requests for a ninety-nine-year franchise on gas, streetcars, and elevated railways, exhibiting at the same time an eagerness to pay well for aye votes. Greased by money, Yerkes' bills slid handily through the legislature. Altgeld, though offered upward of a half million for his signature, killed all three franchises in a stinging veto message; they were all, he said, barefaced attempts to legalize monopoly, to "increase the riches of some men at the expense of others by means of legislation," and he would have nothing to do with them. Brand Whitlock, then a young Chicago reporter, saw lobbyists on the floor of the legislature openly offering $2,000 a vote to pass the bill over Altgeld's veto, but it stood.

There were other experiments in government during Altgeld's reign. With the Haymarket and Pullman affairs in mind, he recommended a system of compulsory investigation and voluntary arbitration in strikes, a system long approved by labor leaders and recently popularized by Henry Lloyd's study, *A Country Without Strikes*. Backed by Jane Addams, Clarence Darrow, and the Chicago Civic Federation, the proposal finally passed, creating a state labor arbitration board that worked with fair success. In addition, Altgeld suggested one of the first collective bargaining acts, designed to protect employees from dismissal because of union activity and to give unions some right of recognition. Altgeld won a partial victory over a corrupt patronage system with a civil service law for city governments—not a wholly satisfactory plan, but it paved the way for later and better ones. Again with the help of Jane Addams and Darrow he pushed through a child- and female-labor law, which the powerful Illinois Manufacturers' Association immediately took to court. The state courts invalidated the act—a decision that retarded social legislation by a full decade—but at least the groundwork was laid for a better legal settlement in 1910. In the same way Altgeld, one of the first real students of penology, made Illinois' prison and welfare system the most enlightened in the Midwest and probably in the nation. Fearful of the influence of private capital on universities (Chicago had recently accepted a huge gift from Rockefeller), Altgeld built up the state university, instituted teachers' colleges, and constructed state libraries and museums.

Altgeld was responsible for putting a great deal of liberal legislation into the statutes, but his greatest contribution to the larger cause of Midwestern progressivism was by the example that he set for the political and social reformers who followed him—for Bryan (who ran in 1896 on a platform Altgeld wrote), for the reform governors and mayors of the turn-of-the-century period, later for Norris and Cummins and La Follette. His influence was strong on such people as Jane Addams of Hull House, Clarence Darrow, Brand Whitlock, Edgar Lee Masters, Carl Sandburg, Vachel Lindsay, and dozens of major and minor reformers and politicians. "No man ever lived whom I respected and loved outside my blood relations as I did John P. Altgeld," said Darrow, and hundreds felt the same. Pardoning the Haymarket rioters (an act which condoned anarchy less than it supported justice) meant his political death, but Altgeld plowed ahead, destined to be forgotten except as the man who set anarchists free.

When Altgeld went to Springfield in 1893 he was a wealthy, popular, and respected public leader. When he left after his defeat in 1896 he was practically penniless, and perhaps the most bitterly excoriated man in public life. Darrow, out of pity, took him into his law firm, where he sat in his office seeing callers—cranks, down-and-outers, curiosity seekers—until, as Darrow put it, his desk became a sort of shrine. He died shortly after a losing campaign for mayor of Chicago in 1902. Darrow and Jane Addams supervised the funeral, for there seemed to be no clergyman in Chicago who would lead the ceremonies. Yet Altgeld's ideals lived on in all of those who found inspiration in the ugly little German's incorruptible honesty and mammoth courage. "Wrong may seem to triumph," he said late in life. "Right may seem to be defeated. But the gravitation of eternal justice is toward the throne of God. Any political institution which is to endure must be plumb with that line of justice."

Jacob Coxey of Ohio was a very different kind of reformer. An old Greenbacker and a wealthy man, he conceived the idea in 1892 of beating hard times by issuing paper money, hiring the unemployed with it, and putting them to work building good roads. This scheme would apparently solve three problems at once by putting more money into circulation, providing employment for the needy, and improving transportation.

As an extra attraction he offered a plan for the issuance of non-interest-bearing bonds by which any municipality could finance civic improvements through a series of bond issues and a complex system for their retirement. Coxey himself was a vague, gentle, somewhat impractical man whose cause had few enlistments until he met Carl Browne, an Iowa-born radical who had once tinkered with the Populist Industrial Legion. Browne was a thorough eccentric (he wore cowboy clothes, never bathed, and held some peculiar theories of religious incarnation) but he was also a clever organizer and a convincing talker. Coxey was a heaven-sent opportunity for him, and together they planned a march on Washington, a "petition in boots," to present Coxey's ideas to Congress. The idea of a mass petition was not new, since the Farmers' Alliance had once planned such a march, but under Browne's direction it speedily became something utterly novel and almost fantastic.

The year 1894 was a bad one. The statistics showed that between forty and sixty thousand unemployed roamed the nation, some of them in bands of one to three hundred under semimilitary discipline, and Cleveland, who believed that the best way to cure a depression was to pretend that it didn't exist, did practically nothing to help matters. The time was ripe, actually overripe, for action, and Coxey's scheme, which was not so harebrained as it sounded, offered at least some hope to the victim of hard times.

From Coxey's headquarters in Massillon, Ohio, organizers and lecturers spread his doctrine, and the badges and banners of "Coxey's Army" began to appear in various parts of the country. Browne, having converted Coxey to his own particular brand of religion, named himself the reincarnated "Cerebellum of Christ," the general "the Cerebrum of Christ," and the movement "the Commonweal of Christ," thus injecting a quasi-religious flavor into the proceedings. An odd assembly of ideological odds and ends came together in Massillon—"Cyclone" Kirtland, a Pittsburgh astrologer; Douglas McCallum of Chicago, who wore a top hat and was the author of a queer pamphlet called *Dogs and Fleas;* a half-breed Indian who was under contract to the *Chicago Times* to report how it felt to live on oatmeal and nothing else; a real cowboy named "Oklahoma Sam" Pfrimmer; and a mysterious rich man who refused to give his name. The newspapers sent up dozens of reporters for a heyday. But underneath the sport they made of Coxey was real uneasiness. "Armies" were organizing in California, Massachusetts, Colorado, Oklahoma, Washington, Indiana, Wisconsin, Michigan, and Maryland, and the thing was not so comic as it looked.

Coxey's Army had the sympathy of labor and Populist groups, if not their support. "This is a protest against wrongs which have become quite universal and intolerable," said General Weaver. "These armies represent the vast excluded multitudes." Senator Peffer of Kansas agreed to introduce Coxey's bills into Congress, explaining that while he did not favor their passage he thought they deserved consideration. Allen of Nebraska asked for a Senate committee to meet Coxey when he arrived in Washington. So Coxey left Massillon, riding in a carriage with Mrs. Coxey and their infant, Legal Tender Coxey, at the head of a column of perhaps a hundred men. Despite its *opéra bouffe* flavor, the army began to pick up recruits, and reports arrived of Kelly and Fry, coming with an "army" from the West Coast, Fitzgerald, leading a group from Massachusetts, and others.

Coxey's Massillon group, augmented by divisions from Pennsylvania, New England, and Texas, reached Washington first. Congress wanted no part of Coxey or Browne and police nabbed the two on the capitol steps, manhandled a few followers, and drove the rest into encampment on the outskirts of the city. Most of the other armies never arrived. Coxey and Browne were tried for disturbing the peace and walking on the grass, convicted, and sentenced to twenty days in jail, which was far too light for the tastes of some. The attention of the nation was shortly focused on the Pullman strike in Illinois, and Coxey went back to Ohio to run unsuccessfully for Congress on the Populist ticket. "Coxey's Army" became a national byword for the tatterdemalion and comic, for the stage tramp with patched pants and an aversion to work.

Yet the Army of the Commonweal was not wholly a failure. Coxey's "petition in boots" was a sign of the times, and despite its humorous overtones, it dramatized a national problem. A few men noted the difference in Congress' reception of Coxey and that accorded a corporation lobbyist. The Western *Midland Monthly* disagreed with Coxey's scheme, but pointed out that "labor as well as capital has claims which governments are bound in duty and in self-interest to respect, and, within reasonable limits, to allow." And then, too, a public works program to assist the unemployed made sense to many who thought it over. Coxeyism was, essentially, not too far from Populism, a logical extension of the Populist theory that if things went wrong it was the function of government to do something about it.

Coxey, Altgeld, and the Populists kept alive an issue that had been the stock in trade of the Midwest since Granger days —the fight against monopoly. To the Granger the chief symbol of monopoly was the railroad, but by 1890 the trend toward concentration in business had accelerated so swiftly that it seemed to the Midwestern farmer and laborer that there was a monopoly (now called a "trust") wherever he looked. The trust issue had been forced on both major parties by aroused public opinion in the campaign of 1888, and both had promised antimonopoly legislation, resulting in the somewhat unsatisfactory Sherman Act of 1890. The Sherman Act interfered only slightly with the operation of big business, and corporation lawyers had a field day with it. As one court ruefully said, "Combinations are Protean, and we are baffled by shadowy communities of interest which seem to have no bodies we can grasp." Weaver, in 1892, claimed there were trusts in oil, sugar, oatmeal, starch, paper, grain, lumber, castor oil, cement, linseed oil, paint, salt, beef, gas, whisky, rubber, steel, railroads, copper, lead, coal, agricultural implements, warehouse facilities, granite, watches, silver, and milling. Ignatius Donnelly even discovered an undertaker's trust in the Northwest, claiming that possibly on resurrection day the dead would awake to find Gabriel controlled by a trumpet trust, "with no toots except for spot cash."

The political failure of the Populists in the early nineties did not kill the trust issue in the Midwest. Governor Knute Nelson of Minnesota, an anti-trust Republican, called for a convention of Midwestern states to be held in Chicago in 1893. Over a hundred delegates attended, Weaver, Donnelly, Lloyd, Darrow, and Thomas Morgan among them, but a hastily formed "Anti-Trust Association" of corporation lawyers and coal men also came and more or less sabotaged the meeting. Donnelly's motion that trusts ought to be denied legal protection and their properties confiscated seemed far too drastic to most of the delegates, so a disgruntled minority withdrew and held its own discussions. The meeting came to no definite conclusions beyond a few generally worded condemnations of trusts, and although Donnelly labeled the whole convention a humbug, the fact that more than a hundred representatives of Republican, Democratic, and Populist parties, drawn from several states, met to discuss more effective means of dealing with monopoly was in itself an indication of the strength of antitrust feeling.

The argument against the trusts in the nineties remained much the same as it had been since Granger days. The trust, it was believed, delegated too much economic power to men not responsible to the public. "The great storehouse of nature is locked," said one editor, "and monopoly holds the key." The trust, said others, also stifled economic competition, driving out small business and killing individualism. "Enlightened public policy," stated Weaver, "favors competition in the present condition of organized society," whereas the aim of monopoly was chiefly "to destroy competition and restrain trade." Government intervention, the Populist assumed, would restore the principle of competition to business; thus the public, as consumer, might regain some of its ability to control business and business would feel greater responsibility to the public. That the corporation had certain legal privileges, Weaver and other Populists were ready to admit. But the corporation must not abuse them, else "the people must put hooks into the jaws of these leviathans and control them."

Another common objection to the trust was that it corrupted politics. Under pressure from corporate wealth, government represented not the people, but the trusts. "The enterprises of the country are aggregating vast corporate political power," warned Chief Justice Ryan of Wisconsin. "For the first time really in our politics money is taking the field as an organized power." Business must be kept out of politics, lest politics become the creature of business. "Liberty and monopoly cannot live together," wrote Henry Lloyd. "If the corporations are to continue, a popular government cannot live."

The trusts themselves, however, quickly developed a defense. Big business, they said, was the result of an inevitable economic tendency, the end product of an evolutionary process. It was useless, possibly dangerous, to attempt to interfere with this natural, irresistible trend toward consolidation in business. Furthermore, standing firm on the right of a man to do what he pleased with his property, the businessman questioned the right of the public to stick its nose into the matter at all. James G. Blaine, campaigning in 1888, asserted that "trusts are largely private affairs with which President Cleveland nor any other private citizen has any particular right to interfere." Charles Yerkes once said that since the public was quite ignorant of his business, he could see no reason for the public to tell him how to run it. In the same vein Sidney Dillon of the Union Pacific, in answer to a question about his railroad's finances, thought it "an impertinence" to question the right of a corporation to do anything it wished with its property.

There also began to appear in the late eighties the concepts of the "good" and the "bad" trust. The "good" trust expanded production, lowered prices, and increased the distribution of its products, simply because it was more efficient, as Andrew Carnegie and John D. Rockefeller pointed out and as statisticians proved with columns of comparative figures. "Combinations of capital are indispensable," averred William Graham Sumner, "because we have purposes to accomplish in no other way." To hamstring the trust, therefore, was economic suicide.

That there were "bad" trusts businessmen willingly agreed, but the crime lay in the use, not the tool. Combinations to regulate prices and restrict trade were evil, but they never lasted long. Competition, said the economist Franklin H. Giddings, was always bound to assert itself; the "bad" trust that tried to circumvent that inflexible economic law was doomed. Any business that "attempts to exact from the consumer more than a just return upon capital and service," wrote Carnegie, "writes the charter of its own defeat." And the amount of public good accrued from the trust far overbalanced its evils. "The burden from them is so light as to be scarcely felt . . . ," thought Judge E. H. Gary. "But none of these evils, unless in very rare instances, deprive anybody of the necessities of life."

Exactly what to do about trusts was everybody's problem in the early nineties, but no one could agree when and how to control them, if they were to be controlled at all. Was it proper to regulate the trust only when it conflicted with public interest (the old Granger theory) or when it prohibited "fair and open competition" (a slippery term)? Did "regulation" mean control of profits, working conditions, relations with labor and markets, financial affairs? Should trusts be prohibited entirely? Possibly, thought some, "natural" monopolies of natural resources ought to be taken over by the state through government ownership; a few were willing to take the full socialistic step to collective ownership of all big business. And always the laissez-faire thinkers argued, leave business alone, have faith in private enterprise, competition, and natural economic evolution.

Midwestern thinking on the trust issue was strongly conditioned by three influential reformers, Henry George of California, Edward Bellamy of Massachusetts, and Henry Demarest
Lloyd of Chicago. George was a product of poverty, the gold-
rush frontier, and Jeffersonianism. As a young man he was
driven by hard times to California, where he worked as a
printer. So poor that he begged on the street while land sold
at a thousand dollars an acre, he was struck by the inescapable
fact that in the midst of huge material progress and economic
plenty there was poverty, suffering, and unrest. Suddenly, he
said, the answer came to him in an "ecstatic vision"; the cause
of poverty was a monopoly which deprived the majority of
the people free use of the land, and which enabled the few to
attach, in the form of rent, the earnings of the many. To destroy poverty one must first destroy the monopoly in land,
which to George meant "natural resources and all the products
of nature." In a a pamphlet, *Our Land and Land Policy*,
written in 1871, he discussed the idea, and then in *Progress
and Poverty*, written in 1879, he developed his solution. Monopoly should be destroyed by confiscation of unearned
"rent," that is, profit which accrued to the owner simply by
reason of his ownership. This could be accomplished by a
single tax which returned to the state all income which the
owner did not earn by his own labor on the land or his improvements on it.

After *Progress and Poverty* appeared, George dropped all
else to crusade for the single tax. Single-tax clubs began to
spring up, and George's paper, *The Standard*, went into thousands of homes. George himself wrote and lectured tirelessly in
the United States, Ireland, England, and Australia. He ran for
mayor of New York in 1887 against Abram Hewitt and young
Theodore Roosevelt, was defeated by a questionable count,
and died in the midst of his second mayoralty campaign in
1897. In the meantime his followers founded the Single Tax
League, a semipolitical organization, and gathered considerable political strength. The Populists absorbed most of the
single taxers (the platform of 1892 contained a thoroughly

Georgist plank), and the movement waxed and waned for several years.

After the fall of Populism the remaining Georgists were absorbed politically into the progressive movements, where their influence was apparent as late as 1924. Joseph Fels, the wealthy soap manufacturer, founded a Single Tax Commission and financed it to the extent of more than a million dollars. C. H. Ingersoll, the millionaire watchmaker, contributed to it and such men as Frederic C. Howe, Lincoln Steffens, and William U'Ren took positions in the Commission. Louis Post's Chicago *Public* served as the chief organ of Georgism up to 1913, John Z. White lectured on it for a decade, Henry George, Jr., went to Congress, and single taxer John Garvin served a term as governor of Rhode Island. In England both Sidney Webb and George Bernard Shaw attributed much of the impetus behind the Fabian Society to George's influence. Occasionally yet it finds some support in high places, while the Schalkenbach Foundation still carries on the educational work of the Fels fund and contributes to the maintenance of the Henry George School of Social Science in New York City.

George's idea was not really new. A long line of economists before him had discussed the economics of land use, but George's single tax was novel, practical, and original, though fitted much more to an agrarian than to an industrial society. Whatever its practicality, its aim was clear—to humanize and democratize the national economy so that it might serve social rather than selfish ends, extending the Jeffersonian tradition of natural rights and equality into the economic sphere. "The equal right of all men to the use of the land," he wrote, "is as clear as their equal right to the air—it is a right proclaimed by the fact of their existence."

The single-tax movement left practically no mark on legislation, but the influence of George on the thought of his times was so pervasive that it is no easy matter to assess it. By the turn of the century the sale of *Progress and Poverty* approached five million copies, and the number of converts and sympathizers must have been near that figure. Many Populist leaders were Georgists to varying degrees, among them Jerry Simpson, Peffer, possibly Donnelly. The reform mayors Tom Johnson of Cleveland and Sam Jones of Toledo were avowed single taxers, Hamlin Garland wrote Georgist stories, B. O. Flower's *Arena* and Post's *Public* published Georgist articles. Scholars like Richard T. Ely and John R. Commons, philanthropists like Fels and Ingersoll, and politicians like Bryan and Donnelly showed traces of George's influence. His anti-monopolism, his insistence upon the duty of the state to guarantee social and economic justice, and his interest in the plight of the economically underprivileged—these, over and above any specific tax scheme he proposed, percolated deep into the mind of the late nineteenth century. A nameless Midwestern farmer in the nineties expressed George's influence best, saying, "If I had not read two books, Henry George and later Bellamy, I should have grubbed along and never thought anything was wrong. Those books set me thinking."

Edward Bellamy represented a different strain, the tradition of New England reform that stretched back to the Puritan commonwealth of God. Like George, Bellamy puzzled over the great contrast between political freedom and material progress on the one hand, and economic inequality and poverty on the other. The Haymarket riots of 1886 set him trying "to reason out a method of economic organization by which the republic might guarantee the livelihood and material welfare of its citizens on a basis of equality corresponding to and supplementing their political equality." The result was *Looking Backward,* published in 1888, a Utopian novel projecting a picture of American society some two hundred years in the future.

Bellamy's twenty-first-century America was a socialist state in which the government owned and controlled all for the public good. State socialism, he assumed, was the ultimate end of monopoly; as trusts grew, they merged into fewer and larger trusts, until in the end there would come one huge trust which

the people, in self-defense, would take over. Nineteenth-century industrial society, reasoned Bellamy, is based on the Darwinian principle of survival of the fittest. It should be founded
instead on the principle of collectivism, of the brotherhood of
man, on Christian ethics. "The principle of the Brotherhood
of Humanity is one of the eternal truths that govern the
world's progress," he wrote, "on lines that distinguish human
nature from brute nature. The principle of competition is
simply the application of the brutal law of survival of the
fittest and most cunning. Therefore, so long as competition
continues to be the ruling factor in our industrial system, the
highest development cannot be reached, the loftiest aims of
humanity cannot be realized." Drawn from a multitude of
sources—from George, Ruskin, Robert Owen and the British
socialists, from Christian socialism and possibly Marxism—
Bellamy's socialism was a blend of native and foreign brands,
and peculiarly his own.

Bellamy's novel never approached George's book in popularity, but it was selling ten thousand a week by 1890 and for
years was given away by the Farmers' Alliance as a subscrip-
tion bonus. It hit the public fancy at the right time—"A Jay
Gould demands an Edward Bellamy," said Frances Willard.
Bellamy organized Nationalist Clubs (so named from the idea
of "nationalizing" the economy), published the *Nationalist
Monthly,* and later founded the *New Nation.* By 1890 there
were 150 active Nationalist Clubs, especially strong in New
England and the East, less numerous in the Midwest, where
industrialism was less of an economic factor. By 1892 the
Populists had absorbed much of Bellamy's following, and
Bellamy himself, writing in the *North American Review* that
year, admitted that the Populist program had the gist of his
principles in it.

Henry Demarest Lloyd of Chicago had a more direct, if less
pervasive, influence on Midwestern thinking of the nineties.
As a young Columbia law student Lloyd made a name in
New York as a young liberal. Moving west, he took a job as a

reporter for the *Chicago Tribune*, shortly taking the post of financial editor. In the course of his editorial work he became interested in the trust question, probing into the railroads (the usual point of attack at the time) and then into Standard Oil. His article on Rockefeller's empire, which William Dean Howells rather courageously published in the *Atlantic* in 1881, marked a decided turning point in journalistic history, since it was the first documented and authoritative study of industrial concentration to appear in the journals. So great was the demand for his article that seven printings of that particular issue of the *Atlantic* had to be run off. Lloyd followed with a series of articles in the same vein, studies of Jay Gould, the Chicago Grain Exchange, the "Lords of Industry," and others that focused national attention on the same problems that the Grangers and their followers had discussed for twenty years.

Lloyd reached a decision in 1886, the year of the Haymarket riots. He resigned from newspaper work to defend the so-called anarchists, ran for Congress on the Union Labor ticket, and mixed into a miner's strike in southern Illinois. Then too, he met Altgeld, joined the group of reformers who followed him, and threw himself into politics. Nominally a Republican, Lloyd worked for a third party in 1890, attended the Populist convention of 1892, and eventually joined the party. He was convinced of the necessity of a farmer-labor alliance and did yeoman work with Darrow in 1893 in attempting to consolidate the two in Illinois politics. "If all the forces of discontent should unite on the candidates of the People's Party," he wrote, "we would revolutionize the politics of the country." The Chicago Populist platform of 1894 came chiefly from his pen, and he was its unsuccessful candidate for Congress that year.

Lloyd's real bombshell exploded in 1894 with the publication of *Wealth Against Commonwealth*, a complete, careful study of trusts, and perhaps the most damning indictment of monopoly ever written. "Our industry," he concluded, "is the fight of every man for himself. The prize we give the fittest is monopoly of the necessaries of life, and we leave the winners of the powers of life and death to wield them over us by the same self-interest with which they took them from us." Survival of the fittest, he agreed with Bellamy, was a principle as unfit for business as it was for civilized life; economy should be motivated not by jungle ethics, but by brotherhood. The answer to the trust, said Lloyd, was state ownership of monopoly; then only could liberty and democracy survive. This doctrine he named the "new *laissez-faire*," which was neither laissez faire nor socialism but a compound of the two. "Let the individual do what the individual can do best," he wrote, "and let the community do what the community can do best. The laissez faire of social self-interest, if true, cannot conflict with the individual self-interest, if true, but must outrank it always. . . . The general welfare demands that they who exercise the powers and those upon whom they are exercised must be the same."

Lloyd's book was a major contribution to Populism. *Wealth Against Commonwealth* became a rallying point for the somewhat confused reform movements of the period, for the agrarian Populist, the urban reformer, the socialist radical, all of whom could find in it some area of agreement. Here was a native, non-Marxian, essentially conservative socialism, with none of Bellamy's regimentation or George's panaceas, a link between collectivism and traditional democratic individualism. Let us go back, he said in effect, to the principles of Jefferson—to equal privileges for all, economic and political—and there will be no need for reform.

Wealth Against Commonwealth, and Lloyd's subsequent *Man the Social Creator* and *Men the Workers,* aroused considerable opposition (especially from economists like George Gunton of *Gunton's Magazine* and Professor J. Laurence Laughlin of the University of Chicago) but it started a blaze. The newspapers and magazines woke up. At Lloyd's heels followed a parade of "muckrakers"—Ida Tarbell, Lincoln

Steffens, Ray Stannard Baker, and others—who contributed so much to the progressive uprising after 1900. Lloyd himself kept on writing against what he called "the Old Enemy," the trusts, and working in the political and labor movements. He helped John Mitchell of the Miner's Union in the anthracite strike of 1902, and died in 1903, as he wanted to, in the middle of a hot campaign, this time against the traction ring in Chicago.

As Populism waned, Lloyd moved closer to the Socialist Labor party, though he felt it was too much under the thumb of Eastern radicals and too despotic in its discipline. Eventually he decided to support the Socialist Democratic party after its secession from the parent group. Yet Lloyd was never a Marxist and disliked Marxism's class aspects. "Workers of the World, Unite!" he said, ought to read, "People of the World, Unite!" He took what he needed from Populism, socalism, Marxism, or any other handy system, evolving his own compromise between collectivism and individualism. "Man will prohibit individualism from taking what belongs to the public," he believed, "and will see to it that what belongs to the individual is not taken from him."

Trusts gave the politicians of the nineties one hot issue to handle. Free silver gave them another. There was, of course, nothing new about currency-reform schemes, for they had been common in politics since the earliest days of the Republic. The theory was that the whole trouble lay in a shortage of currency; if the government issued more, and managed it better, all would be well. It was true that after the Civil War there was a dearth of currency in the South and West. Much of what there was in the form of national banknotes, which tended to concentrate in the industrial East. In the seventies it was argued that more notes, backed by government silver, would solve practically all economic problems, and both Greenbackers and Grangers, supported by Western mining interests, wanted more money. But even at the time silver was gradually passing out of the picture as a medium of exchange. Gold was better—more value in less weight and more durable—while gold strikes in California, Russia, and Australia speeded up the displacement of the cheaper metal. By 1890 all western Europe operated on a gold standard, and America was approaching it.

Congress in 1792 set the mintage ratio of silver to gold at 15 to 1, about the prevailing market price. In the next thirty years, however, the value of silver decreased until the actual market ratio was about 15.7 to 1. It was profitable, therefore, to use 1 ounce of gold to buy 15.7 ounces of silver, and then to use 15 ounces of silver to buy back 1 ounce of gold, leaving .7 of an ounce of silver as profit. In 1834 Congress changed the ratio to 16 to 1, thereby making it profitable to use silver to purchase gold. Another act of 1853 did not change the ratio, for it was clear that gold was displacing silver, but it did establish a gold standard, relegating the use of silver to subsidiary coins.

The act of 1873 (called by the Grangers "The Crime of '73") did little more than openly recognize the gold standard, practically demonetizing silver. The Grangers, Greenbackers, and silver interests claimed it favored Eastern creditors, since it forced debtors to pay back in gold what they had borrowed on a bimetallic basis. Under pressure Congress passed another act in 1878 (sponsored by Bland of Missouri and Allison of Iowa) making silver dollars legal tender and providing that the Treasury purchase monthly between two and four million dollars in silver bullion at market price. Actually the compromise satisfied nobody, and in 1890 the Sherman Act changed the amount of monthly purchase to four and one-half million ounces. Silver and debtor interests believed that this represented a lessening of silver purchases and demanded a revised bimetallic standard. The act was repealed, no substitute provided, and the nation went on a "limping standard" of gold and silver.

Silver was not a legitimate Populist issue, except in so far as it represented an attack on the Eastern "money interests," but the panic of 1893 and hard times threw it in the party's lap. There were a good many Midwestern political leaders who had run the full gamut from Grangerism to Greenbackism to Populism and who were quite willing to accept free silver as an extension of the old currency quarrel.

After 1890 Populists and silverites showed great interest in each other. The Populist campaign of 1892 made a definite bid for silver support, and Bryan and Donnelly both attended the Bimetallic League's convention as interested spectators. Magazines with large Western circulations ran articles on free silver with increasing frequency, while the *Arena* averaged one per issue during 1893 alone. Agrarian politicians looked closer at the argument and found it had possibilities. "The Western farmer," said Lewelling of Kansas, "believes the prime cause of all his woes is the manipulation of the money system of the country by unscrupulous and mercenary interests." And Senator Allen of Nebraska wrote, "We believe it possible by legislation so to regulate the issue of money as to make it of approximately the same value at all times. The value of money ought to bear as nearly as possible a fixed relation to the value of commodities." The farmer seized the issue, the Populists embraced it, and it ran away with them.

Free silver, a dry-as-dust, complex, technical question of currency, thus became the chief issue of a quasi-religious political crusade that ended with Bryan and the fervid evangelical campaign of 1896. The reason lay in hard times, in the bottled-up resentment of thirty years of one section of the nation against another—"monetary sectionalism," George Gunton called it. Silver was sectional in its support and its appeal; the West considered the East a selfish creditor with little understanding of and less sympathy for its problems, and the silver issue provided a point on which all the disparate reform elements of the West could unite. "The money power," said Congressman John Davis, "seizes all the means of life and agencies of commerce and then bids men live or die as best they can. It has established a slavery less merciful than chattel slavery." Free silver was simply another manifestation of the old Midwestern demands for freedom from depression, liberation from the "interests," and restoration of economic freedom. The parallel between the chattel slavery of prewar days and the economic slavery of postwar industrialism was not drawn by chance.

The thunderheads in the West were clearly visible on the Eastern seaboard by 1894. Lloyd, George, Weaver, Bellamy, Simpson, Peffer, Donnelly, and the whole nameless horde of Grangers, Farmers' Alliance men, and silverites were not to be brushed off lightly. "We are today facing a situation of discontent," warned the *American Journal of Politics* in 1894. "The army of discontent is organizing . . . , involving a great many elements and tendencies dangerous to the state."

What was the source of Midwestern agitation and dissatisfaction? Politicians and editors discussed the matter at length in the journals. E. L. Godkin of the *Nation* thought that the West was simply ignorant of economics; another Eastern commentator believed its weakness lay in its lack of great statesmen. A writer from the *Forum* believed that the Midwestern states formed "a community unfortunate and dangerous from the possession of power without a due sense of corresponding responsibilities." Bishop Worthington of Omaha was more specific. The whole trouble in his estimate came from educating farmers; farm boys "who have absolutely no ability to rise get a taste of education and follow it up."

What the writers called "ignorance" and "fanaticism" was of course nothing more than the expression of a feeling that the average Midwesterner had entertained for some time, that something (he was not certain what) was riding him hard. He called it variously the Money Power, the Rich, Invisible Government, Plutocracy, Wall Street, the Trusts, the Interests, or the Gold Bugs, and he struck at it where and when he could, wisely or unwisely, temperately or intemperately. As J. K. Miller explained in the *Arena* in 1895, all those ideas that the East called "crank" or "communistic" were nothing more than variations of the Midwesterner's traditional belief that government should yield the greatest good for the greatest number.

Getting ready for the presidential year of 1896, the Midwestern farmer added up his grievances and found the total impressively large. Thirty years of politics had gained him practically nothing. The trust, the railroad, the "gold power," the alliance of wealth and politics, the tariff—all his old opponents were safely entrenched, perhaps more deeply than ever before. There was still a depression, for the nation climbed slowly, very slowly, out of the trough of 1893. Wheat was 40 cents a bushel, butter 10 cents a pound, chickens 8 cents, eggs 6 cents a dozen. The Populists could ask nothing better.

Hard times and the constant pressure of agrarian and silver interests stirred up interest in Populism in both Republican and Democratic parties. The Republicans had a silver faction, led by Senator Teller of Colorado, and in Democratic ranks men such as Bryan of Nebraska and Bland of Missouri thought that the party might well take a definite silver stand. Cleveland's handling of the labor, currency, and tariff questions during the depression was a source of worry to the Democrats, while Republican victories in the 1894 elections indicated a definite waning of Democratic popularity. If the Populists might be lured into joining them, and a candidate acceptable to both nominated, the Democrats stood a much better chance of winning in 1896 than if they stood on Cleveland's record alone. In a three-cornered contest a good Populist candidate might conceivably carry enough anti-Cleveland votes to insure a Republican victory.

The problem of absorbing Populism therefore became highly important to the Democratic managers. Feelings were mixed on both sides. Conservative Democrats feared that Populism might capture the party, while gold Democrats feared both Populists and silver Democrats. Then there was the Omaha Populist platform, in the opinion of many Democrats a thoroughly radical document; if fusion meant accepting that platform, it seemed to them a long stride to the left.

Leading Populists were also suspicious of Democratic overtures. Henry Lloyd called the silver issue "the cowbird of the reform movement," likely to push all the other eggs out of the nest. Donnelly, who produced the 1892 platform, declared he would not jettison it for the comparatively minor issue of silver, and Peffer of Kansas predicted the collapse of Populism as an independent organization if it co-operated with either major party. Some Southern Populists who had already left the Democratic party saw no reason to go back to it. Weaver had believed in fusion since his Greenback days, Simpson and national chairman Taubeneck favored it, and so did Allen of Nebraska, who once talked for fifteen straight hours in Congress on the benefits of free silver. More and more the silver issue became the chief topic of conflict within the Populist party. If silver were to be the most important plank in both Populist and Democratic platforms, as some claimed it should be, fusion seemed right and proper. If there were more important issues to consider, perhaps Populism might better go its way alone.

The Republicans held their convention first, nominated McKinley, and announced a gold-standard plank as expected, giving the signal for Teller and his silver Republicans to bolt. The Democratic convention met in Chicago not long after, controlled largely by Altgeld, Jones of Arkansas, and "Pitchfork Ben" Tillman of South Carolina. Silver sentiment was strong, but the gold Democrats were there in force, too. Since the Republicans had already declared for gold, it was apparent that opposition, if it came at all, ought to come from the Democrats; there was in fact some talk that unless it did, the silver men might bolt the party to join Teller's silver Republicans in a third party.

The silver Democrats were simply too well organized for the opposition. They swept the convention—temporary chairman, platform committee, permanent chairman, credentials committee—and the platform was everything they wished, containing a strong declaration for free coinage of gold and silver at the old ratio of 16 to 1. Most important was the choice of a candidate, one who should be friendly to the Populists, and preferably from a Western state. Former Governor Boies of Iowa was an old-line Democrat; McLean of Ohio was too conservative; Altgeld was foreign born and ineligible; "Silver Dick" Bland of Missouri was a colorless campaigner. It perhaps might have been Bland if the convention had not suddenly exploded.

The detonation came during a rather dull discussion of the platform committee's report on July 9, 1896, a hot afternoon in Chicago. Tillman spoke first for the silver group, followed by Hill of New York, Russell of Massachusetts, and Vilas of Wisconsin, all gold men. Last came William Jennings Bryan of Nebraska. Bryan was not well known in the party, though he had achieved some popularity in his home state as a friend of Populists and had come to Chicago with a fair number of supporters. He had actually been defeated in the election of Nebraska delegates by J. Sterling Morton's gold men, but the credentials committee had seated him nevertheless. The hall was stifling when Bryan rose to speak, but his words cut through the apathy, confusion, and heat like a knife. The convention stilled under the magic of the greatest spellbinder in political history.

Those who heard it knew they were hearing history. Bryan traced the background of the silver question, bowed in the direction of the pioneer, made a defiant gesture at Great Britain, damned the Republicans, declared for Christianity, and climaxed the speech with an inspired image: "You shall not press down upon the brow of labor this cross of thorns, you shall not crucify mankind upon a cross of gold!" It was oratory—superb oratory—but oratory enunciating a principle much broader than silver alone, a concept of government that Grangers and Populists knew well. "There are two ideas of government," Bryan said.

There are those who believe that if you will only legislate to make the well-to-do prosperous, their prosperity will leak through on those below. The Democratic idea, however, has been that if you make the masses prosperous, their prosperity will find its way up through every class which rests on them.

When the last phrase of the "Cross of Gold" speech died in the air, the convention for all practical purposes was over. It came as close to riot as a convention ever came, and the hall echoed with the beat of "Bryan! Bryan! Bryan!" for half an hour. No one else stood a chance after that. Bryan was the West speaking, the Grangers, the Greenbackers, the Populists, the farmer with mortgages, and the worker in the street. Bryan said nothing new (Altgeld turned to Darrow and asked, "What *did* he say, anyway?") but he had said it in a way no one else had or could. He won the nomination on the fifth ballot, easily, his victory marred only by the secession of some gold Democrats who withdrew to nominate John Palmer of Illinois. "The Great Commoner" had arrived, and the leaderless West was leaderless no more.

The Populist convention met later under the long shadow cast by Bryan's cross of gold, faced with the dilemma of endorsing Bryan and riding the Democrat bandwagon or of nominating its own candidate and splitting the vote. It was a lively and colorful meeting, one at which everyone had something to say and said it, and it was an earnest convention—a reporter there sensed that too—made up of hundreds of people who felt "shut out, fooled, and put upon," ready to follow a leader. There were songs, parades, pageants, humor (the sergeant at arms' suspenders broke and he lost his trousers), but all the while the convention was being shepherded toward Bryan by Kyle, Weaver, Allen, and the silver-fusion leaders.

It required skill to do it. The independent Populists mentioned Eugene Debs of the railway unions as a candidate (too far to the left) and Donnelly (too close to the lunatic fringe). The Southern Populists thought of Tom Watson of Georgia (no Western appeal). Weaver, the 1892 nominee, was a fusionist, anyway. Populists, silver Democrats, and silver Republicans, he argued, were fighting the same battle and if Bryan might "plant the flag one foot nearer the citadel of plutocracy than we did," the Populists should help him. The result was never really in doubt. "That matchless champion of the people, that intrepid foe of corporate greed, that splendid young statesman," William Jennings Bryan, was the Populist nominee. Thus the old Middle Western tradition met the new—Weaver had been Greenbacker, Union Laborite, and Populist, and now he passed the torch of insurgency on to Bryan. Certain independents, however, bucked at Bryan's running mate, Sewall (a Maine banker), and nominated Watson for Vice-President, so that a Populist could at least vote for Bryan, as Donnelly said, "without having to vote for plutocracy too."

The nineteenth-century Midwestern revolt culminated in Bryan. He was its final product, the embodiment of its spirit, the sum of its strengths and its shortcomings. No matter what his party affiliation, Bryan represented Populism in its final phase; in Donnelly's words, "We put him to school and he stole the schoolbooks." With him the Democratic party picked up the Jeffersonian-Jacksonian tradition it had dropped before the Civil War, the tradition that the Populists, Greenbackers, and Anti-Monopolists barely kept alive. Bryan was a throwback to prewar frontier politics, the leader of the debtor, the farmer, the small-time commercial interests, and when he declared in his Cross of Gold speech that the Democrats stood with Jackson "against the encroachments of organized wealth," he put the party back into politics as the party of the West. Notably, Jefferson and Jackson were the only two statesmen Bryan ever quoted consistently, and it is equally notable that after 1892 the Republicans stopped celebrating Jefferson's birthday and organized Hamilton clubs. When Bryan was nominated, the wheel turned full circle.

Bryan's sweep of the 1896 convention was the end of a long and shrewdly planned strategy. Born in Illinois, he moved his law practice to Nebraska in the eighties, into the middle of agrarian discontent, and entered Democratic politics. The Democrats sent him twice to Congress in the early nineties, where he followed the party line faithfully and without much distinction. In 1894 he ran for the Senate against Republican John Thurston, knowing he would lose but hoping in the process to capture the Democratic party in Nebraska from the iron grasp of J. Sterling Morton. He lost as expected, but nevertheless he polled about half the Populist vote, an indication to him of the possibilities of co-operation. He had already supported Populist Senator Allen in 1893, and in 1894 he smuggled some fusionists into the state Democratic convention. Defeated, but still struggling with Morton for control of the party, he joined the staff of an Omaha newspaper and went on the Chautauqua platform. His appearance at the national convention of 1896 was a fortuitous conjunction of the man, the place, the time, and the issues.

Bryan was a big man, broad but not fat, giving an impression of suppressed physical power. He was not a great thinker nor a clear one, nor a student of public affairs, nor an efficient executive, nor an able statesman. He had practically no ideas of his own, dealing in other men's much as a merchant dealt in stock; the books he read and digested would have fitted into much less than a five-foot shelf, and to the end the single real source of his thinking was the Bible. His principles were elementary, the clear and simple issues of the West, and he never changed them—equal rights, popular rule, hatred of monopoly, suspicion of centralized government.

Bryan's power lay in his voice and in his appearance, as nearly everyone who heard and saw him in his early years agreed. His speeches never read well, and as the unsuccessful attempts of countless schoolboy orators proved, it took a Bryan to give them. One listener remarked that you could drive a prairie schooner through one without scraping a hub on a solid thought; it is significant that of all he said in his lifetime only the closing sentence of the Cross of Gold speech remains. Powerful, straight, piercing-eyed, with a mane of dark hair and the mien of a Roman senator, Bryan on the platform generated tremendous voltage, swaying crowds like a strong wind. Even when he was a tired old man, playing the Chautauqua circuit, audiences occasionally felt again the electric quality of the earlier Bryan, saw beneath the sagging figure a flash of the young Knight of the Platte, and stilled in respect. Bryan, in a degree granted to a few men, had Presence.

In the last analysis it was his voice that gave him almost hypnotic power. It was a baritone, not deep, with a silvery quality just short of metallic. With it he could run the scale of expression—sharp and hard for scorn, slow and intense for emotion, stirring and exciting for exhortation. He was never carried away by it himself, always perfectly in command of the instrument no matter how great the tumult. It was how he said something, and how he looked when he said it, that provoked belief. The correspondent of the London *Daily Mail* noted that the question of crowds was never "What did he say?" but "Did you hear him?"

It is a thorough misconception of Bryan to consider him a demagogue, a mere exhorter who appealed to the gullible masses. Bryan was a shrewd, realistic politician who stole two parties, welded them into one, and dominated that one for almost fifteen years. His principles were honestly held, and it is not on record that he ever compromised them. His love for the common people was sincere, and there was nothing he liked better than sweating with them under the hot prairie sun, a handkerchief around his neck and a Panama hat on his head, while he flayed their enemies. His personal tragedy was that he was born out of his time (what Bryan might have done in politics a century earlier almost staggers the imagination) and never adapted to it. The Bryan to remember is not the senile, querulous Bryan of the 1920's, selling real estate in Florida, booed at the 1924 convention, harried by the

cruelly adroit Darrow at the Scopes trial, but the younger
Bryan, the Peerless Leader of the West.

Bryan faced two opponents in the 1896 campaign, William
McKinley, the Republican nominee, and Mark Hanna, his
campaign manager. The two of them made a team, each
supplying qualities the other lacked, and their careers were
so closely bound together that they merged into a single political personality. Mark Hanna, a Cleveland millionaire who
drew his wealth from coal, iron, shipping, and traction holdings, entered Republican politics as a campaign worker in the
seventies. He first met McKinley when the young Canton
lawyer defended some strikers from one of Hanna's mines,
and the two men were immediately attracted to each other.
Hanna retired from active business in the eighties with two
aims, to build a machine within the Republican party and to
make McKinley President. Studying politics as he would a
business in which he was about to invest, he concluded that a
political party was simply a corporation and ought to be run
like one. He went to work quietly, appeared at conventions,
sent talkers to the delegates, paid the bills, and disappeared,
but he built swiftly. At the Republican convention of 1896
few knew him really well, but his Ohio machine ran over the
Eastern bosses to nominate McKinley on a gold platform.
After that Hanna was undisputed master of the Republican
party and the nearest thing to a national political boss that
politics had seen.

Hanna's concept of politics was neither broad nor idealistic.
Cutting directly to the heart of the matter, he said, "Politics
are one form of business, and must be treated strictly as a
business." Another time he observed that in a democracy all
questions of government were eventually questions of money—
who has it, and who gets it. It was neither graft nor corruption
that Hanna wanted from politics, but power—power to run
the country as the Republican corporation thought best. An
intellectually honest man, Hanna never pretended otherwise.
For the average corporation tycoon he had little respect and

not much affection; he thought Pullman a fool for refusing to arbitrate his strike, and George Baer's pious dictum that the coal operator was "chosen by God to govern the workingman" he dismissed with a snort. Homer Davenport's brutal cartoons of Hanna as a bloated moneybag made him familiar to the public as the archetype of all bosses, but in reality he was a charming and refreshingly realistic man whose famous corned beef breakfasts (his own recipe from the mining camps) and honest friendliness swung many a doubting delegate or legislator into line.

McKinley was the other side of the Republican coin, a smooth, handsome, party regular. The last of the Civil War soldier-Presidents, he had neither deeply held ideals nor overwhelming personal charm, but he was a clever and honest party politician of more than average ability. Contemporary cartoons of Hanna as a paunchy plutocrat with the monkey McKinley tied to a string were wrong. McKinley had a mind of his own, a good one, and was no simple tool of Hanna's; the two men were simply stronger together than apart and both knew it. McKinley supplied the presence, the speeches, the unifying personality. Hanna supplied the machine. McKinley knew people and issues—Joe Cannon said he had his ear so close to the ground it was full of grasshoppers—while Hanna handled the apparatus of politics.

The campaign of 1896 was a contest between a highly efficient machine and an emotionally aroused rabble. Bryan's campaign was an effective one. He left crowds of wildly cheering voters behind him as the great crusade took shape—the people against money, the people against the machine, public good against special privilege, free silver against the cross of gold. Henry George, Edward Bellamy, W. D. P. Bliss of the Christian Socialists, and Victor Berger of the Socialists worked for him along with hundreds of anonymous volunteers, and there were mass meetings, processions, banners, songs, and torchlight parades.

Bryan swung first through the Midwest, then through the

East into "enemy territory," and in the last weeks of the campaign through the Midwest again, into the South, up the coast into New England, a total of seventeen thousand miles. Everywhere the crowds gathered—some hating him, others loving him, but all eager to hear him. It was a bitter campaign, one of the bitterest of all time. There was, said the *New York Tribune* later, "such a flood of blasphemy, of taking God's name in vain, as this country at least has never known before." Arrayed against Bryan were the press, the pulpit, and business, who could find nothing too bad to call him. The *New York Tribune* said he was "a puppet in the blood-imbued hands of Altgeld the anarchist, Debs the revolutionist, and other desperadoes." The *Philadelphia Record* "spit upon this communistic, Populistic deliverance," whose "very essence was anarchy." Bryanism, said Professor Laughlin, stemmed from "ignorant, unthinking minds, oppressed by a sense of inferiority." *Gunton's Magazine* called it "a combination of the destructive elements of society . . . , a violent, infectious, political disease . . . , unpatriotic charlatanry and economic hypocrisy." Bryan's principles, explained "Mr. Dooley," Finley Peter Dunne's Irish commentator, were "anny ol' thing that the other parties has rijicted. Some iv thim is in favor of coining money out iv baled hay an' dhried apples, at a ratio of sixteen to wan, and some is in favor iv coining only th' apples."

The churches followed the lead of the newspapers and, if anything, outdid them in abuse. The Republican National Committee circulated church bodies with pamphlets pointing out that free silver would curtail donations and damage ecclesiastical financing. Dr. Charles Parkhurst of New York told his congregation that Bryan's attempt to foment class hatred was "accursed and treasonable," and the Reverend Thomas Dixon said free silver clearly violated the tenth commandment, "Thou shalt not steal." Bryan, said Dixon publicly, "was a slobbering, mouthing demagogue, whose patriotism is in his jawbone." Unaccountably, free silver gradually turned into a moral rather than a financial issue, something clearly un-American and probably un-Christian.

Business was not far behind the pulpit and press in name calling. Railroads, express and telegraph companies, and manufacturers sent instructions to their agents in every town. If Bryan won, said the manufacturers, wages would fall, shops close, and industry stop dead in its tracks. Bankers threatened to call in loans if Bryan were elected, and every farm mortgage would be called as soon as it fell due. There would be, said Senator Allison of Iowa, "no lasting security for either life or property in America." "We must all stand together," said Congressman Wolcott, "against this socialism, populism, and paternalism which is running riot." John Hay reported that many of his friends were preparing to buy homes in Paris if Bryan won, fearing actual personal harm at the hands of mobs. "Probably no man in civil life," said the *Nation* later, "succeeded in inspiring so much terror, without taking life, as Bryan." However, Mark Hanna remained unperturbed. He had the money, the machine, and the bosses. Bryan disturbed him very little.

McKinley's campaign, a rather dignified one, revolved about two major issues—Americanism and prosperity. By good fortune the Republicans picked up a bitter editorial written by a Kansas Republican editor, William Allen White, called "What's the Matter with Kansas?" "The American idea is today in the balance," wrote White. "The Republicans are upholding it. The Populists and their allies are denouncing it. The election will sustain Americanism or it will plant Socialism." White's attack on the "farmer radicals" and agrarian ignoramuses filled the Republican bill exactly. Hanna marked the author down for advancement, and the newspapers broadcast the editorial over the nation. White's editorial completely muddied the real issues of the campaign, but it said what Hanna wanted said, and it gave the voter a good reason for voting against Bryan even though he might feel there was some merit in Bryan's platform. Elect McKinley, "The Advance Agent of Prosperity," and keep your pocketbook full. Let Bryan leave his trail of fire through the states; McKinley, in respectable contrast, conducted a quiet campaign from his back porch in Canton and talked about prosperity and patriotism.

Meanwhile Mark Hanna called in the bankers, the railroad men, and the industrialists. When they left he had their checks. Exactly how full Republican coffers were is a matter of speculation, but estimates ran from as low as six million to as high as twelve million dollars, which Hanna poured out in speakers and pamphlets. The Chicago Republican headquarters sent out a total of one hundred million handbills in ten languages. The New York office sent out twenty million, and no one knows how many were mailed from Washington under congressional franks. In Iowa alone the Republicans put six thousand speakers in the field and mailed out six million pieces of literature. During the last week of the campaign there were eighteen thousand Republican speakers on tour through the nation. This was big business, and Bryan, valiant as he was (he spoke twenty-seven times the last day), could not beat it.

The result was never really in question, though at times it looked like a narrow squeak. McKinley won by a little more than a half million popular votes and a larger margin in electoral votes. Bryan and Sewall polled approximately six million votes, but Bryan's total fell short of the combined Populist-Democratic vote of 1892. He lost every state east of the Mississippi and north of the Potomac, and also the upper tier of trans-Mississippi states. He won the South, the Southwest, the plains states, and parts of the Far West, but wherever industry was strong he was weak. The gold Democrats, the Bryan-Watson Populist ticket, and the silver Republicans made practically no showing. The wreckage of Bryanism littered the states as well. The old Northwest states went Republican, along with Iowa, Minnesota, and North Dakota. Altgeld lost in Illinois. In South Dakota the Democrats, silver Republicans, and Populists elected Arthur Lee governor, and a similar fusion worked successfully in Kansas and Nebraska. Otherwise Populism was gone, lost in free silver and Democratic defeat.

The results of 1896 were viewed generally as a triumph for stable and conservative government over demagoguery and class prejudice. "God's in His heaven," telegraphed Mark Hanna when the decision was known, and the *New York Tribune* by rather tortured reasoning proved McKinley's victory to mean that "right is right and God is God." In an exclusive Chicago club financiers and merchants joyfully began a spontaneous game of follow-the-leader over chairs and tables when the news came, but on second thought, they sobered at the six million votes that Bryan had received.

What were the reasons for those six million votes? What did they mean for the future? After the victory celebrations were over, commentators analyzed and argued, but all agreed that six million was a frighteningly large figure, and that respectability and stability might not win the next time. *Gunton's Magazine* laid Bryan's vote to the rise of socialistic thinking, to the hatred of wealth by the poor, and most of all to Republican indifference to the new economic problems of industry and agriculture. The Republicans, warned Gunton, would have to do some constructive thinking before 1900, or meet defeat. The *Atlantic Monthly* thought most of Bryan's vote came from the farmer; that "sturdy yeoman" had somehow turned into a "hayseed," lacking "habits of thrift and commercial morality," and was an easy mark for "demagogic witchery."

The *Forum's* symposium on the meaning of the election came to some bleak conclusions. Goldwin Smith, who called his contribution "The Brewing of the Storm," advocated increasing the regular army to prepare for the riots certain to come after the next election. David Mears was not at all certain that he could answer the question "Will Government by the People Endure?" Andrew D. White of Cornell thought rich men should give more money to universities, so that "our leading schools should be strengthened . . . as fortresses against future outbursts of demagogism and Jack Cade-ism." Frederick Jackson Turner, the Wisconsin historian, provided the clearest and most sensible summary of what Bryanism meant. "This," he wrote, "is the real situation: a people composed of heterogeneous materials, with divers and conflicting ideals and social interests, having passed from the task of filling up the vacant spaces of the continent, is now thrown back upon itself and is seeking an equilibrium. The diverse elements are now being fused into national unity."

Bryan's adherents were disappointed but not downhearted. Bryan wrote a book, *The First Battle,* and prepared for the second. "We entered the contest with a disorganized army," he wrote. "We emerge from it a united and disciplined force without the loss of a soldier. We are ready for another contest." His army, in fact, was neither unified nor disciplined. A good many Populists were convinced that they could do better next time alone, and probably as many Democrats were not sure whether Populist support in the election had been a liability or an asset.

The defeat of Bryan and the split between Populist and Democrat left the Midwestern "hayseed radical" thoroughly confused. Where could he go? The Republican party was hopelessly out of the question. The Democratic party, without free silver, was not much more to his taste—even Andrew Carnegie said he could not explain the difference between the two parties—and Populism was dying of internal disorders. The National Press Reform Association, composed of Populist editors who wanted to establish independency of the People's party once more, met with the Populist national committee in 1897 but reached no decision. Another conference in 1898 dissolved in bickering between "middle of the roaders" and the fusionists, and another that same year, steered by Donnelly and Coxey, decided to run a separate Populist ticket in 1900. Weaver, observing that "nothing grows in the middle of the road," stuck by the Democrats until he died in 1912, while Donnelly and his paper, the *Representative,* worked for Populism until his death in 1900.

McKinley lived up to his billing as "the advance agent of

prosperity" with the help of prosperity and a war against Spain. Good times took over—dollar wheat, rising wages, higher corporate profits. Business boomed, fortunes grew, and the stock market was crammed with undigested securities. "A carnival of trusts is now in progress," said Henry D. Lloyd, and the figures bore him out. In 1898 the *New York Herald* listed ninety-two trusts formed during the year; in 1900 the census reported seventy-three combinations whose capital exceeded ten millions each, of which only twenty had existed prior to 1898. Mark Hanna refused a cabinet post lest it appear that he was being rewarded for his campaign management, but McKinley's cabinet, composed mainly of Midwesterners and Westerners, showed the power of Hanna's machine. Hanna himself entered the Senate and the inner circle of the "Big Six" who controlled it, Aldrich, Allison, Hale, Platt, and Spooner. "Reaction was in the saddle," remarked the sociologist E. A. Ross, "and rode like a drunken bully."

But the spirit of protest that cast the six million votes for Bryan was by no means gone. It was hampered, certainly, by Populism's internal dissension, the revival of prosperity, and most of all by war with Spain, which shifted attention from domestic to foreign policies. Bryan enlisted in a volunteer regiment (with poorer press relations than Theodore Roosevelt), leaving Donnelly and Weaver and others to argue over whether or not Populists and Democrats should join forces, or whether or not free silver was a dead issue. Some of the reform leaders continued efforts to concentrate and unify forces. "We are not fools," wrote one Midwesterner in 1897, "though we may appear so to you; we know what we want and we are trying to get it."

McKinley rode into office again in 1900 on the crest of a victorious Republican wave along with his running mate, Theodore Roosevelt. Bryan almost automatically ran for the Democrats, relaxing his free-silver stand on the ground that the discovery of gold in Alaska changed the currency situation. The "middle of the road" Populists put up Wharton Barker, a Philadelphia bimetallist, who received only fifty thousand votes. The Populist revolt was over, and though the party struggled on until 1908, it was no use. It died with free silver, and while Bryan searched for an issue to replace the "cross of gold"—antimonopolism, government ownership of railroads, anti-imperialism, and so on—neither he nor the Populists ever found one that fitted the requirements.

So far as immediate practical results were concerned, the Populist revolt accomplished exactly nothing. The political system that had been in power since the Civil War remained in power, its branches shaken by the winds of 1896 but its roots firmly embedded. When Mark Hanna died in 1904, the kind of politics he represented seemed to be stronger than ever before. It beat Weaver in 1892, Bryan in 1896, and Bryan again more thoroughly in 1900, and Hanna himself, the incarnation of the system, had just been returned to the Senate after a frankly conservative campaign—one for which he had coined the term "standpat" to make perfectly clear what he stood for. Politicians in 1900 proudly called themselves "conservative"; the nation liked things as they were, and stood pat.

But the old Midwestern tradition of revolt did not die, even though Bryan lost and Populism withered. It had accomplished more than it seemed, nor were the forces of the opposition quite so powerful as they appeared to be. The constant hammering of Grangers, Alliance men, Greenbackers, and Populists, the cumulative attacks of the Weavers and Donnellys and Simpsons and Lloyds and Bryans were beginning to shake the walls of complacency even during the reign of King Hanna. A half century of campaigning had its effects on public opinion, and a great many people, even if they did not vote for Bryan, perceived that the things of which they complained were compounded of an alliance for profit between politics and business. Bryan and his predecessors stirred people up. Lloyd and his followers made them angry and inquisitive. The more they looked where these men pointed, the more they saw. The public was being educated.

The Republican triumphs of 1896 and 1900 bore in them the germs of defeat. Encouraged by success, the conservatives in business and politics pushed on toward the limits of tolerance, forgetting that the old issues were not dead, but only defeated. By making "conservatism" the ally of graft and privilege, they shifted the connotations of the word until it no longer implied protection of the constant values of American life, but instead meant reaction, self-interest, protection of the corrupt and privileged. The Grangers and Greenbackers and Populists did not lose after all. The essence of Midwestern political thought was its desire to place government more closely under the people's control so that it might answer more directly to the people's needs. That was what Weaver and Donnelly and Bryan, often in a dim and stumbling way, were trying to do, and though they failed, others carried on the tradition.

Thirty years of agitation in the Midwest farm belt laid the foundation for what was to come, sometimes under other auspices—under Theodore Roosevelt, under Wilson, under La Follette and the "reform" mayors and governors who came after 1900. As William Allen White said later, the progressive politicians of the early twentieth century "caught the Populists in swimming and stole all of their clothing except the frayed underdrawers of free silver." In the twenty-five years after Bryan's defeat, twenty-one states (only six of them east of the Mississippi) adopted either some or most of the Granger-Populist platform, and by 1942 the federal government itself had accepted in one form or another every principle common to all the Midwestern "radical" programs except free silver and government ownership of communication and transportation. Granger-Populist reforms in election machinery—the Australian ballot, direct election of government representatives, direct legislation in the form of the initiative and referendum—all appeared in the states in varying forms. The war against the banks and for freer money found fruition in the Federal Reserve Act of 1913, which, though not so sweeping as the paper money and free-silver platforms of the eighties and nineties, nevertheless provided a similar elasticity in control of money and banking. The much-ridiculed subtreasury and farm-credit plans of the seventies and eighties reappeared in the Farm Loan and Warehouse Acts of 1916 and later in the Commodity Credit Corporation. The Granger's cries for railroad and antitrust legislation were reflected in act after act by both state and federal governments after 1900; postal savings banks, income taxes, corporation taxes, and conservation of natural resources came in the twentieth century much as the Midwesterners had asked in 1880 and 1890.

The great nineteenth-century Midwestern revolt grew from the feeling that if the great promises of American democracy remained unrealized, there must be a reason for it. The long line of reformers from Donnelly to Bryan showed the Midwest what the faults were, and it turned to government for aid in correcting them. This was a shift, a marked shift, from the old frontier philosophy of self-reliance and laissez faire to a new one of social co-operation—a shift, as Turner phrased it, "from the ideal of individualism to the ideal of social control through the regulation by law." Government became on the one hand a policeman to restrain those who would repress or victimize the people, and on the other an instrument controlled by the people's will and responsive to their needs. Governor Lewelling of Kansas defined it best:

The Government must make it possible for the citizen to live by his own labor, for the citizen to enjoy liberty and pursuit of happiness. If the Government fails in these things, it fails in its mission . . . , the State has failed, and our boasted civil compact a hollow mockery. But Government is not a failure, and the State has not been constructed in vain. The people are greater than the law and the statutes, and when a nation sets its heart on doing a good or a great thing, it can find a way to do it.

The Capture of the Ivory Tower

IV

When the later twentieth century looks back at the 1890's and the early 1900's, it is prone to see them nostalgically as a naïve and happy era, when fashions ran to tight-bottom trousers, bustles, hard hats and hair puffs, when emotions and dancing styles were unsophisticated—the proverbial "Naughty Nineties" of "Ta-ra-de-boom-de-ay" and the frilled bottoms of cancan girls. The twentieth century sees the era in terms of what William Dean Howells called "the smiling aspects of life," finding amusement in the abundance of whiskers in Congress, in songs of betrayed servant girls and birds in a gilded cage, in corn-belt fundamentalism, in gas lamps, buggies, and Peck's Bad Boy.

It was not like that at all. The period from 1890 to 1910 was an age of uncertainty, shaken by a revolution in science and theology and a real and terrible ordeal for democracy. The twentieth century forgets the upsurge of angry farmers that washed at the pillars of Wall Street, the bloody steel and coal strikes, the assassination of a President, the ominous clowning march of Coxey's ragged "petition in boots," the great depressions, the rage against the "plutocrats" and the "bosses" that made Rockefeller and Hanna symbols of hate to a generation. It forgets the emptiness of faith that followed Darwin, the ruthless realism of thinkers like Sumner and Brooks and Henry Adams. It forgets the huge political machines, the organized graft and corruption of the cities where "Hinky Dinks" and "Bathhouse Johns" represented democracy. The old America was gone, and the new America seemed barren. The faith, optimism, and manifest destiny of the Golden Age disappeared.

But in the midst of doubt and unrest there existed an island of hopefulness. The new America might yet find itself, adjust to science and industrialism, retrieve something of the old American dream of a commonwealth of justice. The political leaders of the Midwest, defeated in the debacle of 1896, served as rallying points for the forces that refused to succumb to materialism, mechanism, and corporate power. The problems that grew out of the collision of old pioneer ideals and the new industrialism were peculiarly theirs. They were among the first to test the solutions.

THE POPULIST REVOLT was a political manifestation of the changing attitudes of late nineteenth- and earlier twentieth-century thinkers toward certain aspects of American life. Bryan was a political candidate, it is true, but beneath Bryan's candidacy lay a whole substratum of social, economic, and religious thought without which he never could have happened. Bryan was an outward symptom of an internal irritation, and while his leadership was important—almost decisive—he must be separated from more fundamental forces at work, if the social or political situation of his time is to be properly examined.

Midwest progressivism was part of a larger ethical as well as political movement, of a major shift in social and political and economic philosophies, and of a redirection of Christian thinking. Charles Eaton, writing in the *Forum* in 1898, believed that the majority of thinkers in the years after 1890 were most concerned with improving the social, the political, and the economic situation in America. This movement was, for the most part, a national rather than a regional manifestation, but the Midwest shared largely in it, contributed to it, and developed it.

The periodicals of the eighties and nineties were filled with discussions of wealth, its function, its right to leadership.

The arguments of the sociologists, the revision of the concept of education, the debate over the application of Darwinism to social and economic problems, the attacks on the monopolist—and the ordinary man's plain and unvarnished fear that something was radically disconnected in the American system—forced the supporters of life-as-it-is to evolve a defense. The paradox of economic inequality and political equality had been apparent for a long time, and with the rise of a postwar industrial economy, the opening of new markets, and the tapping of the greatest store of economic resources the world had yet seen, the ancient debate of have and have-not flared up hotter than ever. It was perfectly clear to the average man that a few—a very few—were gathering a disproportionately large share of the nation's economic blessings to themselves. "The real issue," said Sumner in 1900, "that men of the future have got to meet is the struggle between plutocracy and democracy."

The defense of wealth evolved by the end of the century was strong, well grounded, and credible. Much of it needed no proof, so deeply embedded was it in the American-Christian tradition. Men such as Jim Fisk, Daniel Drew, Jay Gould, Rockefeller, and Carnegie, and even a fair share of those who questioned them, were certain that what they were doing was right, but felt some necessity of explaining why. A few millionaire sports—Joseph Fels, the soap manufacturer, E. A. Filene of Boston, Tom Johnson of Cleveland, and Charles Crane of Chicago—used their fortunes to endow "crackpot" movements against the system that had made them rich, but usually the capitalist felt that laissez faire needed only dusting off and rearranging to justify it. Some way had to be found, as Abram Hewitt, the iron magnate, remarked, of "making men who were entitled to political liberty and equality content with inequality in the distribution of property."

This "gospel of wealth," as it was worked out and substantiated by economists and sociologists (less systematically by the wealthy themselves), consisted of a restatement of certain traditional principles—scientific, religious, and economic—and of their application to contemporary life. Essentially the idea was that an individual possessed the right to acquire and use wealth, and that the economic and social system founded upon his right to do so was better than any other.

Economic individualism itself was deeply rooted in the American tradition. The natural-rights concepts of the eighteenth century clearly supported it; thus Justice Field referred to the Declaration of Independence for proof that each man possessed the right to obtain and use property in his pursuit of life, liberty, and happiness. The Spencerian doctrines of the late nineteenth century buttressed it, for as Sumner explained, the right to own and control property was essential to the selective process. The millionaire was quick to agree. George Baer thought the rich were "gifted and capable men who are obeying the primitive mandate to subdue the earth and have dominion over it." George Gunton thought they were men who were simply better able to follow the principles of nature than their neighbors; Rockefeller tied both Darwinism and Christianity in one neat package by saying that business was "merely the working out of a law of nature and a law of God." Spencer himself, when he visited America, was amazed at how literally American business had accepted his ideas, warning that they had been carried so far that unless government interfered, competition might disappear—a warning few heeded. The age stressed individualism, an industrial individualism that justified the acquisition of wealth in any form or by nearly any method.

More than the Declaration of Independence or Spencer, the ingrained American tradition of self-help and self-attainment reinforced the defense of wealth. Americans, since the days of the Puritans, believed in the moral rightness of getting rich by industry and frugality. James McCosh of Princeton said in 1892, "God has bestowed upon us certain powers and gifts which no one is to take from us or interfere with. All attempts to deprive us of them is theft." Christianity considered man a free agent, free to sink or swim according to his abilities. There was a long tradition of respect for the man who swam—Franklin's *Poor Richard,* Noah Webster's spelling-book adages and McGuffey's moral tales, the Lincoln-Jackson-Garfield-Grant allegories of log cabin or towpath to White House, Alger's *Ragged Dick* and *Frank the Cash Boy,* Carnegie's rise from bobbin boy to steel king, Ford's climb from bicycle shop to River Rouge. The possession of wealth meant, according to the American *mythos,* that its owner had succeeded where other men failed. Thus the president of the Board of Trustees of the University of Chicago, in accepting the gift of a painting of John D. Rockefeller, remarked that his great fortune was "both a badge and a reward of intelligence and energy." Work hard and aim for the highest, Carnegie told the young men of Curry Commercial College in Pittsburgh; never enter a bar room, never speculate, never endorse beyond your surplus cash; put all your eggs in one basket and watch the basket. There was no stigma, Carnegie explained, to poverty. It came when you stayed poor, for failure to rise showed the lack of those qualities necessary for rising. Poverty was a blessing, for it brought out the best qualities of mankind in the struggle against it.

With the right to gain wealth solidly founded on both the religious and secular tradition, the only plausible basis for complaint was over its use. Money was power, there was no doubt of that; what guarantee was there that this power would be used in the proper spirit? It was the rich man's responsibility, his defenders replied, to employ the blessings God had given him in a manner consistent with accepted religious and social principles. If acquisitiveness existed in human nature by divine decree, explained Daniel Gregory's *Christian Ethics* in 1875, it is there for a moral purpose; and, said Mark Hopkins in 1868, "the acquisition of property is required by love, because it is a powerful means of benefitting others." The rich man was a steward of the Lord who must use his wealth, as Carnegie phrased it, "so that the ties of brotherhood may still bind rich and poor in harmonious relationship."

The doctrine of the stewardship of wealth was most fully developed by Andrew Carnegie, who was not only a disciple of Spencer but also a devoutly religious man, anxious to align the apparently contradictory views of Spencer with orthodox Christianity. The man of wealth, he wrote in 1889, is "to consider all surplus revenues which come to him simply as trust funds, which he is called upon to administer in the manner which, in his judgment, is best calculated to produce the most beneficial results for the community." So Carnegie endowed his libraries and philanthropies; Rockefeller his foundations; Drew a theological seminary; Brady a medical research institute; Stanford, Duke, and Rockefeller universities; Folger, Huntington, Newberry, and Clements libraries, and so on. "The good Lord gave me my money," Rockefeller once said, "and how can I withhold it from the University of Chicago?" "I say *get rich, get rich!*" said Russell Conwell in *Acres of Diamonds.* "Money being power, it ought to be in the hands of good men and women."

The defenders of wealth projected a shining picture of the new society that would appear in America under a Christianized capitalism in which enlightened wealth served society. The poor man of 1900 enjoyed things the rich man of 1800 could never afford, things of which he had never dreamed. Wealth had done it, wealth properly used. If the market is open and competition free, agreed economists John Bates Clark and George Gunton, the public benefits by more and cheaper goods produced by invested wealth. The rich will grow richer in the new society, "but it will not mean that the poor need grow poorer." As the "rich man enlarges his holdings . . . from one million dollars to ten, from ten to a hundred, and from a hundred to a thousand—the typical laborer will increase his wages from one dollar a day to two dollars, from two to four, from four to eight." "Don't shoot the millionaires," warned Carnegie, "for they are the bees who make the most honey, and contribute most to the hive." It is a fact, he added, "that the masses of people in any country are prosperous and comfortable just in proportion as there are millionaires."

Still, the rich man's defenses were not attack proof. Before the Civil War riches were popularly respected as evidences of thrift, hard work, and a certain admirable Yankee "cuteness." In the postwar period there was a growing suspicion that perhaps this was no longer so. What the tycoon did was not always consistent with those motives which, Carnegie explained, really actuated his desire to amass wealth. In the sordid seventies, the antics of the pirates and stock riggers—Gould, Drew, Fisk, and others—did not appear to be Christian-inspired, while the mishandling of the railroads and their almost complete financial collapse in 1893 did not impress the public with the superior intelligence of their owners. Big business did not always have full public confidence. The rise of the trust and the exposures of the muckrakers made some of the rich men look more like robber barons than Christian stewards. In 1907, when Theodore Roosevelt in his message to Congress officially placed the blame for the current panic on "law-defying wealth," the rich man struck bottom in public esteem—in the same year that Rockefeller's fortune hit an even billion. If these were the leaders, the stewards, the "naturally fit," the flowers of competition, there was something wrong with the system.

The "gospel of wealth" looked to some like plain nonsense. "The business ideal is the very lowest ideal that can actuate people," said the St. Louis *Mirror;* instead of the desire to serve society, the rich man's motive was "simply greed complicated by fear." Fortunes are immoral, wrote Louis Post of the *Public,* for they represent nothing but "the capitalization of the legal power to exact tribute." "Men of wealth," the sociologist Cooley said, "are liable to certain moral deficiencies," since they deal in matters which have "no settled rules of morality." "Between a Life of Jesse James and a Life of Jay Gould," remarked an editor who caught his office boy reading dime novels on company time, "the former would seem to me less likely to corrupt a boy's ideals." And if the manner in which the rich gain wealth is immoral, said the *American Magazine of Civics,* think of how they spend it—riotous living, all-night balls, showy dinners, foreign titles for marriageable daughters, race horses for sons, snobbishness, lazy seasons at Newport, ostentation, extravagance.

Using the term "the survival of the fittest" to describe the wealthy aroused loud guffaws in some quarters. Some men, their critics pointed out, simply had lower moral standards than others; they were more unscrupulous in improving their opportunities by devices far better hidden than boasted about. Finley Peter Dunne's Mr. Dooley neatly deflated the doctrine of stewardship, remarking that Rockefeller had issued a statement.

. . . sayin' that he's a custojeen iv money appinted be himself. He looks afther his own money an' th' money iv other people. He takes it and puts it where it won't hurt thim and they won't spoil it. He's a kind iv a society f'r th' previntion iv croolty to money.

Though the Reverend Newell Dwight Hillis was certain that "the loftiest positions of the nation are open to the boys of workshop and factory," there was widespread doubt that this was the case. It was perfectly clear that when somebody moved up he closed off an opportunity for someone else, and that the person who held power was more than likely to do his level best to secure it against competition. It was useless to talk to a Nebraska farmer about "competing" with the Burlington, or to the small oil producer about "surviving" against Standard Oil. You might have the "opportunity" of engaging in a clawing match with a bear, said one Populist, but who the hell wanted to?

"To prove any harm in aggregations of wealth, it must be shown that great wealth is, as a rule, in the ordinary course of social affairs, put to a mischievous use," William Graham Sumner wrote in "The Absurd Attempt to Make the World Over." "This," he concluded, "cannot be shown beyond the very slightest degree, if at all." There were a good many who were quite willing to show him. As the abolitionists once warned of the danger of rule of the "slavocracy," so the reformers of the nineteenth and twentieth century raised the specter of rule by the "plutocracy." Chief Justice Ryan of the supreme court of Wisconsin inveighed against this "new and dark power" in 1873. The Grangers and the Farmers' Alliance battled against the railroads and the "interests" in the eighties; the Greenbackers talked of "this aristocracy of wealth . . . , a curse of any country." Weaver, in his 1892 campaign, pointed out that the limited slave power had been superseded by an unlimited aristocracy of wealth, "infinitely more dangerous and powerful . . . ," while Bryan fulminated against plutocracy at every Democratic convention from 1896 to 1912. Resistance to the doctrines of wealth and stewardship was strong and real in the eighties and after.

The fear of the power of wealth, as Bryan's campaign showed, was deeply rooted in the popular fear of the *political* use of wealth. Carnegie and his fellows might talk interminably of the rightness of riches and their socially advantageous uses, but the shadow of the "plutocrat" always hung over and behind the argument. He was, in Sumner's definition, "a man who, having the possession of capital, and having the power of it at his disposal, uses it, not industrially, but politically." Other definitions were less temperate. The *Kansan,* of Pittsburg, Kansas, said he was "a parasite who believes in the rule of the rich"; the Chicago *New Time* thought he was out "to rule the world through the power of gold." He intended, said another, "to suborn popular government in the interests of aristocracy," and a Minnesotan called him "a grave and startling menace to the democratic order."

No amount of "gospel of wealth" logic could erase the fact that contemporary legislation really *did* reflect the influence of wealth. Flower's *Arena* and other magazines pointed it out in the nineties, and the Granger and Alliance and Populist political leaders emphasized it. The captain of industry was the man to catch, his was the trail to follow. The reformers followed it, and what they found at its end was unpleasant and frightening—bribery, corruption, special privilege, a self-seeking, cynical subversion of democracy. Instead of leading mankind forward to the new order, the "plutocrat" seemed to be leading it back to an old one, to "a despotism of wealth more corrupting and subtly poisonous than that of church, king, or aristocrat."

The "gospel of wealth" assumed that the public would willingly accept the right of the wealthy to rule. It assumed that those who were not rich would cheerfully admit that they had lost in the competitive struggle, and that they would submit to the leadership of those who had won. There was always the possibility that the losers in the race might disagree with the rules, refuse to abide by them, and band together to gain by co-operative political or social action what they failed to obtain as individuals. The Christian-Spencerian argument was a fine one—logical, flawless, convincing—but some simply did not believe it and saw a way to beat it.

In the study of the social sciences the "gospel-of-wealth" and Spencerian conservatives found both their best defenders and their most spirited opposition. The argument was, it is true, largely academic, but it was not at all divorced from reality. Rather, it was closely related to the contemporary scene, for the theories advanced by economists and sociologists provided necessary bases for political, social, and economic action. The Populist concept of government, and later the progressive, owed much to economics and sociology; so, for that matter, did their opposition. Sumner supported Hanna, Carnegie, and Rockefeller. Ward, Ely, and the rest gave ballast to the ideas of Bryan and La Follette.

The sources of the conservative defense of things as they were rested on the traditional American principle of individualism. The Bill of Rights, the individualistic heritage of the pioneer, the laissez-faire theory of classical economy, the Darwinian theory of the survival of the fittest—all these added up to the conclusion that every man was responsible for his own destiny. The true conservative placed supreme confidence in the ability and the right of the individual to make his own way, and supported his position by science, economics, and Christianity itself. The great body of plain people accepted individualism without too much question; the existing system, by the simple fact of its existence, needed far less defense than might be assumed in the light of contemporary economic and social protest.

Economists after the Civil War simply reapplied the laissez-faire economics of the eighteenth and early nineteenth centuries to the new industrial age. Those who were busy developing the country had little time or desire to speculate about economic principles. Most Americans were taught, and believed, that private property was the foundation of society; that absolute individualism was the only proper base for economic life; that wealth was the reward of intelligence, skill, and enterprise. Everyone knew that a man was happiest when he got what he wanted. Since only he knew what he wanted, the government had no right to interfere wtih his pursuit of happiness, economically or otherwise, for the happiness of society was in the last analysis the sum total of the happiness of the individuals. Books on economic theory preached these ideas as Holy Writ.

Contemporary discussions of economic life, however, involved discussions of society itself, of what it was, how it ran, and what it existed for. The appeal to laissez-faire economics alone was insufficient. The status quo needed support from sociologists as well. Probably the most influential of social thinkers was William Graham Sumner of Yale, who provided the best possible defense against the political and social reformers. A Yale graduate who studied in Germany, Switzerland, and England, Sumner drew his theory of social action from the post-Darwinians, particularly Spencer, and elucidated it tirelessly in books and articles, his most descriptive being *What Social Classes Owe to Each Other* (1893) and "The Absurd Effort to Make the World Over" in 1894.

The primary fact of life, Sumner explained, is the struggle for existence, in which the greatest advances come from the production and retention of capital. Thus the right to amass wealth—and to use and transmit it—is vital in the struggle to survive and advance. As in the biological world physical inheritance determines the fit, so does economic inheritance in the world of society. Money, to Sumner, was a measure of social fitness, and talk of liberty and equality in eighteenth-century terms was plain nonsense. "Let it be understood," he wrote, "that we cannot go outside of this alternative; liberty, inequality, survival of the fittest; not liberty, equality, survival of the unfittest. The former carries society forward and favors all its best members; the latter carries society downward and favors all its worst members." Inequality is ingrained in nature; it must be, else survival of the fittest is meaningless. The only liberty a society must possess and protect is the liberty to compete, to engage in the struggle for survival.

Sumner's rugged realism comforted few, since the reformers attacked him from one side and the conservatives from the other. True, he did label the millionaire as "the finest product of competitive society," but he also accused him of constantly stacking the cards against the poor man. But in the main his interpretation of economic and social questions from a strictly Darwinian-Spencerian point of view reinforced the conservative, individualistic position. This was a world of "root, hog, or die," he believed, a world in which "the longest pole knocks down the most persimmons." A competitive society "develops

all powers that exist according to their measure and degree."
In open competition "courage, enterprise, good training, intelligence, perseverance" will succeed and the lack of them will
fail. This was exactly what businessmen of the time thought
and said, but not half so well nor so authoritatively as Sumner.
It was what Chauncey Depew meant when, speaking at a dinner of wealthy industrialists in New York, he looked about
him and remarked that they were all there by reason of
"superior ability, foresight, and adaptability."

The offensive against the Spencerian conservatives and the
"let alone" school of business theory took the form of a movement in economics, political science, and social thought toward
collectivism—based on the belief that the state could do certain
things for society with greater efficiency and justice than any
individual could. It was partially a revolt against the Darwinian-Spencerian attitude, and partially a feeling that only
through group action could the dream of the American
commonwealth came true. It was the result of a new trend in
the social sciences, away from the older classical, laissez-faire,
individualistic school of thought.

Before 1880 there were practically no systematic research
techniques employed in the social sciences; indeed, before 1890
only four American universities offered sociology courses. However, a whole new group of social theorists appeared, many of
them trained in Germany. They founded new organizations
for the exchange of information and to attack social and economic problems from new viewpoints—the American Historical Association, the American Economic Association, the
American Political Science Association, the American Sociological Association, and others. What they had to say squared
not at all with the older prevailing theories.

The most incisive answer to Sumner and the individualists
came from Lester Frank Ward, Western-born lawyer, botanist,
geologist, war veteran, professor of sociology at Brown, and
author of *Dynamic Sociology*. The survival-of-the-fittest theory,

said Ward, is simply not applicable to human society. Men are men, not beasts, and need not follow the law of beasts. Nature is wasteful and irrational in its workings, blind, accidental, unintelligent: note the number of seedlings needed to produce one tree, or the false starts and blind alleys nature encountered in evolving the horse. Men do a better job than nature, as every animal breeder and botanist knows. Intelligent elimination of wasteful competition in nature and society permits the superior individual to demonstrate that superiority. Man can and should interfere with natural law to his own advantage, biologically, economically, and socially.

There were, Ward believed, two levels of economics. One was an "animal" level of unlimited competition on which creative energy is dissipated in the simple attempt to survive. Another was a "human" level where, by rational planning, new and better species and patterns of living are possible. The latter is man's level—the plane of ideas, not force, the plane of progress. Thus far, he continued, society has developed by natural law in an irrational, hit-or-miss fashion. It was time to plan, to take care of society rather than let it take care of itself, to apply man's reason to the betterment of his environment, to improve society by "cold calculation." This, Ward said, meant social progress by "dynamic action," rational action guided in constructive channels. Man should control his own destiny.

The state, said Ward, is not merely a policeman, but a positive constructive agency for social and economic progress. It must be a "sociocracy," a medium for "social engineering," a channel through which the popular will expressed its desire for regulation. Its laws should be the results of intelligent experimentation, based on neither laissez faire nor communism, but on social co-operation. It must allow people to use the government to attack and solve collectively problems too large to be solved by the individual alone. "Individual freedom," remarked Ward, "can come only through regulation."

Ward cut away the very foundations of social Darwinism.

Where science showed the struggle for survival to be the first law of nature, Ward countered that men lived not biologically but ideologically. To those individualists who warned that it was against nature to tamper with the status quo, Ward answered that only by so doing could society progress. His answers were exactly those that the social planners and the "radical" politicians needed. It was no longer necessary, after Ward spoke, to tolerate trusts, monopolies, millionaires, social or economic injustices as "inexorable results of a natural evolution." Laissez-faire individualism went out the window and ethics came in.

Others were also hacking at the foundations of Darwinism. The line between economics and sociology seemed to many to be too finely drawn; both were *social* sciences, dealing with man in an interdependent society. To the younger scholars it seemed that the social sciences were splintered, atrophied, crusted over with precedent and tradition, and in the middle eighties a group of them founded the American Economic Association as a protest against the old school. "We regard the state as an educational and ethical agency whose positive aid is an indispensable condition of human progress," their manifesto said, echoing Ward. "While we recognize the necessity of individual initiative in industrial life, we hold that the direction of *laissez-faire* is unsafe in politics and unsound in morals, and that it suggests an adequate explanation of the relations between the state and the citizens."

The most prominent of the young rebel economists was Richard T. Ely, a New Englander who studied at Dartmouth, Columbia, and Heidelberg before coming to Johns Hopkins in the eighties. At Hopkins he became interested in the labor movement and in socialism, both delicate topics for a university professor to discuss. His interests, and his investigation of George Pullman's experiment in company living, made him suspect; eventually in 1892 he left Hopkins, under attack as a "radical," for the University of Wisconsin, where he became director of the School of Economics, Political Science, and

History. The atmosphere of Midwestern radicalism suited him precisely (La Follette greeted him with the words, "You have been my teacher") and despite the constant sniping of the *Nation* and other journals against him as "a socialist and an anarchist," he helped to build Wisconsin into perhaps the most liberal university in the nation.

The key to Ely's economic thought was his belief that economics was a humane, ethical study, not "a science to be used as a tool in the hands of the greedy and avaricious for keeping down and oppressing the laboring classes." Once ask the question "What is the *purpose* of economic life?" he said, and its ethical basis becomes clear. Economics concerns itself not with what is, but with what ought to be. "The ethical school of economists," he once wrote, "aims to direct in a certain definite manner, so far as may be, the economic, social growth of mankind . . . , the most perfect development of all human faculties in each individual which can be attained in harmony with the ethical ideal of Christianity." The businessman, the employer, the man who owned or controlled the materials or means of production, assumed certain social responsibilities. Organized society, through the institution of private property, recognized his ownership as a social trust and expected him to utilize his property for social good. But, Ely made clear, this did not mean socialism. He evolved instead what he termed "the new individualism," which fell somewhere between complete socialism and complete individualism. By the term he meant that men deserved the right to acquire and hold property gained through their individual enterprise, and that it was the duty of the state to preserve that right. But the state recognized too that private property existed for public as well as private good, and that if the use of any particular part of it could benefit the public, it should be made to do so. Thus, for example, Ely inclined toward public ownership and management in the case of natural monopolies; in fields where monopolies might exist to public detriment, he recommended their control by tariffs, patent laws, commission regulation, and inheritance and corporation taxes. In other areas of business, where monopoly was unlikely, competition could be allowed free play.

Where Ely humanized economics, his friend John R. Commons gave it the practical touch. "The place of the economist," he said, "is that of adviser to the leaders, if they want him, and not that of propagandist to the masses." A Vermonter who grew up in Ohio and Indiana in a hot abolitionist-Quaker tradition, Commons graduated from Oberlin and went to Johns Hopkins to become Ely's assistant. Already strongly influenced by Henry George, Commons quickly picked up the Ely point of view and went out to teach at Wesleyan, Syracuse, Oberlin, and Indiana. After his unorthodox economic theories forced him temporarily out of teaching, he joined with Edward Bemis (a refugee from the University of Chicago) and G. H. Sibley to found the Bureau of Economic Research, which failed. After a brief period with the United States Industrial Commission, he was retained by the National Civic Federation, a body interested in labor-industry disputes, to work on the settlement of the great steel strike of 1902. Ely invited him to Wisconsin in 1904 to join his little "radical" group of economists and sociologists, and there Commons stayed for the rest of his life.

Commons was as much political scientist and sociologist as he was economist, and his contributions in all three fields were practical rather than theoretical. He leaned neither toward socialism nor laissez faire, favoring like Ely a middle way he called "progressive individualism." As a teacher his influence was great, but his ideas and experiments had a wider significance. The role of the economist in providing expert advice to government, the creation and use of the commission and bureau in attaining efficiency and justice in solving socioeconomic problems, the benefits of socioeconomic planning, the value of combining the findings of the social scientist with the practical needs of humanity—in these things Commons' importance lay. Men of the Ely-Commons stamp gave La Follette and other Midwestern progressives a scientific ballast that the early Grangers and Populists lacked, a basis for action without which progressivism could not have successfully developed.

There were of course many others like Ely and Commons who gave direction and support to progressive politics. Simon Patten of the University of Pennsylvania, another German-trained AEA member, questioned the view that "economic problems will solve themselves" or that "individual action instead of collective action can promote the best utilization of our natural resources." His thesis that prosperity comes through spending rather than saving is traceable through his students, such as Rexford Tugwell, to the 1930's. Edwin Webster Bemis, another product of Johns Hopkins and Ely, championed municipal ownership of utilities. A tireless writer of books and articles, Bemis was perhaps the most prominent of economists in propagandizing his causes and was dropped from both Kansas Agricultural College and the University of Chicago for it. Frank Parsons, whom the *Arena* called "the economist of revolt," was a Boston University law professor who became interested in municipal ownership, direct legislation, election reform, and trust regulation.

Thorstein Veblen, a Midwesterner of Norwegian parentage, stood on the border line between economics, political science, and sociology. Though he studied with John Bates Clark and William Graham Sumner and received a post at Chicago with the help of J. Laurence Laughlin, he had little use for the brand of sociology and economics they taught. Nor did orthodox economists have much for Veblen. Laughlin, though recognizing his brilliance and protecting him for fourteen years at Chicago, disagreed with him and could do little to help him. President Harper considered him a somewhat uncertain asset, and it is significant that Veblen, who reached an assistant professorship only after the appearance of *The Theory of the Leisure Class,* remained unpromoted after several later important articles and books.

The Capture of the Ivory Tower

In his *Theory of the Leisure Class* in 1899, his *Theory of Business Enterprise* in 1904, and in his numerous articles and reviews, Veblen turned Darwinian individualism against itself. Academic economics, to his view, was shamefully outdated, simply a perpetuation of ancient myths and preconceived "normal" standards, entirely disconnected from modern economic facts. Economic life had to be understood as a conflict between the man who makes goods and the man who makes money, between the worker and the businessman. The latter, under the protection of institutions and the guise of ethics, profited by the wealth created by the former. The aim of business, said Veblen, is not social service but profit.

The wealthy "leisure class," as Veblen drew its picture, bore little resemblance to Sumner's "fittest." They were directly descended from the robber and the pirate; they gained by fraud and chicanery the wealth their ancestors took by force, all the while informing the public that the theft was for the common good. These "fit," these "captains of industry" displayed most of the "destructive and pecuniary traits,"—stealing, lying, cheating, selfishness—whereas the "peaceable and industrial virtues" existed chiefly among the lower or "unfit" strata. Business (or distribution), thought Veblen, had gained ascendancy over industry (or workmanship) and economic life had settled down to an unending war between seller and consumer. Thirty years later, in the 1930's, Veblen's message seemed more pertinent. New Dealers such as Henry Wallace, Isador Lubin, Rexford Tugwell, and Thurman Arnold picked him up again, finding in him a prophecy of depression economics.

The study of sociology underwent an internal transformation in the period after 1890, strongly affected both by developments in economics—many sociologists joined the American Economics Association—and in psychology. The emergence of the school of Lester Ward, culminating in his election as president of the American Sociological Society in 1906, marked a definite break with the past, widened further by the influence of the Russian Kropotkin, who visited the

United States in 1897 and 1902. Though Sumner and his followers formed a stoutly Darwinian opposition, the new sociology tended more and more to become a protest against laissez-faire individualism. Social life, said the Ward school, is made up of individual lives, and the individual human life is thus of the highest importance. The study of society, then, is the study of individuals, groups, activities, and their inter-dependence; social values are the sum of individual values. Sociology, to men like Small, Ross, and Cooley, was not simply a science for the study of the "fit" and the process by which they survived; it was not, as Edward Allsworth Ross called it, "a caricature of Darwinism, invented to justify the ruthless practices of businessmen."

Albion Small, a professed disciple of Ward, was probably the most influential early proponent of the new sociology. Another German-trained Johns Hopkins man, Small went to the University of Chicago in 1892 to head the first department of sociology installed in any major American university. It was not until 1913 that he allowed himself to apply his theories to contemporary conditions, but when he did, in *Between Eras: From Capitalism to Democracy,* he made a notable contribution to social thought. The book was a spirited attack on the right of the individual to hold and bequeath great fortunes and a strong argument for governmental supervision and control of wealth. Capitalism, it said, must be motivated by social rather than by acquisitive sentiments. Both capital and labor must be recognized as possessing valid social functions and given proper representation in social and economic life. The distribution of wealth should be fixed on the principle of social service, fixed by voluntary agreement between capital and labor with the state as arbitrator.

E. A. Ross, more definitely than Small, represented the affiliations between the new sociology and economics and contemporary political thought. Born in the Midwest, and a Populist, Ross was educated at Coe College (where he smuggled forbidden copies of Henry George to fellow students) and at Johns Hopkins. Suspected of radicalism by both Stanford and Nebraska, he came to Wisconsin at Ely's invitation in 1906. His books, *Social Control* in 1901, *Foundations of Sociology* in 1905, *Sin and Society* in 1907, and *Social Psychology* in 1908, were in their quiet, academic way as great an attack on the status quo as ever Bryan or the muckrakers undertook.

Sin and Society, especially, caused murmurs. Society, Ross said, pins the blame for social sin on vague and inescapable forces, when actually society itself is responsible. Society displays a sort of double standard; public and private morality seem to be quite different things. A corporation, for example, may commit acts which for it are perfectly legal, but for which an individual would be hanged. Talk of the biological survival of the fittest in the sociological world was nonsense. Ross could see no logic in relating "the repulsive dog-eat-dog practices of current business and politics" with that "struggle for existence" that Sumner wrote about. Bryan wanted a special paper-bound edition of the book to distribute to *Commoner* subscribers, and Ross himself considered it to be "a variety of sociological muckraking."

The revision of ideas in economics and sociology released the pent-up energies of the social workers and reformers. So long as a survival-of-the-fittest philosophy prevailed, so long as the poor and the unfortunate were regarded as the unfit who had failed in the struggle of life, there was little theoretical justification for charitable and remedial social work. The reformers wished to do in society much as the Populists and progressives wished to do in politics—that is, rehabilitate institutions to provide for and guarantee social justice. In the late seventies, through the efforts of S. H. Gurteen, dozens of poorly run and disorganized public and private charities were associated and co-ordinated for greater effectiveness. Particularly in the Midwest and West, state and municipal boards of health and departments of charities and corrections were formed, many of them staffed by qualified sociologists. The settlement house, a British importation, appeared in the cities, where problems of housing, education, and immigration were of paramount importance. Lillian Wald's Henry Street Settlement in New York and Jane Addams' Hull House in Chicago became models for more than a hundred similar projects in the cities after 1900. Many of these settlements were closely allied with municipal political reforms, while the social workers themselves turned into supporters of progressive politics. Jane Addams was a member of the national Progressive committee in 1912, a friend of La Follette and Roosevelt, and the holder of an honorary degree, the first of its kind awarded a social worker, from the University of Wisconsin. The Chicago Commons, founded in 1896 by the Reverend Graham Taylor and others, sponsored political meetings and appointed a committee of fifteen to watch grafting aldermen. The Commons and Hull House established an Industrial and Economic Union for discussions of socialism, Georgism, labor unions, and direct legislation, and invited before it speakers of the caliber of Clarence Darrow, Washington Gladden, John Dewey, Henry Lloyd, single-taxer John Z. White, and Charles Boring, a specialist in co-operatives. It ran also a School of Social Economics and a magazine, the *Commons,* which published articles on strikes, municipal ownership, and political reforms.

The universities in the later nineteenth century faced a situation common to all educational institutions in a time of dislocation. Criticisms of the existing order by economists and sociologists in faculty posts brought them squarely against the problem of the position a university ought to take on contemporary issues. The schools had but recently emerged from a bitter controversy over the teaching of Darwinian science, and while the argument over economic and social issues was less acrimonious, the question of how far a university should go in freedom of thought and speech was still an open one. The businessman who endowed a university, or contributed to its support through taxes, could see no reason to allow its professors to criticize the policies that paid their way. No teacher, in George Gunton's opinion, ought to be allowed to express political or financial opinions which do not "represent a considerable consensus of the community."

The argument over the proper attitude of the schools toward contemporary issues was of course an old one, dating from the earliest days of public-supported education. As a class, educators were traditionally anything but swift to embrace political or social reforms. They were acutely aware of the taxes paid by the businessman and of the gifts which came to private schools from men such as Rockefeller, Frick, Carnegie, Gary, and Ogden. The National Education Association, in fact, frequently expressed its indebtedness to the rich man for his munificences, and tended to agree with the Chicago *Interocean* that "young men are sent to college to be educated, not indoctrinated." As Fred Rich, a trustee of the University of Chicago said, the duty of a university was to see that "no unsound financial doctrines nor anything of a dangerous nature be taught."

The dispute over academic freedom was part of a larger argument over the place of education in the existing social order. The stresses and strains of the social fabric that came in the eighties and nineties led some to suspect that education was not doing its duty—else why Bryan and the Populist "fanatics"? President Eliot of Harvard, viewing the disorderly Midwest in 1892, wrote in the *Forum* that popular education had evidently failed. If, as he held, the aim of education were to promote "general contentment," and the West was obviously discontented, one could hardly escape the conclusion. If the farmer and laborer believed in such irrational things as free silver, strikes, and greenbacks, then plainly the farmer and laborer could not think straight, and the schools, whose duty it was to teach them to reason, were at fault. A good share of the fault, in the opinion of another, lay with "those professors and preachers [who] of recent years have bestirred themselves vigorously to fan the passions of the poor into flame . . . , the mischievous result of the socialistic doctrines of our so-called ethical economists."

But the current of educational philosophy was running in the other direction. While Eliot wrote, John Dewey experimented in Chicago with what later became "progressive education," designed to develop habits of multiple leadership, self-reliance, and democratic co-operativeness. Hamilton Mabie, making a survey of Midwest universities a few years later, found that state universities of the caliber of Michigan, Illinois, Wisconsin, Nebraska, and Minnesota, and private schools like Kenyon, Knox, Beloit, and Oberlin, were intellectually energetic, aggressive, liberal, and ardently patriotic. They were teaching people to reason, though perhaps not in the way Eliot assumed they should.

The state universities, those uniquely Midwestern institutions, sparked the new liberal movement in higher education. Since they were supported by taxes, they grew to be regarded as public property, as agencies whose aim was service to the state rather than simply service to the individual—a democratized concept of education that stemmed from the Jeffersonian heritage common to the whole Northwest Territory. The mission of the university, in the Midwestern way of thinking, was to produce educated leaders, to recruit from the ranks of democracy those administrators, legislators, judges, and scholars needed for the social, political, and cultural progress of the state.

The political philosophy of progressivism, as it developed out of the agrarian troubles of the postwar period, was partially based on this Jeffersonian concept of education. Placing the trust of the government in the hands of the people, as the Virginian long before pointed out, demanded a well-informed, intelligent, interested electorate, aware of social needs and well versed in history and economics. Democracy postulated more education for more people, a broadening of the educational base of society, and implied the existence of a close relationship between the university and the life of the state. It did not mean a de-emphasis of the humanities and the less practical sciences, but rather an increased emphasis on the university as a functioning unit in the citizen's daily life. The university, said President Van Hise of Wisconsin in his inaugural address of 1903, must be "a fortress for the protection of the people and a watchtower of progress." "It rests with each of us," said another university president, "as with all men, to help or not to help in making this world more habitable, a better place to live in."

The University of Wisconsin perhaps illustrated the trend of Midwestern education best. Founded in 1848, a few months after the admission of the state, the institution grew swiftly in size and importance after the Civil War. John Bascom, trained under Mark Hopkins, came as president in 1874 with the intention of making the university the "home of a keen intellectual life" as well as "an influence in the state." Wisconsin, he remarked, had a tremendous investment in its citizens, and the university was a form of insurance that the investment would pay a rich reward. A recognized scholar himself in philosophy, economics, psychology, ethics, and sociology, Bascom's influence at Wisconsin transcended scholarship. He perceived at once the new forces at work in the Midwest and the responsibilities of the university in channeling and directing them. Economics and politics, in his opinion, had a moral basis; since economic, political, and moral laws ran parallel, the violation of one usually involved the violation of another. The pursuit of wealth or political power might, but need not, follow the laws of intelligence and virtue; the university was to see that it did. It was this that prompted Bascom to say to young La Follette in his first term as governor, "You will doubtless make mistakes of judgment, Robert, but never mind the political mistakes so long as you make no ethical mistakes." Bascom represented the new spirit in university education, encouraging new ideas and experimentation, searching for new ways of binding relationships between university and state, and he sent out a group of young men who spread the "Wisconsin Idea" far and wide.

His successors—Thomas Chamberlain, Charles Kendall

Adams, and Charles R. Van Hise—carried on the Bascom tradition. Chamberlain hired Ely and encouraged the appointment of men like Ross and Commons, acts of real courage for a state university president in the nineties. Van Hise, a classmate of La Follette's and the holder of the first Ph.D. given by Wisconsin, became its president in 1903. He possessed a great ally in La Follette and under the direction of both men the faculty and the legislature worked together as a team. La Follette formed a "lunch club" of professors and legislators to meet each Saturday to discuss state problems; professors became government consultants, sat on civil service, railroad, and tax commissions, wrote tax and utilities laws. In 1912 the university listed thirty-seven faculty members who held posts in the state government, and many others who had direct but unofficial connections. La Follette later said in his autobiography that the reformer should always make sure that the underpinning of his structure—the education of the people— was secure. What Bascom and his followers did at Wisconsin was done on a less spectacular scale throughout the Midwest, providing reformers with the underpinning they needed.

These universities established a liaison between education and social responsibility, but the business of mass education was most thoroughly covered by an institution which reached a portion of the public wholly untouched by the universities. The Chautauqua movement grew out of the postwar religious ferment, out of the conflict between Darwinism and orthodox theology, at the time when Darwin, Spencer, and Huxley seemed to be hacking at the roots of Christian faith. Perturbed at the confusion of the man in the street, Lewis Miller and J. H. Vincent instituted a conference for Sunday school teachers (two weeks for $6.00) at Lake Chautauqua, New York, to discuss contemporary problems and to help solve them by education.

From this modest beginning the movement spread, until in 1874 Miller and Vincent decided to establish the Chautauqua Literary and Scientific Circle, a four-year course in home reading that reached hundreds of communities, especially the small towns of the Middle West. Soon the program included correspondence courses on labor, social economics, and political science as well as on the Bible, and Chautauqua began to publish its own texts. Summer institutes patterned after the original at Lake Chautauqua sprang up; Vincent listed thirty-nine of these by 1886, more than half in the Midwest, where their strong Methodist flavor continued the old pioneer camp-meeting tradition. Bryan, Donnelly, Ely, Commons, Sam Jones, Washington Gladden, and others attended Chautauqua conferences or taught at them.

The "Chautauqua idea," said Vincent, had four aims: to establish a relationship between culture and daily life; to teach the equality of intellect and worth; to emphasize the brotherhood of man; and to teach that wealth, won by honesty and prudence, had a benevolent function. Each of these aims, consciously or unconsciously, implied some connections with the political ideas of the Grangers and the Populists. Chautauqua was formed to combat the scientific materialism and determinism that threatened orthodox Christianity, but it also erected a defense against Darwinian-Spencerian individualism, stressed the traditional Christian and democratic virtues, and carried a message of hope and progress into the home of farmer and laborer. Technically nonreligious, Chautauqua nevertheless reaffirmed the evangelical faith of the frontier and certainly provided some impetus for the agrarian revolt sweeping the prairies in the eighties and nineties. Populism would have come regardless, considering the Midwestern political and economic situation after 1865, but Chautauqua helped it.

Economists, sociologists, and educators were not the only ones who answered the "gospel of wealth" and its social, political, and economic implications. There were others who believed that the answer lay in the substitution of a new system of morality—a system based not on acquisitiveness, but on co-operation and brotherly love. One school of thought, the so-called "Social Gospelers," was willing to keep capitalism, but on a different ethical basis. Another, the Christian Socialists, believed that capitalism was simply against Christianity, and proposed socialism (as taught by the New Testament and not by Marx) as a replacement. Though their methods differed, the two had the same end in view—the establishment of a new society on orthodox Christian foundations. Both were basically religious in inspiration, yet both had strong political connotations. Neither was essentially Midwestern in origin or support (though the Social Gospel probably had its greatest following there) but both contributed significantly to the rise of progressivism in that area after 1900.

Protestant churches after 1870 lived under a cloud. The prevailing philosophy of business, especially as represented by the "gospel of wealth," seemed to some an implicit denial of Christian ethics. The teachings of science, popularized by the publicists of Darwin and Spencer, ran counter to the moral teachings of the New Testament: what became of the Golden Rule in the struggle for survival? The church, some felt, had refused to accept its social responsibilities; it was affected with "moral astigmatism and dry-rot." Few churches, in Brand Whitlock's opinion, "had a glimmer of a ray of light on social conditions and problems, or economic, or in a word, of life." A symposium of ministers in the *Forum* concluded that "our churches are social clubs pure and simple." Henry Lloyd said most churchmen were "restricted to intermittent moods of emotional fervor embellished with occasional charities and surrounded by the accessions of song and stained-glass windows." The *Public* thought many ministers were simply "spiritual Pinkertons, guarding the loot of the unrighteous rich," while H. C. Vedder once wrote that "this bastard, cringing, sycophantic thing that our age calls Christianity is nothing more than the organized worship of Mammon." The Church had lost touch with life. How to regain it?

The error of organized religion, replied the Social Gospelers, was its failure to "open wide the doors . . . , preach fearlessly the gospel of Christ, and apply it to the problems of our day." It must function as an organized conscience, providing a positive philosophy for society. The mainspring of social action should not be the animalistic philosophy of Darwin and Spencer, but the Golden Rule. The gospel should be made *social,* hence the name "Social Gospel." Emphasis on the spiritual side of Christianity must be balanced by an equal emphasis on its practical side—a religion not of faith alone but of faith and works.

The Social Gospel movement set itself directly against Spencerianism, against the competitive principle, and against all its social and economic implications. Unbridled individualism placed the forces of society in opposition rather than in harmony; it placed a premium on acquisitiveness and materialism; it created economic inequality, class division, antagonism; most of all, it placed economic above human values. It was simply un-Christian. "The maxim 'every man for himself' must yield," wrote Washington Gladden, "to the other regarding motive." "Social and economic individualism," said John Bascom, "is out of harmony with the Gospel." And a minister in Chicago wrote, "It is the individualistic and competitive order of our day that is filling our national horizon with storm clouds." One aim of the Social Gospel, said Gladden, was "to make abhorrent and detestable, in the sight of youth, the conduct of men who are amassing great wealth by methods which tend to the overthrow of free government and the destruction of the social order." For this reason Gladden and the board of his church refuséd to accept a gift from John D. Rockefeller.

The Social Gospel stood for "the recognition of the Golden Rule, and the mind of Christ as the supreme law of society and the sure remedy for all social ills." Its real beginnings came in 1885 when the Reverend Josiah Strong of Cincinnati called a conference to discuss the relation of the church to contemporary problems. Washington Gladden, Richard T. Ely, Lyman Abbott, and other churchmen and laymen attended, and from their discussion grew the Evangelical Alliance, formed in 1887.

It organized local groups to study and discuss social and economic issues, attracting people like Jane Addams, John R. Commons, and Frank Parsons. The Alliance was superseded by the Brotherhood of the Kingdom in 1892, which held meetings for twenty years and supported nearly every liberal economic and political cause during the period. Though it drew from all denominations and from the laity as well, the Social Gospel found its greatest support among Congregationalists and Methodists. In 1908 the Methodist Episcopal Church, largest of the American Protestant denominations, adopted its social creed, and the Federal Council of Churches shortly did the same.

The Social Gospel was especially strong in the Midwest during the Populists and Progressive years. Its most prominent leader was Washington Gladden, who came from the East in 1882 to take a Congregational pastorate in Columbus, Ohio. Gladden evolved most of the early principles of the Social Gospel during the eighties and applied them directly to social and economic problems, mixing personally into labor-capital disputes, backing co-operatives and public ownership of utilities, working in political campaigns, censuring the rich and the trusts. The church should lead, not follow, he said, in solving social problems. Co-operation, not competition, must be the basis of social action; "the principle of Good Will" must "supplant the principle of *laissez-faire* in society." A brave, stubborn, and honest fighter for the Lord, Gladden kept up the battle on Spencerianism and the "gospel of wealth" until his death in 1918.

Following Gladden's path, other reformer-ministers joined the movement. The Reverend William Dwight Bliss took out membership in the Knights of Labor, formed a workmen's church in Boston, and organized the Church Association for the Advancement of the Interests of Labor, a ministerial group designed to help the labor unions. Charles M. Sheldon, a Congregational minister in Topeka, Kansas, wrote *In His Steps* in 1898, a Social Gospel novel which to date has sold about twenty-five million copies (ranking it with *Uncle Tom's Cabin* and *Ten Nights in a Barroom*). "Religion as I have understood it," said Sheldon before his death in 1946, "is simply putting the teachings of Christ to work in every part of life," and *In His Steps* was the story of what happened to a community that tried it. Herbert Bigelow of Cincinnati's Vine Street Church was one of the most militant Social Gospelers. The church, in his opinion, "ought to be so democratic that no plutocrat will apply for admission. . . .Let the new cause be won not by fighting but by preaching." Educated in the old abolitionist tradition of Oberlin, Western Reserve, and Lane Seminary, Bigelow chose to live in Cincinnati's worst slums and created a furor by admitting Negroes to full church membership. He spent two years as an assistant to Cleveland's Mayor Tom Johnson, and in 1902 ran unsuccessfully for Democratic secretary of state in Ohio. He withdrew from active politics in 1905, but kept up the battle from the pulpit for twenty more years.

The most colorful—and the most controversial—figure in Social Gospel ranks was George D. Herron. Born in Indiana, Herron entered the Congregational ministry in 1883 and gained a national reputation in 1890 with a famous sermon, "The Message of Jesus to Men of Wealth." The success of this sermon brought him a pastorate in Burlington, Iowa, and in 1892 Iowa College, at Grinnell, Iowa, invited him to give lectures on labor, business, and social problems. They were so successful that a wealthy woman endowed a "Chair of Applied Christianity" on the faculty especially for him. Taking to the platform, Herron toured the Midwest and the East, poured out articles, books, and collected sermons in a stream, and edited a magazine, the *Kingdom*. His summer schools, held at Grinnell, were nationally famous and featured speakers like Commons, Ely, Gladden, T. C. Hall, and Josiah Strong.

Herron, however, moved progressively leftward. Graduates of Iowa College, it was claimed, found it difficult to obtain pastorates when they were known as "Herron men," and it was feared that his attacks on wealth and business might frighten away gifts and endowments. In 1897 Iowa College ran into serious trouble when President Gates, a strong Herron supporter, "exposed" a schoolbook trust in the columns of the *Kingdom* and the American Book Company sued the Kingdom Publishing Company—of which, incidentally, Henry D. Lloyd was treasurer. Clarence Darrow came from Chicago for the defense, and though Gates was not convicted, the costs of litigation broke the *Kingdom*. The suit was not Herron's fault, but the alumni and trustees of Iowa College began to have grave doubts about the advantages of "Herronism" on the campus.

Herron himself was not disposed to help matters. His attacks on capitalism became more violent and his sympathy for socialism increasingly evident. "I think the people are ready," he announced in 1899, "for a great socialistic movement that shall be political in its aspects and yet wholly religious in its spirit." This was too much for the trustees, who asked both Herron and Gates to resign. Herron's dismissal, the college trustees made clear, was strictly the result of his socialism. It was better, they said, to teach men "their present duty rightly to use what wealth shall properly come to them" than "to attack directly systems that can best be changed but slowly."

Herron's reply stated his position unequivocally. "Our system of private ownership of natural resources is a crime against man and God . . . ; natural resources are not property, and cannot be held without destroying the liberty of man and the basis of the religion of Christ." He left Iowa College, but he was by no means finished. He joined the Social Democratic party in 1900 and campaigned for Debs. After denouncing marriage as "a coercive institution," he was successfully sued for divorce by his wife in 1901 and in a civil ceremony married the daughter of the sponsor of his college chair—an act for which the Congregational Church expelled him. Then, after flooding the magazines with articles on socialism and lecturing widely "against capitalists as a class," he suddenly left America for a villa in Italy, turning up as a diplomatic negotiator for the State Department during World War I.

The Social Gospel brought the church directly into political, social, and economic reform. It was a Populist religion, well suited to the restless times in which it developed. "We are in the beginning," said Herron, "of a revolution that will strain all religious and political institutions." Social Gospel churchmen joined forces with politicians, labor leaders, economists, sociologists, and social reformers to guarantee that the revolution reached desirable Christian ends. The Social Gospel conceived politics to be one method of guaranteeing justice for all, by smashing monopoly, privilege, and graft. "We ought to harmonise our citizenship and our Christianity," said the Reverend John G. Smith of Tomah, Wisconsin. "A religion that cannot be applied on election day is not worth having."

Social Gospelers also disagreed with traditional laissez-faire economic theories. They proposed compulsory arbitration of labor disputes, advocated profit-sharing plans and consumer co-operatives, and mixed in strikes and walkouts. The labor-capital struggle, they assumed, could be resolved simply by obedience to the Second Commandment—thus Richard T. Ely explained in his book, *The Labor Movement*. "Let the church become identified with the labor movement," repeated Bigelow. "Let it preach a message calling men to the work of the hour. . . . The fight is on and will not end until we put industrial slavery where chattel slavery now is."

The influence of the Social Gospel was wide, especially among sociologists and economists. Ely was strongly affected by it and the organization of the American Economic Association was intended, in his opinion, to "reemphasize the social aspects of economics," as he did in his book, *The Social Aspects of Christianity*. Bascom's *Sociology*, published in 1887, stated that social progress depended on emphasizing the second rather than the first Christian commandment, and most of the new school of sociologists, fathered by Ward, showed Social Gospel leanings. Ely and Herron in 1894 founded the American Institute of Christian Sociology at Chautauqua to stimulate churches and colleges in the teaching of sociology as "the study of Christianity at work." Commons was hired as secretary of the Institute, but Herron's increasing radicalism made it suspect and it accomplished little. Graham Taylor, of the University of Chicago Theological Seminary, provided a good practical illustration of what he called "sociology with God in it." He headed the Chicago Commons Settlement, spoke out against tariffs, monopolies, and civic corruption, and interested himself in practically every social agency in the city. Frank Parsons suggested a system of "mutualism"—profit sharing, public ownership, woman suffrage, proportional representation, civil service, direct legislation, tax reform, stable currency, postal savings, prohibition, slum clearance, prison reform, abolition of child labor, wage-hour laws, better schools —a complete roster of current political and social reforms, to be accomplished by putting the Social Gospel "law of love" into politics, society, and economics.

None of the political action groups planned by the Social Gospelers materialized, but the National Christian Citizenship League of Chicago, supported largely by them, called a conference in Buffalo in 1899 to form the Social Reform Union. Headed by W. D. P. Bliss, the union was endorsed by Herron, Sam Jones of Toledo, Hazen S. Pingree of Detroit, Henry D. Lloyd, Edwin Bemis, Frank Parsons, Ely, William Dean Howells, George McNeill the labor leader, N. O. Nelson of the co-operatives, and Annie L. Diggs of Kansas—a fascinating conjunction of Georgists, Populists, socialists, labor men, Greenbackers, and academic economists. It called for the usual reforms—direct legislation, public ownership of utilities, tax reforms, income, land, and inheritance taxes, more currency, no monopolies, and so on; took over the *Social Forum;* staffed itself with ousted academics like Commons and Bemis; and affiliated with the National Cooperative Library Association to distribute books by Ruskin, Morris, Ely, Herron, Commons, Henry George, and Bellamy. Bliss, however, leaned strongly toward socialism. Arguments over how socialistic the Union should be and how much political activity it should have eventually broke it up.

From its earlier or Populistic phase (well represented by Wilson and Herron) the Social Gospel passed into a more settled and practical stage. Walter Rauschenbusch's *Theology for the Social Gospel* provided it with a more definite theological system that it has retained to the present day. What the Social Gospel did in the nineties and after, however, had close bearing on Midwestern progressivism. The movement reactivated Protestantism, gave it strength to replace that sapped by science, business, and cynicism, made it aggressively militant, and threw the "gospel of wealth" out the window. The Social Gospel reaffirmed faith in the American system. Co-operation, equality, social and economic justice—these were basic beliefs of democracy—and the Social Gospelers gave them religious foundations. They held out, as the political reformers did, the hope of reorganizing society in such a way as to make democracy something more than a dream. Social Gospel's basis was theological; Bryan and La Follette's was political. Both were different paths to the same goal.

The Social Gospel, it is true, lay not far removed from socialism. Although, as in the case of Bliss and Herron, the transfer from one to the other was not hard to make, the two were neither the same nor did they come from the same sources. The Social Gospel was a native movement, growing naturally out of the New England tradition of Ralph Emerson and Horace Bushnell, reinforced by the evangelical strains of Western Methodism and Congregationalism. Most Social Gospelers did not advocate an overthrow of the capitalistic system; they simply attempted to apply Christian principles to very definite and serious human problems. The Social Gospel did not attack capitalistic democracy but rather its ethics—it wished to make capitalism square both with Christian practice and democratic ideals. It did not censure the businessman per se, but rather that kind of businessman who said (as did H. O. Havemeyer of the sugar trust), "I don't care two cents for ethics and I don't know enough of them to apply them." It did not attack the politician as such, but only the one who said (like Ingalls of Kansas) that "the Decalogue and the Golden Rule have no place in a political campaign." Invitations to join with the socialists—Christian or Marxist—were consistently refused by Social Gospel leaders. As Gladden put it, "Though we could not wisely go all the way with them, we might safely go only part of the way with them."

Christian socialism came directly from earlier Utopian social experiments in Europe and America—from Brook Farm, Icaria, New Harmony, and other communities that appeared on both sides of the Atlantic in the 1840's. Socialism of the gentle Christian variety was already known in America from sources as diverse as Bellamy and Tolstoy.

Like the Social Gospel, Christian socialism visualized a Christian commonwealth, founded on Christian principles and particularly on the Golden Rule. Since all men were brothers, it reasoned, they should co-operate rather than compete. God was the owner of the earth and of all things therein; all men were stewards of his property, not the wealthy alone, and all shared in its riches. Therefore, private ownership of public resources was, as Herron said, "inherently and elementarily immoral." The competitive system, which set one human being against another, violated Christian teachings.

The remedy lay, said the Christian Socialist, in public ownership (varying from a few to all properties), in organizing for social justice, in social and political reforms, and most of all in the substitution of co-operation for competition as the mainspring of economic life.

Christian socialism was loosely organized, vague, individualistic, but its influence was undoubtedly large. Many different brands of socialism existed within the movement, all based on the same elementary New Testament ethics. Some, unwilling to accept socialism completely, preferred to join co-operative movements. Others, like Herron, moved into the Socialist party itself, though he proved too much the individualist to be a good party man. The roster of the *New Time,* edited in Chicago by B. O. Flower and Frederick Upham Adams as an unofficial Christian Socialist organ, showed how varied a group it attracted—Hamlin Garland, Edward Bellamy, and Hazen Pingree subscribed to it, Parsons, Debs, Bemis, Jerry Simpson wrote for it, and of these only Debs was a party Socialist. The average Christian Socialist was very likely someone like Ernest H. Crosby or William Dean Howells, who drew his ideas from George, Jefferson, Tolstoy, Whitman, and the Bible. Sam Jones of Toledo was an exception in that he carried its principles into active politics. Few others did, depending instead upon a program of education and explanation (as in Howells' *Traveller from Altruria* and *Through the Eye of the Needle*) to bring about the Commonwealth of Christian socialism.

Marxian socialism was an entirely different matter. It was avowedly political, as neither Christian socialism nor the Social Gospel were, and it was admittedly foreign. It always ran somewhat outside the main channel of native radicalism, though the two had common enemies, and in some cases common objectives. Marxism was relatively new in American politics. The National Convention of the International in 1872 founded the Social Democratic Workingmen's party of 1874, which a year later became the Socialist Labor party. The Socialist Labor platform, first presented in the presidential campaign of 1892, seemed not too far removed from the Populist—government ownership of transportation and communication, municipal ownership of utilities, income and inheritance taxes, ballot reforms, and so on. But the similarities were only on the surface. Daniel DeLeon, the rigid Marxist who controlled the movement after 1890, considered the Populists "a capitalist bourgeois party" and their program "one of the most conservative and even retrograde attempts ever recorded in the history of economic evolution."

The difference between the native and the Marxist socialist

traditions was partly historical and partly ideological. The native brand, running from Bliss and Howells back through Bellamy and George and Brook Farm to eighteenth-century sources, never went far enough to satisfy the European socialists. Nor on the other hand was Marxism ever able to naturalize itself or adapt to American conditions. At late as 1896 probably not more than 10 per cent of its strength came from native-born elements.

The two radical groups could occasionally work together on a small scale, but not for long. When George's *Progress and Poverty* swept to popularity in the eighties, the Marxians welcomed him and their enthusiasm for the single tax grew with the sales of the book. They warmly supported his United Labor party in New York City—"A born American, Henry George, takes up our standard!" exclaimed *Der Sozialist*—but Marx himself called the single tax "a socialistically fringed attempt to save the rule of capitalism," and the courtship lasted only so long as George campaigned. His idea that "exploitation" arose from private ownership of natural resources simply did not jibe with the Marxist idea that it resulted from private ownership of the means of production and the machinery of exchange.

In 1888 Bellamy's *Looking Backward* apparently offered another chance for co-operation between native and Marxian socialists. But neither did Bellamy's "national socialism" fit the Marxist pattern. He was not at all ready to endorse Marx's class struggle, nor was his evolutionary socialism cut of Marxist revolutionary cloth. Bellamy's following was swallowed up in Christian socialism and Populism, while DeLeon and his group kept sternly on their own narrow path.

The closest American equivalent to Marxism came from a sort of maverick socialism best represented by J. A. Wayland, the "One-Hoss Philosopher of Kansas"—a home-grown variety compounded out of Greenbackism, antimonopolism, Coxeyism, Populism, and simply plain frontier fractiousness. Wayland's *Appeal to Reason* was of considerable influence in Midwest thinking at the turn of the century, and his following among farmers (not all of them socialists) fairly large. But Wayland was a Marxist only when he felt like it, and the party disciplinarians did not look favorably on his peculiar brand. He refused to follow party lines and he enjoyed, so DeLeon thought, independence and prestige far out of proportion to his importance. Wayland was really more Populist than Socialist, a strict individualist and a born rebel. His paper was willing to whoop it up for almost any reform, regardless of Marx (it was Wayland who discovered Upton Sinclair and serialized *The Jungle*), and he refused to accept advertising, bank notes, bank drafts, or checks. His suicide in 1912 (his farewell note said, "The struggle under the capitalistic system isn't worth the effort. Let it pass.") removed the last real native socialist leader in the Midwest, but the tradition Wayland represented continued in the *Coming Nation,* later in the *New Appeal,* and later yet in *Haldeman-Julius' Weekly.*

The agrarian politicians of the Midwest and the Marxists never took kindly to each other. Both attacked capital, but the Midwestern radical never adopted the European idea that political power should rest in a single class, nor did he believe that all means of production and distribution should be owned by the state which this class controlled. Unaccustomed to thinking in terms of classes, the American farmer preferred instead to transfer political power to the majority of the people, irrespective of class, and to break the power of the giant corporations either by controlling them (not necessarily owning them) or by splitting them up into smaller units. From him came the Midwestern demands for more representative government on the one hand and antitrust laws on the other, neither of which had any parallel in European socialistic thinking.

The Populist, unlike the Christian Socialist or the Marxist, was unwilling to surrender the economic principle of individual competition, except in the case of those natural monopolies and resources which he assumed were public properties anyway. He simply wanted to make sure that the competitive principle worked in economic life. The difference between the true socialist and the Midwest radical was never so clearly stated as by Debs in his reply to a request from Ignatius Donnelly in 1899 to join socialism with Populism. Said Debs:

The real issue is the means of production, that is to say, the means of life. As long as these are privately owned and operated for private profit, the present conditions will continue and grow worse, no matter what disposition is made of the money question and other side issues. Nor will it be possible to long harmonize any party which fails to go to the logical conclusion of the program of economic emancipation by declaring in favor of the complete overthrow of capitalism.

Marxian socialism represented an offensive movement for the overthrow of capitalism and the public possession of the means of production and distribution. Populism and its predecessors and successors represented a defensive movement, offering specific remedies for specific capitalistic ills—remedies which occasionally involved public control or ownership of certain facilities of production and distribution. The one was urban, industrial, ideologically foreign; the other native and agrarian. Both of them were clearly distinct from the nonpolitical Christian Socialists, whose interests and objectives ran parallel but whose sources and methods differed. Midwestern progressivism wanted honest, representative political organizations that might extend the functions of government for the purpose of social and political progress. The Socialist wanted immediate economic reforms and a wholly different economic system. The progressive believed that once the people gained power, they could be trusted to use properly for their own advancement. If the people wished under such conditions to adopt any or all of socialism, well and good, but the first problem was to give the people political power.

Public opinion of socialism was consistently muddied by misinformation, misinterpretation, and prejudice. Christian and Marxist brands were often lumped together with communism and anarchism as something foreign, distasteful, violent, and—to the farmer—suspiciously urban. The uncompromising stand of DeLeon made any sort of lasting co-operation between milder liberals and Marxists impossible, while the Marxist policy of reform by revolution rather than by political action never appealed to the American electorate. The most common objection to Marxian socialism was its iron regimentation, its belief that the individual was subordinate to the movement—something most American liberals could never stomach. Some of the Socialists realized this, and led a successful revolt against DeLeon's Socialist Labor party, creating in 1898 the Social Democratic party under Eugene Debs of Indiana and Victor Berger of Wisconsin. Berger, who converted Debs from Populism, was himself an evolutionary socialist, and under the guidance of these two men the movement received greater sympathy from Midwestern liberals. The new party favored peaceful political action rather than outright revolution, and stressed its intention of creating a socially just state in orderly fashion. Native thinkers like Charles E. Russell, William Walling, James Mackaye, Walter Weyl, Henry Lloyd, and others joined it, along with intelligent immigrant leaders like Morris Hillquit and John Spargo, and brought to the Socialist movement a greater flavor of respectability.

Socialism never attained a large following among Midwestern or Western radicals, though it always showed some strength in larger urban industrial centers. The reason lay partially in the split between DeLeon's revolutionary and Debs's evolutionary parties, in the movement's appeal to labor rather than agriculture, and in its predominantly foreign and class composition. Furthermore, the activities of the revolutionary socialists alienated great segments of Midwest opinion. The syndicalist theory, developed after 1905 as a countermove against the increasing conservatism of the Socialist Democrats and the American Federation of Labor, brought the IWW, strikes, bloodshed, and disorder. Captured by syndicalists and anarchists after 1908, the old DeLeon group remained thoroughly Marxist and thoroughly revolutionary. It was very difficult for evolutionary socialists of the Debs and Berger group to disengage themselves from the other variety in the public mind.

But by its very presence, though its direct influence in Midwest thinking was small, socialism was a factor in political events after 1890. The cry of "socialism" drew a red herring across the trail of every reform movement during the period. Bellamy's book was attacked as "communistic slavery," full of "theories imported from the overcrowded industrial centers of Europe" and "unfitted to the free and open West." Justice Samuel Miller of the United States Supreme Court, speaking at the State University of Iowa in 1888, defined as "socialistic" any scheme which undermined the principle of private ownership or modified the traditional system of laissez faire—and he meant to include Grangerism and Populism without a doubt. The question "Is Socialism an Element of Bryanism?" was debated hotly in 1896. In the opinion of one Nebraskan in the *Forum* in 1893, "only the most blind observer" could fail to see "the half-developed germs of pure socialism" in the Grange, in the Farmers' Alliance, in free silver, in the single tax, in Greenbackism, in antimonopolism, in Populism, and evidently in almost anything except the Republican party. As Bryan remarked bitterly, "The poor man is called a socialist if he believes that the wealth of the rich should be divided among the poor, but the rich man is called a financier if he devises a plan by which the pittance of the poor can be converted to *his* use."

Socialism engendered in the Midwest a tolerance for radicalism, and recruited some support for the Populists and later for the progressives. Many too timid or uncertain to travel the whole distance with the socialists gladly fell into step with the halfway measures of Populists and progressives. A correspondent from Michigan reported to Donnelly in 1899 that even among those who "scorned" socialism, interest in antimon-

opolism and public ownership was growing fast, and George
Herron thought in 1900 that one third of the American people were socialists of one sort or another at heart. Socialism
contributed to the softening-up process that allayed the fears
of the skeptics toward the proposals of the middle-of-the-road
liberals and progressives after the turn of the century.

Neither the Socialist Labor nor the Socialist Democratic
parties was ever a significant factor in Midwestern politics.
Debs, the candidate of the latter, drew roughly 90,000 votes
in 1900, 400,000 in 1904, and in 1908, with Taft pulling down
much of the reform vote, 417,000. However, in 1912, he polled
nearly a million, exceeding the Republican vote in seven
states, a feat he repeated in 1920 and a good indication of the
dissatisfaction that motivated the Progressive parties of 1912
and 1924. But socialism's successes were for the most part local
and urban; Milwaukee elected Socialist mayors in 1910, 1911,
and 1916; sent Victor Berger to Congress; and after 1916
usually elected a fairly large legislative minority that worked
with La Follette. Most of socialism's local strength, thought
Louis Post of the Chicago *Public,* came from liberal Republicans and Democrats who crossed party lines. Nationally, these
dissatisfied elements were captured by Republican and Democratic progressivism under Theodore Roosevelt and Wilson.

The revolt of the late nineties never quite came to a full
boil. True, the elements were there for a real political consolidation. Christian socialism attained respectability with Howells,
Herron, Bliss, Ely, and others; remnants of Populism remained
in the strong antimonopoly, antiwealth groups of the Midwest;
shreds of Bellamyism and Georgism were scattered here and
there. There was the moral indignation of the muckrakers, the
social consciousness of Jacob Riis and Jane Addams and
Graham Taylor, the semisocialism of Johnson and Jones, the
Christian capitalism of the Social Gospel and the socially
aware economists and sociologists of the Ely and Ward schools
—all these were in the air. But the ideas did not crystallize

into any coherent political or social movement. The protestants were too scattered, their reforms founded on too widely disparate principles—from Marx to the Golden Rule to the single tax—and their energies too dissipated. The growing insurgent-progressive movement, centering in the Mississippi-Ohio-Missouri basin, gave a better outlet for the pent-up forces of reform, and provided a better group of intelligent political leaders. The reforming energy of the period was rather to be channeled into politics, into an attack on big business, the trusts, and the boss, into an attempt on the part of the Midwestern radical to gain control of the system rather than to overthrow it.

Ideas of exactly how to gain this control took different forms. The Greenbackers and free-silver men once thought it might be done by tampering with the currency. The Grangers and the Populists thought monopoly should be smashed and governmental authority extended over economic affairs. Twentieth-century progressives instead advocated the reformation of political machinery—direct elections, direct legislation, corrupt-practices acts and the like—to make government more responsive to popular will and less vulnerable to organized wealth. Theirs were for the most part attempts to tinker with the mechanics of government, reforms based on the progressive faith in the ability of the people to rule if given the proper tools. Their aim was to retain the form and direction of capitalistic democracy while attempting to change its spirit. "Don't rant at the individual," said Tom Johnson. "Get after the system." They did.

Progressivism at Flood Tide, 1900–1908

V

The wave of agrarian protest washed itself away in Bryan's defeat. The crusade of 1896, and the "dull and colorless reign of privilege" (Altgeld's phrase) that followed it, settled nothing. The issues of the eighties and nineties were driven underground by the Spanish war and militarism, the upsurge of prosperity, the to-be-or-not-to-be of imperialism. But the old difficulties were still unsolved—the trust, the "plutocrat," the twin problems of good government and representative government. What were the economic and political functions of wealth? What were the social and economic functions of government? What of Big Business? What of the farmer and the worker? They all boiled down to a single question, what is democracy?

The plain fact was (and many saw it clearly) that the American dream was simply not coming true. America, "the hope of the human race" as Turgot had called it, was not realizing its promise. The difference between what was and what might be was very great.

The nineteenth-century Midwestern radicals tried to change the system and, with Bryan, lost "the first battle." The twentieth-century leaders reformed the army and mapped new offensives. They were a new kind of captain, trained in the West Point of state politics, with the same objectives as the tattered militia who preceded them.

T HE INITIAL BLOW of the twentieth century was struck by the "muckrakers," who provided a sort of cutting edge to a three-pronged reform movement in politics, society, and economics at the turn of the century. Henry D. Lloyd, and before him Bellamy and George, warned of the dangers of wealth and corporate power. B. O. Flower, an Illinois-born editor who imbibed Midwest radicalism at its source, ran energetic attacks on business and privilege in his magazine, the *Arena,* and shared with Lloyd the credit for pioneering in the journalism of exposure. Flower (who edited the *Arena* from 1889 to 1896, then the Chicago *New Time,* and then rejoined the *Arena*) was undoubtedly one of the most influential of the early reform editors before 1900. His magazines published articles by such well-known dissenters as Henry George, Hamlin Garland, Eugene Debs, George Herron, Frances Willard, and Frank Parsons and were filled with discussions of railroads and trusts, the Australian ballot, municipal ownership, and co-operatives.

The real upswing of muckraking journalism came, however, with the appearance of the cheap popular magazine. The four old standards (*Scribner's, Harper's,* the *Century,* and the *Atlantic*—all sedate, literate, and Eastern controlled)—were hardly the proper outlets for exposure of corruption and graft. The newer inexpensive ones (*Munsey's, Cosmopolitan, Colliers,* the *American, Everybody's, McClure's*) and the more radical intellectual ones (the *Arena, Review of Reviews,* the *Outlook*) suited the purpose admirably. The ten-cent magazine quadrupled the magazine-reading public after 1893.

"Muckraking" (as Theodore Roosevelt later named it) came into being after 1900. Lloyd, Flower, and the editors of

Everybody's and the *Independent* started it, but when S. S. McClure in 1901 put Lincoln Steffens on the trail of the grafting politicians and later sent Ida M. Tarbell after Standard Oil, the lid was off. Every politician, every corporation, every executive was under suspicion, every public and private citizen open to investigation. Most of the writers were newspapermen rather than political scientists or economists, sentimental rather than doctrinaire liberals, but they all hated social and political injustice and pursued it relentlessly in print.

Steffens found political corruption of the grimiest sort in St. Louis, Minneapolis, Pittsburgh, New York, Philadelphia, and Chicago, and wrote it up in *The Shame of the Cities*. Next he inspected Ohio, Rhode Island, New Jersey, California, and Wisconsin; except for Wisconsin, he did not like what he saw and said so in *The Struggle for Self-Government*. As the time came to draw some generalizations from his observations of democracy in action, Steffens turned into less of a muckraker and more of a political philosopher. The trail of boodle, he discovered, led from city hall to state capitol to Washington itself—corruption was simply characteristic of the American political system on all levels. Reluctantly he was forced to the conclusion that the people themselves preferred "bad" to "good" government, that machines and corruption existed because the voter wished them to. America was so involved in business, and business so in need of special privileges, that it was more satisfactory to wink at someone else's "pull" while getting your own than to live under rigidly honest government. The remedy lay, Steffens decided, not in reforming politics but in reforming the voter (a point already noted by Jane Addams in *Democracy and Social Ethics*), by entirely removing privilege from politics, and by reverting to a co-operative economic system—a path that eventually led Steffens straight to Russia.

Steffens' articles set the journals afire. McClure himself took to the road; C. E. Russell, Ben Lindsey, C. P. Connolly, George Kernan, Burton Hendrick, and others found Pennsylvania,

Montana, Colorado, and Delaware as "corrupt and contented" as the states on Steffens' beat. When Steffens trained his sights on Washington, as did David Graham Phillips, Ernest Crosby, Alfred Lewis, and Benjamin Hampton, he found corruption rife in the Congress itself.

Meanwhile, others put big business under the microscope. Ida Tarbell's scholarly and damning study of Standard Oil set the pattern for Russell's study of the beef trust, Ray Stannard Baker's of the railroads, Welliver's of General Electric, Lewis' of International Harvester, Hendricks' of life insurance, Lawson's of Wall Street, and a dozen more. Muckraking moved on to other fields, too. Gentle Jake Riis wrote on the slums; Samuel Hopkins Adams investigated pure food; Will Irwin, Upton Sinclair, and others probed journalism. Churches were scrutinized for commercialism and connections with wealth, and the journals went to work on Belgian rule in the Congo, prison reform, loan sharks, prostitution, literary immorality, various sects—the thing was getting out of hand by 1910 when the public began to tire of it. It became harder to find new muck to rake, and big business discovered that withholding advertising from unco-operative magazines robbed them of a great deal of reforming zeal. Business also launched a counter-offensive of its own, beginning when the anthracite coal industry hired Ivy Lee in 1906 as publicity agent (he later was hired by the Pennsylvania Railroad and Standard Oil), a practice followed by other corporations until the "public relations counselor" became standard business equipment.

Muckraking, both good and bad, was part of a wider political, social, and intellectual reaction to industrial expansion and political corruption, a result of the same forces that produced Bryan, Theodore Roosevelt, Wilson, and La Follette. It was an exposure of fraudulent, misrepresentative government, of monopoly, of industrial immorality, of the trust—essentially the same tendencies in political, social, and economic life criticized by the agrarian radicals of the 1870's. The

Grangers, and their descendants the Populists, had said the same things in a general way. The muckrakers offered proof and gave dates, names, places. The Grangers and Populists turned to government for help with little success. Now it was clear why. Government itself was under the thumb of the very forces they were fighting, as the Midwestern farmer and small businessman suspected all along. Like Populism and later progressivism, muckraking was an attack on privilege, on the exploitation of the many by the few, on social and economic malpractice. Steffens' conclusions were not so far removed from those of Jerry Simpson, nor Ida Tarbell's from General Weaver's.

The investigations of the muckrakers into city governments accelerated a trend toward municipal reform that reached back to the nineties and the Populist tradition. The Populists, and their agrarian predecessors, demanded clean, efficient, and representative government on a state and national scale; their urban counterparts demanded the same thing in the city.

The city undoubtedly needed reforming. It had for a long time. Philip Hone, whose term as mayor of New York ended in 1827, noted in his diary the alarming amount of graft in his day, but he would have been staggered by the extent of municipal corruption after the perfection of the "boss" system in the eighties. Lord Bryce, that observing Englishman, labeled city government in 1888 as "the one conspicuous failure of the United States," and President Andrew White of Cornell remarked in 1890: "With a very few exceptions, the city governments of the United States are the worst in Christendom, the most expensive, the most inefficient, and the most corrupt." The great bosses were in power then and long after—Magee in Pittsburgh, Croker in New York, Lomasny in Boston, Butler in St. Louis, and dozens more. The tremendous growth of cities after 1870 made them especially vulnerable to boss rule. An expanding city needed transportation, gas, water, electricity— needed them swiftly, and were often careless in granting franchises to get them. Immigration to the cities provided large blocs of easily handled, poorly educated voters. City government was likely to be antiquated and weak, councils inexpert and unwieldy, courts disorganized, election systems complex and easily controlled. The situation was made to order for boss rule.

The city boss, as he evolved in the late nineteenth and early twentieth centuries, was an interesting character—never quite socially respectable, but shrewd, intelligent, expert at his business. He stood at the center of a web that reached down through each level of politics to the lowest stratum of the heeler; he was allied with vice (gambling, liquor, prostitution) and with business (utilities, corporations, manufacturing) as the intermediary between both of these and the government, obtaining for each the special privileges it needed to operate successfully, collecting a fee for so doing (of which he kept a percentage), passing it on down to the next level (the council and police) through to the small fry at the bottom. In return, he got the votes he needed to maintain his power. The boss ran the machine and took the blame; the ones who received privileges paid him to do so. As one politician, caught in a probe, remarked bitterly of a bribe-giving businessman, "He sucks eggs like I do but he hides the shells." The political machine was built on a kind of crude socialism, actually, on a general feeling that the right to vote ought to bring some tangible return, some betterment, some privilege.

In the 1870's there had been some agitation for municipal reform, producing Franklin MacVeagh's Citizen's Association in Chicago and similar "good government" committees in other cities. However, it was not until the nineties that real reform began, marked by the formation of the National Municipal Reform League in 1894, the publication of journals on the order of the *American Magazine of Civics,* and the election of three pioneer reform mayors—all Midwesterners—who broke the ground for the muckrakers and the crop of reformers who followed. These were Pingree of Detroit, Jones of Toledo, and Johnson of Cleveland.

Hazen S. Pingree, a relatively well-to-do shoe manufacturer, was elected mayor of Detroit in 1889 and three times thereafter. Detroit, like most large cities at the time, was controlled tightly by a combination of businessmen and politicians. Pingree intended to break it by taking business out of politics. "I have always said," he wrote in 1895, "that government should exercise proper control over the corporations, especially those operating public franchises. I still say it." The focal point of his attack was the utility franchise, especially the street railway. He tried to force the company to reduce fares, helped striking employees, and tried to prevent the consolidation of competing companies. (Oddly enough, one of his opponents in this last affair was Tom Johnson of Cleveland, not yet a reform mayor himself.) But Pingree's most publicized venture (and his least important) was his "potato-patch plan," a form of public works assistance whereby vacant lots in Detroit were donated to needy families for vegetable growing. Eventually this experiment involved more than a thousand Detroit families and was copied by many other cities. Except for the "potato-patch plan," most of Pingree's reforms were unsuccessful, and he passed to the governorship in 1896.

Pingree combined the Grangerism that had passed and the Populism to come, applied on a municipal level to municipal problems. The key to his political philosophy was antimonopolism. "The growth of corporate influence," he said, "is a decided menace to the free institutions of our country," and again, "I do not condemn corporations and rich men, but I would keep them within their proper sphere." Pingree knew firsthand the pressures applied by business to city governments and the corruption that usually accompanied it; he was once offered $75,000 to sign a gas franchise, and later $50,000 to sign a street car franchise. Thus, in Pingree's view, the key to better city government simply lay in controlling the influence of corporations in politics—a rudimentary program, it is true, but one that cut to the root of the matter.

Samuel Milton Jones of Toledo represented a different tradition. Born in Wales, Jones came to Ohio from the oil fields of Pennsylvania. Having invented an improvement in oil-pumping machinery, he set up a factory in Toledo in 1894 to manufacture it. A wealthy man himself and accustomed to the high pay of the oil fields, he was shocked at the low wages and poor working conditions of factory life. He decided therefore to run his business on the socialistic principle that "every man is entitled to such a share in the products of his toil as will enable him to live decently, and in such a way that he and his children may be fitted to be citizens of a free Republic." The foundation of his business would be the Golden Rule. So he tacked it up in his factory and became "Golden Rule" Jones.

His Acme Sucker Rod Company was a thing of industrial wonder in the nineties. Jones established a minimum wage of seventy-five cents a day above the average, an eight-hour day, a system of welfare benefits, a 5 per cent yearly salary dividend, and a week's vacation at full pay. The plant served meals at cost, sponsored a band, a singing club, family gardens, a ball park, "Golden Rule Park" for recreation, and "Golden Rule Hall" for a lecture series which brought people like Washington Gladden, Jane Addams, George Herron, and Graham Taylor to Toledo. In 1904 Jones turned over $10,000 worth of stock to his employees, to be handled by trustees elected by the men, and he eventually abolished the foreman-timekeeper system, allowing each worker to keep his own time.

Jones slipped into the mayoralty of Toledo in 1897 almost by mistake. The Toledo Civic Federation, a reform group, was in conflict with the local Republican machine and Jones's name was offered to break a deadlock in the Republican nomination meeting. Surprisingly, he won, and the Golden Rule went into politics. His program was concrete and comprehensive—municipal ownership of utilities; civil service in city government; home rule; popular approval of grants of extensions of city franchises; public parks, baths, and playgrounds; a referendum; better schools; and penal reforms—and he set about putting them all into effect. Horrified Republicans refused to support him in 1899, so he ran as an independent, receiving more than 70 per cent of the votes cast. In 1899 Jones took time out to run for governor of Ohio, losing to Mark Hanna's man, but in 1901, as an independent, he won the Toledo elections and again in 1903.

Jones belonged to the most powerful type of reformer, the man with a clear, simple, and definite purpose backed by ideals. Essentially he was a Christian Socialist, and his politics, his economics, and his social philosophy were all simply extensions of the Golden Rule. By the force of his personality and his example, the big sandy-haired Welshman joined Christianity to politics and manufactured a revolution in city government. For nearly ten years Toledo was in the unusual position among American cities of finding the Golden Rule the chief topic of political discussion.

Jones, it is true, was an eccentric and simple man, "as naïve as a child" in Brand Whitlock's estimation. He always slept out-of-doors on his back-porch roof (suspicious radicalism in the nineties), wore a big cream-colored hat, and campaigned in a buggy drawn by a gray mare named Molly, with his son Paul along to play the saxophone. He simply brimmed over with Christian love; he used the park department equipment to give free sleigh rides to the children in winter, organized a police band, put golf links in the public parks, gave his salary to the poor, and wrote weekly letters of exhortation to his employees and to city workers. Since as mayor he also sat as police magistrate, the public was amused and occasionally alarmed at his view of justice. He took clubs away from policemen and substituted light canes; drunks he dismissed with a lecture on temperance and thieves with one on the evils of stealing; a man caught illegally carrying a gun was sentenced to smash it in public with a sledge; an assault case received a lecture on the uselessness of force and the power of love. The state legislature finally stopped him by repealing the law allowing mayors to serve as magistrates.

Jones saw all political and economic conflict as a war between wealth and democracy. "I am one," he said, "who believes there is no hope for political peace except as it is reached through political and social justice. The most conspicuous evil of our present system is found in the fact that it gives some men arbitrary power over others. . . ." He was concerned, therefore, with extending political democracy by reforming government and with guaranteeing economic democracy by curbing and redirecting business—principles which made him eventually into a socialist, though he never read Marx, never believed in the class struggle, and never joined a party. His socialism took the concrete form of public ownership, which he advocated at first for municipal utilities and later as the basis for a national co-operative commonwealth. "Private ownership," he once said, "is a high crime against democracy." At the time of his death he was trying to find a way to give his own business to his employees, and he lost no chance to impress on Toledoans the co-operative nature of government. Signs in the parks read "Citizens, Protect Your Property," not "Keep Off the Grass."

Tom Johnson of Cleveland came to political maturity by a quite different route. Born in Kentucky, he had his first job as a messenger boy for the Louisville Street Railway, invented a fare box and an automatic switch, and at twenty-two was sufficiently wealthy to buy the only street railway in Indianapolis. He put on horses instead of mules, painted the cars, uniformed the employees, and with his profits bought a bankrupt line in Cleveland. He built his own steel mill in Ohio, bought up a whole network of trolley lines in Pennsylvania and in Brooklyn, and additional holdings in Detroit, Chicago, and Boston. Then he bought a copy of Henry George's *Social Problems* from a train butcher and read it.

The single-tax doctrine hit Johnson like Paul's vision. When he finished the book he was a man dedicated to the defeat of the monopolism that he himself represented. He went to New York to assist George in his mayoralty campaign, returned to Cleveland to run for Congress as a single-tax Democrat, and served two terms as one of the little Georgist group in Congress. In 1901 he returned to Cleveland to serve as mayor until his death in 1907.

Johnson was no simple, naïve soul like Jones. He was a crack politician, a realistic thinker, and an ambitious man. Large, handsome, full-bodied, bearing a rather remarkable resemblance to Mark Hanna, Johnson had a subtle charm and a colorful personality. He was a boss, and he admitted it. "It all depends," he said, "whether a boss is a good one or a bad one. A bad political organization is worse than a good political machine." He therefore proceeded to build a machine in Cleveland that blew the old Hanna organization sky high. Like Jones, he campaigned unsuccessfully for governor, losing in 1902 to Hanna's candidate, Myron Herrick, but his main interest always lay in Cleveland. The city became, under Johnson, a political laboratory in civic affairs, in Steffens' opinion the best-run city in the land.

Johnson aimed primarily at monopoly and privilege. He wanted home rule, equalization of taxes, municipal ownership, and efficient government. He put good men in office and saw to it that bribery and corruption stopped. Peter Witt, a Populist with a sharp tongue and an incorruptible conscience, went in as city clerk and revised the city's tax structure. Newton D. Baker, a brilliant young lawyer, became city solicitor. The Reverend Harris Cooley, a topflight sociologist, became head of charities and corrections. Professor E. W. Bemis, an authority on municipal ownership and a recent assistant to Pingree in Michigan, became superintendent of waterworks. Young Frederic C. Howe, an expert on city government, entered the city council. As a result, *Gunton's Magazine* in 1903 labeled Johnson as one of the most dangerous men in public life, a man with "radical ideas, few scruples and much money."

Essentially Johnson was radical only in his blend of Jeffersonian and Georgist ideas. He was no socialist, nor was he ever close to socialism. As a businessman he knew that monopoly led straight toward social and economic injustice, and, since a monopoly always needed special privileges, toward political corruption too. The best way to forestall the influence of monopoly in city government was municipal ownership, which was to him one step toward his ultimate goal of the single tax. Trusts, he said, were not by nature bad; monopolies were, for they depended on privilege, "controlling something they should not own and the people do." His most important battles he lost by veto of the Ohio legislature, which prevented him in one instance from making Cleveland's utilities publicly owned and in another from taxing street railways for capital to build competitive municipally owned lines. Yet he started something in Cleveland—the belief that government should extend the greatest good to the greatest number, that it should be clean, honest, and efficient.

Following the lead of the three Lake Erie cities, a wave of reformers swept into city politics in other sections of the nation. Brand Whitlock followed Jones as mayor of Toledo. Newton Baker succeeded Johnson as Democratic leader of Cleveland. Ben Lindsey of Denver, Hovey Clarke of Minneapolis, Moran of Boston, Mark Fagan of Jersey City, Emil Seidel and Dan Hoan (both Socialists) of Milwaukee, Devereaux of Springfield, Low and Jerome of New York, Folk of St. Louis, Rose of Kansas City, Weaver of Philadelphia, Dempsey and Hunt of Cincinnati—all spearheaded reform drives in their respective cities.

The movement for civic reform knew no regional boundaries (though perhaps it was strongest in the West), for municipal corruption was not specifically a regional problem. But certainly the Grangers and the Populists paved the way for it. Like them, the civic reformers had one aim—to make government more representative and more efficient—and they encountered (as the agrarians did) the monopoly, the corporation, and the machine. All intended to abolish privilege in government, whether it be the corporation working against the farmer or the traction tycoon against the city dweller. The personnel of the two movements showed some similarities and later greater differences. The early reform mayors—Pingree, Jones, and Johnson—came from Populist trust busting, Georgism, and Christian socialism, whereas the later reformers of the muckraker era were academic, well schooled, urbane young attorneys, not crusaders but efficiency experts. The city reformers would no doubt have arrived had no Grangers or Populists existed, but the Grange, Farmers' Alliance, and People's party awakened the public conscience, drew the lines of conflict, and started the argument. Civic reform tied in with the Midwest agrarian radical tradition, doing locally what the Populists wished to do nationally. The cities, said Brand Whitlock, were really "working models of the larger democracy" that earlier Populists and later progressives visioned.

The twentieth-century progressive movement was, like its predecessors, deeply rooted in the social and economic soil of the times. American politics has been usually a direct reflection of current patterns of thought—embracing attitudes in business, science, education, economics, the church, and the home —and a manifestation of contemporary ideas that expresses itself among other ways in platforms and candidates. Thus the Grangers, the Farmers' Alliance, and the Populists were compounds of many elements, expressions of what the people (or a considerable segment of it) believed at a particular time. The elements themselves were concentrated for the most part in the agrarian Midwest, where the conflict between the old and new economics was most apparent, where the traditions of frontier discontent were strongest.

From the extreme right to the extreme left, there were in 1900 roughly five discernible answers to the old Populist question "What is Democracy?" To some of the Neanderthal conservatives (admittedly a minority) it meant political, social and economic leadership of the untrustworthy many by the intelligent few. George Baer's statement that the ruling power in democracy rested with "those Christian men to whom God in His wisdom had blessed with property" was a good summary of beliefs honestly held by some businessmen. Others, like Carnegie, believed that democracy meant laissez faire, Christian individualism, restricted government, protection of monopoly and individual rights, stewardship of wealth. The socialists meant to "democratize" economic life through the power of the state by instituting certain politicoeconomic reforms. The syndicalists, despairing of political action, proposed using revolutionary means to attain a communist industrial organization under a different state, while the anarchist opposed the state, *ipso facto.*

Roughly in the middle, between the laissez-faire conservative and the socialist, stood the Midwest "progressive." He did not, like the conservative, distrust the majority or rely on the leadership of the Darwinian survivor; nor at the same time did he, like the socialist, contemplate a shift to a new economic or political state, either by evolutionary or revolutionary means. He did not wholly reject collectivism, being willing to use collectivistic methods if necessary to gain his ends; nor did he believe solely in individualism (despite his frontier heritage) if by individual action he failed to gain his democratic objectives.

"The word Populist has disappeared from the Congressional directory," noted the *Forum* in 1902, "The question that remains unanswered, however, is: Has it been entirely eradicated or is it merely latent? Unfortunately, the latter condition is more probable." The *Forum* was quite correct, for "progressivism" (the usual term after 1905) replaced it. The lineal descendant of nineteenth-century agrarian revolt, progressivism represented the same ideas traveling in the same direction, with new leaders, new vitality, and new weapons, against the old forces of privilege and corruption. Before progressivism was finished it had swept the states, captured a party, advanced into Congress and almost into the White House itself.

The progressives' answer to the question "What is democracy?" was much the same as that of the Populists and the Alliance, of the Greenbackers and Anti-Monopolists. Louis Post of Chicago, in 1906, explained that progressives have been forced to the conclusion that the masses of the people are better to be trusted than any one class, however assertive of its superiority that class may be; they have been forced to the conclusion that what the cause of good government needs is more intense democracy, with easier methods of expressing popular opinion and putting it into law, not harder ones; and they are beginning to appreciate the wholesome theory that that government is best which not only leaves all private functions to private enterprise, but executes all public functions as a public responsibility.

"Progressivism" therefore simply meant that the rule of the majority should be expressed in a stronger government, one with a broader social and economic program and one more responsive to popular control. It was certainly not a new political philosophy to the Midwest. Populist programs before 1900 asked for all the things demanded by the progressives and almost unanimously embodied in successful legislation later. La Follette's program had clear resemblances to Bryan's, and Bryan's showed similarities to Weaver's and Jerry Simpson's. The progressives owed much to their predecessors, as La Follette freely admitted in his autobiography. Like them the progressives attacked capitalism, not in its essentials but in its operation. Keep it, they said, but control and direct it; stop collectivism this side of socialism.

Though their programs were similar, the new progressivism and the older agrarian radicalism differed in procedures and personnel. Its leaders came not from the uncombed third-party groups of single taxers, Grangers, and Populists, but from the ranks of smart young Republican lawyers, district attorneys, and young career politicians who followed in the wake of the Donnellys, Simpsons, and Peffers after 1896. They were sharp, well educated, efficient and practical men, capable of giving direction, organization, and cohesion to the scattered forces of reform. A few of the old rebels, men such as Bryan and Pingree, remained, but the new-style hero of the Midwest reformers was someone like Albert Cummins of Iowa, Beveridge of Indiana, George Norris of Nebraska, or La Follette of Wisconsin.

Despite the dozens of young leaders it developed after 1900, the Midwest never really produced a politician of major stature (with the exception of La Follette) who might have tied Midwest progressivism into one neat bundle and delivered it bound and sealed on the White House doorstep. Neither did the Granger or Populist movements, whose leaders were colorful, astute, and sincere, but none of whom possessed the qualities needed to organize a political movement on a national rather than a regional scale. Bryan, the best of them, had neither the gifts to begin with nor the ability to develop them. Excepting La Follette, the later progressives—honest and skillful men all—were no more than good noncommissioned officers, while La Follette himself was too inflexible, too rigid, too much the lone wolf to become the prairie Jackson that the Midwest progressive tradition demanded. The reason for the Midwest's failure to produce a national leader lay in the fact that the movement itself was a distinctively Midwestern thing that developed regional politicians who were chiefly concerned with regional problems. Progressivism in its Eastern phase— as represented by Theodore Roosevelt and Woodrow Wilson— attained national power and dealt with national issues, but it was not the same thing.

The drift of Midwestern progressive thought in the early 1900's was away from its Jeffersonian-Jacksonian-frontier sources. The ends remained the same, but the methods changed. As the frontier faded, the old eighteenth-century idea of untrammeled individualism and decentralized political power disappeared with it, for in the industrial nineteenth century individualism by itself was hardly enough to secure democracy. Jefferson thought he had secured it when he established the principle that there should be no political or legal check upon the individual's life, liberty, and pursuit of happiness. But the feudalism and royal tyranny he feared might threaten his democracy were replaced in the industrial age by the lords of the trusts, the knights of transportation, the corporate kings, the ministerial bosses. The Jacksonian period believed that in spoils, in the ability of the ordinary man, in the complex safeguards of intricate governmental machinery—there lay safety for the common people; but the boss and the corporation took over the machinery and bought the office. The Granger and the Populist dimly realized that the goals of the old democratic tradition could be attained only by modifications of the old methods and principles. Paradoxically, he found that the preservation of individualism required the introduction of certain restraints upon it. He could restrain it through the only agency—the government—that lay more or less under his direct control.

The most distinctive tendency in twentieth-century Midwestern progressivism, therefore, was its shift away from pure individualism toward social control, a trend already noticeable in the agrarian radicalism of the nineteenth century. Here was an effort to fit the individualism of the old frontier (and of Darwinism) to the new circumstances of an industrial society, an adjustment designed to give the citizen the same advantages under new social and economic conditions that he had enjoyed under the old. . . . "[We must stop] trying to apply a logic, true and proper for an individualistic era, to a new socialistic era," C. L. Deyo wrote in the *Public*. "All our fundamental conceptions will have to be exchanged for new ones in which the *social* side shall have due emphasis." If the individual's welfare—his pursuit of happiness—was the object of democracy, how might one, in trying to evolve a democratic capitalistic society, avoid the perils of a dog-eat-dog individualism on the one hand or the regimentation of socialism or communism on the other? The progressives chose a middle path between the two extremes. Their aim was not simply to restrict individualism, but to restrict in order to conserve the values of democracy.

This course was called by Charles McCarthy of Wisconsin "The New Individualism." It was not socialism, nor was it close to it. True, the Midwest progressive was occasionally willing to accept a so-called "socialistic" method to gain his desired objective. But the progressive, McCarthy explained, believed he could fulfill the promises of socialism wtihout losing the essentials of private ownership and private enterprise. As Jane Addams remarked, since no political party or economic school possessed exclusive right to any device for eradicating poverty or obtaining political and social justice, the progressive had a right to borrow from socialism if he wished. Restrictions on laissez faire were, to the progressive, merely effective ways of preserving laissez faire itself.

Another major principle, a bequest of Populism, was the progressive's faith in and trust of the popular majority. The assumption was that every normal citizen who was mentally and morally qualified had both the right and the duty to participate directly in his government. "The composite judgment is always safer and wiser and stronger and more unselfish than the judgment of any one individual mind," wrote La Follette. "The people have never failed in any great crisis in history." The real cure for the ills of democracy, the Midwest progressive believed, was more democracy. His aim in politics therefore was simply to make government responsible and representative. Or as La Follette put it, "The very backbone of true representative government is the direct participation in the affairs of government by the people."

To insure a government that was both responsible and representative, Midwestern progressives believed it vitally necessary that the people control their government, both before and after elections. Machines and bosses controlled it only when they were allowed to steal the political machinery—something that pre-election measures such as the short ballot, the direct primary, the corrupt-practices act, and revised registration and voting systems were intended to prevent. As postelection controls they suggested the initiative, referendum, recall, and city home rule. Special influence must be removed, the structure of government so modified as to allow a greater direct participation by the citizen in the conduct of public business. The whole purpose of progressivism, said La Follette, was "to uphold the fundamental principles of representative government." It was an attempt to adapt the old democratic system to the needs of a new society, "a movement of a new generation toward more democracy in human relationships."

A third major principle of progressivism was its belief that the functions of government should be extended to meet the growing needs of the people. The state was not to be simply a negative factor in society, its influence happiest when least, but a positive factor, doing some things that no other agency could do, and others that no other agency could do so well. "He is really a Progressive," wrote Walter Owen in *La Follette's Magazine,* "who first discovers any wrongs and suggests the appropriate governmental action to prevent further abuse." Progressivism represented the culmination of an old frontal attack (the Grangers were its vanguard) on the laissez-faire concept of governmental do-nothingism, an assault seconded by economists like Ely and sociologists like Ward. It was the last phase of a movement away from the agrarian-Jeffersonian idea that government was merely a way to keep the individual's pursuit of life, liberty, and happiness within bounds, that government was "anarchy plus the street constable." The earlier agrarians never foresaw that the new industrial capitalism would find that "hands-off" concept of government exactly to its liking. The Populists realized, and the post-1900 progressives knew it more surely, that the tradition of government noninterference defeated the ends of democratic government itself. It had to be modified and adapted to secure democracy and extend it—hence the name "progressive."

The progressive wished to extend the power of the state in two ways: negatively, to use the power of government to limit and regulate capital and business, and positively, to use it to promote and protect the public social and economic welfare. The first aim produced such measures as antitrust laws, regulation of railroads and other corporations, taxes on corporate property and gross earnings, banking and insurance acts, fair-trade and corrupt-practices laws, public service and utility acts, and conservation programs. The second aim motivated proposals such as workmen's compensation and employers' liability laws, child- and female-labor regulations, industrial safety and inspection standards, wage-hour laws, old-age and mothers' pensions, educational expansion and extension programs, and the like. Political democracy, the progressives reasoned, was useless unless it furthered social justice; social justice, in turn, depended upon the fullest and most intelligent expression in politics of the popular will. Either, divorced from the other, was meaningless.

To make government both responsible and representative naturally required efficient and effective administration. "Good laws," said Charles McCarthy, the chief expositor of Wisconsin progressivism, "are ineffective unless accompanied by good administration." The progressive was therefore deeply interested in such matters as the use in government of the commission, the expert adviser, and the special consultant. Building on the foundations already laid down by the Granger railroad commissions, progressives after 1900 made greater use of the nonpartisan, appointive commission or bureau, manned by experts, to administer public affairs in the public interest. La Follette's Wisconsin became a progressive laboratory. It had tax, railroad, conservation, insurance, banking, public service, and industrial commissions, a state bureau of efficiency, a legislative reference service for the drafting of bills, and other similar commissions and bureaus staffed by economists, scientists, and engineers from both academic and private life. The progressives' use of the commission, the bureau, and the expert did not resemble socialism, nor was it intended to.

The progressives used the commissioner, the expert, and the specialist simply so that government might bring to bear upon political, social, and economic problems the best minds and materials. By drawing a clear line between those who determined policy (the legislature and the elected executives) and those whose special skills fitted them to administer it, and by making the latter answerable to the people through the

legislature and executive, they hoped to avoid the characteristic evils of bureaucracy. Commissions, bureaus and consultants, said La Follette, were "simply the executive or administrative branch of the people's will"—servants, not masters, of
government. Thus democracy and efficiency worked together.

In its earliest phases Middle Western progressivism was a
state rather than federal thing, regional rather than national.
Grangerism and Populism had been chiefly concerned with
those issues which presented themselves most directly to the
Midwest farmer—railroads, grain buyers, the price of corn and
wheat, the machinery "ring," monopolies, mortgages, credit,
currency. The problems remained still unsolved after 1900,
and like his grandfather, the Midwest progressive tried to
solve them first at home. This localistic approach was entirely
logical. The state governments, under the American constitutional system, controlled most affairs of a social and political
character—the machinery of nominations and elections, suffrage, civil and criminal law, domestic and industrial relations,
education, municipal government, prisons and corrections,
transportation, its own taxing power. Both the boss and the
seeker of special privilege were most vulnerable on the state
or municipal level, where the progressive reformer found it
easiest to seize control of vital political and social institutions.
The state government was important, therefore, to the progressive as a point from which both to assail bad government
and to launch constructive reforms. The state was to him a
positive force to insure social and political progress and a co-
operative planning board to chart it.

Twentieth-century Midwestern progressivism operated
mainly within the Republican party. Populism in its later
phase had been a manifestation of much the same spirit within
the Democratic party. Certainly the Granger and Populist
failures were partially rooted in the fact that their revolt,
strong as it was, attempted to find its expression through third
parties or through the Democratic party in an area that was
traditionally committed to Republicanism. The new Repub-

lican progressives, while retaining much of the spirit of 1896—
its faith in the common man, its program of remedial legislation, its agrarian suspicion of urbanism, its hatred of monopoly and big business—grafted Populistic and Bryanistic principles on the Hamiltonian-Republican tradition. In the process
they exchanged the Jeffersonian concept of limited government
for the Hamiltonian concept of strong government as the tool
by which to fashion Jeffersonian ends.

Of course, progressive Republicanism was also plainly a
matter of expediency. The GAR still dominated politics in
the Midwest after the turn of the century, and it was wiser, in
those states where the Republican party was deeply dug in, to
seek to capture it than to create diversionary third parties.
"Your party," Bryan wrote to a Republican in 1901, "is entering upon a struggle by the side of which our contest will seem
a love-feast." Bryan was right. The subsequent internecine warfare between progressive and conservative within the Republican party cracked it at the seams, and 1912 split it wide open.

The real leader of Midwestern progressivism, and its greatest, was Robert Marion La Follette. The Midwest had been
laboring to produce a leader for thirty years when he appeared
on the scene in 1900. Under him progressivism captured a
state and in turn furnished the pattern for the capture of the
region; he carried it himself into the Senate and up to the
doors of the White House. He had what the others lacked,
expressed the tradition best, gave it its wisest and clearest
direction, and when he died, it died with him.

Wisconsin, like most Midwestern states in the late nineteenth century, was a tightly held Republican bailiwick controlled by a group of politicians and industrialists who ran
the party with a strong hand. Philetus Sawyer, "Uncle Ike"
Stephenson, and John C. Spooner—all railroad or lumbering
men—held the offices. Henry Payne, a railway, bank, and
public utilities magnate, C. F. Pfister, a banker, and Emanuel
Philipp, a Milwaukee corporation man, supplied the cus-

tomary link between the party and business. They all did their jobs well. Between 1855 and 1890 every governor of the state was a Republican except for one Democratic hiatus in the Granger seventies.

Wisconsin's was Gilded Age government—lobbyists wandering in and out of the legislature, assemblymen selling votes over "bowls of hot Scotch," the corporations running the show. One railroad attorney claimed that during sixteen years in Madison he knew of no single bill that ever passed without railroad approval. The men who ran the state were old-style politicos, pioneers who had come West, to wrest fortunes out of the railroads and the logging camps—hard, crude, wealthy men, believing that power naturally followed wealth. Yet they were, according to their own lights, honest men; they knew how politics operated, and they saw no reason why it should not continue to do so. They were of a different breed from the Goulds and Harrimans, for their wealth was based on power and skill, not adroitness, and they had a dignity and integrity that the robber barons of Wall Street and the pirates of finance lacked. The type was dying in the nineties, and the new progressive spirit showing itself in politics left them puzzled and doubtful. The old days were gone, and they were not certain of the direction of the new. "I have seen the functions of government change," wrote Stephenson in his old age, "from the stimulation to the regulation of effort. In the cycle of progress and the growth of a country so blessed with abundance as ours, this is no doubt necessary. But in the light of the philosophy of my own experiences, I should choose my steps very carefully."

La Follette, who represented the new politics, was born in 1855 in Primrose Township, Dane County, Wisconsin. His father, a Kentuckian who came to the state via Indiana, died soon after, and as the youngest of four children La Follette knew poverty at its source. He grew up in a hot Granger community, read Henry George while still in his teens, and when his mother moved to Madison in the seventies, entered the state university under the great John Bascom—three successive contacts with the original roots of Midwestern progressivism. His university days were hard, for he contributed to the support of the family by outside work while carrying a full course of study. Fraternities dominated university life, and La Follette had his first taste of politics in organizing the "scrubs" to defeat them in the student elections. Like Bryan, he was a budding orator, winning state and interstate titles, and also an editor, founding and editing a college paper. After graduation at twenty-four, he read law with a local law firm, attended law school (he was so poor the university remitted his fees), and was finally admitted to the bar after only five months' preparation. Though he was a good lawyer, politics always interested him more than law, so he decided to run for district attorney, a decision that brought him squarely up against the Republican organization.

Dane County in 1880 was the political property of Colonel E. W. Keyes, Madison postmaster, a one-time Republican state boss now satisfied to control Dane and near-by counties. Keyes, as La Follette described him, was a hard, bluff, dominating man, and a strict party disciplinarian. He caught La Follette in the post office one day and brusquely told him, more for the young man's own good than from any malice, that he was wasting his time running for district attorney. The nomination was already taken care of, and next time La Follette would do well to consult the party before making any plans. As La Follette perceived, all Keyes really wanted was recognition of the machine's authority.

La Follette's reaction was characteristic. He refused to have anything to do with Keyes and set out on his campaign, stumping the county tirelessly, promising to clean up the district attorney's office, cut down expenses, and give his personal attention to all county cases. The university students rallied round him, and by convention time La Follette had considerable backing. Five candidates for the office appeared, and though Keyes threw his support to the Democratic candidate to head him off, La Follette won on the fifth ballot. So La Follette had challenged Keyes on his home grounds and won. In the process he learned a valuable political lesson: a machine can be beaten by going beyond it to the people.

La Follette's two terms as district attorney taught him a great deal more. Trial work especially appealed to him, for it taught him the great importance of facts, a lesson he carried over into his political life. "In no other thing does a public man more surely indicate his quality than in the ability to master actual conditions and set them forth with clearness," he wrote later. "Neither laws nor opinions, nor even constitutions, will finally convince people; it is only the concrete facts of concrete cases." Keyes made a grudging peace with him, allowing him to run unopposed on the Republican slate at the next election, but La Follette by no means appeased the organization. He saw a good deal of the seamy side of politics, and it outraged his sense of honesty. The wife of a political boss, hauled into court on a minor charge, put pressure on everyone from judge down to constable, but La Follette forced the case to its conclusion and the lady drew a fine. Another time the chairman of the state Republican committee was robbed while lying drunk in a Madison hotel room. Asked by La Follette to make out a complaint against the captured thief, he told La Follette to forget it, since he wanted no publicity, However, La Follette chased him to Milwaukee with a subpoena, brought him back, and tried the case—but lost when somebody bribed his witnesses. And Keyes was a constant thorn in his side; witnesses had a habit of fading away after talking to the postmaster. Once during an illness La Follette got word, that Keyes intended to have an adultery case dismissed in his absence. La Follette went to court wrapped in a blanket and racked by chills, got a postponement and later a conviction.

After four years as district attorney, though his private law practice was flourishing, La Follette set his sights on Congress. The "Madison Ring" notified him he had no chance—

Spooner warned him no Wisconsin congressman in fifteen years had been elected without the organization's permission— but La Follette remembered his 1880 campaign and again went directly to the people. Quick, intelligent, confident, a tireless and brilliant speaker, he covered his district thoroughly, swept the caucuses, and went to the convention with the delegates from Dane and Grant, the largest counties in the district, safely wrapped up. Keyes's men tried to stop him, but he had done his work so well that he was nominated on the first ballot. By now it was clear to the Republican organization that La Follette was a real threat to its control. At election time Keyes switched his support to the Democratic nominee, but nevertheless La Follette squeezed in by four hundred votes. Thus Robert La Follette, who was twenty-nine years old and had never been east of Chicago, went to Congress, where he was to spend twenty-five of his forty-odd years in public life.

Wisconsin's congressional politics was supervised in 1885 by the veteran Philetus Sawyer and his protégé, John Spooner. Sawyer was a shrewd, forceful old man, able, intelligent, a typical politician of the Grant era who frankly believed in getting all he could for himself and his associates. Money, he believed, was the real mainspring of politics. Men could always be bought and the transaction usually bothered Sawyer's conscience no more than a deal in lumber, the business in which he had made his fortune. La Follette had defied the machine, it was true, but still he had won, and Sawyer assumed that he was no different from any of the other politicians he had seen come to Washington.

Sawyer took La Follette under his wing, introduced him to President Cleveland and the cabinet, and left word around that this young man was to be treated right. What committee would La Follette prefer in the House? La Follette chose Public Lands, for he was extremely interested in land-grant forfeitures. But Sawyer was not that naïve: land was an object of great interest to lumber and railroad men, and La Follette ended up instead in Indian Affairs, with a more dependable Wisconsin representative, "Uncle Ike" Stephenson, on Public Lands. Unfortunately for Sawyer, he forgot that there were huge stands of timber on the Indian reservations.

La Follette worked hard at being a congressman, sat up nights studying the House rules, read the *Congressional Record* carefully, and dug into Indian affairs. It was a most distinguished and polished Congress that session—Edmunds, Hoar, Sherman, Evarts, Allison, Ingalls, and Blaine were in the Senate, and Reed, McKinley, Joe Cannon, Carlisle, Mills, and Randall in the House—and La Follette missed few sessions or speeches. The more he heard, the more he wondered. Were these men really representing the people, or were they representing special interests? "Even then," he wrote, "the two diametrically opposed ideas of government had begun a death grapple for mastery in the country." From what he saw there was reason to believe the special interests were winning.

The fact first caught La Follette's notice in a bill introduced by the congressman from Sawyer's home district to sell off the rich pine lands of the Menominee Indian reservation in Wisconsin. Suspecting a lumber steal, La Follette consulted the Commissioner of Indian Affairs, who turned thumbs down on the deal, so La Follette killed the bill in committee. Sawyer, who may or may not have been behind it, said nothing, but La Follette began watching bills more closely. A little later he looked into a bill for river and harbor appropriations and found that of sixty-three projects begun by the government, the bill continued only five and added one hundred new ones— a clear piece of "pork-barrel" legislation. He used the bill as the basis for his first major speech in Congress, and though the bill passed, his speech against it attracted a good deal of attention.

La Follette came up for re-election in 1886 facing the usual opposition from Keyes and the state bosses. It was an important election for La Follette and he knew it. If he could get to the voters, he believed, he stood a good chance, so he devised a plan whereby he might counteract the pressure from Keyes's machine in his district. Taking a list of voters in the 1884 elections, he broke it up into townships, sent it to his supporters and requested that they return the lists with the names of local leaders checked. To these names he sent copies of his speeches and long accounts of his Washington record, an expense that ate heavily into a congressman's $5,000 salary but one he felt eminently justified. As results showed, he was right. The Republican convention renominated him over Keyes's opposition, and he won the election and returned to Washington for a second term.

This time La Follette's relations with Sawyer, who remembered the Menominees' pine trees, came close to the breaking point. A bill appeared before the Committee on Indian Affairs opening up eleven million acres of the Sioux reservation in Dakota. In it La Follette found tucked away a provision handing the Milwaukee and the North Western railroads almost a thousand acres each for terminal sites and a plot of 160 acres every ten miles along the track for stations. These looked, thought La Follette, very much like the beginnings of town sites. The railroads could sell the lands (160 acres meant an exceedingly large station) to speculators, and furthermore, since no time limit was set on the possession of the land, they might hold it indefinitely for speculative purposes without building a mile of track. La Follette had not been raised in railroad-hating Granger country for nothing.

La Follette held the bill up, and when Sawyer came to him for a friendly talk, he caught the point, especially when within forty-eight hours he received a visit from Henry Payne, secretary of the Wisconsin Central Republican Committee and lobbyist for the Milwaukee. Payne and Sawyer called on him every evening for a solid week, but he refused to be moved. The bill eventually passed, but not before La Follette tagged it with an amendment limiting station grants to twenty acres, another prohibiting the sale or use of the lands for any purposes except construction, and another placing a three-year limit on construction time, after which the land reverted to the government if no track appeared. Payne became La Follette's lifelong enemy over the affair, but Sawyer, to his credit, held him no ill will, being apparently both puzzled and respectful.

La Follette was re-elected in 1888 for a third term but lost his seat in the Democratic landslide of 1890, returning to Madison to practice law. He had a good record in Congress and a large local following, and furthermore he had successfully challenged the state machine six times. The state Republican committee, out of respect for both his ability and his success at the polls, had never really fully accepted or rejected him, but the time for decision was very near, for La Follette, when he returned to Wisconsin, was aiming at the governorship. He was perfectly aware of the fact that unless he played ball with the bosses he had very little chance of getting it. Payne and Keyes hated him; Spooner and Sawyer were still more or less neutral. Sawyer was the key figure, the man whose approval La Follette must have, and it was Sawyer who finally determined his course.

The new Democratic administration in 1891, probing into the financial affairs of preceding Republican state treasurers, uncovered the fact that several of them had withheld interest payments on state funds they had handled. Sawyer was a bondsman for one of them, and was therefore liable, if the state's suit for recovery of the interest was successful, to lose more than $150,000. The cases were to be tried in Dane County Circuit Court, with Judge Siebecker, La Follette's law partner and brother-in-law, presiding. Calling La Follette to Milwaukee, Sawyer conferred with him in a hotel room, and according to La Follette's account, offered him a retainer fee and a vaguely worded invitation to handle the case. La Follette was horrified. He stamped from the room and in a few days the whole state knew of Sawyer's attempt at "influence." La Follette broke with the machine clearly and definitely when he labeled its acknowledged leader as a corrupt bribegiver.

The truth of the matter is that both men probably misunderstood the nature of the incident. Sawyer said that he did not know of the relationship between La Follette and Siebecker; La Follette believed he did, and that the "retainer" was an attempt to get Siebecker out of the case and secure a favorable decision. Sawyer probably was guilty of an error in judgment, for La Follette's touchy sense of honor was notorious, but it is also true that Sawyer knew little of legal ethics and could have blundered quite honestly. Whatever the case, the incident showed La Follette quite clearly what course he must take. His whole career, he said, crystallized in that Milwaukee hotel room. "I knew that the struggle would be a long one," he said, "but my resolution never faltered."

The struggle was longer than he thought. He had no money, no organization, and only the support of his home district. In 1892 the bosses tried to read him out of the party, but he notified them he intended to campaign anyway and in self-protection the party grudgingly certified him as a campaign speaker. In 1894 he attempted to organize a revolt against the machine, persuading Nils Haugen, a progressive assemblyman, to enter the battle for the gubernatorial nomination, but Sawyer and Payne shut both of them out at the convention. In 1896 La Follette ran himself, but the machine captured his delegates and Scofield, the Payne-Sawyer choice, won the nomination and the election—a victory they repeated in 1898.

La Follette looked like a dead duck politically, but he was not without hope. He had acquired a newspaper, a rudimentary organization, a following of enthusiastic young supporters, and a growing reputation as a fighter against machine politics. He was ready to speak at any time or place, and his fiery, brilliant oratory made him widely known in the state. The presence of La Follette men was beginning to be felt at Republican conventions; somewhat unwillingly, the party in 1899 found itself with a corporation tax, an antipass law, and certain mild election reforms in its platform, while La Follette and his followers agitated for direct primaries and higher railroad tax assessments. After eight years of work, he gained ground steadily. When the party refused to send Stephenson to the Senate in 1899, "Uncle Ike" broke with the machine and came over to La Follette's side. Though always somewhat uncertain of his strange bedfellow, Stephenson worked with him for many years.

By 1900 La Follette could be held off no longer. Sawyer died in April. The Republican convention in August nominated La Follette for governor over the protests of Payne, and he won the election by a hundred thousand votes. Spooner, Payne, and Pfister were still alive and active, but the machine was broken. The legislature was split, unfortunately—the assembly pro-La Follette and the senate anti—and the party, too, into "stalwart" organization men and "half-breed" La Follette men. But progressivism was in the driver's seat, not to step out for twenty-odd years.

La Follette went to work at once. Haugen, now state tax commissioner, drew up a railroad taxation bill and E. R. Stevens a direct primary bill. Both ran into trouble in the stalwart senate, a pattern repeated a dozen times in La Follette's first term. Not one single bill on La Follette's program came through successfully. The stalwarts organized the Wisconsin Republican League to fight him, and Pfister purchased the *Milwaukee Sentinel* for the same purpose, labeling him a "demagogue," "socialist," "anarchist," and "Populist," and accusing him of "imperial ambitions." But having once captured the party, La Follette retained it; the state convention of 1902 renominated him and endorsed his program. Spooner, despite his dislike for La Follette, valued party unity above revenge and prevented a stalwart bolt to David Rose, the Democratic nominee, an act that saved both La Follette and the party. The election was an easy victory for him and he got a fair proportion of the legislature as well. In the 1902 session, with a working majority, the progressive program took shape. The railroad tax and the direct primary bill went through. An inheritance tax passed, but an antilobby bill lost and a pro-

posal for a railroad commission aroused such hot protest from
shippers that it was suspended for the session.

In 1904 the stalwarts found their second wind. For governor
they put up Emil Baensch, an honest and respected Republican
who made a strong preconvention showing. The railroads
dead-headed train crews to strategic towns to vote for anti-
La Follette men where stalwart delegates were in danger of
losing. Thus the stalwarts delegations came to the convention
(the last to be held under the new primary law) with some
strength. Five contested delegations could spell the difference
between a stalwart or La Follette victory. Feelings ran high;
the university gymnasium, the site of the convention, put up
barbed wire and called police guards. The Central Committee,
after some close dealing, finally seated fifty-nine pro-La Follette
delegates and thirty-six stalwarts from the disputed counties,
enough to secure La Follette control, and the stalwarts withdrew to hold a rump convention. Baensch would have none
of it and withdrew from the race, but Spooner, sensing a kill,
went along with the bolters.

The "gymnasium" convention nominated La Follette for
governor and chose delegates to the national convention; the
"opera house" rump put up S. A. Cook and elected delegates
too. Wisconsin thus had two Republican candidates, two state
platforms, and two sets of national delegates. The national
convention in Chicago almost automatically chose the stalwart
delegation and sent the La Follette men home, where they
found that the rump group had legally enjoined the secretary
of state from labeling La Follette's ticket "Republican" on
the ballot. The injunction went to the state supreme court,
which settled the matter in La Follette's favor, and running as
a Republican he won by 50,000 votes—the narrowest squeeze
of his career in state politics.

In the meantime, however, Senator Joseph Quarles, a stalwart who had served since 1899, died, leaving an open Senate
seat. La Follette wanted to return to Washington, and accord-
ingly one of the first acts of the 1905 legislature was to appoint

him to Quarles' place. He stayed in Madison until the railroad commission act and the antilobby bill passed, a civil service system was set up, a merit system for minor offices organized, collection of back railroad taxes begun, a state board of forestry appointed, a new capitol building started, and plans made for labor and industrial boards. Then, in January, 1906, he was sworn in and joined Payne in the Senate, leaving Lieutenant Governor Davidson in charge with the understanding that the mantle of state progressivism was to fall on Irvine Lenroot, his friend and protégé. La Follette never held state office again, but in the nineteen years that followed, his progressive Republican party dominated Wisconsin politics.

Wisconsin was the proving ground of Midwest progressivism in its twentieth-century phase. La Follette and his successors provided continuity of political leadership; Ely, Commons, McCarthy, Van Hise, and others like them supplied the philosophy of government and the social and economic skills needed for the consumation of the "Wisconsin Idea." Nothing like it had been seen before, and it could have happened only in the Midwest. For a quarter of a century, Wisconsin was the agrarian-democratic commonwealth that the Grangers and Populists visualized. And once rolling, progressivism was hard to stop. Even stalwart and Democratic platforms and candidates in the ensuing years took on a progressive look.

The "Wisconsin Idea" was not simply a theory, but a practical and coherent program actually in effect between 1900 and 1914. To insure and enlarge the functions of representative government, the progressives of Wisconsin, before the opening of the first World War, put into operation a direct primary, an initiative and referendum, a corrupt-practices act, a law governing campaign expenditures, a civil service law, and an antilobbying law. To protect the citizen against organized economic power, the state set up transportation, industrial, and public utility commissions to fix rates and guarantee services. It also had a tax commission, a state income tax, an inheritance tax, regulatory life insurance and banking laws, an act to assist co-operatives, an unfair-trade-practices act, new weights and measures regulations, and laws governing stock and bucket shop operations. To promote public safety and welfare it had child- and female-labor laws, industrial safety laws, public health and pure food laws, a workmen's compensation act, a conservation law, and an excellent system of education and extension work. The "Wisconsin Idea" was a progressive experiment in democracy that worked.

The theory of government behind it was simple—that government should be representative, responsible, active in promoting social progress, honest, and efficient. A case in point was provided by its handling of monopoly. The railroads and public utilities in Wisconsin, as in most Midwest states, had been almost immune from attack since the seventies, when the Grangers tried unsuccessfully to hamstring them by regulation and taxation. La Follette kept up the offensive in the early years of his career until in 1903, with the progressives in power, study of the railroad question began afresh under the direction of State Senator William Hatton. It was the duty of the state, in Hatton's opinion, to furnish adequate transportation facilities to its citizens; if that duty were delegated to private corporations, it was the state's business to see the job done properly, with provision for adequate facilities at reasonable cost without discrimination. Thus in 1905 a commission was established to supervise the railroads. Its members were experts on railroad affairs, its appropriations were automatically renewed each legislative session, and its reports and bookkeeping were open to the public. Much the same plan was applied to the regulation of public utilities, highways, stocks and bonds, dairy and food, taxes, life insurance, and banking—each an area of public interest controlled by commissions. This multiplication of bureaus led the Wisconsin Manufacturers' Association to complain of "exasperating meddling . . . with private and corporate affairs," but the theory behind commission government, as La Follette explained, was that if social and industrial life grew more complex and required regulation, government must provide it. "Expert knowledge in the framing of legislation and in the administration of the laws becomes more and more of a public necessity," he said. "So long as the commission is the creature of the legislature, subject to prompt control or abolition, we need not be alarmed."

Drawing upon Danish, Swiss, German, and Canadian precedents, the Wisconsin progressives set about making government honest as well as efficient. In 1900, when La Follette took office, lobbyists wandered in and out of the legislative chambers, bills were sent up to the speaker on odd scraps of paper or old envelopes, and a staff of seventy women wrote out all legislation in longhand for engrossment or distribution. Committees overlapped, their functions hardly clear to the committees themselves; clerkships were patronage footballs; parliamentary rules were only casually observed. In short order an antilobby law got rid of the worst features of lobbying, stenographers and printing appeared, civil service rules were applied to the clerical force, rules for orderly legislative procedure were adopted, and the committee system was overhauled. La Follette set up the State Board of Public Affairs, whose duty it was "to supervise and develop the resources of the state," but which really functioned as an efficiency bureau. The governor and secretary of state sat on it as representatives of the executive branch; the chairman of the senate and assembly finance committees represented the legislature; and a member each was appointed from agriculture, manufacturing, and labor.

One of the weak points in legislative procedure in Wisconsin—and in other states as well—had been the inability of the average legislator, unfamiliar as he often was with such matters as bill drafting and parliamentary law, to obtain information about legislation or its proper form. To remedy this, La Follette called in Charles McCarthy, a brilliant political scientist, to set up a legislative reference service. McCarthy's Legislative Reference Library, developed from modest beginnings in 1901, was one of progressivism's greatest contributions to good government; five states had adopted the plan by 1907 and twenty more by 1917. Legislative reference service provided the legislator with a constant stream of information on bills and hearings and made available to him a staff of experts who could give him facts, statistics, precedents—any information he needed for the proper discharge of his duties—and who drafted any bills he wished to introduce. McCarthy pointed out that one of the reasons for the failure of Granger legislation was that it was usually badly written, often in conflict with constitutional law, and therefore always open to attack. The legislator, working from public opinion, and the courts, working from legal precedent, frequently collided, and the courts always won. McCarthy's staff gave the legislator a chance to avoid this conflict. If a legislator told them what he wanted, the reference service gave him a bill properly drawn, legally sound, and based on proper precedent. Nonpartisan and nonpolitical, McCarthy's service was intended solely as an instrument to promote efficiency in the democratic process. It once even drafted, for a stalwart legislator, a bill to abolish itself.

The "Wisconsin Idea" had its opponents, of course. La Follette's program would drive capital from the state, they warned —his vaunted reforms were nothing but vote-catching demagoguery aimed at creating a "machine" of his own. While it was true that La Follette was occasionally arrogant and dictatorial in his methods, it was also clear that he was impeccably honest and mercilessly efficient. Steffens, probing into his regime, could find no real evidence of self-interest or dishonesty, even from his bitterest political enemies. The charge most often leveled at him was that he was at heart a socialist. "There is no question that pure socialism and progressivism," one critic wrote, "are rapidly approaching each other, steered together by young lawyers trained for the work at Van Hise's spellbinder factory."

In reply, McCarthy pointed out that all of La Follette's bills had been carried through without killing industry, that manufacturing and utility holdings had actually increased in wealth while the reforms were going on. The whole La Follette program, he asserted, was quite the antithesis of socialism. It was really an attempt, he said, "to give the individual a better chance to possess property," based on the idea that "the welfare of the state is the welfare of the individual." The state was never intended to become a socialistic operator of business, but rather an agency by means of which a fairer field—fairer in justice and fairer in fruits—could be given to private business in so far as it was consistent to other operators and consumers. The "Wisconsin Idea" was "a new individualism," in McCarthy's phrase, a median between socialism and complete laissez faire—the realization of Lester Ward's "dynamic action" and Henry Lloyd's "positive progressive instinct for the conscious creation of the public welfare."

La Follette's own political philosophy was grounded on an old-fashioned American individualism of agrarian-Jeffersonian origins. He was a defender of capitalism against itself, he said, believing that capitalism, unless checked, was almost certain to commit suicide, dragging democracy down with it. To him, the preservation of democracy depended upon the people themselves. "Get and keep a dozen or more of the leading men in a community interested in and well-informed upon any public question," he wrote, "and you have laid firmly the foundations of democratic government." In the press, on the Chautauqua platform, at hundreds of county fairs and Grange meetings, from the back of a wagon or later a Ford, La Follette always went directly to the people. "I don't know how the people will feel toward me," he said on his deathbed, "but I shall take to the grave my love for them, which has sustained me through life."

The direct primary, the initiative and referendum, the abolition of the caucus and convention, these and other reforms to him were simply devices by which the people might speak. "To insure a more direct expression of the people's will,"

La Follette said, "in all things pertaining to government, is the dominating thought in American politics today." But having once spoken, the people needed assurances that their voice would be heeded. Thus the responsibility of the elected official to the voter, and of the party to the voter, became a La Follette shibboleth. An officeholder, to his mind, represented the individual citizen in person and the party in the aggregate; he could not therefore play fast and loose with either personal or party obligations. Political parties made a contract with the voters, expressed in party pledges. The party which adopted a program and the candidate who endorsed it were honor bound to observe the contract. Violation of it or failure to execute it was not only "an assault upon party honor," but "a betrayal of the public." This, in La Follette's view, was the chief danger to democracy—not the people's inability to govern themselves, but the betrayal of the people by their representatives.

To beat the machine and the boss, La Follette depended upon the people's wisdom. Therefore a free press, a free and extended educational system, and pitiless publicity of campaign and corporate financing were fundamental to the democratic process. Recalling his own career, he wrote: "Machine control is based upon misrepresentation and ignorance. Democracy is based upon knowledge. It was clear to me that the only way to beat the boss and ring rule was to keep the people thoroughly informed."

La Follette's forty-four years of public service coincided with the antimonopoly era, and his progressivism was an extension of the Anti-Monopoly-Greenback-Granger struggle with the giant corporation. Modern business, he said in his message of 1904, needed large concentrations of capital to operate, but it should never be allowed to use that capital to destroy competition, control prices, milk the public, or corrupt government. Self-interested, organized, economic power was a threat to public welfare and to democracy, too strong to be curbed by any agency other than the state. Government therefore must regulate business in the public interest, and if necessary, break it. "It's as plain as a pikestaff," he said, "that you cannot yoke private monopoly with honest, impartial public service." Nor can you live under an economic and industrial oligarchy and retain political freedom. "We may have the privilege of the ballot, we may have the form and semblance of democracy," he remarked, "but in the end industrial servitude means political servitude."

His method of dealing with monopoly was concrete, factual, and objective. Let us take as an example, he said, United States Steel. Let a government commission ascertain the valuation of its holdings and its actual investment in business. With this sum in mind, figure a reasonable rate of return, ascertain a fair price for its products, and publish it. U. S. Steel would then know what price it could justifiably charge; if it did not charge that price, the government could use more drastic methods of inducing it to do so. Railroads, whose rates should be calculated on the basis of a fair return for investment and service, could be handled the same way. In the case of natural public resources such as oil, coal, iron, timber, and so on, the government should own them and either operate or lease them, controlling both production and price. Private enterprise, La Follette thought, ought always to be allowed to do its job fairly, but if it did not, government ownership or operation was the only other alternative.

As a practicing politician, La Follette ranked among the best. An organizer of great ability, he built up from scratch a party (or a "machine") that controlled Wisconsin for a quarter century, one whose influence was apparent in state politics for more than twenty years after his death. If he did not always inspire affection in his followers, he certainly inspired loyalty and respect. His party was always held together by the force of his own personality and the trust its constituents placed in him. Supreme as a leader, he yet lacked certain qualities to enable him to develop a national following, as Bryan and Theodore Roosevelt did. The austerity and rigidity of his nature and his inability to adjust to changing political and human situations narrowed his appeal. His thinking was Midwestern—typically so, reflecting the prejudices and the traditions of his state and region; the nation and the world were to him merely bigger Wisconsin. He lacked what historians call the "world view"; it was characteristic of him to remark, after his trip to Russia in the twenties, that he wished the Soviets could "come to Wisconsin to see what a real people's commonwealth was like."

La Follette was closer to the people and closer to the Midwest than any politician after Bryan. Unlike Bryan's, his appeal to the public was rational, rather than emotional. He had none of Bryan's crowd-swaying hypnosis, speaking instead in a rapid, intense fashion, flooding his audience with statistics, figures, and examples. The fact that he could keep a crowd of farmers on the edge of their seats for three hours by reciting tariff schedules and tax rates (as he once did on Chautauqua) is a tribute to a skill less flamboyant than Bryan's but one certainly equally effective. He once spoke for fifty-three consecutive nights, without the slightest flagging of his own energy or the audience's interest, a political feat only Bryan himself could equal.

La Follette was a small, wiry man, with a shock of black (later iron-gray) hair and a tendency toward swift and sharp gesture. He was honest, serious, almost inhumanly intense, and thoroughly uncompromising. He was perfectly willing to jeopardize his career, as he did a dozen times, to keep his principles, and the hate and vituperation that often came his way affected him not one iota. "I can no more compromise, or seem to compromise . . . ," he said," than I could by wishing it add twenty years to my life." His principles were always clear, his course equally so. Cold, severe, almost austere in manner, La Follette did not invite easy friendship. He never had fun in politics (as Theodore Roosevelt did), nor did he inspire the devotion that Bryan did. It would be difficult to choose, from the group of men who knew him best and followed him, one who was a really close friend, for his complete and selfless dedication to his cause wrapped him about like armor. In truth, with his solid, lined face, his tremendous idealism, his rigid indifference to any blandishments of friendship, party, place, profit, or power, La Follette was a trifle frightening. No one ever took Bob La Follette lightly or disinterestedly. "The politician cannot exist without absolute, unyielding, uncompromising honesty," he said, and he lived it out to the letter.

La Follette's Wisconsin cut the pattern, and the whole Midwest copied it. Progressivism after 1900 at one time or another had complete control of every state but Illinois, Michigan, Ohio, and Indiana. For that matter, it spread elsewhere under the leadership of men like Hiram Johnson in California, Charles Evans Hughes in New York, Woodrow Wilson in New Jersey, Bass in New Hampshire, and so on. But in the Middle West, where it started, progressivism was considerably more than simply a swing toward honest government. It was a definite and coherent political philosophy, a concept of democracy that grew naturally out of Grangerism and Populism. Behind it were Weaver and Bryan, Donnelly and Lloyd, Altgeld, and Simpson, and a distinctively Midwestern, agrarian, Jeffersonian, frontier tradition.

After La Follette's capture of Wisconsin, Iowa caught the progressive spirit, too. The state was held closely in conservative Republicanism by Senator William Allison, a director of the Union Pacific; J. W. Blythe of the Burlington, who held the party reins; and J. H. Gear, Blythe's father-in-law and a former governor, congressman, and senator. But, as in Wisconsin, the revolt came from within the party, led by Albert B. Cummins, a man who had something of the La Follette stamp and whose career paralleled La Follette's.

Cummins came to Iowa in the seventies from Pennsylvania, by way of Indiana and Illinois, to set up a law practice in Cedar Rapids. Though nominally a Republican, he entered politics on the side of the Grangers and was one of the lawyers retained by the farmers in 1881 to fight the barbed-wire syndicate. His success put him into the state assembly in Larrabee's time, when the Granger-railroad contest was at its height. After 1892 he became known as a left-wing Republican with Populist sympathies, running against Gear for the Republican Senate nomination. He lost, though he built up a good following among farm groups, and again in 1899 he lost after a terrific struggle with the railroad interests. By this time he was definitely labeled as an untrustworthy Republican, slated to be killed off by the party leaders. Gear's death in office left his Senate seat vacant, a seat for which Cummins was a logical contender on the strength of his 1899 election showing. But Governor Shaw chose Jonathan Dolliver, a friend of Allison's, an act that was a clear rebuff to Cummins and supposedly his political epitaph.

Cummins was not easily rebuffed. He immediately entered the 1900 gubernatorial campaign and surprisingly won it. Under him progressivism took over in Iowa, and he remained a leader of the state party until his defeat for the Senate in 1926 by Smith Brookhart. Cummins' inaugural defined his course clearly. He was, he said frankly, a reformer; "Reform and betterment in laws are as essential to the advance of the republic as is the growth of its industrial life." Monopolistic business, specifically, was in his opinion the enemy of democracy and his target was special privilege. "Wealth, and especially corporate wealth," he said, "has many rights; but it should be remembered that among them is not the right to vote. . . . Corporations as such should be rigorously excluded in every form from political affairs." His ideal of government, defined in a later inaugural, was the progressive ideal of the Midwest, not "the desire to change simply to effect a change in the existing order," but "an effort to make it better."

Cummins, like La Follette, turned his guns on the railroads, the tariff, and the corporations. Almost immediately after his inauguration he ran into the Molsberry bill, a piece of legis-

lation engineered by Blythe of the Burlington which removed
debt limitations on corporations and paved the way for a
Burlington-Great Northern merger. Cummins refused to sign
it, broke definitely with his party, and for the rest of his
career ran either as an independent or as a progressive Republican with only token backing from the party. The legislatures
of 1902 and 1904, generally hostile to his program, did not
give him much assistance, but by 1906 the swing toward
progressivism extended his strength. A good corporation
lawyer himself, he was quite familiar with business in politics,
and he proposed a series of laws covering corporation contributions to campaigns, all of which went on the books. He
also suggested antipass laws, a two-cent passenger rate, a commission to fix freight rates, and railroad service regulations,
most of which he saw put into effect.

Cummins' reforms, directed first at railroads, eventually
affected all corporations in the state. Size in business, he felt,
was no objection, "being in itself no menace to the prosperity
and welfare of the people." But the monopoly and the trust
had naturally bad attributes as well as naturally good ones,
tendencies which must be controlled in the public interest.
Thus, said Cummins, no company should incorporate in Iowa
without examination and approval by a qualified state agency;
no corporation should be allowed to issue capital stock until
carefully investigated by the state (a device to outlaw over-
capitalization); no corporation should be allowed to escape its
proper tax burden; and no corporation should be allowed to
engage in any sort of political activity. His program was based
on the principle that the chief evils of big business were sup-
pression of competition and unfair trade practices. The duty
of the state was to guarantee competition and fair trade, not
to "bust the trust" but to keep it in its place. "I believe in
the maintenance of the rule that opens the channels of trade
fairly and fully to all comers," he wrote, and in his twenty-five
years in politics he tried to keep those channels open.

The tariff, long an object of Midwest ire, came next. A believer in competition as the life of trade ("There is always room for three or four firms in any field of business"), Cummins opposed both those tariffs that overprotected and destroyed competition by giving unfair advantage to the few and those that underprotected, destroying competition by opening the door to unfair trade practices. A proper tariff, he said, should "prevent unfair competition from abroad and unwise competition at home"; it should protect neither too much nor too little. So he developed the "Iowa plan" for a tariff whose rates shifted as needs shifted, adjusting to reflect the constantly changing relation of industry to tariffs. Later, in the Senate, he became an outstanding authority on tariffs and the author of an article for the *Encyclopedia Americana*. Consistent in his stand, he refused to vote for the Payne-Aldrich tariff of 1909 and the Fordney-McCumber tariff of 1922 on the ground that they favored industry too much, or for the Underwood tariff of 1913 on the ground that it favored it too little. A tariff, he thought, was closely tied up with the trusts. It should never, in any way, "afford shelter to monopoly."

After he became governor in 1904, Cummins turned his attention more to political and social legislation. His first message emphasized the need for a direct primary law, direct election of senators, initiative and referendum, life insurance company regulation, inheritance taxes, child-labor laws, anti-lobby laws, commission government for cities, and the limitation of hours in certain industries—the usual progressive program. He suggested also a wider use of the constitutional convention and an easier method of constitutional amendment, both in state and nation, as a means of keeping government close to the people. Life insurance, child-labor laws, a pure food act, and the direct primary did pass, but Cummins' program remained far from complete.

The year 1906 brought Cummins' hardest fight. The "standpat" Republicans opposed his re-election, the Burlington fought him tooth and nail. Since he was the first governor in Iowa history to ask a third term, precedent was against him, but he won. He simply picked up where he had left off, asking for regulation of commerce, further curbs on corporations, tariff revisions, uniform marriage and divorce laws, restrictions on lobbyists ("a stench in the nostrils of a decent community"), abolition of the railroad pass, higher corporation taxes, corrupt-practices acts, and so on. A majority of these became law, but Cummins, like La Follette, saw that progressivism was bigger than the state, that while the state might do much to insure responsible and responsive government, the road to reform really lead to Washington. In 1908, refusing to run again, he replaced Allison in the Senate after the latter's death, leaving Lieutenant Governor Garst to fill out his term. In the Senate he met La Follette and joined the small band of Midwestern insurgents who harried Taft and Aldrich. B. F. Carroll, who succeeded Garst, followed Cummins' example, but Iowa went back into regular party channels after the first World War.

Cummins' theory of government resembled La Follette's rather closely. Government, he thought, must be kept near to the voters ("I am not afraid of the people," he said) and responsive to them. The state must be a positive agency for social and economic progress, "constantly adapting itself to the changing relations of men and the varying tendencies of the age." Government should be fluid, without "idolatry for things that are," but progressing always toward things as they might be. Like La Follette, he came out of the Granger-Populist tradition, retaining all its faith in the common man, its concept of the state, its ideals of social and political and economic justice. But he lacked the color and the intensity of the older man, and his genius for leadership. Cummins was a gentle dray horse, as Beveridge called him, courageous and industrious, gaining his points by patient, quiet work rather than by storm.

Of all the Midwestern states, Minnesota was perhaps the most completely in the grip of organized business. The Minneapolis Chamber of Commerce exerted tremendous influence in political affairs, in league with powerful railroad, mining, and milling interests. Despite Donnelly and the others, Populism never made much actual headway in the state, and even under Populist-Democratic Governor Lind, in 1898, reform legislation got nowhere.

The first indication of a break in standpat Republicanism in Minnesota came with the election of Governor Van Sant, who won in 1900 on a program of trust busting, tax reform, and railroad regulation. But Van Sant's brave platform never materialized. Requests for new tax laws failed to elicit any response from the legislature, and a bill to add authority to the railroad and warehouse commission (so that it could fix railroad rates) came to nothing. Yet Van Sant, with the help of Attorney General Douglas, did initiate the Northern Securities case in an attempt to prevent the consolidation of three great railroads in violation of Minnesota statute. The application was denied in the state supreme court, so Van Sant sued in Minnesota county courts. Here again he lost, but the case was later broken by Theodore Roosevelt. Van Sant's vigorous pursuit of Northern Securities insured his re-election in 1902, and in his second term he was able to secure, as Wisconsin had, both a state board of control for state institutions and a primary election law.

Progressivism, when it came to Minnesota, came through the Democratic party, where the Granger-Populist legacy was strongest. John A. Johnson, who followed Van Sant as governor in 1904, was a Swede, a typical product of the interaction of frontier and immigrant. Born in Minnesota when the state had more Dakota Indians than citizens and not a mile of railroad, Johnson came into politics via a small newspaper, the *St. Peter Herald,* which he bought in 1887. Unlike most Minnesota Swedes, Johnson joined the Democratic party, served in it through the Populist era, and had one term as a state senator in 1898. Yet Johnson's party ties were always tenuous. At heart he was more than anything else a throwback to the Donnelly type of independent. "I care not for the party I choose," he once said, "so long as it stands for the rights of the people." Defeated for the state senate in the Republican land-slide of 1902, he was nominated for governor in 1904, 1906, and 1908 and won each time, but he died shortly after his last victory.

Johnson's two full terms paralled those of La Follette and Cummins. A big, slow-moving man with a quick mind, he began with no definite or carefully worked-out pattern of re-form but worked piece by piece and month to month, tinker-ing here and there with progressive ideas. He gathered around him no staff of expert advisers, as La Follette did, nor did he have Cummins' roots in law and economics. Politically John-son had little of either's legislative skill. A somewhat naïve politician, he was incapable of fast and hard political maneu-vering, making his way usually by simple, candid honesty. "Equal rights to all, special privileges to none" summed up his theory of government, and he carried his political philoso-phizing not much further.

But Johnson, for all the seemingly casual nature of his program, arrived at about the same destination as La Follette and Cummins. He asked for the nomination and election of the judiciary on a nonpartisan basis; for the prohibition of railroad passes; for income, corporation, and inheritance taxes; for stricter regulation of railroad rates; for municipal ownership of certain public utilities; for better rural schools; for conservation laws; and so on—a true Midwestern progres-sive program. For the most part he was successful in getting it. He set up a tax commission, passed an inheritance tax law, and fought the mining companies successfully over a tonnage tax slapped on ore production. The railroad and warehouse commission investigated and lowered freight rates, an act that caused a great deal of litigation settled eventually in the state's favor by a 1913 decision of the federal Supreme Court. In addition, Johnson established a state employment bureau and a state immigration bureau, abolished private banks, built a state factory to make harvesting machines in competition with the harvester trust, passed laws regulating bucket shops, and instituted a state insurance code. Like La Follette, Johnson was a strong conservationist, and though he never succeeded in breaking the hold of the lumber barons on the state's natural resources, he did get new timber laws to replace the outmoded acts of 1895.

Johnson's attitude toward the trust and the monopoly represented a modification of that of the nineties. A farmer himself, and the inheritor of the old agrarian distrust of the corporation, he considered the trust a threat to political and economic democracy. Yet as an alert student of twentieth-century affairs he could not accept the simple trust busting of Donnelly as the answer. The trust, in his estimation, was a natural result of economic forces, impossible to abolish but certainly subject to rigid control by the state. As Steffens observed when he swung through in 1902, big business held Minnesota in the palm of its hand, and the solution, said Johnson, lay in properly regulating business by legislation and then properly administering it, except in the case of natural resources where municipal ownership was in order—a position not unlike that of La Follette and Cummins.

Johnson's sudden death after the 1908 elections removed a powerful figure from Midwest politics. Had he lived, Johnson might have been a more significant political influence than he was. As matters stood, he had gone a long way down the progressive road, and though his program was left unfinished, he had gained notable success in a tightly controlled Republican state. In his haphazard way Johnson brought progressive politics into Minnesota to stay. Out of the strong progressive tradition Johnson left, Minnesota passed a corrupt-practices act and child-labor laws, voted in the direct election of senators, and ratified the income tax amendment. By 1914 the progressive program was relatively complete, but the "dry" issue tangled up Minnesota politics after that date and a few years later the entrance of the Non Partisan League into the state introduced another factor, culminating in the Republican-

Farmer-Labor battles of the twenties and the eventual victory of the Farmer-Labor party under Governor Floyd Olson in 1930.

In the Dakotas progressivism faced the same powerfully entrenched Republican opposition as in Minnesota. Alexander McKenzie of the Union Pacific reputedly ran Dakota politics from a hotel room in St. Paul, Alfred Kittredge of the Milwaukee and A. C. Johnson of the North Western distributed the patronage, and Kittredge and Gamble (another railroad man) supervised business interests in the senate. Under Governors Frank White and Elmore Sarles, North Dakota Republican progressives staged an unsuccessful revolt—though they did force a revision of state banking and insurance laws—and in 1906 the liberals threw their support to John Burke, the Democratic candidate, a man much like Johnson in temperament and La Follette in ideas. His victory in 1906, and again in 1908 and 1910, gave North Dakota a really progressive regime.

Opposed at every turn by the Republicans and allied interests, Burke and his party eventually succeeded in passing a primary election law, a corrupt-practices act, the initiative and referendum, railroad regulations, antitrust laws, the commission system for city government, conservation laws, tax revisions, and grain-grading laws, and created a public service commission. Heavily settled by farmers from Wisconsin, North Dakota followed the La Follette pattern quite closely, and Burke's Republican successor, Louis Hanna, continued his work. Under his direction the state passed election reform laws, a state hail insurance act, a tax commission law, and returned to the state-owned elevator idea urged by the Populists in 1892. In 1916 the Non Partisan League entered North Dakota politics and shifted its direction abruptly to the left.

South Dakota had very much the same experience. The Farmers' Alliance, after the termination of Populist power in 1896, finally succeeded in 1898 in passing one of the first initiative and referendum laws. The Populist-Democrats, however, could make little real headway in a traditionally Republican state, while progressive-minded Republicans found the regular Republican organization too strong for them to buck. The first breakthrough came in 1903, when Coe Crawford, counsel for the North Western, resigned from both the railroad and the Republican party to run as an avowedly progressive candidate for governor. He lost the nomination, but his defection broke the party in half. In 1906, with a strong progressive element behind him, he won and put South Dakota on the progressive map for twenty years.

The legislature of 1907 quickly caught up to the progressive procession and routed the North Western and the Milwaukee (both then building extensively in the state) in a no-holds-barred battle. Crawford saw through a primary election law, an antilobby law, and a law forbidding corporation campaign contributions. His administration reduced railroad rates, revalued corporation property for tax purposes, and placed new taxes on corporations. Crawford himself finally followed Cummins and La Follette into the Senate in 1908, but his successors, Vessey, Byrne, and Norbeck, followed his line closely. By 1917 the 1907 program had been augmented by a rural-credits law, budget, tax, and markets commissions, a workmen's compensation law, and other common progressive measures.

The ground in Nebraska had been well fertilized by twenty years of Granger-Populist disturbance. Triumphant in 1896 and 1898, the combined Populist-Democratic party took a head start on progressivism by passing the first initiative and referendum law in the United States, along with strong codes regulating utilities, an antitrust act, and a corrupt-practices act. In 1900 a disagreement between the Democrats and the Populists over the question of fusion let the Republicans back into power under Governor Dietrich. By 1902 the Republicans had consolidated their gains and were moving rapidly back toward their old-time dominance, but at the same time a new group of young Republicans were attracting support from in-

dependents, progressive Republicans, old Populists, and dissatisfied Democrats. The Republican party in Nebraska was
by no means progressive in 1902, but there were faint signs of
a shift of the balance of power within it.

The progressive wave finally hit Nebraska in 1906. George
Sheldon, who was elected governor that year, was a self-con-
fessed reformer and he had on his side a liberal-minded Republican legislature. The 1907 session enacted the most complete
progressive program ever accomplished in a single session by
any Midwestern legislature—a primary law, a child-labor act,
an antipass law, reduced passenger rates, various railroad regulations, acts tightening the railroad commission's powers, insurance codes, and various laws governing administrative
efficiency. The prohibition issue muddied Nebraska politics
considerably and contributed to Sheldon's defeat in 1908, but
in 1910 the progressive Republicans swept back to elect C. H.
Aldrich, beginning a new list of reforms finally carried out by
the Democrats, who came in in 1912—better insurance codes,
a blue-sky law, an industrial mediation board, a conservation
commission, and a female-labor law. Furthermore, Nebraska
during the period sent such men as Norris Brown and George
Norris to Congress to join the Iowa-Wisconsin-Minnesota-
Dakotas group of insurgents. Not until the twenties, after a
seesaw of Democratic and Republican rule, did the original
progressive movement lose its force in Nebraska.

Kansas lived always under the shadow of the Populists,
whose ideas dominated state politics for twenty years after
1892. The Democratic party, split over Bryan and fusion with
Populism, gradually lost ground and the state returned to
regular Republican rule. A group of young Republican rebels
emerged in the years after 1900, however, and Kansas began to
display the same standpat-progressive division that characterized Republicanism in the rest of the Midwest. William Allen
White of the *Emporia Gazette,* Joseph Bristow, Victor Murdock, Henry Allen, Arthur Capper, Walter Stubbs, and others
(all except White practicing politicians) campaigned for such

measures as an antipass law, corporation regulations, railroad rate laws, and tax reforms, most of which became law during the terms of Stubbs's governorship after 1909. The "dry" issue, which confused Midwestern politics after 1900, confused Kansas as well, and the Bull Moose revolt of 1912 split its progressive Republicans badly.

The dominant figure in Kansas politics after 1900 was William Allen White, the small-town Kansas editor who spoke not only for Kansas but for the American liberal. White was a progressive, but his progressivism was not that of La Follette, Johnson, or Crawford. It was, more clearly, the progressivism of Theodore Roosevelt and the Easterners, upper middle-class liberalism rather than Granger-Populist "radicalism." Whatever White's fame, or his influence, he was never a true Midwestern progressive, though a progressive he undoubtedly was. His career pointed up the essential differences between Roosevelt-Bull Moose liberalism and the old Midwestern regional tradition, a conflict of principles which characterized the entire progressive movement in the decade preceding the first World War.

White began his political life as a conservative Republican, a bitter foe of Populism, and a hater of Bryan. He helped hang the "sockless" tag on Jerry Simpson, fought Populism as "European, socialist, Latin" radicalism, and considered the Republican party to be the protector of "the American way" as opposed to the Bryanite "un-American doctrine of state paternalism." The only rule of business worth following, White believed, was "be strong or go under," and as late as 1901 he argued the advantages of boss rule over "mob rule" as "the best government there is." His collection of short stories, *The Real Issue,* published in 1896, attacked the "foolish, empty" schemes of Populism and preached "regeneration" through straight Republican politics. In 1896 William Allen White was certainly not a progressive, and his vitriolic editorial on the Populists of that year, "What's the Matter with Kansas?" provided a valuable weapon for Mark Hanna's campaign arsenal.

Ironically, it was White's editorial that undid him as a party man. Paul Morton, vice-president of the Santa Fe, called the piece to the attention of the *Chicago Times-Herald,* who syndicated it throughout the nation. Hanna picked it up as campaign material, and the Republican National Committee distributed more than a million copies of it in 1896. White found himself suddenly in the inner circle of Republican politics, invited by Hanna to speak at rallies, introduced to McKinley, and, after the election, offered the postmastership at Emporia, his home town. White always believed that a newspaperman should never hold office, and went to Washington to convince McKinley of it. There he met Theodore Roosevelt and was converted. White suddenly realized in horror, he said later, that in his blind Republicanism he was supporting a "plutocratic party" and an essentially dangerous cause. He left Washington an ardent Roosevelt supporter for the rest of his life.

Back in Emporia, White's *Gazette* became the party organ of Roosevelt progressivism, of trust busting, income taxes, unemployment insurance, and of all the other measures its editor had once condemned when the Populists sponsored them. Populism, he explained in justification, had "shaved its whiskers, washed its shirt, put on a derby, and moved up into the middle of the class—the upper middle class." Yet White was not wholly at ease in progressive ranks. He was first and foremost a Republican, and the appearance of "radicalism" within the party confused him. He respected La Follette as a crusader, but he did not wholly agree with or support the Wisconsin insurgent, nor (like his master Theodore Roosevelt) did he ever wholly trust him.

White praised and respected Wilson (he was sorry he was a Democrat), opposed both Taft and Harding (but voted for Harding), voted for Coolidge and Hoover, and supported Franklin Roosevelt consistently except at election time. He was bothered always by his inability to break out of Republican regularity, explaining that he felt he could better keep the party honest and alive from within than from without. When progressive Republicans of the order of Bristow, Stubbs, and Murdock ran for office in Kansas, White backed them. But if progressives ran independently, or as Democrats, White still reluctantly voted Republican, a practice that often left him on one side of the fence and his ballot on the other. Unless it was his idol, Theodore Roosevelt, who was breaking out of party lines, White usually stuck with his party. In 1914, when progressive Republicans split over the third-party issue, he very nearly joined them, but eventually stayed in the fold. Only in 1924, over the Klan issue, did White break away, running for governor unsuccessfully as an independent—a decision he regretted and never again made.

The truth was the William Allen White, like Theodore Roosevelt, did not have in him the hell-for-leather heritage of Midwest independency. He was not a Midwestern progressive, but a progressive Republican—with emphasis on the Republican. His great contribution, like Roosevelt's, was to the party itself, keeping progressive ideals alive in it through the difficult war years and the cynical twenties.

The progressive movement in the Middle West, generated in the years 1900 to 1914, represented a protest against the machine (chiefly the Republican machine, since it was dominant) not solely because it was a machine, but because it was evidently controlled by men and interests who were using it for their own ends. For this protest the agricultural class, its roots deep in nineteenth-century agrarian radicalism, provided the impetus, while insurgent Republicanism provided the means of expression. This progressivism did not make its way without opposition of the strongest sort. To combat it, business interests organized into national, local, and trade groups—the National Association of Manufacturers, the National Metal Trades, the Citizen's Industrial Association, the Citizens' Alliance, the Anti-Boycott Association (later the League for Industrial Rights), and others. They sent lobbyists to state capitals and to Washington to harry progressive legislation before its passage and tie it up in the courts afterward. With tremendous resources to draw upon, a keen sense of propaganda values, and long experience in back-room politics, these men were powerful political forces. Nevertheless, by 1908, progressive Republicans and a few progressive Democrats controlled the Midwest and, with occasional setbacks, kept control until 1914.

Ohio, Michigan, Indiana, and Illinois, where Eastern-industrial ties were strongest, were touched only lightly by progressivism. In them (even under the impulse of Roosevelt's Bull Moosers) the regular Republican organizations managed to stay in power. Michigan elected Chase Osborn as a progressive Republican in 1910, but the party saddled him with a conservative platform and a hostile senate. Ohio was controlled during the same period by Republicans like Foraker (corporation attorney), Foster (speculator and businessman), Payne (Standard Oil), Brice (railroads and stocks), and others. For twenty some years after the election of Governor Nash in 1900, the state had a succession of Republican governors representing chiefly business-industrial elements; passage of progressive legislation in Ohio after 1910 came late and primarily as a concession to the Roosevelt influence within the party. Of the more industrialized portions of the Midwest, none was really progressive in the La Follette-Cummins-Johnson-Crawford sense. The tradition of Grangerism and Populism was weak in those states, and their liberalism was Eastern rather than Midwestern in spirit and origin.

Midwestern progressivism after 1900 was a distinctly regional movement, growing logically out of the recent past and consciously local in application. "There must be eventually, and possibly very soon," said John A. Johnson in 1905,

a new political alignment. . . . The great center of political power should be in the Mississippi valley, instead of on the Atlantic Coast. The best brain and the surest brawn of the nation is found here, and it should be organized into one mighty moral, material, and patriotic force to overthrow the new paternalism and plunder, and regenerate politics and the Republic. To the resources, the energies and genius of the West, the nation looks, not only to build up its commercial and industrial greatness, but its moral and political strength.

Progressivism, Johnson shrewdly recognized, was locally powerful but regionally disunited. It needed to be bound together in one huge movement centered in and representing the Midwest.

However, it had no central point of crystallization, no dominant personality to tie it together, no latter-day Bryan, though men like La Follette, Cummins, and the others were supreme on their home grounds. Theodore Roosevelt, after his accidental elevation to the Presidency, might have welded the elements together—indeed, it looked for a time as if he were the one to do it—but he did not. The force of his personality and the apparent liberalism of his program did unite certain disparate elements of progressivism between 1904 and 1908; had he been more of a progressive and less of a politician he might have made the union permanent. But the Square Deal failed in the pinch. The Bull Moosers paraded down a different road to defeat and dissolution. Midwest progressivism, its ranks depleted by the raids of both Roosevelt and Wilson, saw its own procession vacillate, disperse, and ultimately reform more than a decade later under its once-repudiated leader, La Follette.

The assassin's bullet that cut down McKinley put a man already committed to progressivism into the White House. Both the political leaders of the Midwest and the city and state reformers of the East had begun their work, and T. R. seemed to be the national leader they all prayed for. No man ever stepped into the Presidency with a greater following or more personal power than Theodore Roosevelt. Not quite forty-three, vigorous, and energetic, with a sharp intellect, a quick mind, and a thirst for information, Roosevelt certainly possessed superb equipment for a politician. He was an experienced administrator, with a genius for personal contracts and a good sense of public relations, his appeal wide and his personal charm devastating. He could, as John Hay once said, "organize the unorganizable" by sheer personality.

Roosevelt was also a wizard at group diplomacy. He had an ambidextrous ability to please everybody, to have something for everyone, to catch the prevailing tone of any time or the temper of any group—cowboy, war hero, stern prosecutor of graft and crime, brilliant (though superficial) scholar, and so on. When the country went to war, T.R. was there with the Rough Riders and in the headlines. How many knew or cared that he was second in command, and who heard of Colonel Wood, his superior? If the public criticized college football, there was T.R. with a carefully balanced statement on the matter. If the public liked cowboys, T.R. owned a ranch, had cowboys to lunch, and wore a cowboy hat and a red bandanna to the 1900 Republican convention. He knew Bat Nelson, Bob Fitzsimmons, John L. Sullivan, President Eliot of Harvard, Booker T. Washington, Confederate soldiers (his uncle fought for the South), college professors, stockbrokers—name a prominent man in any walk of life and Roosevelt probably knew him. With his gift for phrases—the "big stick," the "square deal," the "malefactors of great wealth"—he said dramatically and concisely what people thought and wanted to hear. "Teddy" was a familiar face peering out of the newspaper and a familiar name in the headlines before he even went to Washington to serve as Vice-President under McKinley. He seemed in 1901 to be the heaven-sent answer to the progressive prayer for a national leader.

However great the promise of Roosevelt seemed in 1901, some progressives looked at the party he represented and wondered about his future. "The bondsmen of plutocracy," as John Bascom called them, held the party leadership—Chauncey Depew of New York, Allison of Iowa, Elkins of West Virginia, Quay of Pennsylvania, Platt of Connecticut, Aldrich of Rhode

Island—mostly Easterners and nearly all businessmen. Could T.R. do more than chip a few flakes off this rock or drive in the wedge La Follette and the rest had fashioned? The Democratic party, badly divided on sectional lines, could furnish only token opposition to the Republican machine. Bryan Democrats, mostly reconstructed Western Populists, were soundly hated in the East, especially in the vicinity of Tammany, and Bryan had been read out of the party several times by Eastern and Southern Democrats.

Mark Hanna made the Republican party a hierarchy of power, a tightly controlled, businesslike corporation, its power centralized in a group of men who were for the most part in the Senate. It was a real cabal, probably the most powerful in Senate history, which formed policy, imposed it on both House and Senate, and ran the government openly in the interests of the organization. Hanna, who entered the Senate after 1900, provided the necessary contacts between business and party. Spooner of Wisconsin, a good debater and a man of fine legal mind, served as floor leader. Allison of Iowa was the cloakroom specialist, the conciliator and adjuster, the tester of sentiment—so pussyfooted, said Ingalls of Kansas, he could walk across the continent on piano keys and never make a sound. Platt was the practical New England boss, a good man to execute the plans others made, like Quay and Penrose and others who stayed on the fringe of the group. The leader, the unquestioned manager of Republican party politics, was Nelson Aldrich of Rhode Island.

Nelson Aldrich, chairman of the Senate Finance Committee, deserves a second look. One of the richest men in Congress (his daughter married Rockefeller's son), he was the only one of the current Republican leaders who possessed a coherent philosophy of government. He believed none of this nonsense about the worth of the masses or the voice of the people, who were "easily led, easily deceived, easily betrayed." His cardinal political principle, said a Washington correspondent who knew him well, was "that mankind is composed of two parts—the

226

rulers and the ruled." This worked out, in practice, into a variety of Hamiltonianism. Allow the people to express their collective will in government, said Aldrich, but give the leaders the power to administer government and to veto that which was unwise, and you would have a stable, efficient, and relatively successful republic. Who were the real leaders? The men of business, naturally; society was hierarchal, its foundation composed of a trusting electorate, a few rulers from the wealthy industrial class over them. Aldrich believed quite sincerely that the future of the nation depended upon "the assured progress and prosperity of our manufacturing," always represented business in government, and never hesitated to say so. Tall, cold, arrogant, dignified, Aldrich was a skilled, intelligent, and ruthless politician. In the Senate he was forever on the move, giving advice here and information there, in touch with all the Republicans in the chambers, impressing his will on them by a combination of authority and charm; Hansborough of North Dakota said he had an influence like chloroform. From his position in the Senate he controlled committee appointments, passed or killed bills with a nod, held the party purse strings, and controlled a good share of the patronage. He represented everything progressivism hated. After 1900 "Aldrichism" was a bitter epithet in the Midwest.

Theodore Roosevelt knew all the rules, yet never played the game wholly by them. An aristocratic and wealthy young Easterner, he began his career in politics after leaving Harvard and worked his way up in the party in the approved manner. During his three terms in the New York state legislature he displayed no pronounced liberal tendencies. He voted against a twelve-hour day for streetcar conductors as "socialistic and un-American," supported a vicious prison labor-contract system, opposed teacher pensions, and in general acted the way a young Republican of the day should. He was given to extreme statements (that he later regretted) such as his opinon that "radical" groups could be suppressed only "by taking ten or a dozen of their leaders out, standing . . . them against a wall, and shooting them dead." Yet in the New York legislature, a notoriously corrupt one, young Roosevelt saw the grimy side of politics and did not like it. Retiring to his Western ranch to regain his health, he bounced back in 1886 into a three-cornered race with Henry George and Abram Hewitt for the mayoralty of New York City. After losing, he traveled abroad, returning to serve as federal Civil Service Commissioner, as gangbusting Police Commissioner of New York, and as Assistant Secretary of the Navy. He resigned to lead the Rough Riders in Cuba, emerging in late 1898 as perhaps its best-known warrior.

His political experience had been slight, and that mostly confined to administration, where he had proved himself to be an able and trustworthy executive. There was little to stamp him as a liberal. He applauded Cleveland's use of troops in the Pullman strike; thought Altgeld one of the nation's most dangerous men (he refused to meet him socially because he felt they might have to meet later "sword to sword" on the field of battle); and was horrified at Bryan's "semi-socialistic agrarian movement . . . supported mainly because it is hoped thereby to damage the well-to-do and thrifty." On the other hand, he possessed a thorough distaste for corrupt politics and had a sincere sympathy for the poor and oppressed.

Roosevelt was already familiar to the New York Republican machine as an honest and not quite regular party politician. Yet he undeniably possessed the greatest of all political assets, popularity, and Boss Tom Platt somewhat unwillingly put him in the race for governor, which he won handily. This was Platt's great mistake, for Roosevelt began a house cleaning that rattled the Republican structure to its foundations. Too strong for Platt to kill off politically, Roosevelt was an intolerable threat to the state machine, so more in desperation than in anything else, Platt decided to bury him safely in the Vice-Presidency. Mark Hanna, at the 1900 convention, first refused to have anything to do with "that damned cowboy" but as a favor to Platt and McKinley finally agreed to accept him as McKinley's running mate.

"I told McKinley," burst out Hanna at the news of the assassination, "that it was a mistake to nominate that wild man at Philadelphia." To the Republican machine McKinley's death was a terrific blow. The whole party program was predicated on the assumption of a regular party man in the White House, and T.R. was not only obviously irregular but possibly uncontrollable. But he upset no applecarts. He retained McKinley's cabinet *in toto*. He reassured the bosses, saying, "I work with such tools as come to my hand. I am not going to quarrel with Platt or any other man. I am going as far as I can in working with the big and little bosses in every state." For the reassurance of business he remarked, "The mechanism of modern business is so delicate that extreme care must be taken not to interfere with it in a spirit of rashness or ignorance." The Republican satraps looked him over and found him good. "Mr. Roosevelt," said Hanna, emerging from a conference with him, "is an entirely different man today from what he was a few weeks since. He has now acquired all that is needed to round out his character—equipoise and conservatism." Platt thought him "a little loose on the relations of labor, on trusts and combinations" but essentially sound, while *Gunton's Magazine,* looking over his record carefully, concluded that he was "eminently practical and truly conservative."

Roosevelt's first term produced nothing sensational. Perfectly willing to work with the Old Guard, he still never quite let them know where they stood. Hanna, Aldrich, George Perkins of the House of Morgan, A. J. Cassatt of the Pennsylvania Railroad, and James Stillman of the Rockefeller group gave him advice, but they were never sure that it sank in. His first message to Congress, a tremendous thirty-thousand-word document, called for practically everything—trust regulation, extension of the powers of the ICC, a new immigration policy, a revitalized merchant marine, a big navy, a Panama canal, extension of civil service, conservation programs, irrigation projects, more money for the Library of Congress, better treatment of the Indians, a stronger Monroe Doctrine, a better pension system for veterans, and so on. Actually, however, little was done to offend the party leaders in spite of the promises of the message.

Roosevelt ordered his Attorney General to proceed against Northern Securities and eventually cracked it, but his widely publicized campaign against the trusts fizzled out quickly. The story was current that in 1902 during a meeting at Oyster Bay Roosevelt, Spooner, Lodge, Hanna, and Allison agreed that if Roosevelt would leave the party's economic and financial policy to Aldrich, he would be granted a free hand in everything else. Whatever the reason, trust busting slowed down appreciably in 1903. The tariff question never came up seriously, and though he urged Congress to add power to the Interstate Commerce Commission, Roosevelt did little about it beyond signing the weak Elkins bill. His intervention in the coal strike of 1902, the creation of the Panama Canal Zone, his conservation program—these were the main products of his first term, none of them burning issues. So well did he walk the line between promise and reality that his nomination for re-election in 1904 was a foregone conclusion, and his two-million majority and 336 electoral votes (the biggest margin of victory up to his time) testified to his tremendous popular appeal.

Progressives in the Midwest, and some of those in the East, were badly disappointed in Roosevelt. Flower of the *Arena,* frankly believed that T.R. offered little hope; there was but one man really feared by "every corruptionist, grafter, and exploiter of the people," thought Flower, and that man was Robert La Follette. Edgar Lee Masters, the Chicago poet-reformer, called Roosevelt an opportunist, a man of no set principles, a believer in "sheer animalism." A Kansas editor commented that there was "no known instance of his alienating a strong politician of his party," and Joseph Miller of Cleveland, comparing him to Tom Johnson, believed him "an incipient Tory," a "man of unapplied maxims." To Louis Post of the Chicago *Public* it was quite significant that "there is no real hostility cherished at the present time against President Roosevelt by the trusts, the railway corporations, and the privileged interests." The most careful and perhaps the most damning analysis of Roosevelt's three years as "progressive" President came from Frank Parsons, the economist and lawyer. First of all, Parsons pointed out, Roosevelt stood in with the party bosses far too well. He had failed signally to break the railroads and, except for Northern Securities, he had likewise failed to prosecute trusts with any real vigor. On the civil service, tariff, and other important questions he had shown no signs whatever of constructive thinking. Parsons could find no place for Roosevelt in progressive ranks, but he recognized the great potentials the man possessed. "A word from you," he wrote Roosevelt, "will set men and machinery and influences at work that will accomplish wonders."

Parsons represented fairly well the progressive hope that Roosevelt's second term would accomplish something worth while. Most progressives supported him. They recognized that as an "accidental president" he possessed no clear mandate from the people, and that saddled as he was with McKinley's cabinet, McKinley's program, and McKinley's bosses, he could hardly turn the world upside down in three years. The progressives tended to blame Aldrich, or Hanna, or somebody else for Roosevelt's lack of direction and to retain faith in the man while damning his party.

But the Republican convention of 1904, the platform, and the campaign itself did very little to encourage progressive elements in or out of the Republican party. The convention, said Louis Post, was "a mass meeting under the management of corporation directors." La Follette's contesting Wisconsin delegation was ousted in favor of Spooner's, and the steam roller crushed all other opposition. Nor was Roosevelt's program a progressive document, promising prosecution of "bad" trusts and protection to those "lawfully formed for lawful purposes," a statement so vague as to be practically meaningless.

The 1904 campaign, except for the vibrant personality of Roosevelt, was colorless and uninteresting. The Democratic candidate, Judge Alton Parker, was an honest, dignified man,

and his party, controlled by the same set of interests that controlled the Republican, offered a mildly liberal program.
Roosevelt made much of a supposed remark by Boies Penrose
that the corporations had put up five million to defeat him,
but it added little spice to the campaign in the light of the
well-known fact that Rockefeller, Morgan, Depew, H. H.
Rogers, Harriman, Mellon, Hyde, Frick, and others had contributed largely to his own campaign funds. (The trusts complained later when T.R. attacked them, claiming that their
1904 campaign contributions were understood to have granted
them immunity. "We bought the son of a bitch," remarked
Frick, "and he didn't stay bought.") Whether Roosevelt knew
the implications of his backing, or whether he cared, is beside
the point. The progressive elements still supported him,
trusted him, believed in him, and thought he deserved a
chance to do what he could on his own in the Presidency.

After 1904 Roosevelt looked better to them. He very skill-
fully maintained party harmony while enunciating liberal
principles and, it is true, produced some concrete results. The
plain fact remained, however, that he left a great deal undone.
Separating the spectacular promise from the measurable
achievement, progressives found in 1908 that Roosevelt had
to his credit the Hepburn Act of 1906 extending the powers of
the ICC (but not enough); the Meat and Pure Food Act of
1906; the Employers' Liability Act of 1906; the law of 1908
limiting trainmen's hours; and an act of 1907 prohibiting
corporation contributions to campaign funds. His attitude
toward trusts was difficult to assess. "We must draw a line,"
Roosevelt said over and over, "against misconduct, not against
wealth." He wished, he said in his 1903 message, "to hold in
check the unscrupulous man, whether employer or employee,
but to refuse to weaken initiative or to hamper and cramp the
industrial development of the country." He discriminated, he
repeated in 1906, "between those combinations which do good
and those combinations which do evil." All this Mr. Dooley,
Finlay Peter Dunne's Irish commentator, neatly explained as

meaning. "Th' trusts are heejous monsters built up be th' inlightened intherprise iv th' men that have done so much to advance progress in our beloved counthry. On wan hand I wud stamp thim under fut; on th' other hand, not so fast."

Nevertheless, many progressives still clung to the belief that "Teddy" had done the best he could. When in the last months of his term he outlined a sweeping program of reform—physical valuation of railroads for tax purposes, workmen's compensation, regulation of stocks, a stronger ICC, tariff revision, real trust busting, and so on—they took heart again. It all sounded, remarked a St. Louis paper hopefully, "like the preamble to the Populist platform." Roosevelt named Taft, his Secretary of War, as the man to carry the program out, and most of the Midwest progressives followed along, but the election results reflected their suspicion. Five Midwest states voted for Taft over Bryan, but the same five states elected Democratic governors. They would accept what appeared to be Republican progressive leadership on the national level, but not Republican leadership at home.

Whether or not Roosevelt was really a progressive during his two terms as President is an open question. It is doubtful that he possessed, during the years 1900 to 1908, a coherent and organized theory of politics beyond his general desire to institute honest and efficient government. It was not until after he had retired from the Presidency that he developed, under the influence of Eastern intellectuals such as Herbert Croly, a more distinctively progressive political philosophy. From 1900 to 1908 Roosevelt's three chief interests, as shown in his speeches and actions, were regulation of corporations, conservation, and the extension of governmental power in social and economic areas, all of them in agreement with Midwestern progressive aims. Yet his policy toward corporations was certainly not that of Bryan and the Populists, nor that of La Follette and the post-1900 Midwesterners. "As a matter of fact," he confided to a friend in 1908, "I have let up in every case where I have had any possible excuse for so doing." He took a middle road between the Populist-Granger principle of destroying trusts and the La Follette policy of regulating them to insure competition. Roosevelt chose to take his stand on the principle of *establishing* the right to regulate, a wholly different emphasis. He considered the "rural Tories" of the Midwest, who wished to curb the trust or smash it, as no progressives at all, but simply wreckers. Conservation and social legislation, as La Follette pointed out, were progressive issues indeed, but significantly they were not controversial party issues either. Roosevelt's progressivism, it was suspected, stopped where party politics began. The Midwestern states, said La Follette, had done much more on all counts than T.R. had done in seven and one-half years.

In other words, certain Midwestern progressives felt in 1908 that Roosevelt was either not a progressive at all or (more charitably) a progressive of decidedly limited aims and enthusiasms. He talked a great deal, but failed to produce. "This cannonading," wrote La Follette of T.R.'s crusades, "first in one direction and then the other, filled the air with noise and smoke, which confused and obscured the line of action, but when the battle cloud drifted by and quiet was restored, it was always a matter of surprise that so little had really been accomplished." Louis Post, somewhat to the left of La Follette, thought Roosevelt "incapable of cooperation . . . and generally irresponsible," concluding that "progressivism would be stronger without him." Eugene Debs, on the socialist left and one of the gentlest of men, could barely speak or write of him with restraint. But a good many progressives held their tongues, content to accept what minor progress T.R. had undoubtedly made and to hope for more under Taft.

Roosevelt's real contribution to Midwestern progressivism did not come from the fact that he was part of it (for he was not) nor from what he accomplished for it, for he accomplished little. It lay instead in the leadership he assumed in the progressive movement at large—a leadership that the Midwest accepted with reservations, but nevertheless accepted. There was in the nation in 1900 a vague but powerful drift toward honest, efficient, and representative government. Roosevelt became its spearhead. Whether he led the way or whether he stepped in at the head of a procession that had already formed (Roosevelt believed the latter) is beside the question. He was important to progressivism because he was the first President after the Civil War who understood what had happened to the nation socially, politically, and economically since 1865. He dramatized the conflict between progressivism and conservatism, made it alive and important, and caught the imagination of the people with it, even though he did not resolve it. For reasons of temperament he was unable to resolve it, since his principles dissolved too often into glittering generalities "We are neither for the rich man nor the poor man as such, but for the upright man, rich or poor," is a cheeringly liberal statement, but one difficult to put into law books. Yet his contributions to the rising wave of progressivism were not inconsiderable. The teeth, the eyeglasses, the bouncing vitality, the "big stick" and the "strenuous life," the St. George-like sallies against the trusts—all of these were trademarks of a muscular, youthful, aggressive, optimistic democracy that captured the nation's fancy.

Roosevelt's failure as a progressive leader in the period 1900 to 1908 was the result of certain traits in his own character that were liabilities as well as assets. He hoped to be all things to everybody, something a reformer cannot be. Roosevelt was therefore often led to compromise in order to maintain his standing as an all-round political athlete. "The men who wish to work for decent politics," he wrote in 1904, "must work practically . . . ," a principle he held through his entire career. There was in him none of the tenacity, the grimness, the relentless rectitude that was La Follette's strength as a leader and one of his political weaknesses. "How I wish I wasn't a reformer, oh, Senator!" he whote Chauncey Depew. "But I suppose I must live up to my part. . . ."

Roosevelt also had more than his share of what Mark Twain

called "the circus side of a man's nature." He was an inveterate showman, unable to resist a scene even if it meant a slight stretching of principles. His pursuit of his quarry resembled a Long Island fox hunt, in which the fox was brought to earth amid great hallooing but released to run again another day. He was a spectacular man, taking San Juan Hill, stalking lions or trusts, scolding the "mollycoddles," but never quite making anything more than a game of it. It is hard to imagine Roosevelt sitting down, as La Follette did a few years later, with a mountain of records night after night to become a tariff expert in a few weeks in order to defeat a bad tariff bill. But Roosevelt in 1904 probably represented better than La Follette what the public wanted. The mass of the people did not quite know which way to turn in the titanic conflict between progressivism and the interests, and Roosevelt quite honestly reflected that indecision. As one of his advisers put it bluntly, his real power came from the fact that he "understood the psychology of the mutt."

Certainly the most important political problem of the Roosevelt era was the trust, which displaced free silver as a major issue after 1896. "At the dawn of a new century," wrote William Main in the *Forum* in 1901, "no political question in sight appears to be of more interest. . . ." From 1898 to 1900, forty corporations were formed, among them such mammoths as Amalgamated Copper, Consolidated Tobacco, and the reorganized Standard Oil. "The old foes," remarked a Populist, "with new faces." By 1900 practically all of the worth-while railroad lines were controlled by six groups. In 1901 Harriman merged the Southern Pacific and Union Pacific, placing the whole Southwest under his thumb; the same year Northern Securities tried to do the same in the Northwest; and still in the same year United States Steel combined two hundred and fifty subsidiary companies into Morgan's colossus. The relation of the state to industry was suddenly important, more so than ever before. Streams of articles poured into the *Forum,* the

Independent, and the *Arena,* testifying to the popular interest. In 1899 alone there were published twenty-eight books on trusts and more than two hundred magazine articles.

What was the answer? Leave the trust alone? Harass it out of existence with the Sherman Act? Smash it with a new and stronger law? Prosecute only the "bad" trust? Bar it from politics? Recognize its advantages and regulate it in the public interest? Take it over as state property? Hedge it about with restrictions to insure competition? And at what point did business become "big" or "bad"? It was not a question solely of how to handle the trust, but of how to define it. Both antitrust and protrust forces found it difficult to clear any ground for debate in the midst of semantic and economic confusion.

The Trust Conference of 1899, held in Chicago, illustrated the prevailing uncertainty very well. Gompers of the American Federation of Labor, Hoges of the Knights of Labor, representatives of the steel workers, garment makers, and other labor groups met with Republicans, Democrats, and Socialists and with academics such as Ely, Commons, Bemis, Adams of Michigan, and Folwell of Minnesota—all bent on finding out what trusts were and what to do about them. Conclusions were vague. About sixty delegates favored a "let alone" policy; about the same number wanted "legislation" as a remedy, favoring some sort of commission regulation. A year later another convention in Chicago, attended by delegates from thirty-one states, made somewhat sharper decisions favoring government ownership of railroad, telegraph, and telephone, bank-trust regulations, tariff revisions, and direct legislation to break the alliance of trust and politics. Truly, the *Western Christian Advocate* remarked, the time had come for the people to "call the soulless corporation to account."

It was not easy to do. Perhaps the most difficult distinction to draw was that between the "good" and the "bad" trust. Of the existence of trusts there was no doubt, but at what point did they become pernicious? Louis Post set up three standards of judgment: a trust which consolidates functions to effect economic savings to be passed along to the consumer is good; a trust that brings natural resources or essential services under private control is *potentially* bad; a trust which exists to fix prices or stifle competition is *ipso facto* bad. Albert Beveridge, in 1900, agreed essentially with Post's first and third criteria, while Richard Ely defined as "bad" any trust which precluded competition. Gary of the steel trust made his distinction in 1901 on the basis of responsibility—a trust which is responsible to the public is good, one that is irresponsible is bad. Bryan after 1900 suggested forcing a firm to take out a federal license when it controlled 25 per cent or more of the business in a specified area. Van Hise of Wisconsin would allow a combination to control not more than 50 per cent of a business field, a percentage later reduced to thirty by La Follette. The great difficulty clearly lay in recognizing the trust on the one hand as a normal economic development, while on the other curbing it in such a fashion as to prevent monopoly.

To many businessmen the "let alone" policy was fair enough. Trusts existed as the products of normal laissez-faire economics and by the same economics ought to be able to regulate themselves. The good ones would last, believed J. Sterling Morton, and the bad ones would not; one simply depended on competition to eliminate the undesirables. Roswell P. Flower pointed out in *Gunton's* that trusts were legal, stable, effective, permanent, and efficient; so long as they operated legitimately they should be left strictly alone. George Gunton's *Trusts and the Public* in 1899 arrived at much the same conclusion, and William Graham Sumner's *Earth Hunger and Other Essays* warned that if trusts had evolved by natural economic processes, it was obviously vain to oppose them as well as foolish to tamper with evolutionary law. "No large industry," remarked Gary in 1902, "can last in America unless it is founded on the basis of competition, that is, of survival of the fittest" —a neat use of science to bolster an economic principle.

Generally the public came to accept the Rooseveltian distinction between the "good" and the "bad" trust, recognizing that the trust possibly possessed certain economic advantages that somehow ought to be kept, while at the same time its evil tendencies should be restricted. "When great economic advantage can be shown from concentration of industry," wrote Van Hise in *Concentration and Control,* "such concentration should not be broken up or prohibited, but it must be controlled." Competition alone was evidently insufficient to regulate them, and, since trusts did business in more than one state as a rule, federal control of them seemed to be the answer.

The kind of control to be established over the trust was another question. The *Press Post* of Columbus, Ohio, advocated using taxes, "the Achilles' heel" of trusts, to keep them down to a reasonable size. The *Arena* thought that the only real cure for trusts was proper use of an inheritance tax, to prevent huge concentrations of capital. Another editor suggested a consumer boycott of "bad" trusts; another wanted stiffer regulations governing the formation of corporations and higher corporation taxes; and another believed higher taxes and revised tariff schedules would do the job. Others believed that the competition of co-operatives might serve to keep the monopoly in line, seeing the answer to the trust problems in businesses like the Dan Patch Electric Railroad ("the road built by the People, without Wall Street") from St. Paul to Rochester, Minnesota.

The remnants of the Populists and many of the Bryan Democrats agreed with the Socialists that public ownership of certain key monopolies was the only real cure for the trusts. "A fundamental law of nature, a vital principle," said the *Farmer's Voice,* "is violated every time a private monopoly is permitted to exist." Another school of thought disagreed both with those who wished to leave them alone and those who advocated regulating or owning them. Every monopoly rested upon some special privilege, they said, whether it be use of land, tax concessions, patent grants, favorable operating laws, access to natural resources, transportation, or tariffs. "Privilege," wrote Tom Johnson of Cleveland, "is the advantage con-

ferred on one by law of denying the competition of others."
The "repeal of the laws which give them the privileges under
which they flourish," said the St. Louis *Mirror,* was the single
certain method by which the trust might be controlled. To do
this meant breaking up the alliance between business and
politics, drying up the stream of privilege at its source. Direct
primaries, direct legislation, election reforms, and corrupt-
practices acts struck at the trusts because they struck at "government by special privilege." Get rid of the "menace of the
machine," as La Follette called it, and you also might rid
yourself of the menace of monopoly. The connection between
business and politics, personified most vividly to the 1900's by
Mark Hanna, was the key link of the whole chain of economics
on which the trust depended; its "union with corrupt political
bosses and the money-controlled party machines" must be
broken.

Antitrust legislation passed in the Roosevelt era reflected
the current confusion on the issue. The Sherman Act of 1890
was allowed to languish (only eighteen suits were instituted
under its provisions down to 1901) not only because the act
itself seemed impossible to interpret clearly, but also because
neither courts nor government were willing to go as far as it
went. The Sherman Act did not really smash trusts in theory,
or regulate them in practice. After 1900 fewer people wanted
to smash them and more wanted to regulate them, but no one
seemed willing to introduce into the federal system the device
of regulation by commission already adopted by the Midwest
progressives. Roosevelt's creation of a Bureau of Commissions
in the new Department of Commerce and Labor was a tentative step in this direction, but the bureau possessed only investigative powers.

The railroads seemed to fall into a separate category, quite
distinct from other monopolies in the popular mind. They
were closest to the Midwestern shipper and consumer and most
bitterly hated, and railroad men themselves (such as Chauncey
Depew and Charles Francis Adams) admitted that they were

guilty of flagrant misdeeds. The railroads possessed the best legal talent money could buy, who tore huge holes in the shoddy Granger legislation of the seventies. The Nebraska and Texas rate cases of 1898, in which it was held that state commissions had no right to set "unreasonably low" rates, showed how the Granger railroad laws might be circumvented. Yet these early state commissions, frustrated as they often were, helped to publicize the war against the railroads and forced them to recognize their public responsibilities a trifle more clearly.

The agitation begun by the Midwest farmer and joined by the urban worker resulted eventually in the adoption of the regulatory commission on a federal scale. The Interstate Commerce Act of 1887, administered by a federal commission, was designed to prevent some of the worst railroad abuses, but the act's provisions were often easily evaded by railroad lawyers and its powers were gradually shorn off, one by one. In 1896 the commission did succeed for the first time in obtaining testimony from the railroads themselves, but in 1897 it received a nearly fatal blow from the Supreme Court. After that it languished. In 1900 the commission handled only nineteen complaints, and reported that "the railways still make discriminations, perhaps to as great an extent as before."

The act of 1887, however, showed the trend of public opinion. Despite the constant complaint of railroad men that regulation crippled the industry, sentiment for it grew. J. Sterling Morton pointed out the huge taxes paid by railroads and praised the services they provided; Sidney Dillon of the Union Pacific called them "the means and evidence of the unexampled prosperity of the United States"; and the *Indianapolis Standard* claimed that had it not been for railroads half the West would still live in sod houses. But the stubborn fact remained, said the United States Commissioner of Labor, that about ten men, nearly all of whom lived in New York City, controlled most of the railroads of the country. Following Theodore Roosevelt's lead, legislation for the regulation of industry, and especially of railroads, increased in amount and importance. The Elkins Act of 1903 forbade discriminations and rebates, and the Hepburn Act of 1906 enlarged both the size of the ICC and its powers. An Interstate Commerce Reform Convention in 1904, attended by La Follette, Cummins, Van Sant, and other Midwestern governors, urged Roosevelt to allow the ICC even greater control over business, a request finally answered by the Mann-Elkins Act of 1910, which increased and clarified its authority.

Though there was a tendency to establish tighter governmental regulation of industry during the period 1900 to 1908, the trend toward consolidation and combination in business slowed down, but it did not stop. "It really seems hard . . . ," said Jim Hill, thinking of the old freebooting days, "that we should now be compelled to fight for our lives against political adventurers who have never done anything but pose and draw a salary." But the plain fact was that the public, which had long watched business running politics, could see no reason why politics should not run business. For decades the railroads and other business combinations had bought the people's legislators and packed the people's conventions. It was not much use for businessmen to cry after 1900 that business was private business, removed from politics, for it never had been removed from politics.

The truth was that the era of the businessman was drawing to a close. The temper of national life had changed since 1870, the philosophy of democracy was no longer so popularly nor so solidly based on Darwin and Adam Smith. The issues of 1870 were by no means fully settled—indeed, the real settlement had hardly begun—but the alliance between government and business was not so strong as before, the trust under closer rein, the financier not quite so firmly certain of his ground.

Betrayal and Survival, 1908–1920

VI

"Spotless Town" was the creation of a soap advertising campaign. From magazine after magazine, the clean, happy, orderly community looked out at the reader, a miniature Utopia of smiling, decent citizens—selling Sapolio. The progressives wanted "Spotless Town" too, politically cleansed, honest and upright, without a trace of the grime of graft, privilege, and corruption. They cleaned up the legislatures and scrubbed the city councils, and, picking up the pails and brushes, looked at Washington.

Someone had to lead the procession to "Spotless Town." An assassin's bullet conveniently supplied a leader who seemed to be going in the right direction (though occasionally his compass wavered) and his appointed heir was ready to step in when the leader checked out in 1908. Progress was not all it might have been, true, and the progressives were far from "Spotless Town" when he left, but the road was open. The gleaming vision of "Spotless Town" kept fading as the procession went on. Reform turned into protest,

protest into rebellion, and when rebellion found a new leader the world broke out in flames. Democracy had to help put it out; when it ended democracy was no more spotless, it seemed, than before.

THE RESULT OF THE ELECTION of 1908 was almost a foregone conclusion. Taft campaigned on the promise that he would "devote all the ability that is in me to the constructive work of suggesting to the Congress the means by which the Roosevelt policies shall be clinched." *Everybody's* judged him "the proper successor to Mr. Roosevelt, pre-eminently the man to meet and solve the issues raised by the Roosevelt administration." In the Midwest, however, there was some suspicion that the Republican party was not so progressive as Roosevelt made it seem. This suspicion grew when the minority platform submitted by La Follette's Wisconsin delegation to the national convention was thrown out as "socialistic and Democratic" because it contained such planks as tariff revision, a tariff commission, and revaluation of railroad property for taxation. Yet the platform in its final form did contain an antitrust and a tariff-revision pledge, and since Taft had promised to be a real progressive, most of the Midwestern Republican progressives kept quiet. The Democrats nominated Bryan for the third time and resumed, as *Harper's* remarked, "their usual occupation of electing a Republican President." Eugene Debs ran as the Socialist candidate, and T. L. Higsen as the candidate of William Randolph Hearst's third-party Independence League. There was not much doubt about the outcome. After Taft carried twenty-nine states, the nation settled down to four more years of Republican progressivism, while Roosevelt went to Africa to hunt big game.

Few besides Taft realized that Roosevelt had blithely left behind him a whole bundle of highly controversial problems. Roosevelt had talked loudly about tariffs and trusts, then had happily taken ship for Africa, leaving the thankless and nearly impossible job of carrying out the somewhat vague promises in the Republican platform. Taft thought his was the hardest job faced by any President since Lincoln. After his inauguration it took not much more than ninety days for the Republican machine to show very clear evidences of internal friction. There was in Congress in 1908 and after a hard core of Midwest and Western progressives, men from the Populist and Granger states, who had trailed along with Roosevelt and now expected something to be done. Roosevelt's compromises disturbed them, but at the same time Taft had been advertised as an eighteen-carat progressive and they waited for results. When they did not get them, they nearly blew the party apart.

The original recalcitrant, of course, was Bob La Follette, who arrived in the Senate in 1906 to pursue a lonely path for two years before receiving any reinforcement. He was, Dolliver said later, "the first among the Republican political leaders to realize the character of the irrepressible conflict within the party, between public interests and the present day organization of business." In his autobiography La Follette told the story of those early years—how he had been shunned and covertly insulted by his Old Guard colleagues while he fought alone and unsuccessfully for his principles. The regular Republicans ostentatiously left the chamber when he spoke; once, in 1906, he remarked that unless the senators paid more attention to the public interest, the seats temporarily vacant might be permanently vacated after election.

Jonathan Dolliver of Iowa, La Follette's first ally, was a convert from conservatism. Allison brought him into the Senate in 1901, where until Allison's death he voted standpat with clocklike regularity, but Dolliver, a Methodist minister's son, wondered about the politics he saw around him and tried in 1906 to break out of the party line. Allison, so the story went, begged him to wait—an old man, dying slowly. Allison had played the game for twenty years and wanted to see his protégé follow the rules. A big, shambling man, Dolliver was a charming and friendly fellow (not one of his associates or opponents failed to mention this fact) who possessed the sharpest tongue of any of the insurgents. At his best, Dolliver was magnificent. Beveridge, a speaker of parts himself, thought him the greatest orator in the English-speaking world. Dolliver, alone of the progressives, could penetrate Aldrich's complacency and occasionally drove him off the floor with his barbs.

Albert Cummins, who came into the Senate in 1908 to replace the deceased Allison, teamed up with La Follette and Dolliver almost at once. A handsome, dignified man with sad eyes and handle-bar mustaches, Cummins possessed neither Dolliver's skill in debate nor La Follette's hammering energy, but he did have a hard, solid mind and long experience as a practical politician. Joseph Bristow of Kansas arrived in 1909, a product of Kansas Populism and a long-time hater of railroads. Sardonic, tough-minded, aggressive, Bristow was a throwback to the days of Jerry Simpson. His vocabulary was unpolished, his voice harsh and rasping, and in debate he hit Kansas fashion above or below the belt. But Bristow was a hard worker and an earnest progressive, with an element of La Follette's grimness in his makeup. "It is not always comfortable to be hooted at as an Insurgent," he wrote in 1909, "but I know I am standing for the things that are just to the people of this country and I intend to keep it up."

Moses Clapp of Minnesota was perhaps the least colorful of the group. A slow, tall, serious man, he admired La Follette and looked on him much as a bulldog looks on a terrier. Clapp's conversion to progressivism was slow but inexorable; he found his independence late, but never wavered afterward. "I'm a dyed-in-the-wool Republican," he said, "but I contend that a man should not only have the right party but that his party should be right." William E. Borah of Idaho represented the progressive West and was one of Aldrich's few political errors. When he came into the Senate in 1907, the Rhode Island boss looked him up, found him to be an attorney for seven corporations, and put him on the judiciary committee. A keen constitutional lawyer and expert debater, Borah, though younger than his colleagues, was a mighty addition to the little group of progressives.

Albert Beveridge of Indiana was the golden boy of the Senate—"a geared-up speedster, a show car," in William Allen White's estimation. A brilliant speaker with a facile mind and a gift for phrase, an excellent dinner guest and *bon vivant,* Beveridge took progressivism a little easier than his compatriots. His principles lay closer to Roosevelt's than to La Follette's (progressivism, he said in 1906, was really a matter of "conservative advance") and after following Roosevelt out of the party in 1912 he found it convenient to slip back into regular party ways. Beveridge was not insincere, but while he worked with the Midwestern group, he was never really of them. He contributed much to Senate progressivism, but the hell-raising progressivism of the Kansas-Wisconsin axis simply never suited him well.

The House Republican rebels were never so closely knit into a group as were their Senate counterparts. The central core came from the Midwest, remaining relatively constant as the personnel of the group alternately gained and lost supporters from other areas. John Nelson of Wisconsin, a thoroughgoing La Follette man, served as secretary and co-ordinator of the progressives. Edmond Madison came from Jerry Simpson's old "howling Seventh" district of Kansas, but like Clapp in the Senate his progressivism was slow moving and respectable. Miles Poindexter of Washington was a cool, reasoning man much like Beveridge, urbane, polished, and dignified. Charles Lindbergh of Minnesota was a direct political descendant of Donnelly and Populism, a lone wolf in politics, the most leftish of the group, and a bitter hater of trusts and privilege.

The two leaders of the House group, George Norris of Nebraska and Victor Murdock of Kansas, were young men of the La Follette stamp. Norris was nominally a Republican from a strongly Populist district and a born and incorrigible independent. Parties, he said, robbed a man of his political freedom, and throughout his long and distinguished public life he showed not the slightest qualm at bolting his own. "I would rather be right than regular," he once said, so he followed one Roosevelt in 1912, La Follette in 1924, Al Smith in 1928, and another Roosevelt in 1932 and 1936, which led Arthur Capper of Kansas to describe him as "a perambulating Declaration of Independence." As representative, later as senator, Norris never wavered from the progressive path. He entered the House in 1903 and died in 1944, and during the period every single vote or proposal he made reflected the old Midwest progressive tradition. In 1908 he was already known as a young Republican maverick, a consorter with known rebels like Lindbergh and Murdock, and possibly a La Follette man too.

Victor Murdock was more like his one-time opponent, "Sockless Jerry" Simpson than he probably ever imagined. Technically a Republican, ideologically Murdock was a Kansas Populist out of the rough-and-tough school of the nineties. Like Norris, Murdock worried little about party lines and was likely to kick over the traces on any issue. He leaned toward the spectacular, a fiery and occasionally rough speaker in debate, and as a newspaperman he saw to it that the House rebels made good copy.

After 1908 the progressives in Congress were assisted by Irvine Lenroot, a La Follette lieutenant from Wisconsin, and by Miller and Tawney from Minnesota. Iowa sent a whole set of young progressives and more came in from Nebraska. In the Senate men such as Crawford and Gamble arrived from North Dakota, Knute Nelson from Minnesota, and Brown and Burkett from Nebraska. They were all called "progressives" or "insurgents," the latter term coming into general use about 1911, and mostly they came from the Midwest and Far West. Congressmen from other states voted with them occasionally, but the burden of insurgency was borne for the most part in both House and Senate by the Westerners.

It took only a few weeks for the Senate progressives to size up Taft. "The President," said Dolliver concisely, "is surrounded by good men who know exactly what they want." One of the things they wanted was tariff revision—not downward, as the 1908 platform had hinted, but upward, as commercial interests wished. The platform pledge of 1908—one of the hot potatoes left by Roosevelt for Taft to hold—had to be redeemed, so the Republicans set about doing it. Payne introduced a tariff bill into the House in March of 1909, with enough rate reductions to elicit tempered praise from the progressives but with a number of hidden jokers distributed through it. The House progressives, after objecting briefly, passed it by, feeling that probably it was as good a bill as could be expected.

Aldrich was waiting for the tariff bill in the Senate (he held closed meetings on it even before it passed the House) and took it into committee to hear testimony, mostly from manufacturers. When it came out of Aldrich's hands, it was a queer-looking object. Instead of revising tariff schedules downward, it raised duties on more than six hundred items, lowered them on a few, and was so full of tricks that only an expert could find all of them. Thus was the platform pledge redeemed. The Payne-Aldrich bill revised tariffs, certainly, but in a manner never dreamed of by the platform makers. Finley Peter Dunne's Mr. Dooley, noting the inclusion of opium on the free list, found the reason: "Before ye smoke up p'raps ye can't see where the tariff has been rejooced, but afther ye've had a long dhraw it all becomes clear to ye."

La Follette, Bristow, Clapp, Dolliver, Beveridge, Nelson and Cummins read the bill, then night after night, often until dawn, sat up with volumes of reports, each choosing a set of schedules and reading up on the facts. In a few weeks they had most of the inconsistencies and jokers located and were actually tariff authorities, a feat of concentrated effort rarely matched in congressional history. When debates on the bill opened, they knew more about tariffs on things like glass, lead, hides, cotton, iron, wool, and lumber than anyone else in Congress.

La Follette opened the discussion with some pertinent remarks about gas retorts. Knute Nelson followed, wanting to know about the wool and earthenware schedules, and then Dolliver blasted at the textile rates. Beveridge and Crawford followed Dolliver, who then returned with a devastating three-day speech that sent Aldrich into the cloakrooms to count his votes. Bristow, whose specialty was lead, took the lead schedule apart bit by bit, and Cummins went over the iron rates. La Follette stayed out of it, working over the whole bill, and in early June, nearly a month after the debates began, came on the floor loaded with facts. His three-day speech, one of the finest in his career, was a blistering indictment of Aldrich and his committee, and when La Follette stopped Dolliver began once more.

For nearly the entire summer the insurgents held on. When Dolliver stopped, Clapp began; if Clapp tired, Bristow or Beveridge or Cummins stepped in; when they retired, Crawford, Brown, Burkett, or Knute Nelson took the floor. By July it was clear that there was more than simply a tariff bill at stake. The little group of die-hards were fighting for something more than revised rates. They were fighting privilege, the great trusts, machine rule, "Aldrichism"—fighting for an honest observance of party pledges, for representative government and progressive principles.

In the end it was to no avail. The steam roller, driven by Aldrich and Smoot and Depew and Lodge and the rest, rolled over them. Aldrich knew the result beforehand, and during one of La Follette's most vitriolic speeches calmly took a nap in his committee room. He had a hand full of aces, and when the bill came round for vote only ten Republicans, all from seven Midwestern states, voted against it. It was a victory for Aldrichism, and Taft played along with it. The progressives in the Midwest and West raised a storm of protest. "The history of American government," said the Kansas City *Star*, "furnishes no parallel to the insults which are now being heaped on the doctrine of popular government by the Senatorial boss from Rhode Island."

The tariff fight done with, the insurgents looked for a new issue. It came ready to hand in an argument between Gifford

Pinchot, Chief of the Forest Service, and his superior, Secretary of the Interior Ballinger. Pinchot, a strong conservationist, was a close friend and an appointee of Theodore Roosevelt; Ballinger was a friend and appointee of Taft and, like him, a man of strong legalistic mind. The disagreement came originally over Ballinger's action in throwing open to private entry some timber lands his predecessor, Garfield, had held for public power and reclamation projects. It was true, as Ballinger contended, that the Interior Department had never possessed any legal right to withhold the lands, but the Roosevelt administration had usually assumed an extralegal right to do so. Pinchot protested to Taft that Ballinger's action was in direct contravention of Roosevelt's policies and finally succeeded in having some of the lands withdrawn. But in the meantime Louis Glavis, a Land Office field man, claimed that Ballinger had failed to examine properly certain charges that the Morgan-Guggenheim interests were attempting to "steal" some Alaskan coal holdings. Glavis was promptly dismissed, but not before he and Pinchot gave full accounts of the case to Dolliver.

The insurgents picked up the Ballinger-Pinchot squabble and came charging into the argument. *La Follette's Magazine* blared the facts of the case to the public and *Collier's,* along with other magazines, took it up too. Pinchot was dismissed for insubordination in early 1910, and though a congressional committee cleared Ballinger, the affair left a bad taste in the public mouth. In fact, Ballinger himself resigned a year later under threat of impeachment. The whole affair was a matter of ill luck for Taft, whose support of Ballinger was no more than what a President might be expected to give his cabinet member. Yet the incident provided excellent ammunition for the insurgents as an example to the public of how far Taft had departed from the Roosevelt line. "There is a growing disposition," remarked the *Des Moines Register and Leader* after the dispute had died down, "to look to Roosevelt's return as a signal for a break to progressive leadership."

The Senate furnished most of the fireworks during the early

months of Taft's term, but the House group grew increasingly restive in 1908. The issue was "Cannonism," that is, the power possessed by the Speaker of the House. Joe Cannon, a hard-shelled Republican from Illinois, was a well-liked man, but he ran the Republican machine in the House as domineeringly as Aldrich ran his in the Senate. The Speaker held tremendous power; he made appointments to House committees, chaired the Rules Committee, could give or deny recognition to any speaker, and could, in effect, defeat any legislation with his gavel. And Cannon rode the House hard. Part of the reason that insurgency had come to naught in the House was simply Cannon. Complaints to Taft had no effect, since Taft admitted privately that Cannon was too strong for him.

The elections of 1908 in several of the Midwestern states pivoted on the issue of "Cannonism" and from them a group of insurgents came into the House pledged to clip his wings. In January of 1909 about thirty Republicans met to plan a course of action. They framed a resolution which sheared Cannon of his appointive powers, reconstituted the Rules Committee, and established a "Calendar Tuesday" for the presentation of legislation by committees. But the regular Republicans headed off the insurgent bill with a compromise measure that left Cannon almost as strongly entrenched as before. The failure to "get" Cannon began to raise dust in the Midwestern press, and many Republicans wondered whether it might not be wise to jettison "Uncle Joe" and "liberalize" the party. But Taft stuck by him. Cannon was very useful in shoving party legislation through the House and furthermore Taft was beginning to weary of the insurgents' constant badgering. Strong party and corporate interests were at work in Cannon's behalf, and "Uncle Joe," as tough a politician as there was, refused to budge in the slightest.

The deadlock broke suddenly in March of 1910. Norris, who had been carrying the resolution in his pocket for weeks, saw a chance to slip it in. Cannon immediately overruled him, and Norris called for a vote to determine whether the House would uphold Cannon's ruling. Norris and his cohorts began a fili-buster while missing members were gathered and, though Cannon put up a stiff battle, a coalition of insurgents and Democrats passed Norris' resolution, which created a new Rules Committee and barred the Speaker from membership on it. Cannon, with the dignity of the vanquished, offered to entertain a motion that the Speaker's chair be declared vacant, but nothing came of it. Norris and the insurgents hated the system, not Cannon, and "Uncle Joe" remained as Speaker. But the fact remained that the House insurgents had struck a powerful blow at Taft and the Republican machine. To the people, Cannon represented boss rule, and his defeat was a progressive victory.

By 1910 the Republican party was badly split. The Payne-Aldrich tariff, the Ballinger-Pinchot affair, the deposing of Cannon, and other squabbles had created a clear division be-tween insurgents and regulars within the party organization. For Taft it was a choice between party solidarity and progres-sivism, and his decision was apparent. The Republican na-tional committee publicly censured the insurgent leaders, ad-vised Republicans to vote against them, and organized speak-ing forays into their home districts. The Republican state committees denounced Dolliver, Clapp, La Follette, Bristow, Cummins, and Beveridge and appropriated party money for their defeat. "Is The Republican Party Breaking Up?" Ray Stannard Baker asked in a magazine article, and he concluded that it must readjust or it obviously would.

The insurgent leaders were perfectly willing to fight it out on the line drawn by the Republican Old Guard. La Follette founded *La Follette's Magazine* in 1909 as an unofficial insur-gent organ, while other progressive Republicans had news-papers in the Midwest to use as sounding boards. The Chau-tauqua provided a potent weapon. Most of the insurgents paraded up and down the Mississippi and Missouri valleys on its circuit, carrying their argument with the bosses to the people. La Follette's entire speech on the Chautauqua circuit of 1910, for example, consisted solely of a detailed analysis of the Senate roll call on the railroad rate bill, something only he could carry off. Republican Leagues, Progressive Leagues, and other groups began to appear in the Midwestern states, organized and led by astute young men like Harold Ickes of Illinois and White of Kansas. Every move of the insurgents was widely publicized, and every act of the Aldrich-Cannon group pounced upon.

The struggle was, in essence, a contest for control of the Republican party, to decide whether it would become a progressive party, dominated by the Midwest, or a conservative party, dominated by the East. What did the Midwestern insurgent want? Why had he rebelled against the Republicanism of Taft, Cannon, and Aldrich? Actually he wanted the same things that the Populist—and before that the Granger and Greenbacker—wanted. "Why not admit," asked the *Wageworker* of Lincoln, Nebraska, in 1910, "that the so-called insurgents are but giving louder, and perhaps better voice to the very same ideas that the oldtime Populists, of the late 80's and 90's, voiced? The Populists of 1888 saw first, but perhaps not so clearly, what La Follette and Beveridge and others are making plain to us."

Ray Stannard Baker, who covered Coxey's march as a young newspaperman, asked the general about insurgency. The progressives, remarked Coxey, were saying the same things he had said in 1894, but the difference was, he said wryly, that in 1894 he was jailed for it. Henry C. Wallace, of *Wallaces' Farmer*, wrote in 1910 that the Midwest wanted four things: protection of its natural recources, a stronger ICC, better enforcement of the Sherman Act, and the elimination of special privilege from politics—every one straight from 1880, 1892, and 1896. Insurgency was a continuation of the old Midwestern agrarian protest, originating in the same disaffected regions, differing not at all in its fundamentals from the protests earlier voiced in the same areas twenty years and more before. It was by no means merely a remnant of Rooseveltian policy, but an older, established, regional tradition.

Champ Clark, the Democratic leader in the House, looked at the Republicans in 1910 and remarked that their only hope was "that when Colonel Roosevelt returns he will be able and willing to save them." The newspapers published a popular parody:

> Teddy, come home and blow your horn,
> The sheep's in the meadow, the cow's in the corn.
> The boy you left to tend the sheep
> Is under the haystack, fast asleep.

Looking over the wreckage of the Republican party, Mr. Dooley cried, "Oh f'r a Moses!" In the spring of 1910 Moses was on his way home from Africa, fully aware of what had gone on—Pinchot even took a boat to Africa to meet him. He landed amid hysterical enthusiasm, parades, speeches, and fireworks. "Back from Elba!" shouted the press. Progressivism had a leader again.

The Roosevelt who returned from Africa in 1910 was not the same as the one who sailed fifteen months before. T.R. had had time to think, arrange his somewhat disordered political enthusiasms, and codify his scattered progressivism into a more coherent and organized political philosophy. Over a year of political inactivity had sharpened his desire for power and leadership, for he was not the type of man who could remain a contented ex-President. And furthermore, he had taken a book to Africa with him, Herbert Croly's *Promise of American Life*. Croly's knotty, academic, intellectual exposition of progressivism crystallized in Roosevelt's mind all the half-formed, tentative political principles he held. His philosophy of government, germinating in the years 1901 to 1908, burst into bloom after Croly's watering. Roosevelt, when he stepped on shore, knew where he was heading.

Croly spent ten years preparing *The Promise of American Life,* a cool and careful analysis of the American system. American political life, he said, had been based thus far on two antagonistic principles, one the centralized government of Hamilton and the other the loose, decentralized government of Jefferson. Neither alone provided an adequate political philosophy; to realize the promise of American life it was necessary to mix them. The proper proportion, he believed, involved more Hamiltonianism and less Jeffersonianism. "I shall not disguise the fact," he said, "that, on the whole, my own preferences are on the side of Hamilton rather than Jefferson."

The "promise," according to Croly, was the hope of combining economic independence and prosperity with free political institutions, of making "this economic and political system secure results of moral and social value, the seeking of such results which convert democracy from a political system into a constructive social ideal." The promise could be realized only through a stronger national government. The American people must lose their traditional fear of centralized power, must accept government as a partner in enforcing democracy, must use it as an agency to initiate and realize the reforms necessary to political and social welfare. Following the "will-o'-the-wisp of individualism" led, he pointed out, to the concept of democracy as "live and let live"; combining individualistic effort with governmental organization, the concept became "live and help live," in a semicollective society. Using the nation on the one hand as the unit of political organization, and broadening the social and economic program on the other, Croly reached a position between Hamilton and Jefferson (though closer to the former) that secured the ends of the Virginian by the means of the Federalist. This he called "The New Nationalism," a union of "the Hamiltonian principle of national political responsibility and efficiency with a frank democratic purpose."

The problem, as Croly saw it in his detached intellectual way, was simply what to do with democracy in an age of big business. How could the Jeffersonian, individualistic ideal be made effective in an industrial era? How could dispersed political power compete with concentrated economic power? How could the principle of political equality operate successfully in an age of economic and social inequality? Clearly these were pertinent questions.

In Croly's estimation this was the mistake of Midwestern progressivism: that it was attempting to establish a Jeffersonian government in a Hamiltonian age, that it persisted in acting as if pioneer agrarianism and not big business dominated the nation. Pioneer democracy, to Croly, was an admirable political response to the conditions and opportunities of a pioneer society, but it was limited in usefulness to a pioneer society alone. Frontier political virtues could be, in an industrial age, positive vices and real threats to democracy. The cherished individualism of the frontier, carried into the economic field, produced the boss and the capitalist. Mark Hanna, Croly pointed out in a rather admiring biography of him in 1912, was as typical a product of the frontier tradition as Daniel Boone. The pioneer—living in a frontier society that demanded all-round ability and quick adaptation—distrusted the learned man, the specialist; the new problems of an industrial age, however, needed an expert. The frontier emphasis on equal rights, likewise natural in a pioneer society, became in a complex industrial society "a dangerous weapon in the hands of factious and merely revolutionary agitators." What was needed instead of lip service to "equal rights" was a "responsible representative government," in which people entrusted their rights to responsible leaders. Thus all of the deeply held frontier ideals—equal rights, individualism, independence, and other characteristics of a simple pioneer society —should "be abandoned for the benefit of a genuinely individual and social consummation" in a new and quite different era. That was the trouble, thought Croly, with the whole Midwest progressive tradition. It attempted to solve new problems by old formulas.

The contrasts between the progressivism of Croly and the

progressive tradition of La Follette and the Midwest were sharply defined in *The Promise of American Life*. Noticeably, Croly called his program "The New Nationalism," a term which Roosevelt adopted and sometimes referred to as "Progressive Nationalism." On the other hand, Charles McCarthy, the philosopher of La Follettism, called his brand "The New Individualism." The difference in name was precisely the difference in kind. Neither could quite understand the other; though both the "New Nationalists" and the "New Individualists" had the same end in view, they proceeded there by different routes. Croly (and his *New Republic* colleagues, Walter Lippmann and Walter Weyl) never had any real comprehension of the Midwestern variety of progressivism, which was to them simply something wild and erratic, though laudable in intent. The tradition of the Middle West was Jeffersonian and Jacksonian in its fear of bigness, of concentration and control, its worship of individualism, of decentralization, of frontier equality.

The progressivism of Croly and Roosevelt stemmed from Eastern, Hamiltonian, urban sources. Let us recognize bigness, they said, as a natural development, and inequality as an inescapable concomitant of industrialism. Let us recognize collective partnership as the sole political device by which democratic goals may be assured. Instead of erasing the trust, the machine, the capitalist, instead of attempting to breathe life into old-style democracy, let us strike out in another direction. The "New Nationalism" allows the trust and the machine and the capitalist to exist and recognizes their usefulness, but it directs and controls them for proper democratic ends. Roosevelt himself was a nascent Hamiltonian, before he read Croly. He held great admiration for the Federalist statesman, and had already written a sympathetic biography of Gouverneur Morris, Hamilton's close associate. His historical writings revealed a long and deeply held dislike of Jeffersonianism; indeed, the whole drift of his administration was in Hamiltonian directions.

Croly's "New Nationalism" agreed with what Roosevelt already believed, supplied some missing pieces in the pattern, and convinced him that he was on the right political track. Settling down after his return from Africa as associate editor of the *Outlook,* Roosevelt began to enunciate a broader and deeper progressive program than before. He went on a Western swing, outlining his political ideas, announced his "New Nationalism" in Ossawatomie, Kansas, and later collected his speeches in a book of the same name. Roosevelt's final program looked much like Croly's. He called for federal supervision of all corporations engaged in interstate commerce—the trust, he reminded, was "the result of an imperative economic law, which cannot be repealed by political legislation." He came out, as he had not before, for income and inheritance taxes, for laws regulating child and female labor, for workmen's compensation, for labor organization, in fact, for a program that reflected rather accurately Croly's plea for the use of government to assure social progress.

Still considering himself the unofficial head of the Republican party, Roosevelt set out to heal the breach between insurgent and regular. Although his friendship with Taft had cooled considerably from the "Will" and "Teddy" stage, he carefully avoided a break with the President, who was in the unenviable position of second fiddler to a magazine editor who held no political position at all. As a peacemaker he was not too successful. The enthusiasm of the Midwest for "the New Nationalism" was only temperate. "Insurgency got along pretty well when Roosevelt was in Africa," dryly remarked the *Des Moines News.* Louis Parsons of Chicago thought him only a "relative" progressive; he was far enough ahead of his party to look like a leader, but far behind the real progressive parade. Post, of the *Public,* said Roosevelt's "speed as a progressive is like that of a rocking-horse in violent action"—much motion and no progress. Compared with La Follette, or Bristow, or Cummins, he measured poorly.

The elections of 1910 exposed the wide breach in the

Republican party. The issue was insurgency versus regularity, and regulars fell all over the nation. "A great campaign is on," remarked La Follette, "not for our State alone, but for all the States of this country of ours, and for our country itself, to insure to the people true representative government." The insurgents swept the Midwest and the West, taking Wisconsin, Michigan, Indiana, and all Republican states west of the Mississippi except the four mountain states. A good many of those Republicans who had walked out on La Follette in 1906 were no longer present in the Senate, as he reminded that body with some satisfaction. The Democrats took control of the House, and put into state offices men of the stature of Woodrow Wilson, Franklin Roosevelt, Ben Lindsey, and Brand Whitlock. The balance of congressional power rested, after 1910, in progressive hands.

Recognizing the signs of the times, Taft conferred with progressive leaders, seeking compromise in the interests of party harmony. He accomplished little, even when he covertly threatened to withhold patronage from the recalcitrants, a threat to which La Follette replied, "The support of the progressives for progressive legislation will be given without reference to patronage or favors of any sort. That support will rest on conviction." The victory of 1910 had given the rebels too much confidence to regard either concessions or threats very seriously. As 1912 approached, a presidential election year, the division in the party was far beyond the compromise stage. Taft, said La Follette, had "rendered it utterly impossible for Progressive Republicans to support him for re-election." Taft's position, said Cummins in an interview in Chicago in 1911, was no longer debatable; he must be counted as the representative of special interests. The Midwest, said Henry Wallace, thought Taft was honest and faithful, but at the same time it believed him too willing to follow the wishes of the party rather than those of the people. "The big stick in his hands," remarked one of the insurgents, "has become a billy-dilly."

Since Taft was unacceptable, the progressives planned to capture the Republican party and to nominate a progressive candidate in 1912. As a first step the National Progressive Republican League formed at La Follette's home in Washington in January, 1911. "Under existing conditions," the League's declaration read, "legislation in the public interest has been baffled and defeated," and it listed the negative achievements of the preceding three years. The League did not consider itself as a third party, nor did it plan to put up a candidate. Its aim, said Clapp, was "to place the party beyond the control of reactionaries. There'll be no third party until the people despair of desired changes in the old parties." Ostensibly, the League's purpose was to further progressive legislation and incidentally to defeat Taft's renomination.

The composition of the League was interesting. Its president was Jonathan Bourne of Oregon. Governor Chase Osborn of Michigan and George Norris of Nebraska served as vice-presidents, and its treasurer was Charles Crane of Chicago, a wealthy industrialist who had long dabbled in liberal politics. On the executive committee were Clapp and Bristow from the Senate, Hubbard (Iowa), Lenroot (Wisconsin), and Kent (California) from the House. Gifford Pinchot of Pennsylvania and George Record of New Jersey represented the citizenry. Members included five senators (Brown of Nebraska, Cummins of Iowa, Gronna of North Dakota, Dixon of Montana, and La Follette), five governors (Aldrich of Nebraska, Carey of Wyoming, Hiram Johnson of California, McGovern of Wisconsin, and Stubbs of Kansas), and sixteen representatives, among them Lindbergh, Murdock, Nelson, and Poindexter. About twenty men came from private life—Frederic C. Howe, William U'Ren of Oregon, William Allen White, Ray Stannard Baker, Louis Brandeis (who had furnished La Follette with ammunition for the railroad debates), James Garfield (T.R.'s Secretary of the Interior), and so on. It was clear that the NPRL was little more than organized insurgency. Six of the eight senators came from the Midwest; four of the six governors; and thirteen of the sixteen representatives. The program of the League reflected the principles of its members —direct senatorial elections, direct primaries, direct election of convention delegates, direct expression of popular preference in presidential elections, initiative and referendum and recall, corrupt-practices acts, and the other familiar progressive plans.

The founding of the national League encouraged the establishment of state leagues in Minnesota, Wisconsin, Michigan, Nebraska, South Dakota, and Washington. Soon League members everywhere were talking of running a candidate in 1912. In April, 1911, some of them met with newsmen and congressmen in Senator Bourne's committee room to agree on a nominee to oppose Taft for the Republican nomination. Roosevelt steadfastly refused to lend his name to the League, though La Follette wrote him, "Now Colonel, can't you consistently give this movement the benefit of your name and influence?" If T.R. would accept League backing, he was the obvious choice, but on the other hand, the presiding genius of insurgency and the guiding spirit of the League was certainly La Follette. Eventually the group assured La Follette of its support in case he became a candidate, though Cummins, Pinchot, and others, thinking of Achilles resting in his tent at Oyster Bay, refused to make the endorsement official.

Most of the League members considered La Follette to be their real leader. The Minnesota Progressive League openly endorsed him in June, 1911, and strong support for him appeared in other Midwestern and Western states. "The logical candidate of the Republican Progressives," commented Louis Post in the *Public,* "is Senator La Follette who led the advancing column when others feared or faltered, who has proved his constructive skill, and who does not compromise." The *American Magazine* labeled him "the most characteristic and spirited figure in the so-called progressive movement" and began to run his autobiography in installments. La Follette himself picked up the cue in July and announced that he would run.

Four months later three hundred progressive Republican delegates from thirty states met in Chicago and endorsed him, officially opening the campaign.

Theodore Roosevelt remained a puzzle. Certain that the split in the party was permanent, he chose to follow a tortuous path between the two Republican camps while he waited for developments. He refused to endorse the NPRL, but neither did he attack it. He did not declare himself for La Follette, but he wrote a laudatory article about him in the *Outlook* and on a visit to the Wisconsin legislature in 1911 practically endorsed his program in an informal talk. When John R. Commons, a La Follette worker, asked him point blank if he would support La Follette, he gave what Commons considered a clear, affirmative reply. At the same time Roosevelt was noticeably cool to Taft. The truth of the matter was that Roosevelt wanted to be President and he wanted to control the Republican party. He could not control a party led by La Follette, with whom he agreed neither personally nor ideologically, nor could he be President by breaking with Taft, declaring himself a candidate, and splitting the party.

Roosevelt evidently decided in 1911 to let matters proceed while he bided his time. In August, before the Chicago convention, he asked in a letter to the *Pittsburgh Leader* that his name go unnoticed and that no movement for his nomination be considered. But as 1911 wore on, it became quite evident that neither Taft nor La Follette seemed to have strength enough to guarantee nomination. Progressives like Cummins and Bristow, sure that La Follette could not win even if he were nominated, were giving the Wisconsin leader only token support, and other progressives, convinced that Roosevelt could win—if he would only run—were equally unenthusiastic. Brand Whitlock, in December of 1911, detected a strong movement within the League "to head off La Follette." This was a perfectly understandable move in the light of some of the backers of the League—the wealthy Pinchots, A. T. Cochrane (the "carpet king"), J. Coleman du Pont, Medill

McCormick of the *Chicago Tribune,* H. H. Wilkinson, of Crucible Steel, Frank Munsey of the New York press, George Perkins of the Morgan syndicate—who could hardly have been expected to be strong La Follette enthusiasts. In October, William Allen White (who had not attended the Chicago meeting) wrote Roosevelt that he and others "thought the country not quite ready for La Follette." "If there is no other way out," wrote White significantly, "I am going to be for La Follette bigger than a wolf, yet I do not want to get complicated in the situation."

There was, of course, a way out, as White told Bristow two months later, one that was clear to others too. Roosevelt read the signs carefully. If neither Taft nor La Follette could win, it was highly possible that he could take the nomination himself; he told Herman Kohlsaat he had a whole vault full of letters urging him to run. "I am not a candidate," he wrote in December, 1911, "I never will be a candidate, but I have to tell the La Follette men and the Taft men that while I am absolutely sincere in saying that I am not a candidate . . . , it is yet possible there will be a public demand which will present the matter to me in the light of duty which I could not shirk." A few weeks later, on January 7, 1912, Secretary of War Stimson visited Oyster Bay and announced on his return that he had the impression that Roosevelt would not run. But on January 16, Roosevelt wrote Munsey that while he did not seek nomination, he did not wish "to tie his hands" with any statement that would make it impossible for him to accept if it came from "a real popular movement . . . a literally overwhelming demand."

In other words, Roosevelt's supporters understood that he could be drafted, and they began a quiet campaign in his behalf that Roosevelt did nothing to stop. La Follette's strength ebbed rapidly. Big business began to shift toward Roosevelt, feeling that if Taft couldn't win, Roosevelt was at least less dangerous than La Follette. Progressive leaders themselves began to float toward him, for the main point of politics is to win, and if La Follette could not and Roosevelt could, why cling to La Follette? The thorny problem was getting rid of La Follette. It was inconceivable that he would withdraw in T.R.'s favor. In fact, when the subject was mentioned to him, he replied flatly, "I can enlist in the ranks of no man, unless he adopts publicly, in binding terms, the true principles of progressive government by the people." And since La Follette defined the terms, it was quite certain that Roosevelt could not meet them. So Roosevelt's supporters started to play a double game, developing La Follette strength that could be shifted to Roosevelt when the time came. Pinchot, in December, 1911, openly backed LaFollette while working undercover for Roosevelt. Chase Osborn of Michigan, at least, was more straightforward. In January, 1912, he denounced La Follette and left the League.

The actual jettisoning of La Follette, when it came, was not a pleasant spectacle. In February, 1912, he was invited to speak at the annual dinner of the Periodical Publishers' Association in Philadelphia. His campaign since July had been exhausting; he was at the point of collapse, tired, nervous, his daughter seriously ill in a near-by hospital. His speech, an attack on the control of the press by moneyed interests, turned into a rambling, incoherent rant, stretching on and on, while the guests quietly left, one by one. When the newspapers reported the next day that he had suffered a complete mental collapse, the Roosevelt men saw their chance and took it. Amid expressions of sympathy they began to back away. *Everybody's,* a few days later, came out and said it. "The movement which has seemed to be in his [La Follette's] interests has been, for some time, a cover for a movement in favor of Mr. Roosevelt."

Roosevelt was ready at hand. In answer to questions he stated that while he was still not a candidate he would accept the nomination if the Republican party demanded it of him. Strangely enough, within a week, seven governors (of West Virginia, Nebraska, New Hampshire, Wyoming, Michigan, Kansas, and Missouri) addressed an open letter to him, urging him to consider the nomination as "a plain public duty." Eleven days later, speaking to the Ohio Constitutional Convention, he presented a carefully qualified progressive platform, and on February 26 headlines from coast to coast blazoned the fact that his "hat was in the ring."

Whether La Follette received just treatment in the preconvention campaign of 1911 is still debatable. It was, from a realistic point of view, a matter of expediency versus principles, and expediency won. La Follette's fierce progressivism brooked no compromises, and as White pointed out, Roosevelt's "weakness for compromise" was in 1912 a political asset when the Republican party was split. Was it better to win, or was it better to lose without compromise? Even some of the most staunch La Follette supporters were willing to accept Roosevelt and victory as a desirable half-loaf in lieu of the whole. As Ray Stannard Baker phrased it, thousands of progressives were for Roosevelt, but not for President, and backed him only because he might win where La Follette could not. George Norris, who finally washed his hands of the whole affair, explained that he would have continued to support La Follette "if I had thought that there was any possible show of accomplishing anything. . . . I also realized quite fully that if we expected to defeat Mr. Taft we ought to unite on Mr. Roosevelt."

At the same time it must be remembered that Pinchot, Cummins, Bristow, Stubbs, and others, from the beginning of the League's activities, demonstrated a preference for Roosevelt and accepted La Follette only as a substitute. Thus their desertion of La Follette was not unexpected, but there was also some truth in La Follette's contention that he had been used as a stalking horse for T.R.'s candidacy. After the autumn of 1911 the Progressive Republican League was not wholly behind him, and its organizers had not informed him of the fact. How much Roosevelt knew of the double game being played within the NPRL is uncertain, yet it is unlikely that he remained in total ignorance of it. His course remains the most debatable of all. He wanted to be President, he wanted to win, and he wanted to win for progressivism as he conceived it.

The Republican preconvention campaign in the spring of 1912 was a bitter three-way dogfight. La Follette was soon back on his feet, protesting "the surrender of the progressive movement into the hands of softshelled progressives and re-actionaries." Taft denounced the progressives as "neurotics" and Roosevelt as a fake "third term" progressive who was simply out for revenge; a rumor circulated that Roosevelt was actually insane. He, in turn, lashed Taft as a traitor to progressivism, a creature of the "interests," a man who "means well but means feebly." As the June convention approached, it looked like a draw. T.R. had done well in the primaries, capturing six states as well as the big delegations from Pennsylvania and Taft's own Ohio. But his organization was no match for the Republican National Committee, which controlled the patronage and held a solid bloc of Southern delegations. At convention time Taft had the majority of convention votes, but Roosevelt had the larger primary vote, with two hundred and fifty-four contested seats at the convention still in question.

The National Committee made short shrift of the Roosevelt boom. Elihu Root, the convention chairman, was a Taft man, and the contesting Roosevelt delegates were quickly gaveled down. There were no stampedes for Roosevelt, his delegates gained only a few contested seats, and every demonstration for him was quickly hushed up. Roosevelt himself came to Chicago, sounding his battle cry, "We stand at Armageddon and we battle for the Lord," but the Republican machine ground on. Taft men offered to compromise on a third candidate, but Roosevelt refused and his delegates began to walk out of the convention during the first ballot. It was Taft and Sherman by a landslide.

Roosevelt wanted to win, now more than ever, for he had come too far to turn back. The nomination, to his way of thinking, had simply been stolen. So a call went out for a convention to meet in Chicago in August to choose a "progressive" candidate, and the "Bull Moose" campaign ("I feel like a bull moose," said T.R.) was under way. The August convention had something of the flavor of the Populist uprisings of the nineties. Every shade of political opinion was represented, reformers, hard-shelled bosses, feminists such as Jane Addams and college professors such as Charles Merriam, farmers, socialists, philanthropic rich men, social workers, all drawn to Chicago by the magic of T.R.'s personality. "There was room on the platform," one delegate wrote, "for anyone who had seen Peter Pan and believed in fairies." It was a hysterically enthusiastic meeting, filled with parades and outbursts of "Onward, Christian Soldiers," a convention that looked like a crusade.

The platform showed it. As Frank Munsey commented approvingly, "While splendidly progressive it is, at the same time, amply conservative and sound." There was at least one small plank for everybody, all reduced to four main points: the direct participation of all voters in government, a popular check on the judiciary through the recall, regulation of trusts rather than destruction, and a broad program of social welfare legislation. It was really an impeccably progressive platform, but oddly enough its original strong antitrust plank disappeared in committee, replaced by a milder and more vague statement. (Almost as an afterthought the press reported at the same time the last Populist convention in St. Louis, attended by a total of eight delegates.) La Follette did not go to the Bull Moose convention, and neither did Borah and Norris and dozens of others. About all that it accomplished, in the opinion of the La Follette progressives, was to establish who was for Roosevelt and who wasn't.

Democrats watched the Republican civil war with great pleasure. Bryan, three times a loser, probably would not run. "Do you think I'm going to run for President just to get the Republicans out of a hole?" he asked a reporter. But the Democratic party itself was sharply divided into a more or less liberal Bryan wing and conservative, Eastern, anti-Bryan wing. The anti-Bryanites favored Champ Clark of Missouri, popular middle-of-the-roader, while the liberal wing favored Woodrow Wilson, governor of New Jersey. Bryan stood neutral. Wilson had opposed him in 1904, but at the same time Bryan knew that Hearst and Tammany favored Clark, and there was still a chance that Bryan himself might run for a fourth time.

Clark led the race on the opening ballots, with Wilson second. Neither could gain the necessary majority, and the convention went on, deadlocked. The key lay in Bryan's hands, and when on the tenth ballot the delegation from Tammany transferred its votes from Harmon of Ohio to Clark, Bryan used it, taking the floor to announce that he refused to vote for any man favored by New York. In throwing the convention to Wilson, he made a real contribution to his party and to progressive government. The nomination of Wilson was probably Bryan's greatest political achievement.

The Democratic platform was not unusual, remaining more or less the distinctively Bryan document it had been since 1896. It asked for tariff revision, antitrust laws, bank-law reforms, a rural-credits system, prohibition of the injunction in labor disputes, and railroad legislation. The greatest asset to the Democratic party was not its platform but Wilson himself, the ablest Democratic candidate since Jackson, who, though he excited little hysterical enthusiasm, stated the case for progressivism with dignity and confidence.

The campaign itself was an odd spectacle. Wilson stayed out of the dogfight between Roosevelt and Taft, concentrating on the Croly-Roosevelt concept of the progressive state and debating the wisdom of Roosevelt's opinions on trusts. Roosevelt, between pot shots at Taft, replied that the nation had nothing to fear from a strong centralized government and called Wilson's program "rural toryism." The Republican party, retorted Wilson, hadn't had a new idea in thirty years (later he amended this to fifty), while the Republican press jeered him as "a book-learned politician" and "a professor in politics," as indeed he was. At the same time, the Taft press slashed at Roosevelt, whose real aim, it asserted, was "subversion of the government." Taft accused him of wishing to transform the party from "conservatism and moderate liberalism to extreme radicalism." One of Taft's followers, General Nelson Miles was even more specific; the election to him was "a struggle between constitutional government and *communism*." The *New York Times* accused Roosevelt of "a campaign of reckless ambition desirous of unsettling fundamental principles of government and the Constitution." But the Democrats called Taft "a tool of reactionaries" and appealed to progressives to vote for Wilson instead of for the "fake" progressive, Roosevelt.

The old progressive group reacted in various ways. Gronna and Norris Brown chose Wilson; Borah, Cummins, Bourne, and Kenyon of Iowa favored Roosevelt, but did not favor a third party; Beveridge, Bristow, Garfield, Dixon, Pinchot, and Clapp went with Roosevelt. Norman Hapgood, Ray Stannard Baker, Louis Brandeis, Charles Crane, Herbert Quick, and others supported Wilson as "the better fundamental democrat." La Follette refused to be drawn into "the coarse personal quarrel" between Taft and Roosevelt, and persisted in embarrassing Roosevelt by insisting that he divulge the sources of his campaign funds. Unofficially La Follette favored Wilson and threw *La Follette's Magazine* behind him without actually committing himself. In the election he handed in a blank ballot and never again voted for a President. He would vote only for a progressive, and in his opinion (saving his own campaign in 1924) one never ran again in his lifetime.

Roosevelt's defeat was foreordained. Wilson kept the liberal Democrats within his party and attracted a good many La Follette and anti-Roosevelt votes as well. With a solid bloc of Democratic votes to count on, even a normal party vote would have elected him, without the aid of a Republican split. Roosevelt had to depend upon the progressive Republicans and what conservative Republicans he could muster to his party;

without La Follette's support he could not gain all of the former, and with the opposition of the party regulars he could gain few of the latter. Taft took Utah, Vermont, and the worst beating ever absorbed by a Republican candidate up to that time. Roosevelt took Pennsylvania, Michigan, Minnesota, South Dakota, Washington, and most of California, slightly more than four million votes and a half million more than Taft. Wilson carried the remainder, six million votes, and also a Democratic Congress. So. Dr. Thomas Woodrow Wilson (sometime Johns Hopkins student, teacher at Bryn Mawr and Wesleyan, political historian of note, president of Princeton, and governor of New Jersey) packed his seminar papers into his brief case and went to Washington, carrying with him the hopes of liberals and progressives.

Roosevelt's resounding defeat did not mean that progressivism was dead. The election, said White, was merely an incident; progressive principles were "in the heart of the people and soon they will be on the statute books—that is the chief thing." Louis Post believed that progressivism had defeated Roosevelt and elected Wilson, and hoped that the new President would measure up to expectations. La Follette urged progressives everywhere to support Wilson so long as he held to the true course. There was, actually, much for La Follette to be optimistic about in the outlook after 1912. The balance of political power was now in the South and West, a shift greater than any since the Civil War. The alliance between them was not yet a reality, as Jackson and Bryan had dreamed, but it was evidently not far off. Wilson's victory was certainly in part a victory for the old Granger-Populist-Bryan tradition; Bryan nominated him, but Altgeld, Weaver, Simpson, Donnelly, La Follette, and the rest had a part in his victory too.

The Progressive Bull Moose party was left in a bad position. Roosevelt had succeeded in carving four million votes out of the Republican party; now something had to be done with the orphans. Some believed, as La Follette always had, that progressivism could win only by returning to the regular party and working within it. Others, committed to a third party, thought its organization ought to be maintained. Still others, following Wilson, preferred to contract alliances with the Democrats. Beveridge, writing in the *Saturday Evening Post* after the election, said he would stay with the third party. White, analyzing the situation, believed there was a permanent place in politics for a progressive third party, with or without Roosevelt to lead it in 1916.

Enough Bull Moosers agreed with Beveridge and White to call for a convention in Chicago in December, 1912, a month after the election, for the purpose of establishing a permanent party organization. But the third party did not do well in the 1914 elections. All progressives but one left the House, and the old guard of Cannon, Longworth, and the rest went back into control. Furthermore, Wilson's "New Freedom" stole the headlines, and the Progressive party began to fall apart. White gave up in 1914, saying that Progressives were living on their emotions and needed a rest. Beveridge stayed on the fence for a time, finally made his peace with the regulars, and doffed the insurgency that had never suited him well.

Roosevelt, before leaving on an exploring trip to South America, affirmed his devotion to the Progressive organization and vowed he would never go back to the old party. On his return he repeated the same pledge, and after a trip to Europe announced that the Progressive party was here to stay, picking a Progressive nominee for governor of New York. After 1914 he attacked Wilson (whom he hated) for the weakness of his war policy, and in 1915 the press announced that he was ready to return to the Republican party to run against Wilson in 1916. It was all very puzzling, especially to the Progressive National Committee and his party supporters.

Roosevelt's balancing act between Progressivism and Republicanism was not convincing, nor did his bully-boy jingoism appeal to the strong antiwar minority in the party. As 1916 approached, it was clear to many Bull Moosers that he was not the Roosevelt of 1906 or of 1912. "The very worst policy that can be pursued by this nation is a policy of harassing and jeopardizing business so as to impoverish and damage it," he wrote in 1915—a far cry from the days of the "big stick" and the "malefactors of great wealth"—and there was no longer any mention of "the New Nationalism." Business, banking, and Wall Street looked on him with increasing favor, and Progressive doubts grew when he unburdened himself of such opinions as that "Aldrich was a much better man from the standpoint of the country at large than La Follette." The truth was that by 1915 Roosevelt was less interested in progressivism than he was in three other things—beating Wilson, doing it himself, and doing it without losing progressive support. For the Progressive party he had founded he held little hope. The rank and file had left it, he wrote his son Kermit, and he "refused to head the old-style type of fight."

The Progressive strategists met in Chicago in January, 1916, and announced that if the Republicans nominated an acceptable candidate and adopted a progressive platform, they would return to the fold. Privately most of them professed a liking for Roosevelt, and by March the ball was rolling again. Politicians, delegations, and citizens marched in and out of Oyster Bay. Roosevelt's appearances in Chicago and St. Louis touched off demonstrations reminiscent of 1912. There was no doubt of his popularity, but on the other hand there was definite doubt among the Republican leaders as to his desirability. It was not even certain that of the available candidates he had the best chance of beating Wilson. Charles Evans Hughes, an able man with a good record as governor of New York, looked perhaps a trifle better.

As the June conventions approached, Roosevelt's backers began spinning their web. The strategy of the Progressive leaders, whose convention preceded the Republican, was to nominate Roosevelt first, leaving the Republicans the choice of either seconding the nomination or electing Wilson again in a three-way race. George Perkins, the chairman of the convention, had other plans. He delayed and temporized, trying to hold off a nomination until the Republicans had named their man, which would force the decision on the Progressives, and despite all that White, Ickes, Pinchot, and others could do, he succeeded. The Republicans nominated Hughes, and the Progressives were left with the alternative of returning to the party with Hughes or staying out with Roosevelt. Hughes was simply too much for the old Bull Moosers; "A business man's candidate," said White bitterly, "hovering around the *status quo* like a sick kitten around a hot brick." They rebelled, overrode Perkins, and nominated Roosevelt anyway.

If ever Theodore Roosevelt had the chance to assume the leadership of a real progressive movement, it was in 1916—and he refused, advising the Progressives to follow him back into the Republican party behind Hughes, who deserved the support of "all progressive-minded and patriotic men." By his refusal Roosevelt abandoned progressivism, definitely and irrevocably. The decision whether the Progressive party lived or died remained with Roosevelt, and he killed it dead in its tracks.

Roosevelt was tired and bitter in 1916, and his dislike of Wilson blotted out everything else. Running as a third-party candidate would have kept the Progressive party alive; it would also have guaranteed Wilson's re-election by splitting the Republican vote. Roosevelt wanted to beat Wilson, but in the end he lost on all counts and died a disappointed man. Alongside La Follette's grim and single-minded progressivism, the internal drive that led him to lead a doomed third party at the age of seventy, Roosevelt's refusal to run in 1916 makes a sorry contrast.

The homeless Progressive party broke up in disorder after 1916, though some rebels refused to play dead. John Parker, Roosevelt's running mate, campaigned anyway, and Victor Murdock and a few others formed a short-lived National Progressive party that merged with the Prohibitionists in 1917. Some of the lost orphans went with Wilson, while others, such as White, returned to Republicanism in an attempt to make it progressive. Beveridge, discouraged at Roosevelt's defection, went back into Republican ranks and ended his life deep in the study of history. The real progressive tradition, the one that Roosevelt never touched, came to light again after the first World War from the source it had always come from—the Midwest and West—in the La Follettes, Norrises, Shipsteads, Borahs, Cappers, and Fraziers who kept it alive.

Whatever the fate of the Progressive party, progressivism by 1916 had won most of its points, though it had been led, since 1870, by men of temperaments and ideas as different as Bryan, La Follette, Roosevelt, and Wilson. It had obtained considerable control of the machinery of government through the direct primary, the initiative and referendum, the popular election of senators, corrupt-practices acts, and other devices. The boss and the machine were still powerful but no longer safe. Business had been placed under governmental control by the Midwestern states and to a lesser extent by the federal government, and the corporation was by 1916 more or less answerable to the public—the old "public be damned" attitude terminated dramatically with U. S. Steel's resolution to investigate itself in 1912. Then too, the fourteenth amendment was slowly drawing in its picket lines. The function of government, it seemed to be agreed by 1916, extended to include the social and economic welfare of the people at large; significant legislation had been passed relating to health, employment, and security. In effect, the essentials of the Populist platform of 1892 were on the statute books by 1916, and the man most responsible for putting them there was Woodrow Wilson.

Woodrow Wilson did not enter politics until he was fifty-four. In 1912 he was exactly what he looked like, a cold, austere, aristocratic professor of history. A former student of Ely's at Johns Hopkins, he taught history and political science until he was made president of Princeton in 1902, where for eight years he attempted to transform the school from a country club into an institution of higher learning. He had almost no experience in practical politics when he became

President—one term as governor of New Jersey—and possessed neither commitments to nor strong affiliations with the Democratic party organization that nominated and elected him. What he knew of government he knew from books—from Bagehot, Gladstone, Burke, and Bryce, and not from the hurly-burly of ward politics. He had never faced a really hard campaign, nor had he dealt with political personalities above the level of the state bosses. Yet his record was deceptive. Wilson was no babe in the political woods.

As president of Princeton, Wilson looked and acted like a reactionary. His comments on politics were consistently conservative and narrow. He distrusted Bryan, thought him "foolish and dangerous in his theoretical beliefs," and hoped, he once said, that Bryanism might be "knocked once and for all into a cocked hat" so that the Democratic party might return to "the conservative principles it represented." Nor did he have any greater respect for Theodore Roosevelt, a "radical" whose policies on trusts and railroads he heartily disliked. In fact, it is difficult to discover a single item in either the Bryan-Populist or the Roosevelt-Progressive program that Wilson did not censure publicly or privately before 1908.

Such complete and thorough conservatism in a man of Wilson's prominence deserved attention. Colonel George Harvey, of the Morgan syndicate and the publisher of *Harper's Weekly*, and Cleveland Dodge of the National City Bank both inspected his record and found him up to specifications. A group of industrialists took him to dinner at Delmonico's, quizzed him thoroughly, set the stamp of approval on him, and a deal with Jim Smith, the Democratic boss of New Jersey, made Wilson the Democratic nominee for governor, an office he won without any great effort. Harvey plastered a banner on the *Harper's* masthead, "For President, Woodrow Wilson," and began booming him as a second Cleveland.

The trouble was that Harvey and the kingmakers had not read Wilson's books, especially *The State* and *An Old Master and Other Political Essays*. Whatever his public statements,

Wilson had been moving in the direction of Bryan and La Follette for almost twenty years, slowly but still surely, and by 1910 he was nearly up to them. *The State,* for example, analyzed the function and aim of government, coming to a stand on the middle ground between individualism and socialism. Government, the book said, is simply an instrument of society, its objective the development of society. Government must regulate public affairs to the end that society progresses and prospers (a rephrasing of the La Follette idea), and therefore all combinations or special interests that threaten society's security or progress must be directly or indirectly under state control. As early as 1889, then, Wilson thought along progressive lines. By 1910 "the New Freedom" was about to mature.

It was not the first time that the bosses made a mistake, but this time the mistake was monumental. Wilson as governor of New Jersey proved to be completely unmanageable. He jettisoned Smith and Harvey, coldly informing the latter that his connection with the Morgans made his support distinctly unwelcome, and set about to reform the state. The bosses could not touch him—his wits had been sharpened on the proving ground of faculty politics—and he beat them at their own game. He made his peace with Bryan, praised La Follette, damned the reactionaries in his own party, and gave New Jersey an enviable two years of progressive government. He also took on a political adviser (the closest friend he ever had), Colonel E. M. House, a Texas Democrat with strong Populist leanings. By 1912 Wilson was a strong presidential possibility by reason of his own efforts and no one else's.

The chart that Wilson followed as President appeared most completely in *The New Freedom,* a book which contributed a new phrase to the political lexicon along with the Croly-Roosevelt "New Nationalism" and the McCarthy-La Follette "New Individualism." "The New Freedom" rejected laissez-faire individualism as a philosophy of government which had served an earlier and simpler era well but which was ill fitted to a new and complex society. "There is one great basic fact which underlies all the questions that are discussed in the political platforms of the present moment," Wilson wrote. "That singular fact is that nothing is done in this country as it was done twenty years ago." A government built on the idea that men did best when let alone, in Wilson's view, did not suit the new social organization. To retain and develop freedom, the nation must evolve a new concept of democratic individualism, with the government serving as co-ordinator and protector of the individual's rights.

The things that Wilson feared most were the trust and its political and economic companions, special privilege and concentration of economic power. All business, he believed, was public business, subject to public control in the same manner as a tenement house or a highway. To guarantee freedom, the corporation must submit to regulation. Government must remove that "hindrance of hindrances," the stifling of competition, so that the old days of individual enterprise might return, bringing to the complex and centralized society of the twentieth century some of the economic, political, and social freedom of the eighteenth and early nineteenth.

"The New Freedom" was therefore a rebirth of the old freedom. It meant exactly what it said—the restoration of individual competition—freedom for the small business against the trust, for the farmer against the banker and manufacturer, for the small bank against the chain, for the laborer against the employer. "The New Freedom" meant, Wilson wrote, "a revival of the power of the people, the beginning of an age of thoughtful reconstruction, that makes our thought hark back to the great age in which democracy was set up in America." So "the New Freedom" went into effect in 1913. "We are going to climb the slow road," Wilson said,

until it reaches some upland where the air is fresher, where the whole talk of politicians is stilled, where men can look in each other's faces and see that there is nothing to conceal; and whence, looking over the road, we shall see at last that we have fulfilled our promise to mankind. We had said to the world, "America was created to break every kind of monopoly, and to set men free, upon a footing of equality," and now we have proved that we have meant it.

Wilson's choice of cabinet members encouraged his supporters. It was not a well-known group, but one composed of men of good caliber, not one of whom came from the inner circle of Eastern bosses. His most important appointment, probably, was Bryan as Secretary of State (it was only sixteen years since Bryan had been called a communist and anarchist), a wise choice from both the standpoint of expediency and politics, for Bryan had still a large personal following and Wilson owed him a debt from the convention of 1912. Wilson's inaugural, one of the finest of presidential documents, picked up the tradition of Jefferson, Jackson, and Bryan where the Democratic party had dropped it in 1896. "The great Government we loved," he said, "has too often been made use of for private and selfish purposes, and those who used it have forgotten the people. . . . We have made up our minds to square every process of our national life again with the standards we so proudly set up in the beginning and have always carried in our hearts." The Democratic victory, he explained, was not simply a change of drivers in the same old wagon going down the same old road. It represented, he believed, a plain indictment by the people of the whole course of recent political trends in America, a clear mandate from them for a thorough reorganization and redirection of political life.

What did the people want? Wilson was sure that he knew. He pledged his administration to a revision of the tariff, to a revision of banking and currency laws, to a revision of labor laws, to aid to agriculture, to a program of antitrust legislation, and to the constructive use of the federal power in the service of humanity through social legislation. There was nothing in his program that had not already been suggested by the Grangers, the Anti-Monopolists, the Populists, the Bryan Democrats, and the Midwest progressives.

Wilson redeemed nearly all his pledges in less than two years. His first message to Congress asked for a revision of the tariff while Underwood was already writing a tariff bill in the House—the chief aim of Republican tariffs, Wilson said, seemed to have been to do everything for the nonproducers of wealth and nothing for the producers. The bill passed the House quickly, and when it looked as if the Senate might re-write it as Aldrich had done in 1909, Wilson put his foot down. As a result the bill came out pretty much as it went in. Both La Follette and Poindexter, left over from insurgent days, approved it heartily, and it was, to be exact, the first honest tariff bill in decades. Eventually in 1916 it was augmented by the creation of a Tariff Commission, the same "scientific" investigative body La Follette suggested in 1906.

The ink was hardly dry on the Underwood Tariff when Wilson was back in Congress to consider the old question of currency and banking. His recommendations had a familiar ring—a Granger-Greenbacker-Silver Democrat-Populist ring—asking for an elastic currency, decentralization of banking, and government control of currency and banking. "Control," said Wilson, taking his words out of the eighties, "must be public, not private, must be vested in the government itself, so that the banks may be the instruments, not the masters of business and of individual enterprise and initiative." Congress responded with the Federal Reserve Act of 1913, creating a system of regional reserve banks, recognizing paper as the money of the country, and providing for a contracting-expanding currency. The act contained too a provision for the extension of agricultural credit, a principle finally made permanent in the Federal Farm Loan Act of 1916, which put the finishing touches on the agrarian demands of the seventies and gave agriculture the credit system it had asked for forty years.

Having concluded operations on two problems that brought both Roosevelt and Taft nothing but trouble, Wilson attacked a third, the hot issue of trusts. His ideas on industrial combinations represented a blend of the Populist, La Follette, and

Rooseveltian views. "I am for big business," he said, "and I am against the trusts." Competition was not wrong, but illicit competition was. "All the fair competition you choose," he wrote in *The New Freedom,* "but no unfair competition of any kind." In essence, he had in mind a system of government regulation so designed as "to make men in a small way of business free to succeed as in a big way . . . to destroy monopoly and maintain competition as the only effectual instrument of business liberty."

The argument was not, in Wilson's view, between big business and small business, but between business and unfair monopoly. "I am not afraid of any corporation, no matter how big," he said in 1912. "I am afraid of any corporation, however small, that is bad, that is rotten to the core, whose practices and actions are in restraint of trade." Big business (and here he agreed with Roosevelt and Croly) was perhaps inevitable and possibly desirable, but monopolistic business was neither; it was the result of illegitimate practices, unfair competition, and special advantages. Legislate against unfair business, bar undesirable practices, keep the competition honest and open— this was the Wilsonian principle, not the Roosevelt-Croly idea of allowing the trust to exist and then controlling it, nor the Bryanite aim of making little business out of big by smashing it into fragments. It was, essentially, closer to La Follette's plan for retaining the competitive principle of capitalism while restraining its practices.

The mixed aspect of the Wilsonian attitude toward the trust was evident in the double-headed legislation passed in 1914 comprising the Federal Trade Commission Act and the Clayton Act. The first set up, in place of the old Bureau of Corporations, a Federal Trade Commission with both investigative and regulative powers. It outlawed "unfair methods of competition in business," supplementing both the old Sherman and the new Clayton acts by establishing the facts upon which antitrust prosecutions might proceed. The FTC defined what business could and could not do (definitions which business itself had long desired); corporations thus had a lead to follow so that suits need not be brought against them unless violations of the code were deliberate and continuous. This, thought Wilson, was a more efficient method of regulation than the old practice of allowing a business to violate the law first and then prosecuting it.

The Clayton Act reinforced and clarified the controversial Sherman Act by outlawing certain practices and prescribing correctives, incidentally exempting labor unions and co-operatives from its provisions to forestall the use of antitrust laws as antilabor weapons. Under the act most of the abuses complained of since the eighties were prohibited—price discrimination, consolidations, interlocking directorates, unfair trade practices, and so on. In addition, it made the personnel of corporations responsible for corporation policy, since it was foolish, said Wilson, to punish the process and let the man go free. In effect, Wilsonian legislation recognized big business as legitimate, as Roosevelt had, so long as it remained only big, but curbed it when it became big and bad. In practice the principle seemed to work fairly well. Though Wilson's administration recorded fewer antitrusts suits than Taft's, in a good many instances the trusts came to terms with FTC without recourse to suit, as they did in both the International Harvester and "Big Five" meat-packer cases. However, the development of the "rule of reason" by the Supreme Court hampered trust prosecution after the Court decided that concentration of economic power was permissible if the method by which power was obtained and its use were "reasonable."

Though he had already put more significant legislation on the books than any other President since Lincoln, Wilson did not pause. The ratification of the seventeenth amendment, embodying the traditional progressive principle of direct senatorial elections, came in 1913. The nineteenth amendment, which gave votes to women, was finally ratified in 1920, and a child-labor act passed in 1916. The La Follette Seamen's Act, which liberated an entire group from an eighteenth-century labor system, passed in 1915, something labor remembered when La Follette ran for President in 1924. The Adamson Law established an eight-hour day for trainmen, an extension of an earlier law governing the hours of government workers and an issue agitated by the Populists in the nineties. Later, in wartime, the creation of the War Labor Board and the War Labor Policies Board did much to encourage better wages and working conditions in industry.

America's entrance into the first World War virtually ended Wilson's domestic program, yet it is clear from the record that during his first administration (actually in less than four years) more legislation of a progressive nature was passed, and the groundwork for more laid, than under any previous leader. And it was distinctly legislation of the Midwest-Bryan-La Follette tradition. Wilson's statement in 1912 that "the history of human liberty is the restriction of governmental functions" was a far cry from the "New Nationalism" of Roosevelt and Croly; Croly himself, after analyzing the "New Freedom," thought it neither satisfactory nor progressive. It looked, he remarked in 1914 in *Progressive Democracy,* "like a revival of Jeffersonian individualism," its "eye fastened more on the past than on the future," a "return to a primitive American democracy."

Croly was perfectly correct. Wilsonianism was Jeffersonianism revised, and had Croly looked more closely he would have found Weaver and Bryan and La Follette in it too—currency reform, protection of agrarian interests, antimonopolism, state regulation of business, state planning for social welfare, direct participation of the voter in government, abolition of special privilege, restoration of individualism. Like La Follette and Bryan, Wilson had a hatred of special privilege, of "the invisible empire" of government, as he called it in the 1912 campaign. "The machinery of political control," he remarked, "must be put in the hands of the people . . . ," and again, "The business of government is to organize the common interest against the special interests," a statement that might easily have come from Donnelly or any other of the Midwestern radicals of the nineteenth century. Ray Stannard Baker, who heard both Wilson and La Follette speak in Philadelphia in 1912, noted that both spoke on exactly the same topic, the control of government by special interests, and came to almost the same conclusions by somewhat different routes. Wilson possessed the same faith in the common man that both Bryan and La Follette expressed again and again. "I believe," he said, "as I believe in nothing else, in the average integrity and the average intelligence of the American people. . . ." For all his icy aloofness, Wilson trusted the individual with the faith of the Populists, and ultimately of Jefferson, not the "people is a great beast" school of Hamilton. "In brief," he wrote in 1910, "our program should be a general revival of popular politics, of common counsel, of responsible government."

Yet there were certain clear contrasts between Wilson and the Midwesterners, differences not of aim but of spirit and method. His program was, like theirs, an attempt to adjust the new industrialism to the democratic tradition. Its reforms were less social and political than economic. Of course, much of what progressivism asked in its social and political philosophy had already been accomplished, on both the state and the federal levels, in the form of workmen's compensation acts, employer liability laws, election and nomination reforms, wage-hour laws, social service legislation, and the like, since such laws lay chiefly within the province of state power. But it is true that Wilson's most significantly progressive legislation was economic—tariffs, banks, trusts—and less directed toward social security and social progress. Nor was Wilson, like La Follette, a believer in "scientific" or "efficient" government, being less inclined to use the specialist, the commission, or the expert consultant in the manner of the Wisconsin experimenters.

Wilson's sharpest contrast with Bryan and La Follette and their Midwest forebears was his lack of the frontier spirit. He was an idealist (his statement, "We must believe the things we tell our children" is one of the most striking ever made by an American politician), but his idealism was cold and emotionless. "The New Freedom" was an inspiring, possibly a visionary, blueprint of the commonwealth to come, but it appealed to the intellect rather than to the blood. Wilson ran his program like a class in political science or a seminar in economics. He inspired no parades, no camp meetings or torchlight processions as Bryan did (no one would think of Wilson as "The Great Commoner" or "The Knight of New Jersey") and he aroused none of the affectionate respect for a hard, fair fighter that made La Follette "Fighting Bob" or "Old Bob" to the Midwest. Who could have called him "Old Woodrow" with a straight face? Wilson did indeed inspire respect and admiration, as a brilliant professor does in a bright student. But not crusades. The difference was that Wilson was national minded where Bryan was class minded and La Follette regional minded. Bryan thought America was the farmer and the laborer, and La Follette thought it was Wisconsin and the Midwest, but Wilson conceived of America in federal terms. Though the cast and the play were the same to all three, Wilson's stage was wider. This was Wilson's strength and the Midwestern progressive's weakness.

It seems strange that a Virginia Democrat from Princeton should have provided for Midwestern progressivism both the leadership it needed and the opportunity to put its essential principles into effect. At second glance it is not so strange. Wilson had most of the political qualities possessed by the Midwestern progressive leaders, no matter what his personal and environmental differences—a keen sense of political strategy, a recognition of the forces that make politics tick, a sensitivity to public opinion and a great respect for it, a gift for the felicitous and dramatic phrase, and above all, a high, clear idealism untainted by compromise, self-interest, or narrow party fealty. He had the drive of Jackson, the broad humanity of Jefferson, the democratic principles of both, and a natural independency of spirit that made him an uncompromising if unspectacular insurgent at heart. And from where, except from frontier agrarian democracy, from the democracy of Jackson and Jefferson, had Midwestern progressivism come? La Follette and Bryan and Weaver and Simpson and Donnelly and the rest were inheritors of the same political strain, carried west to be deposited in the Northwest Territory and the plains states by generations of pioneers. Wilson caught the progressive tradition at its source, at the Virginia headwaters of the stream that flowed west, but it was still the same Jeffersonian river, filtered through a century of change and experience and colored by his own admiration for the nineteenth-century British liberals. The tradition lost with Bryan, missed with La Follette, followed Roosevelt down a blind alley, and in one of the numerous ironies of politics, achieved its most concrete victories under the direction of the austere scholar from the East.

The first World War suspended progressivism while the issue of political freedom was contested on a larger field, and the optimism of the great progressive era was lost in a war for the survival of democracy itself. "Men are afraid all over the world," wrote William Allen White. "The fear psychology has replaced the hopeful buoyance that bolstered civilization before August, 1914." Wilson submerged his legislative program in the war effort, and the drive to speed production of war materials took precedence over the desire to restore competition and initiate "the New Freedom." The Midwestern insurgents left in Congress concerned themselves with unsuccessful efforts to keep profits out of war and to keep the country itself out, trying to preserve meanwhile the political gains made before 1914 and to save fundamental liberties in a time of centralized bureaucratic mobilization for war. The fact that of the "little group of willful men" who opposed the Wilsonian policy of "armed peace" five were Midwestern progressives (La Follette, Norris, Cummins, Gronna, and Clapp) hurt their cause badly, and for their opposition to the armed-ship bill they were subjected to a campaign of excoriation and abuse.

If the leaders of progressivism were, as the press called them, "moral perverts," "copper-streaked politicians," "delinquents and dastards," the whole progressive movement itself was bound to be smeared in the eyes of the public. Nothing constructive could be done in wartime, and after the war the opposition had consolidated itself so strongly in both major parties that the progressives faced a stone wall wherever they turned. Reaction was back with a vengeance. The Republican slogan "Less government in business and more business in government" struck the dominant chord of the Wagnerian symphony of the roaring twenties. So the old progressives began the long, slow road back.

The Road Back, 1920–1958

VII

The prosperity of the twenties was the greatest the nation had ever experienced, and the deflating it received in 1929 was likewise the most thorough flattening it had ever undergone. When the merry-go-round broke down, as a popular song of a later period expressed it, the bleakness of the early thirties settled in. In the midst of hopelessness, the shining Utopia of the New Deal took shape, and the promise was so brilliant, so dazzlingly conceived, that the old progressive dream of an agrarian commonwealth looked dated and old fashioned by comparison. The old leaders died, the grim war against the "interests" and the "plutocrats" interred with them. The cadets could not carry on the battle alone, nor were they sure of what the battle was. The Midwest that spawned the tradition was now simply no longer a regional entity, but a part of a larger unit, engaged in a greater offensive against transatlantic ideologies. Of the old crusade, all that remained was the moral energy, diverted into new channels.

THE FIRST WORLD WAR broke the progressive movement, scattered it, and left it in 1920 with no point on which to re-form. "Right now our government is in the hands of

reactionaries and every executive official is afraid for his life
if he undertakes to even be friendly to such men as myself,"
George Norris wrote after the close of the war. In the Midwestern states, where progressivism gained its first solid victories twenty years before, conservatism was in power again
after the Wilsonian interregnum. The progressives did not lie
down quietly under conservative rule. The focal point of revolt, a revolt that was in essence a resurgence of Grangerism,
was North Dakota.

North Dakota in 1914 was in some respects still frontier
territory, sparsely settled by a good many different immigrant
strains. Except for five years under the enlightened governorship of John Burke, the state had been for years in the grip
of a powerful Republican ring. Grain-raising North Dakota
was peculiarly vulnerable to price fixing, since it depended on
the railroad for the transportation of its products and on St.
Paul, Minneapolis, Duluth, and Chicago for its market outlets.
As a result the state was kept under close control by Alexander
McKenzie, the St. Paul Republican boss, and the interests he
represented. Working with McKenzie and the politicians was
the Minneapolis Chamber of Commerce, which was empowered
by the Minnesota legislator to make its own rules stand as
law and which required a $25,000 initiation fee for member-
ship. Since the Chamber of Commerce, along with the Duluth
and Chicago Boards of Trade, controlled the grain market,
the chances of a farmers' representative's gaining a seat on
any of them were obviously small.

North Dakota, because of its late entrance into the Union,
had been touched only lightly by the Granger and Farmers'
Alliance movements. In 1914 it stood about in the position of
the Granger states of the eighties and nineties. The uprising
under Burke from 1907 to 1912 breached the conservative wall
(establishing a direct primary, a railroad commission, direct
senatorial elections, and a state-owned elevator) but by 1914
the Republicans had re-established themselves without much
opposition. "Go home and slop the hogs and stop bothering
us," the state legislature told one farmers' group, and there

was nothing they could do about it. But the North Dakota farmer by 1915 was in a rebellious mood. Rebuffed by his legislature, governed from a hotel suite in St. Paul, robbed by railroads and elevators and millers, he was ready for revolt.

An analysis of his situation showed why. Loans in North Dakota carried 10 to 16 per cent interest, with one recorded high of 24 per cent. Provided the farmer did get credit and raise a crop, he dealt next with the chain or "line" elevator which bought his grain at a price fixed by an agreement among the elevator operators. When his wheat was graded at the elevator, he took what was offered. One elevator chain over a two-year period shipped out four and one-half million more bushels of No. 1 wheat than it took in; another docked farmers for screenings in wheat and then sold the screenings for $8 a ton. It was calculated that a single elevator could make $30,000 a month on grade-shifting alone, and also that 60 per cent of all elevator scales were "defective."

If he managed to escape the elevators, the farmer next faced the railroad. A rebellious farmer who bothered the elevator owners might find the railroad mysteriously unable to provide cars for his wheat, or discover that he owed "switching" charges. Also, the railroads had a peculiar "terminal freight rate" system: no matter where the farmer shipped his grain, he paid charges to the terminal point of the line, which might be Minneapolis, Duluth, Chicago, or Milwaukee. Thus a farmer who sold his wheat to a near-by elevator might pay charges to a city to which his wheat never went; furthermore, when he bought his own wheat back as flour, he paid freight on it from Minneapolis, though it might have been milled less than ten miles away. One farmer, toting up his accounts, found he received $1.30 a bushel for his wheat and paid $17 a barrel for flour; he received nothing at all for wheat screenings and paid $20 a ton for feed made from them. The "Feed D" wheat for which he was paid $658 sold two days later on the exchange for $1,058. He and others tried to do something about it, but never very successfully.

Arthur C. Townley, an ex-Socialist with a genius for organizing, began his political activities in North Dakota in 1915. Townley saw that the key to the situation was political action, and that the key to political action was organization. So he formed an organization, calling for state-owned terminal elevators, state-owned flour mills, packing houses, and storage plants; for state inspection of grain-grading practices; for exemption of farm improvements from taxation; for state hail insurance; and for rural-credit banks operated at cost. What Townley proposed was not new—indeed, most of it had been offered by the Grangers long before—but he offered it at the right time. What Townley really had, one commentator said, was "salesmanship, the promise of action, and a Ford." From these came the Non Partisan League.

The organization of the Non Partisan League was a work of skill. Dues were high ($16 for two years), but Townley was willing to accept notes. He picked up organizers, many of them ex-Socialists like himself, and chose one well-known farmer in each section as a "booster" to help his agents. He established a paper, the *Non Partisan Leader* and hired a good editor (C. E. Russell, later city editor of the New York *World*) and a good cartoonist (John Baer, who later became a congressman). As time passed, he set up more *Leaders* and enlisted the sympathies of more than a hundred independent dailies in the Northwest. In about six months he enrolled forty thousand members in spite of accusations that the League was "a fleecing scheme," a "socialist plot," and a "lust for personal power."

Townley did not intend at first to establish a third party. The main thing, he believed, was to avoid voting for any man who represented the wrong interests, no matter what his party affiliation. "If you put a lawyer, a banker, and an industrialist in a barrel and roll it downhill," he remarked, "there'll always be a son-of-a-bitch on top"—a view of politics that delighted the farmer.

The League's first real test came in 1916 when it ran Lynn Frazier as its candidate for governor. With the help of the poorest wheat crop since 1910, the League won easily, gaining control of the lower house but not of the state senate. The upper house blocked the better part of Frazier's program, but he nevertheless accomplished a great deal. The success of 1916 prompted Townley to announce that he was ready to begin operations in other states of the Northwest as well as in Washington, Colorado, Oklahoma, Texas, and Louisiana, or wherever the farmer needed him.

Minnesota, a grain and dairy state, resembled North Dakota most closely in its economy and background, and the Non Partisan League met most success there. Townley opened offices in St. Paul in January, 1918, founded the *Minnesota Leader,* and sent out agents. By midyear he had about fifty thousand members signed up and forty county newspapers in line. Since Minnesota also had miners and factory workers, he tacked on some labor planks to the League's platform (free employment bureaus, state-owned paper mills, an eight-hour day for industry, and so on) stressing the need for farmer-labor political co-operation. The state League convention in 1918 made overtures to Republican Governor Burnquist, who flatly turned it down, so it nominated Congressman Charles Lindbergh, the old insurgent, who lost.

Townley changed his tactics. Negotiations with the Minnesota Federation of Labor turned the League into a frankly farmer-labor political organization called the Working People's Non Partisan Political League, or the Farmer-Labor party, which put up David Evans against Burnquist in the next election. Evans lost, but the new coalition took about a quarter of the seats in the house and one fifth of those in the senate. It swung enough weight to pass a law legalizing co-operative markets (a fight since Grange days in Minnesota) but that was its only real victory. The war hurt the League badly in Minnesota. Evans lost the primary race for governor in 1920, and Henrik Shipstead, who ran as an independent with League backing, lost to the wealthy Republican Jacob Preus. After that the League disappeared as a political influence, but the

Farmer-Labor party remained, finally electing Floyd Olson to the governorship in 1930.

Oliver S. Evans ran the Non Partisan League in Nebraska, taking over the thirty thousand-strong Farmers' Union as a nucleus for it. But unfortunately much of the League's strength lay in German-settled rural areas, where war hysteria severely hampered its activities. In Wisconsin O. A. Stolen piled up a membership of thirty thousand, soon absorbed by La Follette progressivism. Montana, a mining-agricultural state, developed an organization resembling the Farmer-Labor group in Minnesota. In none of these states did the League exert the influence it had in North Dakota. According to unofficial figures, by 1918 it had 50,000 members in Minnesota, 40,000 in North Dakota, 25,000 in South Dakota, 21,000 in Montana, 30,000 in Wisconsin, and 56,000 scattered through nine other states.

The outbreak of the war gave the opponents of the League a chance to wreck the organization, and they did a thoroughly efficient job of it. The official stand taken by Townley was that it was "a rich man's war." While the League would back the war effort to the limit, he said, it would sanction no wartime profits for industry and would keep on crusading for a square deal for the farmer, a stand not unlike that of La Follette and the other Midwestern progressive leaders. Therefore Townley suggested that an excess-profits tax be levied on industry, that the government control the railroads, and that prices be fixed at reasonable levels.

Whether deliberately or not—and in some cases it was clearly deliberate—League opponents called this un-American, disloyal, communistic, and pro-German. Roosevelt, who had first hailed the League as "progressive," believed that it was now "necessary for every loyal American severely to condemn it." League members and organizers were beaten and run out of Midwestern towns by vigilante groups. Townley himself was tried and acquitted in Minnesota for allegedly discouraging enlistments and later convicted of the same charge in 1919, and La Follette, speaking at a League-sponsored convention in St. Paul, was misquoted by the press in one of the most blatant offenses against truth in the history of American journalism, damned as a pro-German, and very nearly expelled from the Senate.

In Nebraska the State Council for Defense labeled the League as unpatriotic, and when it distributed copies of Wilson's book, *The New Freedom,* the Council officially prescribed the book as "seditious"—an odd decision in the light of the fact that Wilson was at the time President and Commander-in-Chief. Attorney General Reed of Nebraska ruled that League organizers were not engaged in a useful occupation, thereby making them subject to immediate draft. Anti-League forces everywhere, with the exception of North Dakota, used similar tactics to discredit it, despite the fact that George Creel's Committee on Public Information cleared it of charges of disloyalty. But the war killed the League. By 1920 it was no longer a major force in Northwest politics. Townley, discredited by his conviction in 1919, organized the National Producers' Alliance as its successor in the early 1920's and merged it with the Farmers' Union in 1926.

What the Non Partisan League represented was nothing more or less than the renaissance of Grangerism. It was an attempt by the farmer and the laborer to escape the domination of industrial, marketing, and transportation interests, an effort by the producer to gain control of the transportation and sale of his product. So far as it related to the economic problems of grain growing, the program of the League differed not a whit from that of the Kansas-Nebraska-Iowa farmers of forty years before. But the League showed the influence of all that had gone on since the Grangers—the twentieth-century progressives' interest in extension of state services, direct participation in government, and the use of the commission. It drew something quite obviously from socialism too—the native, non-Marxian brand—but its measures were more common sense than doctrinaire. The League was willing to go further toward public ownership than were either Republican or

Democratic progressives, but this did not mean that they were more socialistic or less progressive. Contemporary attacks on the League as "bolshevistic" or "socialistically inspired" may be almost completely discounted. It may have included crackpots and malcontents, but in the long run it was the ordinary farmer who controlled it and made it powerful. It disappeared when its work was done, but the hard core of Non Partisan League support remained for La Follette in 1924 and to some extent for the New Deal in 1932.

By 1920 the nation at large was tired of Wilsonian idealism, of progressivism, of reform, of wartime emotionalism. People wanted nothing so much as to be let alone to enjoy the postwar boom. Roosevelt was dead, La Follette still in the shadow of wartime "disloyalty," the country out of patience with Jeremiahs. "Less government in business and more business in government," the Republican slogan, summed up the prevailing attitude. Republicanism was controlled by conservatives, men such as Lodge, Reed Smoot, Grundy, and Charles Curtis; the progressive element was brushed aside. White, Ickes, Hiram Johnson, and other ex-Bull Moosers tried to inject something of the old spirit into the party, only to see the 1920 presidential convention choose Harding and his "return to normalcy." The Democrats, angry at Wilson and his League of Nations, selected James Cox, governor of Ohio, and as his running mate Franklin D. Roosevelt, a young New Yorker. Neither party platform held out much hope that progressivism might pick up where it left off.

Like McKinley, Harding conducted a "back porch" campaign from his home in Marion, Ohio, and the nation turned to the handsome Ohio editor with relief. America needed, he said, "not heroics but healing, not nostrums but normalcy, not revolution but restoration . . . ," phrases that caught and expressed perfectly the postwar mood. It was not only Harding's campaign that recalled McKinley; the whole temper of the early twenties resembled that of 1900. A victorious war had just concluded, a boom of prosperity was under way, and although the nation suffered a temporary recession in 1921, it was still on the verge of the most prosperous period in its history. Wealth rolled in almost without conscious effort.

The trusts, by no means "busted," were strong and powerful. The older ones and the railroads were bigger than ever. New and equally large were General Motors, DuPont, United States Electric Power, Insull's Middle Western Utilities, and a dozen other later arrivals, some of them so huge and intricate that no one knew where they began or ended or how much they were worth. The House of Morgan, after two decades of defensive retreat, still was estimated to have connections with one quarter of all corporate wealth in the nation.

The businessmen of the twenties who controlled these corporations were not of the same type that Bryan and La Follette attacked a decade and more before. The "capitalist" of McKinley days was something of an individualist, buying the privileges and immunities he needed, identifying his own interests with the public's, following the principle of "what's good for me is good for the country," while the businessman of the twenties were much more united, articulate, and class conscious. They organized into trade associations, manufacturers' associations, chambers of commerce, business protective groups, and so on, cultivating class solidarity to make up for the fact that they were a minority. By steady offensive warfare, intelligent use of public relations, unity of purpose, and sheer energy, businessmen displaced lawyers as the ruling class in politics and used political means to consolidate their industrial and economic positions.

The change in the attitude of the American public toward the rich man reflected the victory of business in the twenties. "The public hatred of wealth has subsided," remarked Arthur Train in 1924. "As the years have gone by and the millionaire era has become the billionaire era, the virus of acquisition has built up its own anti-toxin." Nobody asked questions any more, or at least few did, about huge fortunes. The billionaire was assumed to have made his money by zeal, initiative, ambition, and intelligence, and in many quarters there was anxiety lest foolish legislation impair his genius for productive accumulation. The cycle had run from thorny old Commodore Vanderbilt to Rockefeller to Henry Ford, from admiration to hatred to faith. The same public that hated Morgan and the elder Rockefeller made Henry Ford (a less able man) into a national idol, proposed him for President, and hung on his words as if he were an oracle. The twenties rolled in money, and could not help trusting money or those who had it. As George Norris, one of the few remaining doubters, said, "People flung themselves on their knees at the shrine of private business and industry." Progressivism never flourished in such an atmosphere.

Harding's "normalcy" meant a return to the political temper of Grant's time, to the "great barbecue" of the seventies and eighties. Completely unequipped to deal with any of the nation's major problems, surrounded by as untrustworthy a group of advisers as ever cursed a President, Harding immediately fell among thieves. Congress got down to business at once, and the whole trend of Wilsonian politics went into complete reverse.

The first move was to repeal the wartime excess-profits tax and the taxes on gifts and estates. The income tax remained, but millions of dollars leaked out of legal loopholes the Treasury had failed to notice for more than five years. The railroads returned to private ownership after wartime government operation. Under the Esch-Cummins Law (the same insurgent Cummins, now on the other side of the fence) they were awarded a 5.5 per cent profit return for the wartime period plus one half of all profits over 6 per cent, the latter provision so loosely worded that the railroads collected millions while the courts attempted to define it. The Fordney-McCumber tariff revised rates upward for protection of industry while corporation taxes went downward to provide capital. The Federal Trade Commission turned into a purely research organization, allowing the Sherman and Clayton acts to languish while it found evidence to allow business to do what it was doing. The courts followed the same line. Their acquittal of U. S. Steel in 1920 under the "rule of reason" showed that bigness was no longer wrong, that it need merely to behave reasonably.

Harding's death and Coolidge's succession changed matters very little. The taciturn Vermonter gave the Republican party a desperately needed touch of respectability and steadiness, but his dictum that "the business of America is business" was only a clearer statement of Harding's "normalcy." Coolidge's ideas dated from McKinley's time and exactly represented his party. La Follette dryly remarked of his first message to Congress, "It was an able, concise, and frank presentation of the standpat, reactionary theory of government. . . . There is nothing in the message that will offend the most sensitive of big business interests." Will Rogers caught the Coolidge spirit a little better, saying, "He didn't do anything, but that's what people wanted done."

To the progressive it seemed as if the whole thing had to be done over again. "Where shall the progressive go?" asked George Payne in the *Forum*. The Bull Mooser and Midwest insurgent were out of place in the party of Harding and Coolidge, nor could either find shelter in Democracy. Herbert Croly remarked that the Republican party, once the haven of progressivism, "has since 1912 developed steadily in the direction of conscious dogmatic conservatism." The Democrats were not much better. "There is nothing between the parties," wrote Samuel Blythe in 1922, "save the desire of the Republicans, who are in power, to stay in power, and the desire of the Democrats, who are not in power, to get back in power." Both parties were conservative—the Republicans proudly so, the Democrats somewhat apologetically. Payne's question, in the light of the political alignment of the twenties, simply had no answer.

The progressives, particularly those in the Middle West, did not die easily. There was, even before the beginnings of the Bourbon reign in 1920, quite a good deal of liberal, progressive, and radical thought lying about, scattered and ineffective but very much alive. The Non Partisan League, broken and discredited by war, still had thousands of members in the Northwest. Labor, not present as a political factor in 1896 or 1912, was flexing its muscles. Several labor parties formed in wartime, notably the Independent Labor party backed by the Chicago unions in 1918, and a year later many of them consolidated into the National Labor party. The Farmer-Labor party, particularly in Minnesota, was a going concern and a potential ally for the National Laborites. Then too, there were remnants of the Progressives of 1916, the National Progressive party steered by a few Bull Moosers, and the Socialist party of Berger and Debs. Out of these, and out of a considerable body of unaffiliated independents, it was possible something might develop.

In 1919 a group of die-hard progressives called a meeting in New York to see whether some organization of progressive groups might be perfected. The group gathered—labor men, Socialists, Bull Moosers, intellectuals, old Populists, single taxers, Midwestern La Follette progressives, and all the rest—and dissolved after passing some platform resolutions and calling a second conference in St. Louis late in the year. The St. Louis conference met over some local objection (it was necessary to get a restraining injunction to allow it to proceed) and established the "Committee of Forty-eight," not a political party but the first move toward one. The Committee, as the composition of its board indicated, was run by a rather diverse group. J. A. H. Hopkins, the chairman, was a wealthy New Jerseyite who had once served as a Bull Moose executive; McAlister Coleman was a Socialist of the Debs school; Will Durant, John Haynes Holmes, and Arthur Garfield Hays were prominent intellectuals; Gilbert Roe was a La Follette lieutenant, and Frederic C. Howe a veteran of Tom Johnson's reign in Cleveland. The Bull Moose executive committee, custodians of the Progressive name, officially bequeathed it to these men.

The St. Louis conference stimulated further conferences, and when the Chicago Farmer-Labor convention met in July of 1920, the Forty-eighters attended. They were badly disappointed. The convention settled down into an internal row between labor unions (an anti-Gompers group versus a pro-Gompers group), and the Committee of Forty-eight delegates marched out in disgust. After their departure the convention passed a thoroughly leftist platform and fully intended to nominate La Follette as a candidate for 1920, but "Old Bob" knew better than to allow himself to be tangled up in a labor dispute. He was busy fashioning a third party of his own in Wisconsin, and he knew that the agrarian Midwest was by no means ready for decisive political action.

La Follette refused the convention's nomination on the ground that the platform's public ownership plank was too sweeping for his taste. Instead, the Chicago meeting called itself the Farmer-Labor party and nominated Parley P. Christianson of Utah for President. Without AFL or progressive support, and with Debs running from prison on the Socialist ticket, Christianson drew fewer than three hundred thousand votes. The Farmer-Labor party evidently did not fill the bill. It was too far to the left for the La Follette and Bull Moose progressives, too far to the right for the Socialists, and split within its own ranks. If progressive sentiment were to find expression, wrote Allen McCurdy of the Forty-eighters, it must come through the creation of some other new party.

The whole body of dissident political thought, ranging from the Forty-eighters on the right through to the Socialists on the left, waited in 1922 for some central issue on which to join forces. The fifteen railroad brotherhoods, early in the year, crystallized matters by calling a Conference for Progressive Political Action, to be held in Cleveland in February. "There has been no common understanding to bind the working of all walks of life together," their announcement read. "For lack of this common understanding we have been divided and betrayed. . . . This is not an attempt to form a new political party. It is an effort to make use of those constructive forces already in existence and by cooperation to bring about political unity." Everyone was invited—farmer, laborer, Bull Mooser, Forty-eighter, any attached or unattached liberal—and though the railroad unions denied third-party intentions, something was certainly in the air.

The Socialists, after some deliberation, threw in with the movement, a decision which marked a major shift in their strategy, for they had refused since Donnelly's time to co-operate with the Midwestern liberals. But some new course of action was necessary, for the party was in desperate straits. Since the Debs campaign of 1920 it had declined rapidly, and its leaders did not wish to lose the initiative to whatever new third party might develop from the Conference for Progressive Political Action. Though co-operation with non-Socialist groups might mean, as Morris Hillquit said, "a corresponding loss of clarity and purpose," Socialists preferred to take that chance rather than be excluded. The general feeling among Socialist leaders was that the progressives were headed in the right direction, that a La Follette-led third party might conceivably end up as a true Social Democratic party. Therefore they threw in with the CPPA. Hillquit, in fact, suggested the name.

The first CPPA conference gathered in about every existing shade of opinion except conservative. The Non Partisan League, fifty unions, single taxers, Socialists, the Catholic Welfare Council, the Methodist Federation for Social Service, the Church League for Industrial Democracy—nearly all splinter groups, large or small—had at least one delegate among the three hundred who attended. The conference was concerned chiefly with organizing machinery in the states, setting up a national headquarters, and passing resolutions attacking "the invisible government of plutocracy and privilege" that had "usurped the government." Taking a leaf from the Granger book, the conference decided to run no tickets of its own in the states, preferring instead merely to endorse candidates for the congressional elections of the fall of 1922. The next meeting, scheduled for Cleveland in December of 1922, was to proceed further with a national organization if the situation so warranted.

Whether or not it was the work of Frederic Howe's Committee on Organization, CPPA-endorsed candidates did very well in the fall elections. La Follette returned to the Senate with a smashing victory, as untamed as ever. The Farmer-Labor party in Minnesota sent Magnus Johnson and Henrik Shipstead to Congress, Frazier and Ladd of the Non Partisan League came back from North Dakota and Brookhart from Iowa in place of Cummins (who no longer seemed a progressive), and other CPPA choices won in Nebraska, Kansas, Colorado, Montana, Oklahoma, and Arizona. "The Midwest," commented William Allen White, "is on the rampage again." The West, thought Norris, was tired of political machines, "just as tired of one machine as of the other." *Current History*, counting up the "radical insurgents" in Congress, found in the House fifteen from Wisconsin, five from Minnesota, one each from Kansas and North Dakota, and one (Fiorello LaGuardia) from New York, all in addition to the incumbent senatorial group.

La Follette, who was by seniority and temperament the acknowledged leader of the new CPPA-progressive bloc, called a meeting in Washington in early December in conjunction with the People's Legislative Service League. The meeting had much the flavor of the old National Progressive Republican League. All the recalcitrant congressmen were there—Norris, Brookhart, Ladd, Frazier, Wheeler, LaGuardia, Shipstead, Borah, McNary, and others—with such private citizens as Oswald Garrison Villard of the *Nation*, Herbert Croly of the *New Republic*, Roger Baldwin, and labor men like Andrew Furuseth, Samuel Gompers, and John Moore. The group limited itself to attacks on "special privilege," and to resolutions pledging support to progressive legislation. Led by La Follette, its congressional members sniped incessantly at the Republicans, especially during the graft scandals, and in general comported themselves like the insurgents of 1909. Its 1922 meeting had no official connection with the CPPA, but there it was—a body of progressive strength ready at hand, in Congress and out of it.

At the December meeting of the CPPA in Cleveland, the progressives encountered, for the first time, the Communists who were to hamper their efforts for the next twenty years. The DeLeon Socialists, who split with the Debs-Berger Socialist wing at the turn of the century, had kept up an ineffective existence since that time. But the revolution in Russia and the formation of the Leninist party gave communism a new pattern and a new impetus. After 1919, the Marxist-Leninists reorganized and finally emerged as the Workers' party in 1921. Their strategy, familiar in subsequent years, was to infiltrate and capture a going liberal party, partly as a front and partly as a means of attracting non-Communist support. The Chicago CPPA conference of 1922 turned them down flat, but the Communists had hopes of gaining entrance to the Cleveland meeting and came in force.

William Z. Foster, the most able and aggressive of the Communists, led an uninvited group to Cleveland and got exactly nowhere. A motion to refuse seats to Workers' party delegates found practically unanimous support from progressives, union representatives, and Socialists, so the Workers withdrew. The convention then went on to discuss consolidating the gains in the states made in the 1922 congressional campaigns, but still deferred action on a third party until the national picture was clearer. The unions, traditionally against the third parties anyway, did not want one yet. The Socialists, already a third party of long standing, wanted to form one then and there. The farm representatives favored perfecting an organization in the states first. In the end the unions won, and the conference de-

cided to watch voting trends during 1923 before taking definite action on a third party.

While the CPPA was temporizing, the Workers' party, twice
rejected, almost stole the ball. The Communists needed an
established third party of comparatively unblemished reputation as a Trojan horse, and since both the AFL and CPPA
seemed impregnable, they cast about for alternatives. The
Farmer-Labor party blunderingly gave them their chance
when it called a convention of non-CPPA elements in Chicago
in mid-1923 and included the Workers' party in the invitation.
The Communists, with characteristic discipline and solidarity,
set out to pack the convention. The totally unsuspecting credentials committee seated so many representatives of previously unheard-of organizations that the innocent Farmer-
Laborites, Socialists, Non Partisan Leaguers, and labor groups
had no chance. The convention voted the way the Communist
steering committee directed. Foster, Ruthenberg, and Gitlow
simply steam-rollered the farmers and unionists flat.

The Communists wanted a third party and they got it—the
Federated Farmer-Labor party. The trouble was that the steal
was a little too obvious. With their usual disregard for the
intelligence of the average voter, the Communists tipped their
hand far too much. The original Farmer-Labor group refused
to support the new Federated Farmer-Labor organization, the
unions repudiated it, and the CPPA, perfectly aware of the
theft, ignored it. By the opening of 1924 the name Farmer-
Labor no longer meant what it said, and nearly everyone
knew it.

As the CPPA's organization developed, the creation of a
third party came closer to reality. After it adopted a platform,
disseminated literature, and worked as a party in two states,
the Midwest and the West demanded more definite action.
Herbert Croly remarked in the *New Republic* in early 1924
that he found "profound popular protest in the West," and
again a month later he noted that there was "bitter discontent
among the farmers and political unrest." The *Nation* believed

that a third party ought to be organized at once to lead the nation "out of the dismal wilderness of 'business administration,'" while the *Forum* noted that after twenty years of trying to reform the Republican party, the Midwest seemed about ready to give it up as a bad job and form a party of its own. There were many such straws in the wind, all blowing in the same direction. The Midwest and West, said Henrik Shipstead, wanted a new party, pledged to public ownership of natural resources and key industries, lower freight rates, a stable currency, and honest government. It had waited for these things long enough.

All that the CPPA needed to become an actual party was a name, a convention, and a candidate. For the candidate there was but one choice, La Follette, the last of the old progressive vanguard. Now almost seventy, iron-gray and aging, the senator had mellowed a bit. As a veteran of more than twenty years of campaigning, he obviously possessed the necessary experience. He had a backlog of support throughout the Midwest and West and a stainless reputation, with only his wartime record against him. He was acceptable to labor on the right and to the Socialists on the left, as well as to the whole range of progressivism in between. Morris Hillquit thought his "political conceptions moved wholly within the orbit of the existing economic system"—the traditional difference between Socialist and progressive—but still close enough to socialism to be satisfactory. The Committee of Forty-eight, after a poll of progressives, found him to be an almost unanimous selection. George Soule summed it up in the *New Republic* in the spring of 1924, saying, "The deep devotion felt for the steadfastness and incorrigible honesty of La Follette on the part not only of the Western progressives but also even of the more conservative labor unions has suddenly crystallized into the conviction that he was the one experienced national leader who could unite all the essential constituencies." So the candidate nearly had to be La Follette.

The Communist-controlled Farmer-Labor Federation had much the same idea. If, they reasoned, they nominated La Follette first, the CPPA would be placed in an extremely embarrassing position. It would be forced either to give tacit support to the Federation by naming the same candidate, or kill its own chances by repudiating its best nominee. However, La Follette, perfectly aware of their intentions, ruined the plan quickly and effectively. In May, 1924, he published a letter written to Herman Ekern of Wisconsin, in answer to Ekern's request to explain his stand on communism and the Farmer-Labor Federation.

La Follette's letter was and still is the classic reply of progressivism to communism. "The Communists," he wrote, "have admittedly entered into this political movement not for the purpose of curing, by means of the ballot, the evils which affect the American people, but only to divide and confuse the Progressive movement and create a condition of chaos favorable to their ultimate aims. . . . To pretend that the Communists can work with the Progressives who believe in democracy is deliberately to deceive the public. The Communists are antagonistic to the Progressive cause and their only purpose in joining such a movement is to disrupt it." For these reasons, he concluded, "I most emphatically protest against their being admitted into the council of any body of Progressive voters." The progressive movement's skirts were clean after La Follette's letter was published. The Federated Farmer-Labor convention met in June, and with La Follette's unequivocal reply at hand, named Duncan MacDonald (a non-Communist miner) for President. But a month later the Executive Committee vetoed the convention's choice, put up Foster and Gitlow, both avowed Communists.

A "La Follette for President" committee, sparked by Dante Pierce, editor of the *Iowa Homestead,* Donald Richberg, special legislative attorney for the railroad unions, and W. T. Rawleigh, a wealthy manufacturer from Freeport, Illinois, set up headquarters in Chicago in preparation for the July CPPA convention. The Republican convention met in early June in Cleveland, a dull, cut-and-dried meeting. With no real issue to discuss, and with Coolidge almost certain to be nominated, the convention had nothing to argue about. The speeches were able and without exception reactionary, reaching some sort of high point in Chairman Mondell's statement that the party had "never proposed nor advocated an unwise or unsound national policy." The Wisconsin delegation dutifully submitted the same progressive platform it had been submitting to Republican conventions since 1908, and received the customary flattening from the platform committee. "At its best," concluded William Allen White, who reported the convention, "this party, wholly conservative with no liberal flaw, spot, or blemish in its creed, completely represents the yearnings of a benevolent plutocracy."

The Democratic convention in New York, held later the same month, was vastly livelier but hardly more concerned with the real issues of 1924. Few conventions have been more wide open. It was an aggregate of discordant factions—Bryanite Westerners, city bosses, Southern Bourbons—the same groups Wilson and Bryan had temporarily united, now flying apart. Wilson was dead and repudiated, Bryan a ghost from the past (a newspaperman finally discovered him squeezed between a fat woman and a cub reporter, pressed against the back wall). And again like many Democratic conventions, it opened with no majority for any candidate but with two favorites, Al Smith of New York and William Gibbs McAdoo of California.

McAdoo, who administered the railroads in wartime, had union support and Bryan's backing (for what it was worth) and was a "dry" (especially appealing to the West) and a Protestant. Al Smith, a "wet" Catholic, had the support of the city machines and a surprisingly large following among urban voters, who loved him as the tough city kid who spoke out of the side of his mouth and had risen from fish market to governor's chair. It took one hundred and one ballots to finally convince the convention that neither could win, and on the one hundred and third it chose a dark horse, John W. Davis of West Virginia, a courtly, able, middle-of-the-roader. Quickly Charles Bryan, William's brother, was chosen to run with Davis. If, as the Democrats seemed to feel in June, 1924, the chief issues of the campaign were Catholicism and prohibition, the party was in dire straits indeed.

The Progressive convention in Cleveland in early July was a wholly different matter. William Allen White, there as a reporter, sensed the charged atmosphere, the air of seriousness, purposefulness, sincerity. Its personnel indicated the range of its appeal and the traditions, both old and new, from which it sprang—Lynn Frazier of North Dakota and the Non Partisan League, Shipstead of Minnesota from the Farmer-Labor stronghold, Zona Gale and Edwin Markham of the literati, Peter Witt from Tom Johnson's Cleveland, Andrew Furuseth from the hard-bitten Seamen's Union, Johnston and Wills of the railroad and machinists' brotherhoods, Victor Berger and Norman Thomas and Morris Hillquit of the Socialists, General Coxey of Populist days. Compared to the Bull Moose meeting of 1912, the Progressive convention was less a crusade and more a planned attack. It did not stand at Armageddon, nor did it sing the "Battle Hymn of the Republic" so lustily as Roosevelt's legions. But it sang almost as feelingly such songs as "Twas a long long trail that led us, unto the party of our dreams" and (to the tune of *Maryland, My Maryland*)

> His mind is wise, his courage vast;
>   La Follette, yes La Follette:
> In nothing can he be outclassed—
>   La Follette, yes La Follette.

The credentials committee, remembering the fate of the Farmer-Laborites, inspected delegates carefully. Suspected Communists were quickly and ruthlessly thrown out. The "Red" threat disposed of, the convention got down to business.

Among the delegates, four fairly well-organized blocs could be recognized—the Wisconsin group, the Non Partisan Leaguers from the Northwest, the railroad brotherhoods, and the Socialist party—whose claims and divergent ideas had to be discussed and adjusted. There was some pulling and hauling, but not much. The chief point of conflict lay in the fact that La Follette wished to run as an independent, the Socialists wanted to form a national third party, and labor was not so sure. As an independent, La Follette felt he could avoid the stigma of running as a "class" candidate, and appeal to the whole progressive-radical electorate regardless of party lines. His refusal settled the matter, and the Socialists finally acceded.

Oddly enough, the National Committee asked La Follette to run before the balloting began, a logical move in the light of the obvious impossibility of the convention's asking someone else, and La Follette accepted on the first day of the convention. For Vice-President, they chose Burton K. Wheeler, a hurly-burly Montana Democrat who fought Anaconda Copper in his home state and whose probe of the Department of Justice in the oil scandals had nearly sent the Attorney General to prison.

Compared with the Republican and Democratic platforms, the Progressive document was a model of brevity and pertinence. Its first sentence stated its dominant theme: "The great issue before the American people today is the control of government and industry by private monopoly." Monopoly, it went on, "crushed competition, stifled private initiative and independent enterprise, and . . . now extracts extortionate profits upon every necessity of life consumed by the public." It destroyed "equality of opportunity," ruined the farmer by "extending almost unlimited credit to the great corporations by tariffs . . . , excessive freight rates . . . , gambling on farm products." Monopoly, big business, drove out competition, and this the Progressives chose as the major issue of their campaign. Their target, as La Follette phrased it in his letter of acceptance, was "the combined power of private monopoly over the political and economic life of the American people."

The specific planks of the platform marked out the lines of attack. It asked for a house cleaning of all federal executive departments to insure honest antimonopolistic policies. It asked for conservation of natural resources—especially oil, coal, and iron—for public ownership of water power, and for the development of a super utilities system to provide electricity and nitrates at cost. For railroads it asked a thorough over-hauling of rate and tax policies, and eventually public owner-ship. It wanted a complete revision of tax schedules, with larger inheritance and excess-profits taxes and a corresponding reduction of income taxes in the lower brackets. For the farmer it wanted an extension of federal aid and credit. For labor it asked the abolition of the use of the injunction in strikes and recognition of collective bargaining rights. It asked also that the Supreme Court, which Progressives believed had pushed its control into legislative fields, be curbed both by the popular election of federal judges and a constitutional amendment permitting Congress to override a Court decision. Almost as an afterthought the Progressives turned their attention to foreign affairs, suggesting that the State Department serve less as a "trading post" for imperialists and more as a diplomatic body, that the Versailles treaty be revised, and the war and conscription be internationally outlawed.

Cyrus Curtis of the New York *Evening Post* called the plat-form "raw, red, Socialism, borrowed from the Red Dynasty of Sovietism." The *Wall Street Journal* thought it was simply "Wisconsin Bolshevism," but William Z. Foster declared it "the most reactionary document of the year." Both attitudes made complete nonsense. The platform said nothing that Grangers and Populists and Midwestern progressives had not been saying for forty years. In the last analysis, labor and socialism and Eastern progressivism (in the person of Croly and the old Bull Moosers) had contributed little to it.

A survey of the Cleveland platform showed that beneath each plank were traditional Midwestern progressive principles.

Antimonopoly, its chief issue, had been the central thread in Midwestern political patterns from Simpson and Donnelly to Bryan to Johnson to La Follette. Conservation, public ownership, railroad regulation, tax revision, government efficiency and responsibility, direct government, aids to agriculture and labor—every one of these planks had appeared in Midwestern political platforms after 1892, and most of them had already been made into law in the Midwestern states by 1916. There was certainly nothing foreign and little new in the platform of 1924.

But the charge of "Red radicalism," absurd as it was, nevertheless played an important part in the campaign. The Republicans, the Democrats, and most business groups, in condemning the 1924 Progressives (as they had the Bull Moosers) as radicals, overlooked the trend of events during the preceding twenty years. Progressivism had never yet attained national power, still under both Republican and Democratic administrations practically all of its principles had in one way or another been adopted into law. La Follette's Wisconsin delegation, for example, presented platform resolutions at every Republican convention after 1908, each time being brushed aside. In those sixteen years, the Wisconsin program suggested twenty-seven resolutions; by 1926 nearly all had been embodied in legislation. Evidently the major parties' right hands paid no attention to their left hands when the leaders condemned La Follette's "Red radicalism" in 1924.

The Progressive campaign started slowly. Both Republicans and Democrats had speakers in the field before La Follette, in October, began his tour, first of the East, then of the Midwest, then back to the East again. In all he gave twenty major speeches and uncounted minor ones, no easy feat at sixty-nine. In the Midwest he paid especial attention to agricultural issues, in the East to matters of tariff and business, but he returned again and again to the theme of monopoly. One fifth of his major speeches dealt wholly with it, and all of them devoted some time to the menace of big business. It was apparent, he said, that democracy could not live side by side with monopoly. The nation must choose "on the one hand between representative government with its guarantee of peace, liberty, and economic freedom and prosperity for all the people, and on the other, war, tyranny, and the impoverishment of the many for the enrichment of the few."

La Follette made a good campaign. An aging, rugged little man with a self-invented vest filled with pens and pencils, wearing a specially made Philippine straw hat, in action he was the same old fighter, flaying the trust and nailing the pelt up as he had for twenty years. The weakness of his campaign was that monopoly was not the same bugbear in 1924 that it had been twenty years before. The public in the twenties no longer held the same fear of big business, and in effect La Follette was fighting shadows. The old man's ideas, remarked the *Outlook*, were "survivals of a period when the real struggle in America was between government . . . and its creature the corporation," but that epoch was closed. In a way, there was truth to the charge that antimonopoly was an anachronism, but La Follette himself was anachronistic too. What he was saying differed not a bit from what he had said for twenty years.

The Democratic campaign, handled ably by Davis, centered primarily on the Progressives' attempt to clip the power of the Supreme Court. Davis, himself a lawyer of repute, considered this to be the most important issue and stressed the legal dangers involved in any sweeping judicial alterations. Republican strategy was much broader. Coolidge, as President, could hardly be expected to descend into the undignified brawling of the arena, and since he was assumed to be a strong, silent, imperturbable Yankee, campaigning was for him out of character. The burden was therefore turned over to General Dawes, who was not at all averse to rough politics and whose picturesque profanity and crowd-pleasing mannerisms had already given him a reputation. For the defense, the Republicans simply stood on the record and promised more of the same. "It is well for the country to have liberality in thought and progress in action," Coolidge said, "but its greatest asset is common sense. . . . The people want a government of common sense." From this position they launched a three-pronged attack on La Follette: his wartime record made him suspect in matters of "loyalty" and "true Americanism"; his progressivism was really "Red radicalism"; and his program would hurt business and consequently destroy prosperity.

The Republicans displayed little squeamishness in their campaign tactics, concentrating on La Follette more than on Davis. Leaflets accusing the Wisconsin senator of disloyalty were scattered over the nation. The American Legion founded a "Republican Service League" to defend America against him, and the 35th Division Association called him "an enemy to the country." The Third International had just formed in Moscow, and General Dawes insisted that the Progressives must have some connection with it. They were, he said, "a heterogenous collection of those opposed to the existing order of things, the greatest section of which, the Socialists, flies the Red flag." "The Bolshevism that Russia has been preaching to the world," said former Governor Stake of New Jersey, "is rallying round La Follette—they would make this a second Russia." The *Cincinnati Enquirer* wanted to discharge all school teachers who came out for La Follette, and Barrett Wendell, the renowned Harvard litterateur, called him "a distorted fool-fire, a begrimed Will-o'-the-wisp." Stanley Frost, commentator for the *Outlook*, reminded his readers that after all Wisconsin, which produced La Follettism was "a state quite foreign to the American tradition and American experience and thought"—a direct insult to the German descendants of the Forty-eighters. Even Coolidge stooped to say that the issue of 1924 was "whether America will allow itself to be degraded into a communistic or socialistic state or whether it will remain American." Although the spectacle of Old Bob, in the pay of Moscow, hatching out a revolution in Madison, Wisconsin, was laughable to anyone who stopped to think, the Red scare was a potent weapon in Republican hands. The party, especially Cyrus Curtis and his powerful *Saturday Evening Post*, made full use of it.

The most effective anti-Progressive weapon, however, was the plain fact that in 1924 the nation was on the crest of a boom. "The United States," *Current History* pointed out, "and most of the people are highly prosperous." Why rock the boat? If business was good, then business had caused it—leave it alone. By a rather illogical but understandable transfer of responsibility, the Republicans took credit for prosperity, and Coolidge, silently sitting on the lid, was its symbol. "Keep Cool With Coolidge," "Coolidge and Common Sense," "Coolidge or Chaos," ran the slogans. "Silence and Success," carried the implication that Cal's reticence guaranteed national wealth. For once, even farmers toned down their traditional complaints. After three hard years agriculture boomed in the summer of 1924, and by August farm prices hit the highest peak in forty-seven months. Wheat was a $1.10 in August, and the *Outlook* headlined, "Fortune Smiles on the Western Farmer!" Prosperity worked against La Follette. As the *Independent* said late in the campaign, the nation was thinking "in terms of black and white on ledgers instead of pink and red on rostrums."

The election results confirmed the newspaper predictions. Coolidge gathered slightly more than fifteen million votes, Davis nearly eight and a half, and La Follette a trifle less than five. La Follette carried only his own state of Wisconsin, but ran second in California, Idaho, Iowa, Minnesota, Montana, Nevada, South Dakota, North Dakota, Washington, and Wyoming. His votes, clearly, were drawn more from Davis than from Coolidge, but Coolidge still would have won had La Follette not entered the race, since the Democratic and Progressive total fell two million short of the Republican. Actually the Progressives missed even the Bull Moose mark, for in 1912 Roosevelt polled roughly one third of the votes cast, in comparison with La Follette's one sixth of a total vote that had been doubled by woman suffrage. Of La Follette's vote, 49 per cent came from the thirteen agricultural or semi-agricultural states of the Midwest and West. In those states the percentage of voters actually voting was among the highest recorded up to that time (65 per cent), an indication of the strength of feeling that the campaign aroused in the Granger-Populist regions.

The Progressive party of 1924 was slated for failure from the start. It never possessed either a smooth-working organization or a really unified high command. The central committee, with branches in both Chicago and Washington, suffered from divided authority and lack of co-ordination. The party lacked state organizations, except in Wisconsin, and placed candidates on only a few state tickets. Nor was there more than a handful of experienced politicians in the whole party. Unlike Theodore Roosevelt, who had the best of political help, La Follette was surrounded by labor leaders, Socialists, reformers, and intellectuals—all of them sincere but unversed in political strategy and practice. There were not enough of them to do the back-breaking labor necessary to organize a new party, place it on the ballot, and run a campaign. In New York, for example, the law required signatures on La Follette-Wheeler petitions in every county, a huge task for the pitifully few Progressive workers.

Too many groups had fingers in the Progressive pie. It was almost impossible for the Progressive leaders to persuade the disparate elements of the party, stretching from the IWW and Fabian Socialists to union men, to see eye to eye on exactly what the aims of the party were. The Socialist party and the railroad brotherhoods were sworn enemies, yet they were supposed to work together in harmony with such diverse groups as the Committee of Forty-eight, the Non Partisan League, the Farmers' Council, and the old Farmer-Labor party. The trade-unions' traditional reluctance to join third parties fitted ill with the Socialist dedication to nothing but third parties; the farm groups' old suspicion of both Socialist and labor groups did not encourage unity. Labor's vote never materialized as expected, and neither did the farmer's. Most farm journals supported Coolidge, and the unions, especially in the East, deserted the cause at the last moment.

The fact was that farmer and laborer simply were not yet ready to combine. There was still too much political individualism left, too much flexibility in class division, not enough consciousness of identical interests. And in some cases the desires of the groups within the party were diametrically opposed. The farmer's demand for lower freight rates meant, if granted, lower operating expenses for the railroads, the last thing the railroad unions wished. The Farmer-Labor men and the Non Partisan Leaguers were relatively successful, it is true, in tying labor and agriculture together, but primarily in agricultural states on a state-wide, not national basis. La Follette constantly hammered home the fact that labor and agriculture, while their interests might clash at lower levels, possessed a community of interest at higher ones. Both, he argued, were dominated by corporate privilege and special interests, and both would profit by economic freedom, but it was difficult to convince either group.

The record of campaign expenditures told another chapter in the election story. The Republicans spent four and one-quarter million dollars, the Democrats nearly a million. The Progressives spent a trifle more than two hundred thousand, one sixth of which came from the pockets of a single man, W. T. Rawleigh, the chief Progressive angel. On one day contributions to the Progressive treasury from the entire nation totaled exactly fifteen dollars. The major parties, particularly the Republican, bought space in newspapers for campaign propaganda (a subtle way of buying editorial support as well) and sent speakers into every corner of the states. Until October 27 the Progressives had no more than seventeen speakers in the field; up to election time they had on their side only a few newspapers, the *Nation*, and the *New Republic*. Against the imperial legions of Cyrus H. K. Curtis this was nothing.

It was inevitable that comparisons would be made between

1924 and 1912, but the two campaigns had little in common.
Roosevelt in 1912 had popularity, wealth, astute advisers, and
a powerful press. La Follette had none of these. He had a long
and distinguished record as a progressive and commanded
popular respect as a man of integrity and purpose, but he
attracted little of the very real affection that Roosevelt's personal charm or Bryan's magnetism inspired. Roosevelt's genius
for eliciting co-operation even from those whom he attacked
had no counterpart in the make-up of La Follette. La Follette
attacked the Klan, and Imperial Wizard Evans openly ordered
Klansmen to vote for Coolidge; Roosevelt somehow would
have managed to denounce the Klan and get its vote too. And
La Follette's war record, honest as it was, worked against him,
a handicap Roosevelt never faced. Nor had Roosevelt ever
suffered from the great Red scare; La Follette contended with
hysteria throughout his whole campaign. But in spite of all
these things, five million people voted in 1924 for a man who
stood only a bare chance of election, votes cast for La Follette's
deep integrity as much as for anything else—a real tribute to
the man and the tradition he represented.

The 1924 campaign was rooted in 1896, not in 1912. It was
a throwback to the Populist and the Greenbacker rather than
to the Bull Moose, motivated by the same desire to turn the
clock back to the good old days of agrarian democracy. The
1924 movement was a demand for the recognition of the economic interests of the farmer and wage earner, both of whom
considered themselves to be the targets of discrimination. It
intended to find redress by breaking the grip of the favored
industrial classes on government and by employing the
national resources more distinctly in favor of agriculture and
labor. The campaign of 1924, like that of 1896, was economically motivated, the Progressives advocating the use of political
means to remedy economic grievances—the traditional Middle
Western implement. Bull Moose progressivism instead intended to restore popular control in governmental affairs
through certain political reforms. La Follette's appeal was, like

Bryan's, regional and class conscious; he aimed at a balanced development of both agriculture and industry, at representation and justice for certain sections and classes. The 1924 Progressives wanted to stop certain practices and institute others for the benefit of the West, the farmer, and the worker. The movement therefore was, in Herbert Croly's opinion, "a more realistic political insurrection than that of twelve years ago."

The crusade of 1912 was a joyful affair, with much talk of standing at Armageddon and battling for the Lord. The Progressives of 1924 were angrier than the Bull Moosers of 1912. They wanted a fairer distribution of the economic and political power of the nation, power then concentrated in the business and professional groups who controlled the organs of political authority. They were angry, as the farmers of Jefferson and Simpson and Donnelly and Bryan had been, and they had with them a new political element, the working class. The farmers, laborers, and Socialists who backed La Follette did not want control of the machinery of government in order to pass laws for others' benefit. They wanted to benefit themselves. From their point of view the existing system of government placed certain obstacles in their way—tariffs, special privileges, railroad rates, injunctions, court decisions, taxes. They intended to remove these obstacles, and to improve their positions by substituting new and more favorable laws for the old. Their 1924 platform—concise, concrete, and specific compared to that of 1912—showed exactly how they believed it should be done.

"We will not quit and we will not compromise," La Follette said after the election returns came in. "We have just begun to fight." But not all Progressives were so sanguinary as the old Wisconsin lion. They were in the same position as the Populists after 1892 and the Bull Moosers after 1912. They had not cracked the two-party system; was it wiser to continue third-party action or attempt to capture a major party?.

The last Conference for Progressive Political Action convened in February, 1925. The railroad brotherhoods, regretting their departure from Gompers' time-honored doctrine of non-partisan politics, pulled out almost at once, taking the CPPA name with them. Hillquit, Debs, and the Socialists wanted to continue the party under a new name, and though some Midwestern farm delegates favored the idea, they held strong reservations as to the kind of party it ought to be. The Socialists, it developed, had in mind a labor party modeled on British lines, with a proletarian flavor; the Midwest and Western agricultural delegates wanted very much the same groupings of progressive elements as before, in the traditional pattern of La Follette. Arthur Garfield Hays finally worked out a compromise reminiscent of Donnelly's in 1891. Each organization, he suggested, should go home and decide for itself what name and affiliation it preferred, while an executive committee served as co-ordinator until such time as agreement might be reached. The compromise merely delayed the end.

La Follette's death in June, 1925, cut the heart out of the party. He was more than merely a leader, more than an available candidate, for he was the last link with the militant past, the last surviving embodiment of the rebellious Midwest, the last symbol of the old tradition. "What the battered and scattered insurgents need," remarked the *Philadelphia Ledger* in 1925, looking over the Progressives after La Follette's death, "is a Moses to bring it out of the wilderness, or a Mohammed to lead it against the infidel." They still had Brookhart, Shipstead, Frazier, Johnson, and Borah, but none of them had the driving force of the Wisconsin Mohammed. The National Progressive party headquarters remained, more or less an empty shell, until 1927, and then dissolved. It belonged, as La Follette did, to an age of discontent; this was an age of acquiescence.

"What has become of this movement that promised so much?" asked Frederic Howe. "Was the fight too hard? Did youth burn itself out? May it be so—as some of them feel—that there is little for liberals to do?" The reply was that business was in control, and people liked it. The 1924 election was a clear indication of the "as you were" temper of the public. Comments in the journals after the election reflected the great sigh of relief that passed over the land at La Follette's defeat. "Business began to pick up the day after election," reported the *Cincinnati Enquirer*. "The United States faces the greatest period of prosperity it has ever known." "Coolidge's election will be a powerful stimulus to business," thought one financial expert. "Why are we happy?" crowed Goodbody and Company's market letter. "Because radicalism, if not dead, is scotched for another four years. Because the election restored confidence and removed distractions to labor and trade." The best part of it all was that it would never end. Prosperity had a permanent home in America. It might continue so long, thought Bernard Baruch, that the age would be known to history as "the industrial renaissance." "We in America," Herbert Hoover said, "are nearer to the final triumph over poverty than ever before in the history of any land."

"Business seems to be in the saddle," said *Harper's* in early 1925. "Let us see what it can make of the job." For the next four years it looked as if business was making a very good job of it indeed. Wages were up, production was up, stocks were up (old-timers still nostalgically remember RCA shares at 549), and spirits were up. Coolidge, with a perspicacity historians sometimes deny him, simply sat tight and accepted the credit. Do-nothingism was the temper of the twenties. If a survey had been made of all the issues and problems current in American life during the period of 1920 to 1928, it would have concluded that not a single one was handled, if at all, with any energy or efficiency. This was not the fault of Coolidge, nor of his successor Hoover, nor of the Republican party. The American people, in the midst of war-born prosperity, believed that if they let it alone, they had Utopia.

Coolidge's laconic statement in 1927 that he "did not choose to run" left the way open for a draft that did not materialize. Instead the Republicans chose Herbert Hoover, an able administrator with an excellent record as Secretary of Commerce and as executive of the postwar European relief program. Hoover, who considered himself a middle-of-the-road liberal, did not have the full support of the old-line party bosses, but his philosophy of "rugged individualism" was nonetheless cut from their cloth. Al Smith, his Democratic opponent, carried too heavy a load in being a "wet" Catholic Tammanyite, and Hoover won the election with relative ease. "Coolidge prosperity" favored the Republicans, as it had in 1924, and if La Follette had been running again (as he certainly would have run had he lived) the public would have no doubt rejected him and progressivism as it had before. And Hoover did nothing to dispel the illusion of continuing prosperity under Republican rule. He pledged, in fact, complete support of Coolidge laissez faire and kept his promise.

Hoover believed in a system of enlightened individualism, much as Andrew Carnegie had before him. No believer in the masses, he wrote in *American Individualism,* "Acts and deeds leading to progress are born of the individual mind, not out of the mind of the crowd. . . . The crowd is credulous, it destroys, it hates and it dreams, but it never builds." He envisioned a world in which individual enterprise produced more and more and paid more and more to a public that bought more and more, a world derived from the economics of George Gunton and others of the later nineteenth century. Elected as "the Great Engineer," he approached national problems as an engineer, not as a politician. Hoover was not a happy President, pulled from one side by the Old Guard and pushed from another by a group of Western insurgents led by Norris. He was, Walter Lippmann thought, "in the worst straits that any President has been since 1912," facing "the opposition of the Western Progressives" on the one hand and "losing on the other the confidence of the Eastern conservatives." As a result, Hoover's four years solved no major problems. The do-nothing era came to an end with him.

The prosperity bubble blew up with a bang when the big

bull market broke in September, 1929. It was, in the opinion of the financial experts, only "a readjustment to a more secure technical position," but inexplicably the break in the market continued, despite Irving Fisher's prediction that stocks were bound to "remain on a permanently high plateau." Then in October the bottom dropped out of Wall Street. Sixteen million shares changed hands on "black Tuesday," fifty leading stocks fell forty points in a single day, and messenger boys bought well-known stocks at a dollar a share. Nobody would believe it—except those caught in the wreckage—for nine years of good times had conditioned people to nothing but good times, and this debacle simply could not happen. Prosperity, said Hoover, was "just around the corner"—in sixty more days the break would end. Secretary of Commerce Lamont thought two months would bring full recovery, and Secretary of the Treasury Mellon predicted 1930 would be "a normal year." But it had happened. The Federal Reserve Board, with a classic understatement, admitted finally the existence of "what appears to be a business depression." The rest of the way was all downhill.

The depression hung over the political conventions of 1932 like a cloud. The Republicans faced election year with something less than enthusiasm; they had taken credit for prosperity and now had to take the blame for depression. Though the party leaders did not particularly relish Hoover, they could hardly afford to repudiate him, lest it be construed as an admission that he and his party had failed to meet the crisis. The convention met, nominated him, and submitted a lackluster platform. Walter Lippmann remarked on the "total absence of any evidence of economic insurgency" in it and its complete lack of any token of progressivism. For sheer colorlessness, it was unmatched by any Republican platform since 1912.

The Democrats met in late June, after the Republicans had gone home, with the brightest prospects in years, for the depression had pricked the bubble of Republican prosperity and H. L. Mencken's proverbial Chinaman, the Democrats felt, could win if they nominated him. The most logical candidate was Alfred E. Smith, the seasoned campaigner of 1928. But in the preconvention horse trading, Franklin Delano Roosevelt, governor of New York, began to show up as a strong contender. It did not take long for the Smith-Raskob organization to collapse, and the convention nominated Roosevelt on the fourth ballot. Shattering precedent (though La Follette had done something of the sort in 1924), he flew to Chicago to accept the nomination in person. The platform the Democrats gave him was not much, yet it was a positive document—Lippmann saw in it some of the tradition of Wilson and Jefferson, but it took a long look to find it. However, it was not the platform that mattered, but the man who ran on it.

Roosevelt's acceptance speech, the famous "New Deal" speech, was a positive, ringing, optimistic promise to get something done. He recognized, he said, that this was an industrial civilization, and that this meant "new problems for those who would remain free." What was its great evil? It was the "new despotism" of "industrial dictatorship," the rule of "economic royalists." Opportunity was limited by monopoly. Individual initiative had been crushed in the cogs of a great economic machine. The fields open to business were more and more restricted. Private enterprise was too private; it was privileged, not free and open; there were too many poor, too few rich. "Throughout the nation," Roosevelt said, "men and women, forgotten in the political philosophy of the government of the last years, look to us here for a more equitable opportunity to share in the distribution of national wealth." The Republicans never remembered "the forgotten man," but instead favored business in the hope that some of its wealth would trickle down to him. All this was now over. "I pledge you, I pledge myself," he concluded, "to a new deal for the American people."

On his record Franklin Delano Roosevelt, a distant cousin

of Theodore, was an unlikely candidate for the leadership of a progressive cause. A wealthy, landed New Yorker, with a background that included Groton, Harvard, and Columbia Law School, his career until 1932 was relatively unmarked by progressivism of either the Roosevelt or La Follette varieties. In 1910, at thirty, he entered politics as a state senator, the first Democrat in twenty-eight years to go to Albany from his native Dutchess county. As a legislator he helped organize a revolt against Tammany, was re-elected in 1912, and supported Wilson at the Baltimore convention of that year.

As a reward for his services, Wilson offered him in turn the Collectorship of the Port of New York and the Assistant Secretaryship of the Treasury, both high-ranking patronage positions that he refused. His interest in naval affairs prompted him finally to accept the Assistant Secretaryship of the Navy, a post Theodore Roosevelt had held before him. A strong believer in preparedness, he did outstanding work in building up the navy before the first World War and during it. In 1920 he was judged important enough to pair with Cox in the dismal presidential campaign of that year, going down in the debacle of Harding "normalcy" and retiring from politics to practice law.

A little more than a year later, at thirty-nine, Roosevelt was struck by poliomyelitis, paralyzed from the waist down, his political career seemingly finished. But through a long uphill fight against illness, Roosevelt, like Jefferson, used his time in correspondence. By 1922 he had built up a tremendous acquaintance among party workers over the country and was a potent behind-the-scenes force in the Democratic organization. He appeared in public only once, to nominate Al Smith at the 1924 convention. In 1928 Smith, his close friend, persuaded him to make the race for the governorship of New York, which he did successfully, serving until 1932.

As governor he did a respectable job. He inherited a liberal program from Al Smith, which he tried to complete, but he faced the difficult task of placating both Tammany and the reformers. In the end he did too much to satisfy the one and not enough to please the other. On the other hand, he left an excellent list of antidepression measures and virtually won his fight for the state ownership of hydroelectric developments on the St. Lawrence. But this was not really an imposing record. At the time of his nomination in 1932 he was generally regarded as a charming gentleman of fine radio and platform presence, a loyal party man, and a "safe" candidate. Bruce Bliven judged him to be "the good fellow who talks in terms of restitution to the poor but would not do anything which would seriously hurt the rich." Walter Lippmann saw him as "a pleasant man who without any important qualifications for the office would like to be President," finding his reputation for liberal sympathies hard to explain.

The campaign of 1932 broke Republican solidarity for the first time since 1916, doing far greater damage to it than the Progressives did in 1924. The insistence of the Republicans in running Hoover on a vague, conservative platform sent Bull Moosers like Harold Ickes (who had never been a very good Republican anyway), insurgents like Norris, and old La Follette men right out of the party. In 1928 some of the progressive and liberal elements had formed the League for Independent Political Action, an organization of the National Progressive Republican League type, led by Paul Douglas of Chicago and John Dewey of New York. Although the League endorsed the Socialist ticket in 1932, much of its rank and file went over to Roosevelt. In the same fashion, a band of insurgents met in Congress in 1931 to draw up a program of progressive legislation as other insurgents had done in 1912 and 1924. The support of this group went largely to Roosevelt —Norris, Costigan of Colorado, Cutting of New Mexico, Wheeler, La Follette, Jr., Brookhart—and so did the support of others outside of Congress, men such as Bristow, Hiram Johnson, Donald Richberg, Charles Beard, E. A. Ross, William T. Evjue (an old La Follette editor), and Milo Reno, the farm-strike leader. In effect, the Democratic party in 1932 seemed to be the common rallying point for all the shreds of earlier progressive movements, for the 1912, 1924, insurgent, Wilsonian, and La Follette liberals. The only place left for them to go was the Democratic party, which of the two major parties resembled more nearly the old progressives—though admittedly not very closely. It was not the platform that drew them; it was instead the recoil from Republican do-nothingism and the electric personality of Roosevelt himself.

Roosevelt proved to be the best Democratic campaigner since Bryan and probably the best the party ever had. He exceeded the Great Commoner's man-killing tour of 1896, for Roosevelt had better means of transportation, and his total of twenty-six thousand miles on campaign set a new record. The New Deal, born in his acceptance speech in June, began to emerge as a long-range, sweeping, political, economic, and social reorganization that, if instituted, would mark a major shift in the direction of national internal policy. Holding out the guarantee to every man of "the right to make a comfortable living," Roosevelt seemed like Bryan born again with decorations, assailing the "economic royalists" of wealth as vigorously as Bryan had, attacking the wealth economy of laissez faire with equal energy.

Hoover's campaign, an able one, suffered by comparison. To him the campaign was "a contest between two philosophies of government." The Democratic New Deal was "a challenge to liberty," the supporters of Roosevelt "exponents of a social philosophy different from the traditional American one." Stubbornly blaming the depression on "international causes," Hoover maintained that there was nothing wrong with the economic system that tinkering could not fix if the people believed in it. As the campaign progressed it became clear that the difference between Hoover and Roosevelt was an extremely important one. Hoover talked of returning to the days of early 1929; Roosevelt talked of a new day quite different from 1929.

Roosevelt's early lead in the balloting was never in doubt.

By midnight of election day it was certain that he had been not only elected, but elected by the largest vote in history, to be exceeded only by his vote in 1936. Hoover carried six states in the East by small majorities. Roosevelt and the Democrats swept the traditionally Republican Middle West by a large margin; only eight Republican governors survived in the landslide, and familiar Republican landmarks disappeared from Congress. It was by no means a progressive or a liberal victory as such. It was a victory for the depression, a desperate nation's vote of confidence in optimism. "No administration in recent times," commented *Current History,* "has faced so stupendous a task as does that of President Roosevelt, nor from any one man has more been expected."

The progressives from 1932 to 1936 were uncertain of the future, unable to agree on a proper course. The New Deal after 1932 absorbed many of them, and whether or not they were in entire sympathy with Roosevelt's complete program, they hesitated to leave it. The right wingers and the discouraged returned to their own parties. The left wing vacillated between joining the Socialists and founding another third party. The corps of Midwestern and Western progressives in the Senate—Norris, Johnson, Cutting, Wheeler, La Follette, Brookhart, and Borah—usually followed Roosevelt's lead, and the House group did much the same. Actually, there was little else to be done. Progressivism was geared to the concept of a sound, stable, expanding economy; it was unequipped to meet depression, and surprised and puzzled by it. The New Deal, seizing the initiative, was willing to experiment, to improvise, to make mistakes in a fashion that the older progressive leaders found confusing. "Above all," said Roosevelt in 1932, "try *something*"—a flexibility that those who had evolved their political philosophy over three decades could not fathom.

Despite the rapid succession of antidepression measures passed in the famous "Hundred Days" of 1933 by the new administration, the depression hung on, recovery was slow, dissatisfaction very much alive. Discontent was most evident in the farm belt of the Midwest, where the traditional combination of debt, low market prices, poor crops, and high buying prices still plagued the farmer. Depression compounded the farmer's problems, and while the pump priming of the New Deal did much to alleviate distress, agriculture was by no means well off. In South Dakota, for example, one half of the state's farm families were on relief by 1934; 65 per cent of the state's rural property was owned by outsiders. The Grange and the Farm Bureau, both relatively staid organizations, remained quiet, but other groups, such as the Farmers' Union and the Farm Holiday Association, did not. Drawing on the tradition of the old Grange and the Farmers' Alliance, they resorted to direct methods, particularly in 1933, with farm strikes, milk dumping, and (in some states) an embargo on wheat shipments, intended to maintain the price level. The Farm Holiday Association, most aggressive of the farm groups, organized in 1932 after John Bosch and Milo Reno led a militant wing of the Farmers' Union out of the Union's Des Moines convention to fight, as Reno put it, for "the right to live and enjoy the decent existence that our resources entitle us to." Reno, a leader of the Jerry Simpson type, kept the association on the warpath until his death in 1936. The AAA and the drought of 1934, plus partial recovery, brought higher prices that dampened rural militancy, but the farm bloc after 1935 remained as a not too willing ally of the New Deal and occasionally a source of great irritation to it.

Technocracy, a depression-born elaboration of Veblen's planned economy, appealed temporarily both to progressives and to radicals in the early thirties. Looking forward to the time when machines could do all the nation's work, Technocracy intended to exploit the machine rather than to allow it to exploit society. Conceived in 1919, it hit the headlines in 1932, dotting the nation with societies and publications, filling the air with strange talk of "erg dollars" and machine living reminiscent of the Utopian economics of the late nineteenth century. But Technocracy broke up into schismatic complexity and finally passed over into the realm of cultism. So too Upton Sinclair's EPIC ("End Poverty in Civilization"), a combination of Utopian economics with Bellamyite socialism, flared and died.

From 1932 to 1936 there was no scarcity of what might loosely be called "progressive" thought. Schemes, plans, and remedies appeared and disappeared regularly as depression hung on. Even the constant experimentation of the New Deal failed to satisfy a large number of dissidents from both left and right. Whether Roosevelt was reactionary, reformer, or revolutionary was an open question among those progressives who (much as they had in 1913 and 1925) felt disunified and homeless. "Among the casualties of the New Deal," remarked the *New Republic,* "are the progressives. . . . President Roosevelt and his associates have stolen the spotlight so completely that everyone else has been in eclipse." But though they were in eclipse, they were still there.

The chief repositories of liberal political and economic thought during the New Deal period were the magazines *Common Sense,* founded in 1932 by Alfred Bingham and Selden Rodman, and the *Progressive,* the successor to *La Follette's Magazine.* The *Progressive,* published in Wisconsin and distinctively Midwestern in flavor, took a watchful attitude toward Roosevelt—hopeful, but ready and willing to criticize him on specific issues. As McAlister Coleman said in its columns, "Progressives need not feel it necessary to sneeze every time snuff is passed about at the White House." Edited first by William T. Evjue, a lieutenant of the elder La Follette, and later by Morris Rubin, the *Progressive* kept track of progressive issues and leaders and clung to the old La Follette platform.

Common Sense, published in New York, took a more Eastern-bred, intellectualist, and anticapitalist position. Consciously more highbrow than its Madison counterpart, *Common Sense* favored "just distribution of wealth," unemployment relief, taxation of unearned income, national control of banks and credit and currency, and a "production for use" economy. This last, an adaptation of a Marxist idea, became an increasingly important part of the Eastern liberals' program. It meant, explained *Common Sense,* that "purchasing power must be measured by production, not production limited to purchasing power"—i.e., that people should have the money to buy what is produced, not that production should be restricted by the degree of purchasing power. The scheme was, essentially, a planned economy with buying power and producing power hooked together.

The first move in reorganizing the scattered forces of progressivism came from the League for Independent Political Action, which called a Conference for Progressive Political Action for September, 1933, in Chicago, to discuss the possibility of founding a new party. The acknowledged leader of the convention was Thomas Amlie, Progressive congressman from Wisconsin, assisted by Congressmen Marcantonio of New York and Lundeen of Minnesota. About two hundred delegates attended, the majority from the Midwest. The conference recalled in some ways the CPPA of ten years earlier (Mahoney and Johnston of the machinists' and railroad unions were there) but the union representatives and intellectual liberals made up a smaller minority than before. The large farm groups, the Farmer-Labor party of Minnesota, and the Wisconsin delegates dominated it.

The tone of the conference was highly reminiscent of the twenties. Capitalism, said Amlie in his opening speech, had collapsed; the direction of the New Deal was not yet clear; the major parties served big business. The only progressive answer could be the organization of a "farmer-labor, united people's party," a party aggressively antiwealth, anticapitalism, and anti-big business. In response, the conference founded the Farmer-Labor Political Federation, with headquarters in the Midwest, to prepare the ground for third-party tickets in the states in 1934. The opening sentences of the platform adopted by the Chicago meeting reflected the drift of its political thinking: "We, the masses of the people, must rise up and win economic and political control. We must organize to establish a new social order, a scientifically planned system," to "supply human needs instead of profits." John Dewey was elected honorary chairman of the Federation, Amlie and Howard Williams of Minnesota (secretary of the League for Independent Political Action), chief organizers. Overtures were made to the Socialists, who decided the time was not yet ripe to join. The League for Independent Political Action, though remaining outside the Federation, promised its full co-operation.

Another group of twenty-five progressives met in Chicago three motnhs later, called together by Philip La Follette. They agreed that Roosevelt's program had neither solved the depression nor avoided the possibility of another; while his direction seemed correct, they believed that his leadership left much to be desired. The answer, the conference concluded, lay in the nationalization of banks and the credit system and in government ownership of public utilities, "to break the power of Wall street over the farmer and laborer." Yet at the same time the conference delegates faced the dilemma of all middle-of-the-road progressives in the thirties. Should they recognize what progressivism there seemed to be in the New Deal and continue to support it, or should they join a newly founded third party and exert pressure on the New Deal from without? The Chicago meeting never made up its mind.

The Farmer-Labor Political Federation, another attempt to unity scattered progressive forces, drew its support chiefly from the Farmer-Labor parties of the Midwest and the La Follette progressives in Wisconsin. The Minnesota Farmer-Labor party, which elected Floyd Olson governor in 1930, dominated politics in that state, and while the stalwart Republicans had temporarily come to power in Wisconsin, the La Follette organization was in the process of building a coalition of labor, agriculture, and Milwaukee socialism. The Farmers' Union and the Farm Holiday Association were very active in Illinois, Farmer-Laborites in Iowa had third-party aspirations, and Michigan's Farmer-Labor party was getting an organization started. North and South Dakota—Nonpartisan League territory—supported growing Farmer-Labor movements. California's agricultural and labor groups were caught up in Sinclair's EPIC program, while Kansas and Nebraska, seat of the powerful Farm-Holding Association, were teetering on the edge of third-party action. The Federation established contact with all of these.

The Farmer-Labor Political Federation had two political issues. In the first place, it charged that neither conservative Republican laissez-faire capitalism nor Democratic New Deal capitalism provided a real solution to existing economic and social problems. The New Deal, said Floyd Olson, was a radical-liberal-conservative compromise that satisfied nobody, and *Common Sense* counted up twenty-one progressive issues on which Roosevelt had taken no action whatever. The Federation's chief point seemed to be that capitalism was "a wornout machine, unsuited to the times, and incapable of satisfying the needs of the people." If both Republicans and Democrats wished to keep the machine—one preferring it in its worn-out state and the other repaired—the only thing for a progressive to do was to attempt to substitute a better machine.

So the various Farmer-Labor parties of the Midwest returned to their grandfathers' platforms, recommending public ownership of "monopolistic industries," while the Eastern intellectuals and economists favored a "planned economy of abundance." By 1934 Iowa, Michigan, and Wisconsin Farmer-Labor and progressive platforms were calling for public ownership of key industries; Minnesota's Farmer-Labor party, in a startling document, asked for complete public ownership of *all* industry, banking, and insurance in a "cooperative commonwealth." It was not, as all of them made clear, communism or anything like it (Amlie called Marxism "dialectics adrift"). It was instead a logical extension of the time-honored principle that government and economy existed solely for the people's benefit. Why not, they said, change the system so they would?

The Farmer-Labor Political Federation did not do badly in the 1934 elections. Though it ran no state tickets, it endorsed enough winning candidates to allow it to claim a victory. Wisconsin made Phillip La Follette governor and returned Robert junior to the Senate. Floyd Olson remained governor of Minnesota; William Langer, an old Non Partisan Leaguer, went in as governor of North Dakota (though his ouster later on graft charges hurt the movement locally); Sinclair almost took California; and in Washington a third party sent Lewis Schwellenbach to the Senate. In Iowa and Michigan Farmer-Labor parties made a small showing, but the over-all results were enough for the Federation to claim that "a revolt was going on in the Middle West."

Encouraged by the Republican defeats of 1934, the Federation sent out a message to all "progressive" elements (including Father Coughlin's Social Justice group, the Technocrats, and practically every other dissident organization except outright Communists) for a conference to complete the establishment of a national third party. Roosevelt, said *Common Sense,* had simply not lived up to expectations; he was "an astute politician with excellent intentions, trying to save a system whose basis was exploitation by admonishing it not to exploit." John Dewey pointed out that it was not the Democratic party but only Roosevelt who seemed liberal, concluding that the "only way to preserve as well as extend whatever is good in Rooseveltian measures is the formation of a strong, united, radical third party." The strategy should be, the Federation thought, "independent political action" with "inner guidance" from a "disciplined corps" of progressive leaders, concentrating "upon the most advanced section of the country," the Midwest.

In December, 1934, in response to the Federation's invitation, two hundred delegates met at a Legislative Conference at St. Paul, representing every Midwestern state and several of those in the Northwest. The conference met a rebuff from the American Federation of Labor, which vividly remembered

1924, but the delegates nevertheless drew up plans for a national conference to be held in July of 1935 to take the final step of third-party organization. The new party, it was agreed, ought to include all liberal, progressive, and radical groups except Communists—the elements of Midwest revolt (the Non Partisans, Farmer-Labor alignments, Wisconsin progressives, and farm groups), EPIC from California, the reform Fusion party from New York, the Socialists, the co-operative associations, the Technocrats, the American Federation of Labor (a vain hope), organized professional and union groups, and the miniscule die-hard Bellamyites, single taxers, Greenbackers, and Prohibitionists. Unification of this "mighty but scattered army" ought to result in an imposing and powerful coalition.

Unification involved certain difficulties, however, as it had in 1892, 1896, 1912, and 1924. It was a formidable job to weld together into a single discipline unit organizations as disparate in aim and composition as the Technocrats on one side and the Farmers' Union on the other. Within the progressive group, especially among trade-unions, there still existed strong suspicion of third-party tactics. Furthermore, the traditional strategy of such organizations as the Non Partisan League, the Wisconsin progressives, and the farm groups had nearly always been to infiltrate and capture a major party. The situation in Wisconsin illustrated the reluctance of many older progressives to enter third-party action. Operative since 1900 as a wing of the Republican party, the progressives finally broke off in 1935 to form an independent group, but many were not wholly pleased at the move.

The elements which were to make up this new party were by no means agreed as to the principles on which it should be founded. The "planned economy" program of the professional economists meant little to the farmer who wanted higher farm prices. Soaking the rich, curbing monopoly—those things he could understand—but the intricacies of Technocracy, EPIC, and "production for use" left him cold. Nor did the simplicity of old-time agrarian radicalism attract the intellectuals who festooned the fringes of liberalism; there was a great gap between the thinking of Milo Reno and that of John Dewey and Howard Scott. Public ownership of monopoly meant something to the Farmer-Laborite, but the dictum of *Common Sense* that "the key is necessarily a planned society, with production as a social enterprise" was to him hardly a rousing declaration of war. When it came to rock bottom, the Midwest farmer wanted, as he always had, a good market with high prices, control of his own government, more currency, easier credit, and good times. The intellectual's Utopia was a trifle too complicated for him to take in all at once.

The conference met in Chicago in July, 1935, with about two hundred delegates from twenty-seven states, representing Socialists, farmer-labor groups, various state parties, a few Technocrats, and a few trade-unions. Paul Douglas of the League for Independent Political Action was elected chairman and Alfred Bingham of *Common Sense* secretary, and the business of establishing an organization for 1936 began. The third-party question came up at once. Adolph Germer, a veteran of 1924, warned that any independent party must be based on labor, which was certainly not well represented, while Minnesota and Wisconsin delegates, both of whom had healthy third parties at home, showed an understandable reluctance to throw in with a national movement. Led by Amlie, the independents voted to establish a new organization, "based on the principle of PRODUCTION FOR USE," called the American Commonwealth Political Federation, which was to adopt a platform and nominate a candidate for 1936. "We must have a political realignment," said Amlie, "that will place the exploiting reactionary on one side and the producer, consumer, independent business and professional interests on the other."

The platform adopted by the July conference was an interesting blend of old progressivism and new economics. It declared first for an "economy of abundance" based on "unlimited production for use by and for the unemployed." Complete economic security was to be guaranteed by extending the scope of social legislation, unemployment insurance, health legislation, and old-age pensions. There was to be collective bargaining, but no strike breaking. Reflecting the Populist and progressive demands of earlier years, the platform asked for heavy taxes in the upper income brackets and on gifts and inheritances, for public ownership of basic industries, mines, munitions, and utilities, for federal ownership of banks and credit systems, and for government aid to education. In the tradition of 1924 it suggested an amendment to the Constitution allowing Congress to make "any laws necessary to the progress of the people" without judiciary interference. Except for the "production for use" plank, the platform involved nothing that had not been a part of every Midwestern political platform since 1892, and, for that matter, nothing not already apparent to some degree in the policies of the New Deal.

The chairman of the Commonwealth Political Federation, and indeed its prime mover, was Thomas Amlie. For vice-president it elected John Bosch of the Minnesota Farm Holiday Association, for secretary Bingham of *Common Sense,* and for treasurer Paul Douglas. Amlie represented something new in Midwest progressivism, though he was undoubtedly rooted in the old tradition. Wisconsin-born of Norwegian descent, he grew up during the La Follette-stalwart battles of the early century and as a farm boy lived in the midst of old Granger territory. Educated at the state university, he joined the Non Partisan League as an organizer for Townley during the bitter postwar years when the League was labeled "Red" and "seditious." Back at the university in 1920, he read Veblen and Marx, among others, becoming convinced of the utter failure of laissez-faire capitalism. Entering state politics as La Follette-progressive Republican, he served in Congress during the early thirties, plumped for the creation of a third party, and eventually in 1935 helped the Wisconsin progressives accomplish independency.

The point is, wrote Amlie in 1935, that "what we are now going through is more than a depression; that it represents a new phase of capitalism; and that the suffering and maladjustment we are now experiencing is to a large extent chronic. . . ." Surveying the wreckage of the depression, the liberal seemed to conclude that capitalism could not be saved, that it was not worth saving, and that some way must be found to save it. The escape from this contradictory position, wrote Amlie, was obvious. Either the nation had capitalism, motivated by a desire for private gain, or it had something else. Logically, the liberal must therefore give up capitalism; the best substitute would be "a wholesale planning of the socially-owned machinery of production for the sole use and benefit of society." A third party, he believed, if it offered abundance for all under a properly organized economic system, would certainly be successful.

Among the various radical and liberal movements of the thirties, only the Farmer-Labor and the Wisconsin Progressive contingents really carried on the old tradition. The planners, the Veblenites, the American Commonwealth Political Federation, the Technocrats, and the "production for use" men did not. Midwestern progressives had always been opportunists, attacking evils as they came, finding specific remedies for specific ills and only incidentally making long-range plans. It was an evolutionary, not a revolutionary, tradition, working step by step, proceeding against one adversary at a time.

The older progressive was an individualist, asking only to be let alone to enjoy his guaranteed privileges, advocating public ownership or control of economic and social institutions only when they did not appear to operate correctly. His theme was political; to him political power preceded and postulated economic power. His aim was to control the government for the common good; economic justice he believed would naturally follow. The difference between the old and the new schools of thought was apparent in the remarks of an old La Follette lieutenant who tried to tell Louis Adamic in 1934 just what he thought progressivism was. "We'll try to take the masses," he said, "just as far as we feel fairly sure they'll be willing to go from time to time . . . toward a new social order, to be built on the American pattern, which is a matter of our past and present. . . . We consider the people, their mentality, the fact that they are Americans, which means they are great optimists and inclined to consider and deal with their problems only from moment to moment. That's the American way; whether it is good or bad is immaterial. It was the way of Jefferson, Lincoln, and Old Bob."

The American Commonwealth Political Federation was hardly a ripple compared to the New Deal tidal wave of 1936. A meeting of prominent liberals in Chicago in late 1935 endorsed the President's policies with noticeable enthusiasm, and even *Common Sense,* one of Roosevelt's chief critics, ended in 1936 by declaring for him as "the best we can get." The intense campaign waged by the American Liberty League in 1935 and 1936 against the New Deal further convinced many liberal critics of Roosevelt that if big business was against him, he must be on the right side, and deserved their support. Thus by November of 1936 progressives were being advised to get on the bandwagon on election day but to get off the day after. The 1936 election was a New Deal year, and the day after found liberals more disorganized than in 1932.

Roosevelt took off on his second term with renewed energy. The Supreme Court had killed the AAA, the NRA, and other New Deal legislation, and lawyers were casting eyes at both the Social Security Act and the Wagner Labor Relations Act of 1935. The attack on the New Deal brought most liberal groups rallying to its support, and the *rapport* between New Dealers and various liberal-progressives waxed.

The fact was that after 1936 the New Deal seemed to be all that the third-party men, the Commonwealth Federation, and the Farmer-Labor groups could ask. What Roosevelt was doing, it became clear, was creating within the framework of the Democratic party a third party of his own, an alliance of New Dealers, independents, progressives, and unions, making the

Democratic party itself available to them as a political tool. Third parties were needed only in those states where the Democratic organization was controlled by conservatives. More and more liberals pinned their hopes on Roosevelt for a planned economy, for public control of banking and money and credit, and for social and economic legislation. Some, like Paul Douglas of Illinois, having once entered into two-party politics, found it possible to work for progressive policies within a major party and could see no reason to return to third-party ways. By 1938, *Common Sense,* which had once labeled the New Deal a sham, declared it would support Roosevelt for a third term in 1940, or for that matter support any party he cared to lead.

The only real recalcitrancy came from the La Follette brothers, whose Progressive party in Wisconsin was the sole remaining third party of consequence in the nation. In April, 1938, both La Follettes broke with Roosevelt, and Philip, then governor of Wisconsin, called a convention at Madison in late April for the purpose of establishing a new progressive party on a national scale. Though it came as a surprise to many progressives, the call was the result of carefully planned maneuvering. Phillip La Follette, beginning some time before, had conferred with almost twelve hundred liberals throughout the country, from the ranks of labor, agriculture, and politics. There was, he thought, enough anti-New Deal sentiment and anti-Republican sentiment to warrant the formation of a third party.

Progressives, La Follette announced, had "given up hope." They had felt for some months that the Democratic party as a whole was not interested in coming to grips with the real economic and social problems of the time, though it had progressive and socially conscious leadership for the moment. But the party also embraced Hagues, Pendergasts, Kellys, Nashes, and Tammany, who could hardly be called progressives. Based on fundamentally conservative ideas, following only temporarily enlightened leadership, the Democratic party was not a fit progressive instrument. Reforming the party from within, after that leadership was gone, appeared to be a hopeless task; if the people were forced to choose in 1940 between a conservative Republican and a conservative Democrat (as progressives had been forced to choose before) the gains of 1932 and the following years would surely be lost. The need, therefore, said La Follette, was for a "really dynamic political movement" on progressive lines, to hold and to guarantee advance.

The National Progressive party was launched from the University of Wisconsin stock pavilion in Madison on April 28, 1938, before an audience of 3,500. The emotionalism of the meeting (which included some careful stage effects and a party banner with a circle-and-cross device) disturbed the correspondent of *Common Sense,* who found it unhealthily reminiscent of European political methods. Yet the meeting was spontaneously exciting. Judge Alvin Reis, in his keynote address, praised Roosevelt and his program, but urged the need to prepare for that time "when there are two candidates, neither of whom is progressive." Philip La Follette's able main speech defined the chief issue of contemporary politics as the division "between the earners on one side and the collectors on the other." Neither major party, he believed, represented the first half of this economic division.

Liberals greeted the National Progressive party with something less than enthusiasm. *Common Sense,* once a strong third-party proponent, thought it unwise to break into New Deal strength and advised the progressives to forget La Follette. Villard of the *Nation,* though not wholly a New Deal sympathizer, thought it a most inauspicious moment to begin a third party. Attracting little support from the progressive element outside Wisconsin, the National Progressives unsuccessfully went on the ballot in Iowa and California. La Follette himself was shortly defeated for the governorship in Wisconsin, and the new party disappeared.

The National Progressive movement was the last appearance

of the old Midwestern progressivism, much watered and badly managed. It was founded on a contradiction—that though Roosevelt's New Deal was satisfactory, a different program ought to be ready for an emergency. Since there was no apparent emergency, the party could hardly be expected to elicit fervent response. And furthermore, the "emergency" program offered nothing that the New Deal did not already offer or might offer. The National Progressives had no real issue—monopoly, tariff, free silver, big business, railroads, none of the great traditional rallying points for the discontented. "The very multiplicity of present-day issues," wrote Villard, "confuses people and makes it extraordinarily difficult to unite any large group upon a platform," a comment particularly appropriate to the National Progressives. Nor did the new party possess a leader of the stature of the elder La Follette or of Theodore Roosevelt, who was great enough to override issues. Business was on the upturn, domestic issues dormant, and attention was focused on the struggle against fascism abroad.

Roosevelt dominated the thirties and forties. The New Deal absorbed much of progressivism and some of radicalism as well. Analyzing its relationship to the older strain of progressivism is not a simple task, for the New Deal was eclectic, embracing all, emphasizing some, drawing liberally from everything that had preceded it. Roosevelt could sound and act at times like Bryan, like La Follette, like Theodore Roosevelt, or like Wilson. None of them would have quarreled seriously with certain aspects of his program, but all of them would have no doubt objected strenuously to others.

In 1933 Roosevelt stated the aims of his new order as he saw them: elimination of special privilege, elimination of graft and corruption, and elimination of the power of wealth. These were, obviously, simple restatements of the same problems of domestic policy as the Midwest had observed them since 1870; neither Granger, Populist, Silver Democrat, Wilsonian Democrat, nor Progressive would have stated them any differently. Again, in 1935, he remarked: "Our concepts of the regulation of money and credit, and industrial competition, of the relation of employer and employee, created for the old civilization, are being modified to save our economic structure from confusion, destruction, and paralysis," a statement that might well have come from 1892, 1896, 1912, or 1924.

On the agricultural front, the New Deal handled the old problems of markets, prices, and credits much as the Midwest had always wanted them to be. The Farm Credit Administration was a return to the Granger idea of cheap and easy agricultural credit. The Resettlement Administration could easily have been established in 1880 with Granger and Alliance approval. The Surplus Commodities Act was the old "sub-treasury plan" in new dress. The AAA, admittedly experimental as it was, attacked the troublesome problem of crop surpluses in a different way, but the aim was the same—gear production to demand, and control prices. In none of these acts did the New Deal invent something new.

In his dealings with business, Franklin Roosevelt looked most like Theodore. Like him, he recognized the existence of monopoly and concentration as well as its dangers and its responsibilities. We must, he said, "bring private autocratic powers into their proper subordination to the people's government . . ."; we must restrain the unethical and irresponsible use of the "vast financial and management power" placed in the hands of the capitalist; we must "preserve the American ideal of economic as well as political democracy against the abuse of concentration of economic power that has been insidiously growing up among us in the past fifty years." T.R. himself would have found no quarrel with this language, nor would La Follette.

Roosevelt's aim was, in essence, to work out a scheme of business regulation that prevented concentration of capital and its misuse, and one that was still consistent both with the aims of democracy and with the preservation of the values inherent in industrial combination. It was the same policy, actually, that Theodore Roosevelt searched for and could not find. The answer, Franklin Roosevelt wrote in 1934, "is a coherent body of law protective of the large consuming interests and yet broad enough to afford the necessary play for industry to act as a unit, free from pressure of unrestrained and wasteful competition." "We seek," he said another time, "to guarantee the survival of private enterprise by guaranteeing conditions under which it can work."

To Roosevelt, then, the struggle against monopoly and combination was "a struggle for, not against, American business . . . to preserve individual enterprise and economic freedom" from the restraints placed upon it by "private monopolies and financial oligarchies." Control, yes, in the T.R. tradition—"busting," in the Bryan tradition, no. The NRA, the best example of the New Deal policy toward business, was essentially a compromise between the trust buster and the regulator; as General Hugh Johnson, its administrator, said time and again, the aim of the NRA was to reward good business and punish bad. Its policy was based on a mixture of competition and combination, not too much of either, just enough of both. For this reason co-operatives were encouraged and great utility projects (such as TVA) were launched, not simply as a continuation of those publicly owned projects dear to La Follette and Norris and Wilson but as competitive clubs to keep private business in line.

Roosevelt, as the liberals of the early thirties claimed, truthfully wanted controlled laissez-faire capitalism, not "individualism run wild" (as he called it in 1936) but individualism under regulation. "I believe in individualism," he once said, "up to the point where the individualist starts to operate at the expense of society." The aim of the national economy, he said in Detroit in 1932, "should not be the survival of the fittest," but rather "the fitting of as many human beings as possible into the scheme of surviving." A year later, speaking to the Federal Council of the Churches of Christ, he remarked, "We recognize the right of the individual to seek and obtain

his own fair wage, his own fair profit, in his own fair way—
just so long as in the doing of it he does not push down or
hold down his neighbor." Buried beneath these statements
were two generations of anti-Darwinian political and economic
thought.

Roosevelt believed in individual, private enterprise, but he
believed too that its field of operation was narrowed by concentrations of capital and power. He sought, therefore, to keep
private enterprise alive by that sort of regulation which limited
its capacity to exploit or stifle. The whole thing was a problem
in balance—"balance between agriculture and industry, and
balance between the wage earner, the employer, and the consumer." But unlike "the New Freedom" of Wilson, or "the
New Nationalism" of Croly and Roosevelt, or "the New Individualism" of McCarthy and La Follette, the New Deal was
much more willing to supplant individual enterprise with
government assistance when regulation alone seemed insufficient to preserve it. The New Deal supplied credit, established
and subsidized farm prices, developed utilities and natural
resources, built houses, and was never reluctant to use the
national power to make available what private business could
or would not.

The financial policies of the New Deal dated from the
eighties and nineties. Roosevelt's statement in 1933 that the
nation needed "the kind of a dollar which a generation hence
will have the same purchasing power as the dollar value we
hope to achieve in the near future" had clear Greenback and
Populist overtones. The departure from the gold standard, the
pegging of gold and silver at inflated values, controlled inflation, devaluation and increased flexibility of the "rubber
dollar"—all these went back to the "cross of gold," free silver,
greenbacks, and currency tinkering. The Federal Deposit
Insurance Corporation was nothing more or less than the old
Populist demand for guaranteed bank deposits. The Federal
Securities Act and the augmented powers of the Securities
Exchange Commission both carried out pledges taken from

every Midwest political platform since 1892 for control of "Wall Street," market gambling, and irresponsible speculation. For that matter, the Works Progress Administration (the famed WPA), the Civilian Conservation Corps, and other such measures had a distinctly Coxeyan ancestry.

In his use of the bureau, the expert, and the commission, Roosevelt went far beyond the limits set by the early twentieth-century progressives, approaching closer to the plans advocated by the intellectuals and the "planned economy" thinkers of the thirties. "No one could study the history of our industrial advance," said Roosevelt, "without being struck by its haphazardness." To him the nation's paramount economic problem was "the problem of controlling by planning the creation and distribution of those products which our vast economic machine is capable of yielding." The New Deal planned with a vengeance. By 1934 there were roughly fifty bureaus or commissions responsible directly to the President. These in turn involved hundreds of sub bureaus, boards, and administrative groups—forty-five in the AAA, thirty-five in the NRA, and nearly as many in other agencies, a state of affairs that stirred the conscience of the Midwestern individualist rather sharply.

There were other similarities between the New Deal and earlier progressive programs. Its reforestation, flood control, and erosion projects and its creation of agencies such as the National Resources Board and the Civilian Conservation Corps recalled the conservation policies of Theodore Roosevelt and of the progressives in the Midwestern states. The Non Partisan League had already thought of low-cost, public-financed housing, while the WPA, PWA, and other public works programs mirrored what Coxey, the Populists, and state progressives had thought of years before. The National Labor and National Relations Boards, and for that matter the minimum wage, collective bargaining, and maximum hour provisions of the NRA codes, had been implicit in all progressive platforms after 1900. Roosevelt's "collective effort for social

planning" and his "social justice through social action," culminating in the Social Security Act, were extensions of earlier
ideas advanced by social thinkers and politicians from Altgeld
and Jane Addams through Theodore Roosevelt, Wilson, and
La Follette. And the attempt in 1937 to "pack" the Supreme
Court in order to make it more responsive to public needs recalled the attacks on the judiciary of both La Follette and T.R.
and their demands for constitutional flexibility.

The old-line progressives willingly recognized certain positive achievements of the New Deal and applauded them—the
relief program, the public works and conservation programs,
the encouragement of co-operatives, acts such as TVA, Social
Security, and Labor Relations. To progressives these were
social and economic advances. But at the same time, many of
them asked, was the New Deal initiated for political or for
honestly progressive purposes? Was it founded on a solidly
progressive philosophy of government, or was it simply the
product of political expediency or sudden inspiration? Progressives pointed out that in some cases legislation of a progressive nature (the Rural Electrification Act and the Wagner
Act, for example) was accepted only when its passage seemed
politically advantageous. Noticeably, after 1936, when New
Deal supremacy was firmly established, progressive legislation
diminished and politically motivated legislation seemed to
increase, or so the *Progressive* felt as early as 1937 and as late
as 1943.

Many Midwestern progressives found it not too difficult to
follow Roosevelt in 1932. Though they occasionally viewed
him with suspicion, many were convinced that he was the
nearest thing to a progressive President they could expect, and
at any rate better than Hoover. They recognized the obvious
bonds tying New Deal policies to old-time progressivism and
took some pride in pointing out Roosevelt's borrowings from
Midwestern experience and theory. Yet after 1936 there grew
among the older leaders a recurrent off-the-record criticism of

what they felt was the New Deal tendency to take good, sound progressive policy and botch it up. If Roosevelt agreed with something they had carefully nurtured for decades—bang, there it was, perhaps not quite as it had been planned, but good enough to placate some progressives and infuriate others by its incompleteness.

Though the New Deal did carry out many of the plans long advocated by progressives, there was something about its spirit, and about its methods, that seemed to some to ring false. In banking, as the National Progressives protested in 1938, the New Deal did not radically change things. It increased the authority of the Federal Reserve Board, but progressives claimed that the system was still under the control of the bankers. The New Deal inveighed against price fixing and monopoly; then the NRA suspended antitrust laws, fixed codes and prices for industry, and in effect regimented it. But, some liberals claimed, big business itself wrote the agreements that fixed prices and codes, giving legal sanction to essentially monopolistic practices. Forays against trusts under the New Deal were more numerous than in the Republican twenties, and the New Deal no doubt frightened big business, but progressives doubted that it dealt monopoly any body blows.

In the matter of extending political democracy, the older progressives (particularly those of the La Follette variety) believed that the New Deal should have placed more emphasis on necessary forms and techniques. The recall, the referendum, the initiative, popular election of the judiciary and kindred proposals for broadening direct participation by the people in government were staples of progressivism in the pre-World War I years and in the twenties. Roosevelt never gave them serious consideration.

Perhaps the aspect of the New Deal most unlike Midwestern progressivism was the ruthlessness it occasionally displayed in making and carrying its points. Progressives often received the impression that its leaders held less respect for the intelligence (and possibly the will) of the common people than had La

Follette or Bryan, or even the austere Wilson. The New Deal placed its reliance on the expert, the planner, the man who knew better than the people. No one thought of calling the group of experts who surrounded La Follette a "Brain Trust," but under the New Deal the term had connotations, not always good humored, that made it fit.

La Follette, of course, and the Grangers before him, always regarded the politician, the expert, and the commissioner as servants of the people, responsible to them through the legislature and the executive. Their function was to do the things the people wanted done. The New Deal board of experts was often responsible to the President alone, combining legislative, executive, and judicial functions within itself and offering small chance of appeal from its judgment. The fundamental democracy of the New Deal was never in question, but certainly some of the old progressives felt that it was impersonal, self-contained, and not always the people's own instrument for self-government.

The truth is that the New Deal planners, the Midwestern progressives felt, did not have the root of the matter in them. The New Dealers had the know-how, the statistics, the theories, the techniques of the social worker and economist, but not the insurgent heart. To them progress was a matter of theory, a "let's see if this will work" attitude, and not a crusade for democracy. The La Follette Progressives of 1924 had their "intellectuals" and planners too, but they were hard-bitten, experienced veterans, some of whom had been in politics since 1904 and almost all of them since 1916—Frank Paterson, George Record, David Blauvelt, Allen McCurdy, Arthur Garfield Hays, Oswald Garrison Villard, and others. They were not simply intellectuals, but progressive crusaders with deep democratic convictions.

The Midwestern progressive movement was sectional minded, perhaps provincial in its manner of thinking, concerned with immediate problems solved in local terms. The New Deal was sophisticated, nationalized, and federalized, a combination of long-range planning and political expediency, rarely concerned with local and state perogatives. The Midwestern agrarians called in the federal government when they needed help, but not before. The Wisconsin Idea of "the new individualism" did not propose a leviathan state, or constant subsidization, or consistent federal assistance. It had in mind instead the old Jeffersonian-frontier ideal of a self-reliant individual living in an agrarian commonwealth.

The dilemma of the progressives during the New Deal era was that while Roosevelt did many things with which they agreed, and seemed to carry on the tradition of Bryan and La Follette and Wilson, at the same time he seemed to deny that tradition as a whole while he carried it on in part. They concluded that Roosevelt was indeed attempting to accomplish the old progressive ends—an equitable distribution of wealth, a higher standard of social and economic justice, the abolition of privilege in the democratic process—but that in so doing he came perilously near to federalization and regimentation, neither of which were ever parts of the Midwestern creed. The objective was the same, the method and the spirit different. The Wilsonian program, though it too involved centralization of power, was still essentially Jeffersonian in concept. The New Deal, though it had Jeffersonian overtones, was Hamiltonian in method. It was no accident that Roosevelt himself admired Hamilton for his ability "to bring order out of chaos" and always spoke approvingly of strong nationalists like Theodore Roosevelt and Lincoln. He summarized his philosophy of government himself in 1933, saying, "If Jefferson could return to our councils he would find that while economic changes of a century have changed the necessary methods of government action, the principles of that action are still wholly his own."

The advent of World War II (as World War I had affected the course of Wilsonian progressivism) turned the New Deal from internal to external affairs. If the New Dealers intended to effect a progressive revolution in American political, social, and economic affairs, they had two full terms in which to do it (a privilege denied Bryan and La Follette and Wilson and Theodore Roosevelt) before war intervened. They did not. Before Pearl Harbor and before Roosevelt's death, the reactivation of numerous progressive, liberal, and radical groups indicated that there was current dissatisfaction with the New Deal "revolution." Shortly before Roosevelt's delayed decision to become a third-term candidate, at least nine minor organizations, old and new, splinter segments of major parties or independent organizations, existed—the Union for Democratic Action, the CIO Political Action Committee, the National Citizens' Political Action Committee, the Wisconsin Progressive party, the Socialist party, the Socialist Democratic Federation, the New York American Labor party, the New York Liberal party, and the Commonwealth Federation of Michigan and Illinois. Among them there was some unity of feeling, though it was often obscured by their devotion to different methods of gaining the same ends. Most of them approved of New Deal social and agricultural legislation; many of them agreed among themselves and disagreed with the New Deal on matters of tax reform, the use of public credit for full employment, public control and ownership of certain areas of industry, co-operatives, and the extension of government enterprise for social and economic benefits. The greatest disagreement among them lay in the area of foreign relations.

The Progressive Party of 1948, which nominated Henry Wallace and Glen Taylor on its national ticket, was not related to the older progressive movement, though it claimed descent from both La Follette and Theodore Roosevelt, as well as from Bryan, Norris, Franklin Roosevelt, and Jefferson. The Wallace Progressives' chief platform plank in 1948 (and its chief campaign issue) concerned peace and diplomatic relations with Russia, an issue never raised in any progressive circles before. The Progressives' rather vague plans for abundance recalled the planners' paradises of the thirties, while their proposals for control of monopolies and the nationalization of some carried reminders of the trust-hating Grangers. Unlike La Follette in 1924, Wallace failed to disavow Communist support in 1948; by refusing to do so, he incurred the antagonism of most of the progressive groups and leaders. *The Progressive,* the sole remaining organ of Midwestern progressivism, flatly repudiated the Wallace movement, feeling that it "sullied the name 'progressive'" and that "believers in freedom and devotees of dictatorship . . . cannot live under the same tent." After the outbreak of the Korean War, Wallace made a public break with the Progressive Party he had led in 1948, and its subsequent leaders have been drawn from splinter groups which have little relation to traditional progressivism.

No issue or leader has emerged since Franklin Roosevelt's time to join a few or all of the liberal-radical groups into a temporary alliance, as La Follette united them briefly in 1924 or Bryan in 1896. Midwestern progressivism, old style, died in November of 1932. Depression, New Deal, the shock of a second World War, Korea, Russian imperialism, industrial expansion, cold war, missiles, satellites, and divided atoms destroyed the old framework of political thinking in the Midwest. The classic battles of progressivism on the home front have either been won or lost decisively, or are no longer so important as they once seemed to be in another, older kind of world. Regional in source and provincial in inspiration, Midwestern progressivism as a separate political force began to fade as soon as the Midwest emerged from its colonialism into a larger nationalism. The postwar mood of the forties and fifties was quite different from the temper of La Follette's or Bryan's society, or even that of Roosevelt and Truman.

The problems of an uneasy peace have powerfully conditioned the atmosphere of American political thinking since the defeat of Germany and Japan. Since 1946 the United States has existed virtually on a wartime footing, in a sort of quasi-war in which political and economic reform have usually been subordinated to the immediate needs of a garrison state. So long as American-Soviet relations have remained at a straining point, it has seemed politically desirable to justify almost anything by its relevance to "beating the Russians," including bigger movie screens, longer automobiles, increased installment buying, wider roads, and more emphasis on college football. Under such conditions liberalism in politics has always found it difficult to operate.

The most noticeable result of this has been the post-World War II trend toward an official uniformity of political thought, toward popular suspicion of political reform, experimentation, innovation. Indeed, at the crest of the Red-hunting wave of 1950-1954, almost any principle or institution once approved by the Soviet (even free schools) became automatically suspect; disagreement with the *status quo* was often regarded as disloyal if not actually subversive. The threat of communism, real and imaginary, brought about a severe revision of popular and official attitudes toward non-conformity and criticism, while disapproval of "red" thinking led naturally to uneasy speculation about other bands of the political spectrum. Progressive political thought, Midwestern or otherwise, most certainly never flourished in such a climate. Older Midwestern progressives and liberals soon found themselves regarded with suspicion. Younger ones, with investigating committees harrying the universities, found it wise to say nothing, write nothing, and keep one's record clean. The Eisenhower victory of 1952, its genuflections toward "the best business brains," its embarrassed acceptance of the Neanderthal Right of McCarthy and Jenner, and pervasive "back to normalcy" flavor, dealt a heavy blow to scattered and confused liberals. The Midwest went conservative too, and until 1956 the Republican party enjoyed more complete control of Midwestern politics than it had previously possessed for fifty years. There were obvious reasons for this—"corruption," "time for a change," Korea, farm prosperity, recoil from the *carte blanche* liberalism of the thirties and forties. As the charge of "red socialism" and "pro-Germanism" hurt the old Midwestern progressives after World War I, so did McCarthyism find scapegoats for the frustrations of cold war and Russian rivalry in anything that resembled liberal politics. With the restoration of some sort of partisan equilibrium, however, after 1956, and the gradual decline of political hysteria, words such as *progressive* and *liberal* have begun to regain at least partial respectability. There can be no doubt, however, that it will be some time before political liberalism, in the nation at large as well as in the Midwest, can again achieve quite the status it once attained.

The major theme of American political activity since 1946, by the force of circumstances, has been its military-mindedness. Military influence on domestic and foreign policy has been greater, and of longer duration, than at any other period of American history. For the first time in the history of a nation traditionally committed to civilian control of internal and external affairs, the makers of military policy—as represented by the Department of Defense — possess coordinate authority with the Department of State and in effect with the Executive itself. It is significant that Congress, when asked, quickly passed without appreciable debate special legislation to allow a General to become Secretary of Defense, a post previously restricted to civilians, and that in 1952 and 1956 the figure of an Army general dominated the American presidential elections almost as completely as Washington did. One third of all funds of all national budgets since 1946 have been allotted to the armed services; if defense-related agencies such as the VA and the AEC are included in the total, the percentage is nearly two thirds. Under the Defense Reorganization plan, suggested by the President in 1958, the authority to control most of these funds could be vested in a single man.

The militarization of politics and the semi-military mobilization of industry have stimulated an exceptional growth of corporate business. For the past nineteen years military contracts have provided the greatest single source of American industrial activity, and large segments of the national economy are directly geared to military spending. The net effect of World War II was to make big business bigger; as World War I proved, there is no time in wartime to think seriously about the Sherman Act. Postwar competition with Russia, the "limited war" in Korea, and the demands of a rapidly growing home population have since speeded up the trend toward corporate concentration. The present size of General Motors (the largest corporate business venture in the history of the world) would shock a Populist into insensibility and strike an old Progressive speechless.

At the same time and for much the same reasons, the growth of corporations has been matched by a corresponding growth in the size and authority of the federal government, whose massive contours lie hidden from the casual viewer like those of an iceberg. The United States government today employs more than a tenth of the entire national labor force and disburses more than a quarter of the total national income. Yet the huge corporation and the leviathan state exist, for good or ill, and will continue so to exist into the foreseeable future. The citizen of tomorrow will be forced to learn to live with them, adjust to them, and work out with them a set of satisfactory political, economic, and social relationships. The still unanswered question facing our contemporary society is—how may people meet the problems of a permanent war economy, of ever-bigger business, and of an expanding state, while still preserving unimpaired the traditional body of American values and principles?

The Midwest, over the past twenty years, has undergone swifter and more drastic social and economic changes than in any other period since the passage of the Northwest Ordinance. These changes demand new political approaches to the problems they create, and a regional political philosophy congruent with the times. First of all, the Middle West is now a highly industrialized area. Manufacturing began to move in quantity into the Ohio-Mississippi basin before Pearl Harbor, while the wartime boom of the forties enlarged its industrial productive capacity at a rate unmatched by any other section of the nation except the Pacific Coast. In the eastern half of the region (Ohio, Michigan, Indiana, Illinois, Wisconsin) the Bureau of the Census reported slightly more than 40,000 manufacturing establishments in 1949, 59,000 in 1954, and more than 60,000 in 1958, approximately a fifty percent increase in one decade. In the traditionally agrarian western half (Minnesota, Iowa, Nebraska, Kansas, and the Dakotas) the percent of growth was almost the same, from about 15,000 firms in 1939, to 19,000 in 1954, to approximately 21,000 in 1958.

Of all the regions of the United States, the Midwest by 1954 counted the largest industrial payrolls and the largest industrial work force. With approximately one third of the national population, the Midwest contains about one half of the national productive capacity. The belt stretching from Milwaukee to Chicago to Detroit to Cleveland, about 200 miles wide, is the most highly concentrated industrial area in the world. The Midwest, over three generations of dispute and compromise, has finally succeeded in creating the political machinery and the economic atmosphere needed to release the incredibly powerful productive forces of its economy.

The growth of branch factories and the flow of population into the medium-sized towns of the Midwest have simply changed the face of the land. Today's county seat has a factory as well as a courthouse. The farmer's sons and daughters commute to the nearest city for factory work, nor is it unusual for an employee to work his farm and drive thirty miles to a plant each day. The big cities of the Midwest grew swiftly in the decade 1940 to 1950—Chicago 13%, Cleveland 15%, Detroit 26%, Minneapolis 18%, Milwaukee 13%. But the truly spectacular growth occurred in middle-sized Midwestern industrial cities, such as Lansing, Michigan (33%), South Bend, Indiana (26%), Evansville, Indiana (22%), Lorain, Ohio

(32%), Kalamazoo, Michigan (28%), Rock Island, Illinois (21%), Madison, Wisconsin (31%), Wichita, Kansas (55%), Sioux Falls, South Dakota, (22%), Des Moines, Iowa (19%), or Lima, Ohio (22%). These towns and others like them scattered through what was once, a few years ago, almost exclusively farming country, are focal points in the helter-skelter pattern of a new Midwestern industrial economy. The old rural-orientated Midwest, the "farmer's stronghold," is fast disappearing.

Industrialization and urbanization have had direct and powerful impact on the Midwest's political outlook. Plainly, organized labor is a much more potent political force in the Midwest than ever before. Under the AFL-CIO merger, for example, Michigan now has a million, and Illinois a half million labor union members, each with a vote. Even in the so-called traditionally "farm" states labor is a factor of growing significance. By 1960 there will be 250,000 AFL-CIO members in Minnesota, 140,000 in Iowa, 300,000 in Wisconsin, 75,000 in Kansas, and 45,000 in Nebraska. The temperature of the Midwestern politics no longer rises and falls with the price of hogs and wheat (though when the farmer frowns, politicians still tremble) quite so quickly as it did in the days of the Alliance or the Farm Bloc. Hourly wages, the price of autos and freezers, overtime pay, fringe benefits, and a dozen other things that concerned neither Bryan nor La Follette now condition the Midwesterner's politics and help to decide his vote. The union hall, as the grange hall once was, is often the decisive political forum in parts of the Midwest today.

Unlike the days when Populist headhunters stalked Wall Street bankers, concentrations of money power in the East have been largely dispersed. New York bankers, once regarded by Midwestern politicians as the evil octopi of finance, have lost a great deal of business to their Chicago and Kansas City cousins who live closer to the factory gates of the industrial heartlands. The diffusion of financial power once demanded by Weaver and Bryan is no better illustrated than by the increase in number, and changes in kind, of the sources of money — insurance companies, credit unions, pension funds, mutual investment funds, savings and loan association funds, and so on. Midwestern newspapers still may not love Wall Street, but the old bitterness of Western debtor against Eastern creditor is no longer the political weapon it once was. Today's Kansas farmer would probably fail to recognize the "money king" with his gold watch-chain, fancy vest, and silk hat, and might even vote for him in a good year.

Whereas a generation or so ago the Midwestern farmer usually put up a solid political front against his enemies, he today has far less unity of purpose. Technical changes in farming, diversification of farm production, greater economic sophistication, and the industrialization of certain segments of agriculture itself mean that today's farmers do not always see eye to eye. The Grange, the National Farm Bureau, and the National Farm Union, the three most effective national farm organizations, disagree on political issues as often as they agree. Farm votes are influenced less by sectional alignments and price fluctuations than by such factors as subsidies, size of farm, kind of product marketed, type of land tenure, marketing procedures, and tax policies. Though there are still times when the farmers rise up in unified wrath, the farm vote in the Midwest tends rather to spread itself across a rather wide political spectrum, and farm organizations, like trade unions, often reflect national rather than purely regional issues. But the most important fact about the Midwestern farm vote, of course, is that as the industrial population of the area has grown, so its farm population has decreased. From 1940 to 1950, for example, the farm population of Illinois dropped 21%, of Kansas 27%, of Minnesota 18%, of Wisconsin 17%, and the decrease still continues. There are simply fewer farmers in the Midwest than ever before, and fewer farm votes.

The Midwest today is no longer the rural, agrarian commonwealth of small town joined with farm that it was barely a half century ago. It is instead the center of the greatest industrial productivity in national history. It is a focal point of the most advanced form of industrialism, combined with declining agriculturalism and increased urban growth. It has thus become, one observer writes, "a lab for social experimentation and change more rapid and basic than any previously known in this country." The Midwest holds a key. Because the Midwest holds encapsulated within it most of the social, economic, and political perplexities that plague modern America, what happens there takes on a more-than-regional relevance. New York may provide the eye-patch advertisement and the hand-painted tie, or California the television comic and the home barbecue pit, but the man in Kokomo, Kalamazoo, or Keokuk decides where the nation goes. The staff of a national news magazine, its Chicago bureau chief reports, learned long ago that "if you can spot a fairly basic change underway in the Midwest, it will soon appear all the way from Madison Avenue to Hollywood and Vine."

One of the most striking changes in recent Midwestern political history has been its gradual drift toward international-mindedness. It is difficult to find today, among liberals or enlightened conservatives, the stereotyped "Middlewestern isolationist" so long accepted as typical of its regional political thinking. Two world wars, of course, worked a tremendous change in the general American attitudes toward foreign affairs, the Midwest not excepted. The farmer has realized since 1941, as he never did in Granger days, that he was directly affected by fluctuations in foreign trade or foreign currency, by custom policies, tariff rates, and foreign aid, and by economic upsets in far-away places with strange names. The Midwestern farmer and manufacturer realized that he did not belong to a self-sufficient region, set apart from the world. Chicago, after all, has been an official United States Port of Entry since 1945, and is no more than 10 hours from London or 30 from Tokyo. "We in the Midwest," concluded Governor Adlai Stevenson of Illinois in 1949, "have discarded some of the illusions which beclouded our earlier thinking (*and*) have abandoned the treacherous trail to security by isolation." While now and then there may still emanate blasts from the small towns against the UN flag or protests over school collections for UNESCO, there is in the Midwest very little of the blind, classical isolationism of a generation ago. Public opinion polls consistently show little difference among New England, Middle Atlantic, and Midwestern states on foreign policy issues.

It is not to be assumed, however, that isolationism has ceased to exist west of Cleveland. The Chicago *Tribune* is not yet an internationalist organ. Echoes of Ignatius Donnelly's prejudice against "bloated Easterners and Britishers" may still be found in what the *Tribune* fondly calls its "Chicagoland." Yet the fact is that no influential Midwestern political leaders of either party may be called actively isolationist. The surprising conversion to internationalism of the late Senator Arthur Vandenberg of Michigan, and more recently that of Senator Alexander Wiley of Wisconsin, afford good evidence of the Midwest's shifting attitude. Senator Taft, who angrily voted against the ratification of the North Atlantic Treaty alliance, reluctantly moved toward the internationalist camp after 1946.

Isolationism itself, of course, was never historically a part of Midwestern progressive politics, despite La Follette's admitted provincialism and the narrow nationalism of the early progressive groups. Indeed, as Samuel Lubell has shown, the sources of American isolationism have always been ethnic and emotional, not geographic; given proper conditions, its appearance in Texas or Vermont is as likely as in Wisconsin or Kansas. A generation ago, the strong German, Irish, Scandinavian, and Polish elements in the Midwestern states, remnants of the last great wave of immigration, combined with the regional tradition of evangelical Protestantism to exert a powerful isolationist influence in politics. The absorption of such nationality groups into Midwest society and the impact of two world wars on the second generation have altered the climate of their thinking about the relationship of the United States—and of the Middle West—to the rest of the world.

The changed nature of Midwestern life, and its shifting relationships to the rest of the country, have introduced many new variables into its political life. Today's Midwestern politics may be called "progressive," in the sense that it is a reasoned attempt to adapt politics to new regional conditions, though applying the label to contemporary Midwestern political life might mislead one into false analogies with the traditional progressivism of an older era. The aims of the new politics are direct and simple. First, it intends to establish governmental machinery by which to negotiate some sort of regional equilibrium among agriculture, labor, and industry, all of which today operate within a new set of conditions not even in existence thirty years ago. Second, it hopes to find a satisfactory balance between state and federal power. The fact that the Midwest contains half of the national industrial economy and is the source of nearly a third of the national revenue makes this an extremely delicate search. In simpler days when the Grangers and Populists called for federal help against local enemies, or when Progressives asked the federal government for reinforcements against depression, power boundaries were clearer than today. The increasing prosperity of the Midwest since 1945 has created new pressures to restrain the powers of the federal government from interference in state affairs, or even in national affairs which may affect the regional economy only at second hand. A great deal of energy is expended by the states in attempting to outwit or evade the federal government, and to establish the line where Washington stops and the statehouse begins. Third, the aim of today's Midwestern politics is to maintain at its maximum the wide diffusion of wealth created by the social and economic developments of the last quarter century. Since the emergence of the Midwest as a conscious, regional entity in the latter decades of the 19th century, the major theme of its "progressive" politics (under whatever name) has been a protest against limits set by concentrations of power—railroads, banks, political rings, monopolies — which presumably prevented the widest possible distribution of wealth. The Midwest wanted an open-door economy, and it has almost achieved it. It has come very near to realizing its dream of a pervasive, egalitarian prosperity, and hopes to keep it that way.

For these reasons, the wild, uncurried radical today makes, and will no doubt continue to make, only very rare appearances in Midwestern politics. The Midwest of the nineteen-fifties is far too prosperous, far too self-assured, to produce hayseed radicals or old-style crusading liberals. The contemporary Midwestern liberal is more likely to be the product of a professional (and often intellectual) background than of hard knocks or splinter movements, and his core of support, as a rule, derives chiefly from a labor-liberal-"egghead" coalition, strong in the cities and weaker in the hinterlands. Today's Midwestern "progressive" or liberal politician has an awareness of economic issues far beyond that of his Populist or Progressive grandfather. He is sophisticated and knowledgeable about such things as taxes, labor statutes, corporation legislation, collective bargaining, labor-urban politics, and economic forces, as his predecessors were often not. At the same time, like his grandfather, he is equally conscious of the necessity of positive governmental attitudes toward social problems and he is similarly convinced that government must function as a social agency. The older progressive who stressed the responsibility of state government to promote the social welfare of its citizens, demanded free schools, wage-hour laws, woman suffrage, child labor laws, and equality of opportunity. The Midwestern liberal of the forties and fifties has widened the perimeter of what the earlier century called "social politics" to include programs for mental health, expansion of educational facilities, unemployment and security benefits, old age pensions, fair employment practices, and so on.

It is inconceivable that a Jerry Simpson, an Ignatius Donnelly, or even an elder La Follette will ever again capture the fancy of the Midwestern electorate. The Midwest has changed, matured, and stabilized in its political thinking. The Midwestern progressive movement, so alive, vital, and pulsing with ideas and personalities, has become history, one with the spirit of Daniel Shays' farmers and Jackson's muddy-booted hordes. But as one aging Wisconsin warhorse, once a county worker in Old Bob's organization, put it while recalling the old days a few years ago, "It's gone now, but it was great while it lasted. Maybe someday my grandsons will have the chance to do it again."

General Sources

Aaron, Daniel. *Men of Good Hope.* New York, 1951.

Adams, James T. *Frontiers of American Culture.* New York, 1944.

Adams, Samuel Hopkins. *The Incredible Era.* New York, 1939.

Agar, Herbert. *The People's Choice.* New York, 1933.

Allen, Frederick Lewis. *Only Yesterday.* New York, 1931.

Allen, Paul L. *America's Awakening.* Chicago, 1906.

Arnett, A. M. *The Populist Movement.* New York, 1922.

Baker, Ray Stannard. *American Chronicle.* New York, 1945.

Barnard, Harry. *Eagle Forgotten: The Life of John P. Altgeld.* Indianapolis, 1938.

Beale, H. K. *History of Freedom of Teaching in American Schools.* New York, 1941.

Beale, Truxton ed. *Man Versus State.* New York, 1916.

Beard, Charles A. *Contemporary American History.* New York, 1914.

———, and Smith, G. H. E. *The Future Comes: A Study of the New Deal.* New York, 1933.

Beard, Miriam. *History of the American Business Man.* New York, 1938.

Beer, Thomas. *Hanna.* New York, 1929.

Binkley, William E. *American Political Parties: Their Natural History.* New York, 1944.

Blum, John M. *Woodrow Wilson and The Politics of Morality.* Boston, 1957.

Bogart, E. L., and Mathews, John. *The Modern Commonwealth.* Springfield, Ill., 1920.

———, and Thompson, C. M. *The Industrial State.* Springfield, Ill., 1920.

Bowers, Claude. *Beveridge and the Progressive Era*. New York, 1932.

Brooks, John C. *The Social Unrest*. New York, 1903.

Brooks, R. C. *Corruption in American Politics and Life*. New York, 1910.

Bruce, A. A. *The Non Partisan League*. New York, 1922.

Buck, Solon J. *The Agrarian Crusade*. New Haven, 1921.

———. *The Granger Movement*. Cambridge, 1913.

Burns, James. *Roosevelt: The Lion and The Fox*. New York, 1956.

Carroll, M. R. *Labor and Politics*. Boston, 1923.

Case, Victoria and Robert. *We Called It Culture*. New York, 1948.

Chamberlain, John. *Farewell to Reform*. New York, 1932.

Champlin, J. D., ed. *Chauncey Depew: Orations, Letters and Speeches*. New York, 1910.

Christiansen, Theodore. *Minnesota*. New York, 1935.

Chugerman, Samuel. *Lester Ward, American Aristotle*. Durham, 1939.

Clough, F. C. *William Allen White of Emporia*. New York, 1941.

Cochran, T. C., and Miller, William. *The Age of Enterprise*. New York, 1942.

Coleman, McAlister. *Eugene V. Debs*. New York, 1930.

———. *Pioneers of Freedom*. New York, 1929.

Cousens, T. V. *Politics and Political Organizations in America*. New York, 1942.

Crane, Milton. *The Roosevelt Era*. New York, 1947.

Crawford, Lewis F. *The History of North Dakota*. Chicago, 1931.

Croly, Herbert. *Marcus Alonzo Hanna*. New York, 1912.

Cullom, Shelby M. *Fifty Years of Public Service*. Chicago, 1911.

Current, R. N. *Pine Logs and Politics*. Madison, Wis., 1950.

Curti, Merle. *The Growth of American Thought*. New York, 1943.

Daniels, Josephus. *The Wilson Era: Years of Peace*. Chapel Hill, 1941.

Day, Donald, ed. *Woodrow Wilson's Own Story*. Boston, 1952.

Day, F. A., and Knappen, T. M. *Life of John Albert Johnson*. St. Paul, 1910.

Dell, Floyd. *Upton Sinclair*. New York, 1927.

De Mille, Anna George. *Henry George: Citizen of the World*. Chapel Hill, 1950.

Destler, Chester M. *American Radicalism, 1865–1901*. New London, Conn., 1946.

Doan, E. M. *The La Follettes and the Wisconsin Idea*. New York, 1948.

Dombrowski, J. A. *The Early Days of Christian Socialism in America*. New York, 1936.

Dorfman, Joseph. *Thorstein Veblen and His America*. New York, 1934.

Dreier, Thomas. *Heroes of Insurgency*. Boston, 1910.

Ellis, Elmer. *Mr. Dooley's America*. New York, 1941.

Ewing, C. A. M. *Presidential Elections*. Norman, Okla., 1940.

Filler, Louis. *Crusaders for American Liberalism*. New York, 1939.

Fine, Nathan. *Labor and Farmer Parties in the United States, 1828–1928*. New York, 1928.

Fite, Gilbert C. *Peter Norbeck: Prairie Statesman*. Columbia, Mo., 1948.

Fitzpatrick, E. A. *McCarthy of Wisconsin*. New York, 1944.

Flower, B. O. *Progressive Men, Women, and Movements of the Past Fifty Years*. Boston, 1914.

Fossum, Paul R. *The Agrarian Movement in North Dakota*. Baltimore, 1925.

Friedel, Frank. *Franklin D. Roosevelt*. Three volumes. Boston, 1952, 1954, 1956.

Gabriel, Ralph H. *The Course of American Democratic Thought*. New York, 1940.

Garraty, John A. *Woodrow Wilson*. New York, 1956.

Gaston, Herbert. *The Non Partisan League*. New York, 1920.

Geiger, C. R. *The Philosophy of Henry George*. New York, 1933.

Ginger, Ray. *The Bending Cross: A Biography of Eugene Debs*. New Brunswick, 1949.

———. *Altgeld's America*. New York, 1958.

Goldman, Eric F. *Rendezvous with Destiny*. New York, 1952.

Gregory, C. W. *Samuel Miller*. Iowa City, 1907.

Gue, Benjamin. *The History of Iowa*. New York, 1903.

Gunther, John. *Roosevelt in Retrospect*. New York, 1950.

Gurko, Leo. *The Angry Decade*. New York, 1947.

Hacker, Louis. *A Short History of the New Deal*. New York, 1935.

Harlan, E. R. *A Narrative History of the People of Iowa*. Chicago, 1931.

Haworth, Paul L. *America in Ferment*. Indianapolis, 1915.

Hayes, E. C. *Recent Developments in the Social Sciences*. Philadelphia, 1927.

Haynes, Fred E. *James Baird Weaver*. Iowa City, 1919.

———. *Social Politics in the United States*. New York, 1924.

———. *Third Party Movements Since the Civil War with Special Reference to Iowa*. Iowa City, 1916.

Hechler, Kenneth. *Insurgency: Personalities and Politics of the Taft Era*. New York, 1940.

Helmes, Winifred. *John A. Johnson: The People's Governor*. Minneapolis, 1950.

Hendrick, Burton J. *The Age of Big Business*. New York, 1919.

Hesseltine, William B. *The Rise and Fall of Third Parties*. Washington, 1948.

Hibben, Paxton. *The Peerless Leader: William Jennings Bryan*. New York, 1929.

Hicks, Granville. *The Great Tradition*. New York, 1935.

Hicks, John D. *The Populist Revolt*. Minneapolis, 1931.

Hillquit, Morris. *History of Socialism in the United States*. New York, 1910.

Hinshaw, David. *A Man From Kansas: William Allen White.* New York, 1945.

Hofstadter, Richard. *The American Political Tradition and the Men Who Made It.* New York, 1948.

———. *Social Darwinism in American Thought, 1860–1915.* Philadelphia, 1945.

———. *The Age of Reform.* New York, 1955.

Hoover, Herbert. *The Ordeal of Woodrow Wilson.* New York, 1958.

Holcombe, Arthur N. *The Middle Classes in American Politics.* Cambridge, 1940.

———. *The Political Parties of Today.* New York, 1924.

Hopkins, C. H. *The Rise of the Social Gospel in American Protestantism, 1860–1915.* New Haven, 1940.

Howe, Frederic. *The Confessions of a Reformer.* New York, 1915.

Howland, Harold J. *Theodore Roosevelt and His Times.* New Haven, 1921.

Hubbart, H. C. *The Older Middle West, 1840–1880.* New York, 1934.

Hugh-Jones, E. M. *Woodrow Wilson and American Liberalism.* New York, 1948.

Johnson, Walter. *Selected Letters of William Allen White.* New York, 1947.

———. *William Allen White's America.* New York, 1947.

Josephson, Matthew. *The Politicos, 1865–1900.* New York, 1938.

Kazin, Alfred. *On Native Grounds.* New York, 1942.

Keller, A. G., and Davies, M. R. *Selected Essays of William Graham Sumner.* New Haven, 1924.

Key, V. O. *Techniques of Political Graft in the United States.* Chicago, 1936.

Knoles, G. H. *The Presidential Campaign and Election of 1892.* Stanford, 1942.

Kohlsaat, Herman H. *From McKinley to Harding.* New York, 1923.

Laidler, Harry W. *Concentration in American Industry.* New York, 1931.

Lief, Alfred. *Democracy's Norris.* New York, 1939.

Link, A. S. *Wilson: The Road to the White House.* Princeton, 1947.

———. *The New Freedom.* Princeton, 1956.

———. *Woodrow Wilson and The Progressive Era.* New York, 1954.

Linn, James. *Jane Addams.* New York, 1935.

Lloyd, Caro. *Henry Demarest Lloyd.* New York, 1912.

Lorenz, Carl. *Tom L. Johnson.* New York, 1911.

Lovejoy, A. T. *La Follette and the Establishment of the Direct Primary in Wisconsin.* New Haven, 1941.

Lovett, Robert Morss. *All Our Years.* New York, 1948.

Lowry, E. G. *Washington Closeups.* Boston, 1921.

MacKay, Kenneth. *The Progressive Movement of 1924.* New York, 1947.

McMurry, Donald L. *Coxey's Army.* Boston, 1929.

Macy, John. *Socialism in America.* New York, 1916.

Madison, Charles. *Critics and Crusaders.* New York, 1947–48.

Malin, James C. *An Interpretation of Recent American History.* New York, 1926.

Manning, G. C. *The Fadeout of Populism.* New York, 1928.

Manning, T. G., with D. M. Potter and W. E. Davies. *Government and the American Economy, 1870–Present.* New York, 1949.

Masters, Edgar Lee. *The New Star Chamber and Other Essays.* Chicago, 1904.

Merriam, Charles E. *American Political Ideals, 1865–1917.* New York, 1921.

————, and Barnes, Harry E., eds. *A History of Political Theories: Recent Times.* New York, 1924.

————, and Gosnell, H. F. *The American Party System.* New York, 1933.

Mitchell, Broadus. *Depression Decade.* New York, 1947.

Mitchell, Wesley. *A History of the Greenbacks.* Chicago, 1903.

Morgan, Arthur E. *Edward Bellamy.* New York, 1944.

————. *The Philosophy of Edward Bellamy.* New York, 1945.

Morris, Lloyd. *Postscript to Yesterday.* New York, 1948.

Mowry, G. E. *Theodore Roosevelt and the Progressive Movement.* Madison, Wis., 1946.

————. *The Roosevelt Era: 1900-1910.* New York, 1958.

Mumford, Lewis. *The Story of Utopias.* New York, 1922.

Myers, W. S., and Newton, W. H. *The Hoover Administration: A Documented Narrative.* New York, 1936.

Nelson, Bruce. *Land of the Dacotahs.* Minneapolis, 1946.

Nichols, Jeannette, and Randall, J. G., eds. *Democracy in the Middle West, 1840–1940.* New York, 1941.

Noble, David W. *The Paradox of Progressive Thought.* Minneapolis, 1958.

Odlund, Martin W. *The Life of Knute Nelson.* Minneapolis, 1926.

Odum, H. W., ed. *American Masters of Social Science.* New York, 1927.

————, and Moore, H. E. *American Regionalism.* New York, 1938.

Olcott, C. S. *Life of William McKinley.* Boston, 1916.

Olson, J. C. *J. Sterling Morton.* Lincoln, Nebr., 1942.

Parrington, Vernon L. *Main Currents in American Thought.* New York, 1927–30.

Patton, C. W. *The Battle for Municipal Reform, 1875–1900.* New York, 1940.

Paxson, F. L. *History of the American Frontier, 1763–1893.* Boston, 1924.

Porter, K. H. *National Party Platforms.* New York, 1924.

Putnam, Carleton. *Theodore Roosevelt: The Formative Years.* New York, 1958.

Quaife, M. M. *Wisconsin: Its History and Its People.* Chicago, 1924.

Ramey, W. F. *Wisconsin, A Story of Its Progress.* New York, 1940.

Ratner, Sidney. *American Taxation, Its History as a Social Force in Democracy.* New York, 1942.

Regier, C. C. *The Era of the Muckrakers.* Chapel Hill, 1942.

Rhodes, James F. *The McKinley and Roosevelt Administrations.* New York, 1922.

Rice, S. A. *Farmers and Workers in American Politics.* New York, 1924.

Rich, Everett. *William Allen White.* New York, 1941.

Ring, Elizabeth. *The Progressive Movement of 1912 and the Third Party Movement of 1924 in Maine.* Orono, Maine, 1933.

Ritchie, D. G. *Darwinism and Politics.* London, 1889.

Robinson, Edgar E. *The Roosevelt Leadership: 1933–1945.* Philadelphia, 1955.

Ross, Edward Alsworth. *Changing America.* New York, 1912.

Rusk, Ralph L. *The Literature of the Middle Western Frontier.* New York, 1926.

Russell, Charles E. *Bare Hands and Stone Walls.* New York, 1933.

———. *A Pioneer Editor in Early Iowa.* Washington, 1941.

———. *The Story of the Non Partisan League.* New York, 1920.

Schlesinger, Arthur M. *New Viewpoints in American History.* New York, 1922.

Shannon, Fred A. *The Farmer's Last Frontier, 1860–1897.* New York, 1945.

Sharp, Paul F. *The Agrarian Revolt in Western Canada.* Minneapolis, 1948.

Sheldon, A. E. *Nebraska: The Land and the People.* Chicago, 1931.

Shippee, L. B. *Recent American History.* New York, 1913.

Soule, George. *Prosperity Decade.* New York, 1947.

Starr, H. E. *William Graham Sumner.* New York, 1925.

Steevens, George. *The Land of the Dollar.* New York, 1897.

Stephenson, N. W. *Nelson Aldrich: A Leader in American Politics.* New York, 1930.

Stirn, E. W. *An Annotated Bibliography of Robert M. La Follette.* Chicago, 1937.

Stoddard, H. L. *As I Knew Them.* New York, 1927.

Sullivan, Mark. *Our Times.* New York, 1928–1935.

Symes, Lillian, and Clement, Travers. *Rebel America: The Story of Social Revolt in the United States.* New York, 1934.

Taylor, Walter F. *The Economic Novel in America.* Chapel Hill, 1942.

Thompson, C. W. *Presidents I've Known and Two Near Presidents.* Indianapolis, 1929.

Turner, Frederick Jackson. *The Frontier in American History.* New York, 1920.

———. *The Rise of the New West.* New York, 1906.

Underwood, John C. *Literature and Insurgency.* New York, 1914.

Usher, Ellis B. *The Greenback Movement of 1875–1884 and Wisconsin's Part in It.* Milwaukee, 1911.

Van Hise, Charles. *Concentration and Control.* New York, 1912.

Villard, Oswald Garrison. *Prophets True and False.* New York, 1928.

Wallace, S. C. *The New Deal in Action.* New York, 1934.

Wecter, Dixon. *The Age of the Great Depression.* New York, 1948.

Wheeler, E. P. *Sixty Years of American Life.* New York, 1917.

White, William Allen. *Autobiography.* New York, 1946.

———. *Masks in a Pageant.* New York, 1928.

———. *Woodrow Wilson.* Boston and New York, 1924.

Whitlock, Brand. *Forty Years of It.* New York, 1914.

Wiltse, C. M. *The Jeffersonian Tradition in American Democracy.* Chapel Hill, 1935.

Young, A. N. *The Single Tax Movement in the United States.* Princeton, 1916.

Chapter References

THESE REFERENCES are not intended to be exhaustive, but rather to serve the purpose of indicating the chief sources of material used in the book, and to suggest additional sources of more detailed information concerning men and movements treated herein.

Chapter I

The chief historian of the Midwest is still the late Frederick Jackson Turner, whose *Frontier in American History* contains perhaps the definitive historical treatment of the area, drawn upon liberally here. His *Rise of the New West* (volume XIV of Albert Bushnell Hart's *The American Nation: A History*), Frederick L. Paxson's *History of the American Frontier, 1763–1893*, H. C. Hubbart's *The Older Middle West, 1840–1880*, and A. N. Holcombe's *Middle Classes in American Politics* furnished additional material, while Lois K. Mathews, *The Expansion of New England, 1820–1865*, provided data on the migration of Eastern culture westward. Other sources include T. J. Wertenbaker, "The Molding of the Middle West," *American Historical Review*, LIII (January, 1948), pp. 223–24; H. C. Hockett, "The Influence of the West on the Rise and Fall of Political Parties," *Mississippi Valley Historical Review*, IV (March, 1918), pp. 459–70; C. E. Merriam, "The Outlook for Social Politics," *American Journal of Sociology*, XVIII (March, 1913), pp. 676–88; C. S. Gleed, "The Wealth and Business Relations of the Middle West," *Forum*, XIV (January, 1893), pp. 621–43. Odum and Moore, *American Regionalism*, is a discussion of American sections, and the symposium edited by Nichols

and Randall, *Democracy in the Middle West, 1840–1940,* is a valuable
political guide.

The discussion of the intellectual backgrounds of the nineteenth
and early twentieth centuries is derived in part from Faulkner, Par-
rington, Gabriel, E. R. Lewis, Hofstadter, Jacobson, Merriam, Parkes,
Malin, Curti, and others cited in the general bibliography, and from
an extensive reading of the journals and literature of the period. Use-
ful material was provided by E. L. Godkin, *Unforeseen Tendencies of
Democracy* (New York, 1898); Simon Newcomb, "The Let-Alone
Principle," *North American Review,* CX (January, 1870), pp. 1–33;
E. L. Godkin, "The Real Problems of Democracy," *Atlantic Monthly,*
LXXVIII (July, 1896), pp. 1–13; Henry Brown, "The Twentieth
Century," *Forum,* XIX (August, 1895), pp. 630–38; John Moody,
"The Evolution of the Trust," *Arena,* XXXVII (May, 1907), pp.
476–84; J. C. Redpath, "The True Inwardness of Wall Street," *ibid.,*
XVIII (July, 1897), pp. 9–23; and W. G. Sumner, "The Absurd Effort
to Make the World Over," *Forum,* XVII (March, 1894), pp. 92-103.
The impact of evolution on American thought is treated in Bert
J. Loewenberg, "Darwinism Comes to America," *Mississippi Valley
Historical Review,* XXVIII (June, 1941), pp. 339–69; Bert J. Loewen-
berg, "The Reaction of American Scientists to Darwinism," *American
Historical Review,* XXXV (July, 1933), pp. 687–702; H. W. Schneider,
"Evolution and Theology in America," *Journal of the History of
Ideas,* IV (January, 1945), pp. 3–19; Sidney Ratner, "Evolution and
the Rise of the Scientific Spirit in America," *Philosophy of Science,*
III (1936), pp. 104–22; A. M. Schlesinger, "A Critical Period in
American Religion," *Massachusetts Historical Society Proceedings,*
LXIV (1932), pp. 523–47; R. B. Nye, "John Fiske and the Cosmic
Philosophy," *Proceedings of the Michigan Academy,* XXVIII (1942),
pp. 685–92; and W. H. Roberts, *The Reaction of American Protestant
Churches to the Darwinian Philosophy* (doctoral dissertation abstract,
University of Chicago, 1938).

Chapter II

Chief sources of material on the Granger, Farmers' Alliance, and
early Populist movements are S. J. Buck, *The Agrarian Crusade* and
The Granger Movement; J. D. Hicks, *The Populist Revolt;* Nathan
Fine, *Labor and Farmer Parties in the United States;* Fred E. Haynes,
Third Party Movements, all cited in the general list of sources. Fred
A. Shannon, *The Farmer's Last Frontier,* volume V of *The Economic
History of the United States,* is an especially good treatment of the
economic problems and policies of the period. Other sources include:
J. A. Woodburn, "Western Radicalism in American Politics," *Missis-
sippi Valley Historical Review,* XIII (September, 1926), pp. 143–68;
Hallie Farmer, "The Economic Backgrounds of Frontier Populism,"
ibid., X (March, 1924), pp. 406–27; R. C. Miller, "The Background

of Populism in Kansas," *ibid.*, XI (March, 1925), pp. 469–90; K. L. Butterfield, "The Grange," *Forum*, XXXI (April, 1901), pp. 231–42; J. D. Hicks, "The Origin and Early History of the Farmers' Alliance in Minnesota," *Mississippi Valley Historical Review*, IX (December, 1922), pp. 203–27; J. C. Malin, "The Farmers' Alliance Subtreasury Plan," *ibid.*, XXXI (1944–45), pp. 255–60; H. C. Nixon, "The Cleavage within the Farmers' Alliance Movement," *ibid.*, XV (June, 1928), pp. 22–33; H. S. K. Bartholomew, "The Political Career of Benjamin F. Shiveley," *Indiana Magazine of History*, XXVIII (December, 1937), pp. 251–69; Herman J. Deutsch, "Disintegrating Forces in Wisconsin Politics of the Early Seventies," *Wisconsin Magazine of History*, XV (1931–32), pp. 168–81, 282–96, 391–411.

Contemporary sources include "Farmers' Alliance Songs of the Nineties," *Nebraska Folklore Pamphlets* (Lincoln, 1938); Annie L. Diggs, "Women in the Alliance Movement," *Arena*, VI (July, 1892), pp. 161–92, and "The Farmers' Alliance and Some of its Leaders," *ibid.*, V (June, 1892), pp. 590–604; Hamlin Garland, "The Alliance Wedge in Congress," *ibid.*, V (March, 1892), pp. 447–57; C. F. Adams, "The Granger Movement," *North American Review*, CCXLVII (April, 1875), pp. 394–608; W. A. Peffer, "The Farmer's Defensive Movement," *Forum*, VIII (January, 1890), pp. 464–73; Rodney Welch, "The Farmer's Changed Condition," *ibid.*, X (February, 1891), pp. 688–700; Washington Gladden, "The Embattled Farmers," *ibid.* (November, 1890), pp. 315–22; C. W. Davis, "Why the Farmer is not Prosperous," *ibid.*, IX (June, 1889), pp. 231–41; David Starr Jordan, "Agricultural Depression and Waste of Time," *ibid.*, XII (October, 1891), pp. 238–46; J. D. Forrest, "Antimonopoly Legislation in the United States," *American Journal of Sociology*, I (January, 1896), pp. 411–25; and J. A. Kasson, "The Western View of the Tariff," *Forum*, IV (December, 1887), pp. 357–66.

Other important contemporary sources are James B. Weaver, *A Call to Action* (Des Moines, 1892); James D. McCabe (Edward Martin [pseud.]), *History of the Grange Movement, or, The Farmer's War against Monopoly* (Chicago, 1873); Matt Carpenter, *Speech at the Ripon, Wisconsin, Agricultural Association* (Milwaukee, 1874); and Everett Fish, *Donnelliana* (Chicago, 1892). Also informative are Fred E. Haynes' biography, *James Baird Weaver* (Iowa City, 1919); Annie L. Diggs, *The Story of Jerry Simpson* (Wichita, 1908); and an article, "Jerry Simpson," *Public*, VIII (November 18, 1905), pp. 522–26. Material on Donnelly is drawn in part from J. D. Hicks, "The Political Career of Ignatius Donnelly," *Mississippi Valley Historical Review*, VIII (June-September, 1921), pp. 86–132; Fish's *Donnelliana;* and a study of Donnelly's newspaper, *The Representative.*

Excellent studies of Western credit are J. W. Gleed, "Western Mortgages," *Forum*, IX (March, 1890), pp. 93–105; and J. P. Dunn, "The Mortgage Evil," *Political Science Quarterly*, V (March, 1890), pp. 79–85. For discussion of the early aspects of the currency question, this chapter drew from the works cited in the general list of sources, and from Orin G. Libby, "A Study of the Greenback Movement, 1876–1884," *Transactions of the Wisconsin Academy*, XII (1898), pp. 520–543; Ellis B. Usher, *The Greenback Movement of 1875–1881 and Wisconsin's Part In It;* and Wesley Mitchell, *A History of the Greenbacks.* The struggle of the farmer with the railroad is treated by Hicks and Buck and also by Hallie Farmer, "The Railroad and Frontier Populism," *Mississippi Valley Historical Review*, XIII (December, 1926), pp. 387–97; F. H. Dixon, "Railroad Control in Nebraska," *Political Science Quarterly*, XIII (December, 1898), pp. 617–47; R. E. Reiger, "Western Railroad Pools," *Mississippi Valley Historical Review*, XVIII (1931–32), pp. 364–98; Richard Overton, *Burlington West* (Cambridge, 1941); Sidney Dillon, "The West and the Railroad," *North American Review*, XLII (April, 1891), pp. 443–60; A. G. Warner, "Railroad Problems in the West," *Political Science Quarterly*, VI (March, 1891), pp. 66–89; C. F. Adams, "Railway Problems in 1869," *North American Review*, CX (January, 1870), pp. 116–50; C. S. Wood, "The Farmer, The Investor, and The Railway," *Arena*, III (February, 1891), pp. 288–303; C. F. Adams, *The Railroad Problem* (New York, 1888); Cy Warman, *The Story of the Railroad* (New York, 1888); and *Yesterday and Today: A History of the Chicago and North Western Railway System* (Chicago, 1905).

Chapter III

The discussion of the rise and fall of Populism derives from the definitive work of John D. Hicks and others cited in the general bibliography. Additional material is drawn from G. H. Knoles, *The Presidential Campaign and Election of 1892;* Haynes, *James Baird Weaver;* and Arnett, *The Populist Movement.* Useful articles were H. C. Nixon, "The Populist Movement in Iowa," *Iowa Journal of History and Politics*, XXIV (January, 1926), pp. 3–107; E. D. Stewart, "The Populist Party in Indiana," *Indiana Magazine of History*, XIV (December, 1918), pp. 332–67, and XV (March, 1919), pp. 53–74; G. C. Manning, *The Fadeout of Populism;* T. A. Bailey, "The West and Radical Legislation, 1830–1930," *American Journal of Sociology*, XXXVIII (January, 1933), pp. 603–11; H. R. Burnett, "The Last Pioneer Governor of Indiana, Blue Jeans Williams," *Indiana Magazine of History*, XXII (June, 1926), pp. 101–29; E. N. Barr, "The Populist Uprising in Kansas," in W. E. Connelly, ed., *The History of Kansas, State and People* (New York, 1928), II, 1135–1204; C. H. Moore, "Ohio in National Politics, 1865–1896," *Ohio Archaeological and Historical Quarterly*, XXXVIII (June, 1928), pp. 220–422; J. D. Hicks, "The Persistence of Populism," *Minnesota History*, XII (March, 1931), pp. 3–20.

Contemporary estimates of Populism and Bryanism are numerous, especially in such magaines as the *Arena*, the *Forum*, *Gunton's*, and others. Among the more important sources of information are Albert Watkins, "Bryanism and Jeffersonian Democracy," *Forum*, XXXI (May, 1901), pp. 358–70; James Hyslop, "The Grievance of the West," *ibid.*, XXIII (June, 1897), pp. 476–85; "The Knight Errants of Today," *New Time*, I (December, 1897), pp. 381–83; C. C. Millard, "An Open Letter to Eastern Capitalists," *Arena*, XVIII (August, 1897), pp. 211–17; B. F. Mills, "The New Party," *ibid.*, XXI (January, 1899), pp. 2–4; David Overmyer, "The Future of the Democratic Party, *ibid.*, XVIII (September, 1897), pp. 302–18; W. D. P. Bliss, "Unite or Perish," *ibid.*, XXII (July, 1899), pp. 78–89; "The Political Menace of the Discontented," *Atlantic Monthly*, LXXVIII (September, 1896), pp. 447–50; George Gunton, "The Meaning of Bryanism in American Politics," *Gunton's Magazine*, XI (December, 1896), pp. 385–96; Frank Parsons, "The Issue of 1896," *Arena*, XVI (November, 1896), pp. 881–85; R. J. Hinton, "The New Politics," *ibid.*, XI (January, 1895), pp. 217–26; J. K. Miller, "Are the People of the West Fanatics?" *ibid.*, XIII (June, 1895), pp. 92–97; J. H. Canfield, "Is the West Discontented?" *Forum*, XVIII (1894), pp. 449–61; John Bennett, "Why the West is Discontented," *Arena*, XVI (August, 1896), pp. 393–405; J. W. Gleed, "Is New York More Civilized than Kansas?" *Forum*, XVII (April, 1894), pp. 217–34; Eva MacDonald-Valesh, "The Strength and Weakness of the People's Movement," *Arena*, V (May, 1892), pp. 726–31; Willis J. Abbott, "The Chicago Populist Campaign," *ibid.*, XI (February, 1895), pp. 330–37; William Allen, "The Necessity for the People's Party," *ibid.*, XXX (October, 1903), pp. 410–14; W. C. Mains, "The Radical Movement in the Democratic Party," *Forum*, XXXI (April, 1901), pp. 157–64; "The Probable Benefits and Dangers of the Recent Elections," *American Magazine of Civics*, VI (January, 1895), pp. 81–86; Carlos Martyn, "Un-American Tendencies," *Arena*, IV (September, 1891), pp. 431–39; R. H. Williams, "Populism Considered as an Honest Effort for the Securing of Better Conditions," *American Magazine of Civics*, VII (August, 1895), pp. 195–204; F. J. Turner, "The Problem of the West," *Atlantic Monthly*, LXXVIII (September, 1896), pp. 289–97; F. M. Drew, "The Present Farmers' Movement," *Political Science Quarterly*, VI (June, 1891), pp. 282–310; A. L. Williams, *A Jeremiad* (Topeka, 1896); "The Buffalo Conference," *Arena*, XXII (July, 1899), pp. 71–77; "Union Reform League Activities," *ibid.*, pp. 111–14; "The Social Reform Union," *ibid.* (August, 1899), pp. 272–75.

The campaign of 1896 and Bryan's part in it are treated in Bryan's *The First Battle* (Chicago, 1896), an anonymously compiled Bryan scrapbook in the Newberry Library, and in the books by White, Hibben, Sullivan, Kohlsaat, Dunn, Johnson, and Filler, all cited in the general bibliography; an interesting article is J. A. Barnes, "Myths of the Bryan Campaign," *Mississippi Valley Historical Review*, XXXIV (1947–48), pp. 367–404. Streams of articles in the *Arena*, *Gunton's*, the *Forum*, *Public Opinion*, the *New Time*, *Atlantic Monthly*, Morton's *Conservative*, Donnelly's *Representative*, and

Bryan's *Commoner* cover the anti-Bryan, Populist, Silver Democrat, and Republican viewpoints thoroughly, and have provided much material for this chapter.

The literature of monopoly and antimonopoly is large. Secondary sources used include John Moody, *The Truth About Trusts;* H. W. Laidler, *Concentration in American Industry;* B. J. Hendrick, *The Age of Big Business;* R. T. Ely, *Monopolies and Trusts;* and others cited in the general bibliography. Other important sources include Henry D. Lloyd's monumental *Wealth Against Commonwealth;* Weaver's *Call to Action;* Tom Worrall's *The Grain Trust Exposed* (Chicago, 1905); Henry George, Jr., *The Menace of Privilege* (New York, 1906); George Gunton, *Trusts and the Public* (New York, 1899); and C. W. Baker, *Monopolies and the People* (New York, 1889). Illustrative articles include: B. O. Flower, "The Corporations against the People," *Arena,* XIX (February, 1898), pp. 218–28; Henry Wood, "The Bugbear of Trusts," *Forum,* V (July, 1888), pp. 584–90; Andrew Carnegie, "The Bugaboo of Trusts," in *The Empire of Business* (New York, 1902); John Bates Clark and Franklin Giddings, "The Limits of Competition" and "The Persistence of Competition," *Political Science Quarterly,* II (March, 1887), pp. 62–91; George Gunton, "The Economic and Social Aspects of Trusts," and T. W. Dwight, "The Legality of Trusts," *ibid.,* III (September, 1888), pp. 385–408, 592–632; J. B. Weaver, "The Threefold Contention of Industry," *Arena,* V (March, 1892), pp. 427–35; Nelson Baldwin, "Why the Farmer Does Not Get Rich," *American Magazine of Civics,* VIII (June, 1896), pp. 561–74; Hugh Pentecost, "Poverty and Plutocracy," *Arena,* II (August, 1890), pp. 373–75.

The financial issues of the period are discussed by J. Laurence Laughlin, *History of Bimetallism in the United States* (Chicago, 1897); Ignatius Donnelly, *The American People's Money* (Chicago, 1895); W. H. Harvey, *Coin's Financial School* (Chicago, 1894), and *Patriots of America* (Chicago, 1895). Valuable contemporary articles include F. J. Stimson, "The Ethical Side of the Free Silver Question," *The International Journal of Ethics,* VII (July, 1897), pp. 401–14; L. M. Keasbey, "The New Sectionalism," *Forum,* XVI (January, 1894), pp. 578–87; C. S. Thomas, "Why the West Needs Free Coinage," *Arena,* XV (June, 1895), pp. 887–91; John Davis, "Honest and Dishonest Money," *ibid.,* IX (January, 1894), pp. 359–63; J. Laurence Laughlin, "Coin's Food for the Gullible," *Forum,* XIX (July, 1895), pp. 573–85; R. B. Hassell, "The Independent Party and Money at Cost," *Arena,* IV (August, 1891), pp. 340–52; J. Laurence Laughlin, "The Silver Danger," *Atlantic Monthly,* LIII (May, 1884), pp. 677–81; C. W. Cram, "The Slave Power and the Money Power," *Arena,* VII (November, 1893), pp. 690–701; John Davis, "The New Slavery," *ibid.,* X (November, 1894), pp. 745–55; Jay Cooke, "The Silver Question," *American Magazine of Civics,* VIII (February, 1896), pp. 147–52; and others, especially in the *Arena* and *Gunton's Magazine.*

The estimate of Henry George, his ideas, and his influence is derived in part from Parrington, Gabriel, and Curti. In addition to George's own writings, useful material came from C. R. Geiger, A. N. Young, and Anna George DeMille, whose works are cited in the general bibliography, and from Hamlin Garland, "The Single Tax in Actual Operation," *Arena*, X (June, 1894), pp. 52–55; George Gunton, "The Henry George Candidacy," *Gunton's Magazine*, XIII (November, 1897), pp. 333–42; and F. N. Stockbridge, "The Single Taxers," *Everybody's*, XXVI (April, 1912), pp. 507–22. Sources of information concerning Henry D. Lloyd are the definitive biography by Caro Lloyd; W. G. Eggleston, "Henry D. Lloyd, Messenger," *Arena*, XXXVI (July, 1904), pp. 351–61; Henry Latchford, "A Social Reformer," *ibid.*, X (October, 1894), pp. 577–89; Jane Addams, "Henry D. Lloyd," in *The Excellent Becomes Permanent* (New York, 1932); and the obituary in *The Public*, VI (October, 1903), pp. 407–9. Material on Bellamy is derived from Bellamy's own writings and from A. E. Morgan's twin studies, both cited in the general bibliography, from Lewis Mumford's *Story of Utopias*, W. F. Taylor's *Economic Novel in America*, and from A. B. Forbes, "The Literary Quest for Utopia," *Social Forces*, VI (December, 1927), pp. 179–89. Chief sources of material on Altgeld are Altgeld's own *Live Questions* (Chicago, 1899); Harry Barnard, *Eagle Forgotten: The Life of John P. Altgeld;* Clarence Darrow, *The Story of My Life* (New York, 1932); Wayne Andrews, *The Battle for Chicago* (New York, 1946); Brand Whitlock, *Forty Years of It;* Harvey Wish, "Altgeld and the Progressive Tradition," *American Historical Review*, XXXXVI (July, 1941), pp. 813–32; Harvey Wish, "John Peter Altgeld and the Background of the Campaign of 1896," *Mississippi Valley Historical Review*, XXIV (1937–38), pp. 503–19; and Nicholas Vachel Lindsay, "The Altgeld Temperament," *The Public*, May 24, 1912. Coxey and Coxeyism are treated in D. L. McMurry, *Coxey's Army;* Henry Vincent, *The Story of the Commonweal* (Chicago, 1894); and W. T. Stead, "The Rationale of Coxeyism," *Review of Reviews*, X (July, 1894), pp. 47–59. Excellent accounts of the McKinley-Hanna period are found in Herbert Croly, *Marcus Alonzo Hanna;* Thomas Beer, *Hanna;* and in the general histories cited in the list of sources.

Chapter IV

The chief studies of muckraking drawn upon in this chapter were Louis Filler, *Crusaders for American Liberalism*, and C. C. Regier, *The Era of the Muckrakers*. The muckraking magazines themselves, particularly *McClure's* and the *Arena*, furnished additional information, as did books such as Steffens' *Autobiography* (New York, 1931), his *Struggle for Self-Government* (New York, 1906), and his *Shame of the Cities* (New York, 1904); Brand Whitlock's *Forty Years of It;* Paul Allen's *America's Awakening;* Frederic Howe's *Confessions of a*

Chapter References

Reformer; Ray Stannard Baker's *American Chronicle;* Thomas Spelling's *Bossism and Monopoly* (Chicago, 1906); and Jane Addams' *Democracy and Social Ethics* (New York, 1902). Also useful were Clifford Patton, *The Battle for Municipal Reform, 1875–1900;* Hazen S. Pingree, "The Problem of Municipal Reform," *Arena,* XVII (April, 1897), pp. 707–9; Carter Harrison, *Some Phases of the Municipal Problem* (n.p., n.d.); C. E. Merriam, *Chicago: A More Intimate View of Urban Politics* (New York, 1929); S. S. McClure, "Lawlessness in the United States," and "Tammanyizing Civilization," *McClure's,* XXIV (December, 1904), pp. 163–71; Samuel Davis, "Current Reforms in City Government," *The Kingdom,* XI (December, 1898), pp. 183–84; C. R. Woodruff, "The Progress of Municipal Reform," *American Magazine of Civics,* VI (July, 1895), pp. 66–73; T. E. Will, "The Problem of the City," *ibid.,* VII (September, 1895), pp. 231–42; J. W. Folk, "Municipal Corruption," *Independent,* LV (November, 1903), pp. 2804–6; C. R. Wood, "The Cleveland Conference for Good City Government," *American Magazine of Civics,* VII (August, 1895), pp. 167–70; and Linton Satterthwaite, "Our National Peril," *ibid.,* VIII (April, 1896), pp. 407–9. For the direct legislation movement, sources used included the files of the *Arena* and the *Direct Legislation Record;* Eltweed Pomeroy, "The Doorway to Reforms," *Arena,* XVII (April, 1897), pp. 711–21; "The Direct Legislation Movement, and its Leaders," *ibid.,* XVI (June, 1896), pp. 29–43; and "Needed Political Reforms," *ibid.,* XXII (May, 1902), pp. 471–80; and Duane Mowry, "Some Thoughts on Public Reform," *ibid.* (July, 1902), pp. 464–70.

The career of Tom L. Johnson of Cleveland is treated by Carl Lorenz, *Tom L. Johnson;* sketches in *The Public,* V (April, 1902), pp. 13–15 and the *Chicago Times-Herald,* February 12, 1899; and in Johnson's autobiographic *My Story.* Hazen Pingree's papers are in the Detroit Public Library; additional information may be gained from C. A. Robinson, "Pingree's Potato Culture," *Arena,* XIX (March, 1898), pp. 368–77; "The Potato Patch Plan," *Public Opinion,* XX (January 23, February 13, 1896), pp. 109–10; "A Successful Experiment," *Arena,* XV (March, 1896), pp. 545–54; and from Charles R. Starring, "Hazen S. Pingree: Another Forgotten Eagle," *Michigan History,* XXXII (June, 1948), pp. 129–50. Pingree's collected speeches, *What Constitutes Party Loyalty* (Lansing, 1898), *Facts and Opinions* (Detroit, 1895), and *Address Before the Nineteenth Century Club* (Lansing, 1897), provide further material. The *Arena,* the *Public,* and the *Commons* kept close track of the activities of Samuel Jones of Toledo. Other material is found in Ernest Crosby, *Golden Rule Jones, Mayor of Toledo* (Chicago, 1896); Washington Gladden, "Mayor Jones of Toledo," *Outlook,* LXII (May, 1899), pp. 17–21; F. T. Carlton, "The Golden Rule Factory," *Arena,* XXXII (October, 1904), pp. 408–10; E. Crosby, "Samuel Milton Jones," *ibid.,* XXXV (February, 1906), pp. 126–32; H. N. Casson, "Draining a Political Swamp," *ibid.,* XXI (June, 1899), pp. 768–82; and the obituaries by

Brand Whitlock, Graham Taylor, and Allen Tanner in the *Commons,*
IX (August, 1904), pp. 345–62.

For its discussion of William Graham Sumner, the chapter drew
upon Hofstadter, Starr, Keller, Gabriel, Curti, and Davis, listed in the
general bibliography, and upon Sumner's *What Social Classes Owe
to Each Other* (New York, 1883); his "What is Civil Liberty?" *Popular
Science Monthly,* XXV (July, 1889), pp. 289–303; H. E. Barnes, "William Graham Sumner, 1840–1910," *Sociological Review,* XIV (1922),
pp. 209–12; "Sketch of W. G. Sumner," *Popular Science Monthly,*"
XXV (June, 1889); and Harris Starr, "William Graham Sumner,"
Social Forces, III (May, 1925), pp. 622–25. Definitive treatments of
Ward and Veblen used here are Samuel Chugerman, *Lester F. Ward,
American Aristotle,* and Joseph Dorfman, *Thorstein Veblen and
His America.* Howard Odum, ed., *American Masters of Social Science,*
treats Sumner, Ward, Small, Giddings, and others, whereas George
Gunton is revealed best by the files of *Gunton's Magazine.* Laughlin
and Clark are sketched in *The Dictionary of American Biography.*
J. C. Olson, *J. Sterling Morton,* and the files of Morton's *Conservative*
provide full information on Morton.

Discussion of changing concepts in law, sociology, and education is
based on Gabriel, Parrington, Jacobson, and Merriam, with addi-
tional material from E. C. Hayes, *Recent Developments in the Social
Sciences;* H. E. Barnes, *The History and Prospects of the Social
Sciences;* and Merle Curti, *The Social Ideas of American Educators;*
James Linn, *Jane Addams;* and Graham Taylor, *Pioneering on Social
Frontiers* (Chicago, 1930). Richard T. Ely, *Ground Under Our Feet*
(New York, 1938) and E. A. Ross, *Seventy Years of It* (New York,
1936) are valuable personal records. B. O. Flower, "An Economist
with Twentieth Century Ideals," *Arena,* XXVI (May, 1903), pp.
154–74 is a good sketch of Frank Parsons, while Simon Newcomb,
"The Let-Alone Principle," *North American Review,* CX (January,
1870), pp. 1–53 is an able defense of laissez-faire economics.

The Chautauqua movement is treated by John H. Vincent, *The
Chautauqua Movement* (Boston, 1886); Charles E. Horner, *The Life
of James Redpath* (New York, 1926); J. T. Adams, *Frontiers of Ameri-
can Culture;* and Victoria and Robert Case, *We Called It Culture.*
The section on educational development and academic freedom is
based on Charles McCarthy, *The Wisconsin Idea;* La Follette's *Auto-
biography;* H. K. Beale, *A History of the Freedom of Teaching in
American Schools;* E. W. Bemis, "Academic Freedom," *Independent,*
LI (August 17, 1899), pp. 2195–99; T. W. Will, "A College for the
People," *Arena,* XXVI (July, 1901), pp. 15–20, and "A Menace to
Freedom," *ibid.* (September, 901), pp. 244–57; Henry Holt, "The
Social Discontent, Its Causes," *Forum,* XVIII (February, 1895), pp.
664–78; H. W. Mabie, "The Intellectual Movement in the West,"
Atlantic Monthly, XXCII (November, 1898), pp. 592–605; J. H.
Dillard, "The Blot on the Scutcheon of Higher Education," *The*

Public, VIII (December, 1904), pp. 546–50; and George Gates, "College Endowments and the Freedom of Teaching," *The Kingdom*, XI (January 5, 1899), pp. 239–40.

The argument over wealth and business was seemingly interminable. Representative discussions are Andrew Carnegie, *The Empire of Business* (New York, 1902) and *The Gospel of Wealth and Other Essays* (New York, 1901); Basil Bouroff, *The Impending Crisis* (Chicago, 1905); George Gunton, *Wealth and Progress* (New York, 1888); John Bates Clark, *The Philosophy of Wealth* (New York, 1886); Truxton Beale, ed., *Man versus State* (New York, 1916); John Bates Clark, "The Society of the Future," *Independent*, LIII (July 18, 1901), pp. 1649–51; C. A. Henderson, "Business Men and Social Theorists," *American Journal of Sociology*, I (January, 1896), pp. 385–91; G. F. Williams, "Our Real Masters," *Arena*, XXIX (January, 1903), pp. 8–15; "The Anti-Capital Crusade," *Gunton's Magazine*, XI (November, 1896), pp. 319–25; "The Tether of Large Fortunes," *ibid.*, XV (June, 1899), pp. 401–8; "Wealth," *ibid.*, XXIV (March, 1903), pp. 206–8; "Is Poverty an Obstacle?" *ibid.*, XXIII (May, 1903), pp. 394–97; "Are Millionaires a Menace?" *ibid.*, XXV (November, 1903), pp. 388–91; "Are the Rich Socially Rotten?" *ibid.* (December, 1903), pp. 478–85.

Other articles concerning the rich man and society are F. A. Walker, "Democracy and Wealth," *Forum*, X (November, 1890), pp. 251–54; John Bates Clark, "The New Philosophy of Wealth," *New Englander*, XXXVI (January, 1877), pp. 170–86; Arthur T. Hadley, "Jay Gould and Socialism," *Forum*, XIV (January, 1893), pp. 686–93; "The Influence of Wealth on the Higher Life," *Gunton's Magazine*, XXVI (April, 1904), pp. 300–7; "Large Aggregations of Capital," *ibid.*, XII (May, 1897), pp. 334–41; "Opportunities for Young Men," *ibid.*, XVII (October, 1899), pp. 293–95; C. D. Wright, "Have We Equality of Opportunity?" *Forum*, XIX (May, 1895), pp. 301–12; "The Moral Aspect of Great Fortune," *Public*, II (November 18, 1899), pp. 5–9; John Bates Clark, "Business Ethics, Past and Present," *New Englander*, XXXVIII (March, 1879), pp. 157–69; R. N. Reeves, "Our Aristocracy," *American Magazine of Civics*, VIII (January, 1896), pp. 23–29; Lester F. Ward, "The Use and Abuse of Wealth," *Forum*, II (January, 1887), pp. 555–59; M. W. Howard, "The Menace of Plutocracy," *New Time*, II (January, 1898), pp. 9–11; D. A. Gorton, "The Ethics of Trade and Capital as Related to Popular Government," *American Magazine of Civics*, VIII (February, 1896), pp. 152–64; Eltweed Pomeroy, "The Concentration of Wealth," *Arena*, XVII (December, 1896), pp. 82–96; B. O. Flower, "Plutocracy's Bastiles," *ibid.*, X (October, 1894), pp. 601–21.

Sources of material on the Social Gospel and Christian Socialist movements are C. H. Hopkins, *The Rise of the Social Gospel in American Protestantism, 1865–1915*, and J. A. Dombrowski, *The Early Days of Christian Socialism in America*. The *New Time*, the *Commons*, the *Social Crusader*, the *Kingdom*, and the *Social Forum* also provided much contemporary information. For the career of

Herron, see C. Beardsley, "Professor Herron," *Arena*, XV (April, 1896), pp. 784–96; "Dr. Herron's Confession of Social Faith," *The Kingdom*, XI (December 22, 1898), pp. 203–4; W. T. Brown, "George D. Herron: The Tragedy of Conscience," *Arena*, XXV (May, 1901), pp. 471–85. Also see Herron's articles and sermons, particularly "The New Social Apostolate," *ibid.*, pp. 486–91; "The Sociality of Jesus' Religion," *ibid.*, XIV (November, 1895), pp. 385–91; *The Message of Jesus to Men of Wealth* (New York, 1891); *Christian Society* (New York, 1894); and *Between Caesar and Jesus* (Chicago, 1899). Other articles and books include R. T. Ely, "Some Ethical Aspects of Ownership," *Public*, V (August 23, 1902), pp. 316–17; J. R. Commons, "Progressive Individualism," *American Magazine of Civics*, VI (June, 1895), pp. 561–74; J. O. Benthall, "Why I Am a Christian Socialist," *Arena*, XXXVII (June, 1907), pp. 600–4; Paul Monroe, "English and American Christian Socialism," *American Journal of Sociology*, I (July, 1895), pp. 50–68; T. T. Frickstad, "Competition and Socialism from a Moral Point of View," *The Kingdom*, XI (April 6, 1899), pp. 454–56; C. H. Zimmerman, "The Church and Economic Reform," *Arena*, X (October, 1894), pp. 694–99; Frank Parsons, "The Philosophy of Mutualism," *ibid.*, IX (May, 1894), pp. 785–815; A. A. Johnson, "Steam and Electricity, a Study in Sociology," *American Magazine of Civics*, VII (October, 1895), pp. 343–60; John Bascom, "Individualism," *The Kingdom*, XI (December 8, 1898), pp. 153–54; W. A. Evans, "Preacher and Plutocrat," *Arena*, XIV (October, 1895), pp. 228–38; "The Churches and Social Questions," *ibid.*, XX (August, 1898), pp. 207–22; Howard McQuarry, "Ethics and Politics," *American Magazine of Civics*, VI (January, 1895), pp. 86–96; Washington Gladden, "Civic Religion," *ibid.*, VII (December, 1895), pp. 624–32; F. D. Bentley, "The Survival of the Fittest in the Coming Age," *Arena*, XXVII (March, 1902), pp. 249–53; Walter Rauschenbusch, "The Ideals of Social Reformers," *American Journal of Sociology*, II (September, 1896), pp. 202–19; H. C. Vedder, *Socialism and The Ethics of Jesus* (New York, 1913); R. T. Ely, *Social Aspects of Christianity and Other Essays* (New York, 1899); Washington Gladden, *Recollections* (New York, 1909), *Christianity and Socialism* (New York, 1905), and *Applied Christianity* (Boston, 1886); and William Dean Howells, *A Traveller from Altruria* (Boston, 1894).

Material on the early phases of the socialist movement is drawn from Symes and Clement, Hillquit, Coleman, Ginger, and Macy, all cited in the general list of sources. Interesting articles are F. B. Tracy, "Menacing Socialism in the United States," *Forum*, XV (May, 1893), pp. 332–42; Eugene Debs, "Socialist Ideals," *Arena*, XL (November, 1908), pp. 432–35, and "The Cry of Anarchist," *American Magazine of Civics*, VI (April, 1895), pp. 408–12. Richard Michaelis, *Looking Forward* (Chicago, 1890), is a violent attack on contemporary socialism, while Debs' important letter to Donnelly appears in Donnelly's paper, the *Representative*, February 22, 1899.

Chapter V

General sources used in this chapter include Sullivan, Mowry, Aaron, Goldman, Hofstadter, Rhodes, William Allen White, Malin, Stoddard, Kohlsaat, Binkley, Beard, Dunn, Paul Allen, Howe, Haworth, and Walter Johnson, all cited in the general list of sources. Of great assistance was an unpublished doctoral dissertation by Benton H. Wilcox, "A Reconsideration of the Character and Bases of Northwest Radicalism" (University of Wisconsin, 1933). Discussion of the backgrounds of progressivism in the states is drawn in part from the histories of Ramey, Haynes, Gue, Sheldon, Christiansen, Crawford, Harlan, Bogart, and Mathews, and others listed in the general bibliography. Specific treatments of men and issues may be found in Walter Owen, "The Progressive and Government," *La Follette's Magazine*, IX (August 12, 1912), pp. 8–9; Albert Watkins, "Radicalism, East and West," *Arena*, XXIII (February, 1900), pp. 149–56; B. O. Flower, "The Fundamental Conflict of the Present," *ibid.*, XXIX (January, 1903), pp. 89–91; the three studies of Nelson and Johnson by Odlund, Day and Knappen, and Helmes; W. P. Belden, "Governor Pingree and His Reforms," *American Law Review*, XXXIV (January-February, 1910), pp. 36–50; John Bingham, "Cummins," *Review of Reviews*, XXXIV (September, 1906), pp. 291–95; L. B. Smith, "Albert Cummins," *Arena*, XXXVI (July, 1906), pp. 38–41; H. G. Moorhead, "A. B. Cummins," *World Today*, XI (November, 1906), pp. 1089–91; Elbert Harrington, "The Political Ideas of Albert B. Cummins" (Unpublished master's thesis, State University of Iowa, 1931); and the three biographies of William Allen White by Hinshaw, Rich, and Clough.

For the career and character of Robert M. La Follette, his *Autobiography* is naturally a major source of information; the definitive biography is Belle Case and Fola La Follete, *Robert M. La Follette*, two volumes (New York, 1953). Additional information is derived from E. M. Doan, *The La Follettes and the Wisconsin Idea* (New York, 1947); F. C. Howe, *Wisconsin: An Experiment in Democracy* (New York, 1912); Charles McCarthy, *The Wisconsin Idea* (New York, 1912); E. A. Fitzpatrick, *McCarthy of Wisconsin*; C. C. Platt, *What La Follette's State is Doing* (Batavia, N. Y., 1924); Fred L. Holmes, "The Triumph of the Progressive Movement," in M. M. Quaife, ed., *Wisconsin, Its History and Its People*, vol. II (Chicago, 1924); Ellen Torelle, ed., *The Political Philosophy of Robert M. La Follette as Revealed in his Speeches and Writings* (Madison, 1920); Wallace S. Sayre, "Robert La Follette, A Study in Political Methods" (Unpublished doctoral dissertation, New York University, 1930); A. O. Barton, *La Follette's Winning of Wisconsin* (Madison, 1922); A. M. Thomson, *A Political History of Wisconsin* (Milwaukee, 1902); R. G. Plumb, *Badger Politics, 1836–1930* (Manitowoc, Wis., 1930);

Isaac Stephenson, *Recollections of a Long Life* (Chicago, 1915); Dorothy Ganfield, "The Influence of Wisconsin on Federal Politics, 1880–1907," *Wisconsin Magazine of History*, XV (September, 1932), pp. 3–25; C. H. Crownhart, "Two Wisconsin Immortals," *Blue Book of the State of Wisconsin*, 1927; Nils P. Haugen, "Pioneer and Political Reminiscences," *Wisconsin Magazine of History*, XI (1927–8), pp. 121, 269, 395, XII (1928–29), 41, 176, 271, 379, and XIII (1929–30), 121; William Kittle, "La Follette," *Arena*, XXV (June, 1905), pp. 571–76; and Robert S. Maxwell, *La Follette and The Rise of the Progressives in Wisconsin* (Madison, 1956).

The argument over the railroad and the trust is treated in the sources listed for chapters III and IV; the files of the *Arena*, the *Public*, the *Forum*, the *Independent*, and *Gunton's Magazine* are filled with articles. Those of special interest for this chapter are B. O. Flower, "The Corruption of Government by Corporations," *Arena*, XXIX (July, 1903), pp. 55–68; E. W. Bemis, "The Good and Evil in Trusts," *The Kingdom*, XI (March, 1899), pp. 408–10; A. G. Wall, "The Futility of Trust Legislation," *Arena*, XXIV (October, 1900), pp. 405–11; Frank Parsons, "Remedies for Trust Abuses," *ibid.* (December, 1900), pp. 569–72, and "How Trusts can be Crushed," *ibid.*, XXV (March, 1901), pp. 264–70; Philip Robinson, "Economic Consolidation and Monopoly," *Conservative Review*, IV (September-December, 1900), pp. 33–96; F. B. Thurber, "The Organization of Industry," *Arena*, XXII (September, 1899), pp. 301–12; David Willcox, "The Futility of the Anti-Trust Issue," *Forum*, XXVIII (February, 1900), pp. 732–37; E. W. Bemis, "The Trust Problem," *ibid.*, (December, 1899), pp. 412–27; W. A. Peffer, "The Trust Problem and its Solution," *ibid.* (July, 1899), pp. 513–33; and Aldyce Walker, "Anti-Trust Legislation," *ibid.* (May, 1899), pp. 256–57.

Theodore Roosevelt's early career and first administration are treated by Rhodes, Mowry, Dunn, and Kohlsaat, listed above. Roosevelt's *Autobiography* (New York, 1913); Harold Howland, *Theodore Roosevelt and His Times;* W. S. Parks, "Should Mr. Roosevelt be Nominated?" *Arena*, XXXI (April, 1904); S. C. Parks, "Is Mr. Roosevelt a Failure?" *ibid.*, XXXVIII (May, 1907), pp. 160–62, and W. B. Fleming, "The Good and Bad of the President's Policies," *ibid.* (December, 1907), pp. 625–28; H. L. West, "American Politics," *Forum*, XXXIV (January, 1902), pp. 326–30; and Frank Parsons, "The President and the Trusts," *Arena*, XVIII (November, 1902), pp. 452–56, and "An Open Letter to President Roosevelt," *ibid.*, XXII (August, 1904), pp. 122–28, supply additional material.

Chapter VI

Background material for this chapter derives from substantially the same general sources listed at the beginning of the bibliography for chapter V. The files of the *Public, La Follette's Magazine,* the *Ameri-*

can Magazine, Current History, the *Nation,* and the *New Republic* provided a wealth of additional material. Claude Bowers, *Beveridge and the Progressive Era,* and Kenneth Hechler, *Insurgency: Personalities and Politics of the Taft Era,* were indispensable sources of information, and La Follette's *Autobiography* was of course a primary source of great importance. Useful material is also found in William Allen White, *The Old Order Changeth* (New York, 1911); Albert J. Beveridge, *The Meaning of the Times* (Indianapolis, 1908); Alfred Lief, *Democracy's Norris;* Thomas Dreier, *Heroes of Insurgency;* Nathaniel Stephenson, *Nelson W. Aldrich;* Ray Stannard Baker, *American Chronicle;* "The Meaning of Insurgency," *American Magazine,* LXXII (May, 1911), pp. 59–64; Henry C. Wallace, "What the Middle West Wants," *World's Work,* XX (May, 1910), pp. 12891–98; Hastings McAdams, "The Insurgents," *Everybody's,* XXVI (May, 1912), pp. 780–87; and Ida M. Tarbell, "The Stand-Pat Intellect," *American Magazine,* LXXII (May, 1911), pp. 33–41.

The ideology of Bull Moose progressivism is best explained by Herbert Croly's *The Promise of American Life* (New York, 1910) and *Progressive Democracy* (New York, 1914). Also informative are Walter Weyl, *The New Democracy* (New York, 1912); William E. Walling, *Progressivism and After* (New York, 1914); John Chamberlain's sketch of Croly in *The American Stakes* (New York, 1940); and B. P. DeWitt, *The Progressive Movement* (New York, 1915). The campaign of 1912 is reconstructed from contemporary periodical files; additional studies are William Jennings Bryan, *Tale of Two Conventions* (New York, 1912); A. D. Campbell, "The Bull Moose Movement in Michigan," *Michigan History,* XXV (Winter, 1941), pp. 34–37; W. B. Hesseltine, "Bull Mooses and the Great Betrayal," *Progressive,* August 18, 1947; G. H. Payne, *The Birth of a New Party* (Naperville, Ill., 1912); and Herbert Parzen, *A Comparative Study of the Progressive Presidential Campaigns of 1912 and 1924* (Unpublished doctoral dissertation, Columbia University, 1926). The decline of the Progressive party after 1912 may be traced in Johnson's *Selected Letters of William Allen White* and in Harold Ickes, "Who Killed the Progressive Party?" *American Historical Review,* XXXVI (January, 1941), pp. 191–206.

Wilson and his era are treated by Gabriel, Hoover, Garraty, Blum, Curti, Merriam, R. S. Baker, White, Link, Daniels, Hugh-Jones, and others listed in the general bibliography, and in R. S. Baker and W. E. Dodd, eds., *The Public Papers of Woodrow Wilson* (New York, 1925). The history of the Non Partisan League is derived from Bruce Nelson and S. A. Olsness of North Dakota, and from the works by Nelson, Gaston, Russell, Bruce, and Fossum listed in the general bibliography. Also useful is G. C. Fite, "Peter Norbeck and the Defeat of the Non Partisan League in South Dakota," *Mississippi Valley Historical Review,* XXXIII (1946–47), pp. 217–37 and Fite's study of Norbeck.

Chapter VII

Material for a discussion of the period is drawn in part from the books by Mark Sullivan, Richard Hofstadter, Eric Goldman, George Soule, Broadus Mitchell, Samuel Hopkins Adams, Leo Gurko, Frederick Lewis Allen, Lilliam Symes and Travers Clement, W. S. Myers and W. H. Newton, and C. M. Wiltse, listed in the general bibliography. An excellent recent study is David Noble, *The Paradox of Progressive Thought* (Minneapolis, 1958). Especially useful also were William Allen White, *Masks in a Pageant* (New York, 1928); Arthur Capper, *The Agricultural Bloc* (New York, 1922); and Herbert Hoover, *Addresses on the American Road* (New York, 1938). C. C. Arbuthnot, "The Economic Interpretation of Present Day Politics," *Popular Science Monthly*, LXXXI (August, 1912), pp. 183–92; F. L. Bullard, "Calvin Coolidge as Man and Statesman," *Current History*, XVIII (September, 1923), pp. 897–903, were helpful articles. The files of *Common Sense, La Follette's Magazine*, the *Progressive*, the *Nation*, the *New Republic, Time*, the *Outlook, Harper's, Current History*, the *Independent, World's Work, Literary Digest*, the *Forum*, and the *Review of Reviews* furnished a running commentary on men and issues, while Harold Ickes' *Autobiography of a Curmudgeon* (New York, 1943), Cordell Hull's *Memoirs* (New York, 1948), Fiorello La Guardia's *The Making of an Insurgent* (New York, 1948), and Frances Perkins' *Roosevelt as I Knew Him* (New York, 1947) provided valuable personal records of the period.

Kenneth C. MacKay, *The Progressive Movement of 1924*, is an indispensable source of information and the authoritative book on the progressive movement from 1916 to 1924. C. W. Gilbert, *You Takes Your Choice* (New York, 1924); William Allen White, *Politics: The Citizen's Business* (New York, 1924); Morris Hillquit, *Loose Leaves from a Busy Life* (New York, 1934); and *The Facts: A La Follette-Wheeler Campaign Textbook* (Chicago, 1924) gave useful information on the 1924 campaign.

Articles of interest relating to the period 1916 to 1924 include Clinton Gilbert, "La Follette," *Literary Digest*, LXXXII (August 9, 1924), pp. 41–43; Bruce Bliven, "La Follette's Place in our History," *Current History*, XXII (August, 1925), pp. 16–22; F. A. Ogg, "Robert La Follette in Retrospect," *ibid.*, XXXIII (February, 1931), pp. 685–91; Lewis Gannett, "A Party Struggles to be Born," *Nation*, CXX (March 4, 1925), pp. 240–42; R. M. Lovett, "The Farmer-Labor-Communist Party," *New Republic*, XXXIX (July 2, 1924), pp. 153–54; Benjamin Stolberg, "The Peter Pans of Communism," *Century*, CX (July, 1925), pp. 3–5; Murray King, "The Farmer-Labor Federation," *New Republic*, XXXVIII (April 2, 1924), pp. 145–47; Allen McCurdy, "The 48'ers Position," *Nation*, CXI (July, 1920), pp. 126–27; F. E. Haynes, "The Significance of the Latest Third Party Movement,"

Chapter References

Mississippi Valley Historical Review, XII (September, 1925), pp. 177–86; H. T. Keenlyside, "The American Political Revolution of 1924," *Current History*, XXI (March, 1926), pp. 833–40; "The Business Man's Bloc," *New Republic*, XXXIX (June 25, 1924), pp. 114–45; Arthur Train, "The Billionaire's Era," *Forum*, LXXI (November, 1924), pp. 618–28, and (December, 1924), pp. 746–49; Lincoln Colcord, "The Committee of 48," *Nation*, CIX (December 27, 1919), pp. 821–23; O. G. Villard, "An Honest Convention," *ibid.*, CXIX (July 16, 1924), pp. 63-65; "The La Follette Platform," *New Republic*, XXXIX (June 18, 1924), pp. 88–92; "Progressivism—1912 and 1924," *ibid.* (August 13, 1924), pp. 312–14; "The Outlook for Progressivism in Politics," *ibid.* (December 10, 1924), pp. 60–63; Henrik Shipstead, "What the Progressive Farmer Wants," *Forum*, LXXI (April, 1924), pp. 496–98; E. G. Lowry, "La Follette's Own Platform," *World's Work*, XXXVIII (September, 1924), pp. 513–19; Benjamin Stolberg, "La Follette Crosses the Rubicon," *Independent*, CXIII (July 19, 1924), p. 34; James O'Neal, "The Changing Fortunes of American Socialism," *Current History*, XX (April, 1924), pp. 92–97; David Karsner, "The Passing of the Socialist Party," *ibid.* (June, 1924), pp. 402–6; George Soule, "Signs of a New Party," *New Republic*, XXXVIII (May 14, 1924), pp. 302–4; Benjamin Stolberg, "Third Party Chances," *Nation*, CXVIII (April 16, 1924), pp. 422–25; McAlister Coleman, "La Follette Day at Cleveland," *Outlook*, CXXXVII (July 16, 1924), pp. 425–26; H. L. Varney, "An American Labor Party," *Current History*, XX (April, 1924), pp. 86–91; F. E. Haynes, "Third Party Backgrounds," *Independent*, CIII (August 2, 1924), pp. 71–74; Jane Addams, Zona Gale, Felix Frankfurter, Herbert Croly, John R. Commons, and others, "Why I Shall Vote for La Follette," *New Republic*, XL (September 10, 1924), pp. 36–37, (September 17, 1924), pp. 63–64, (October 1, 1924), pp. 115–16.

For estimates of and commentaries on the New Deal period, see the books by Hacker, Wallace, Goldman, Beard and Smith, and others listed in the general bibliography. Other informative sources are A. M. Bingham and Selden Rodman, *Challenge to the New Deal* (New York, 1934); B. D. Zevin, *Nothing to Fear: Selected Addresses of Franklin D. Roosevelt* (New York, 1946); Henry A. Wallace, *Democracy Reborn* (New York, 1944); Allan Nevins, ed., *Walter Lippmann's Interpretations, 1931–1933* (New York, 1933); A. A. Berle, *New Directions in the New World* (New York, 1940); Franklin D. Roosevelt, *Looking Forward* (New York, 1933); and Roosevelt's *Public Papers and Addresses* (five volumes, New York, 1938). Friedel's three-volume *Roosevelt* (of a projected six), Crane, Burns, Gunther, Robinson, and others provide materials on the political career of FDR. Representative articles dealing with the period include "La Follette Progressives," *Fortune*, XVIII (1938), pp. 90–95; Philip La Follette, "They Wanted Something New," *Nation*, CXLVII (December 3, 1938), p. 586; Francis Brown, "The Power of Progressivism,"

Common Sense, IV (November, 1935), pp. 13–15; Howard Scott, "Technocracy, 1933," *ibid.*, II (December, 1933), pp. 6–8; H. V. Knight, "Poverty in the Farm Belt," *ibid.*, III (December, 1934), pp. 23–24; Claude Fuess, "Roosevelt: The Democratic Hope," *Current History*, XXXVI (August, 1932), pp. 513–20; Thomas Amlie, "How Radical is the New Deal?" *Common Sense*, IV (August, 1936), pp. 21–23, and "A Progressive Looks at the New Deal," VII (November, 1938), pp. 8–10; Robert La Follette, Jr., "The Shame of the Democratic Party," *Progressive*, July 11, 1942; McAlister Coleman, "The New Liberalism," *ibid.*, December 14, 1942; Stuart Chase, "Is the New Deal Dead?" *ibid.*, May 2, 1942; Harry W. Laidler, "Platforms to the Left," *Common Sense*, XIII (August, 1944), pp. 269–71; W. B. Hesseltine, "The New Deal and the Progressive Tradition," *Progressive*, July 7, 1947, "The Failure of the New Deal," *ibid.*, July 21, 1947, and "The Perversion of Progressivism," September, 1948.

For discussions of liberalism in present-day politics, see Arthur E. Ekirch, *The Decline of American Liberalism* (New York, 1955), and Arthur Schlesinger, Jr., *The Vital Center* (Boston, 1949); an interesting brief discussion is in Adlai Stevenson's "The Mission of Liberalism," *New Republic*, September 24, 1956. For material concerning the growth of business and government since 1940 see the report of the Federal Trade Commission, *Summary Report on the Merger Movement* (Washington, 1948); Thurman Arnold, "The Sherman Act on Trial," *Atlantic Monthly*, July, 1953; and Paul Douglas, "Colossus on the Potomac," *Harper's Magazine*, July, 1953. David Lilienthal, *Big Business, A New Era* (New York, 1953) is a thoughtful attempt to work out the problems of big business relationships in contemporary society.

Provocative analyses of contemporary Midwestern politics are K. S. Davis, "East is East and Midwest is Midwest," *New York Times Magazine*, November 20, 1949; Roy Basler, Bernard Duffey, and T. George Harris, "The Changing Role of the Middle West," *Centennial Review*, II (Spring, 1958), pp. 109–51; and John Bartlow Martin's series, "The Changing Midwest," *Saturday Evening Post*, January 11, 18, 25, and February 1, 1958. The isolationist issue in the Midwest is treated by Adlai Stevenson, "The Challenge of a New Isolationism," *The New York Times Magazine*, November 6, 1949; Samuel Lubell, *The Future of American Politics* (New York, 1951), Chapter 7, "The Myth of Isolationism," and R. A. Billington, "The Origins of Middle Western Isolationism," *Political Science Quarterly*, LX (March, 1945), pp. 44–64.

Index

Index

Stimson, Henry, on Theodore Roosevelt, 264

Stoddard, Henry L., on business in politics, 26

Strong, Josiah, and Social Gospel, 153, 155

Stubbs, Walter, campaign platform of, 219-20; mentioned, 261; and Theodore Roosevelt, 266

Sumner, William Graham, quoted, 127, 133; as spokesman for conservatism, 29, 96, 136-37, 238

Taft, William Howard, administration of, 250-53; 1912 nomination, 267-68; and 1908 presidential campaign, 244, 259; and progressives, 244-45, 260, 264, 266-67; and Theodore Roosevelt, 233

Tarbell, Ida, as muckraker, 102, 171

Tariff question, background, 11; and Cummins, 210-12; and Payne-Aldrich, 249-50; Underwood tariff, 280

Taubeneck, Herman, and Democratic-Populist fusion, 108

Taylor, Graham, mentioned, 176; and Social Gospel, 158, 167; and social welfare, 146

Technocracy, and economic planning, 328-29, 334-35; and Farmer-Labor Political Federation, 333

Teller, Henry M., and silver issue, 107-108

Third parties, minor Midwestern, 50-51, 56-68, 74-80

Thomas, Norman, and third party movement, 308

Tillman, Ben, and 1896 Democratic convention, 108, 109

Townley, Arthur C., and Non Partisan League, 291, 292, 293

Train, Arthur, quoted, 296

Trusts, Altgeld on, 87-88; Bellamy on, 99-100; Bryan on, 238; Čroly on, 258; Cummins on, 210-11;

Ely on, 140; and Farmer-Labor Federation, 332; and Farmers' Alliance, 59-68; and Grangers, 53-55; Johnson on, 179-80; Jones on, 178; La Follette on, 201-202, 206, 311-12; Lloyd on, 101-102; Pingree on, 175; in politics, 42-44, 93-96, 236-42, 296-97; Populists on, 79, 163-64, 168, 255-56; and 1924 Progressive platform, 309-10, 310-12; F.D.R. on, 323, 342-43; Theodore Roosevelt on, 229-30, 232-33, 234, 259; Wilson on, 280-82

Turner, Frederick Jackson, quoted, 77-78, 119-120, 124

Union Labor party, and Donnelly, 70; organized, 60

U'Ren, William, mentioned, 261; and single-tax, 97

Vandenberg, Arthur, 359

Vanderbilt, Commodore, mentioned, 297

Van Dyke, Henry, quoted, 74

Van Hise, Charles R., on trusts, 238, 239; and University of Wisconsin, 150; and Wisconsin Idea, 150, 201

Van Sant, Samuel, mentioned, 242; trust busting of, 214

Veblem, Thorstein, mentioned, 328, 336; and *Theory of Business*, 143; and Theory of the Leisure Class, 142-43

Villard, Oswald Garrison, and La Follette, 302, 348; and New Deal, 340

Wallace, Henry A., as 1948 Progressive candidate, 350-51

Wallace, Henry C., quoted, 254, 260

Ward, Lester F., and AEA, 143; on social Darwinism, 137-38

Watson, Thomas, as Populist, 79, 110

Wayland, J.A., socialism of, 162

397